Cairo

Andrew Humphreys

Cairo

1st edition

Published by
Lonely Planet Publications
Head Office: PO Box 617, Hawthorn, Vic 3122, Australia
Branches: 155 Filbert St, Suite 251, Oakland, CA 94607, USA
                    10a Spring Place, London NW5 3BH, UK
                    71 bis rue du Cardinal Lemoine, 75005 Paris, France

Printed by
Colorcraft Ltd, Hong Kong
Printed in China

Photographs by
Glenn Beanland, Kristie Burns, Bethune Carmichael, Geert Cole, Eddie Gerald, Patrick Horton,
Adam McCrow

Front cover: View of Islamic Cairo's domes and minarets (Adam McCrow)

Published
April 1998

National Library of Australia Cataloguing in Publication Data

Humphreys, Andrew, 1965- .
Cairo.

1st ed.
Includes index.
ISBN 0 86442 548 1.

1. Cairo (Egypt) - Guidebooks. I. Title.

916.21604

text & maps © Lonely Planet 1998
photos © photographers as indicated 1998

Andrew Humphreys

Born in England, Andrew stayed around just long enough to complete his studies in architecture before relocating to Egypt. He spent three years in the dust and fumes, among other things mapping out Cairo's decaying Islamic monuments, later going on to work for the country's biggest-selling English-language publication, *Egypt Today*. In 1991 he reluctantly returned to the real world to pursue a career in journalism which took him to the newly independent Baltic States where he co-founded an English-language Baltic newspaper. In 1994 Lonely Planet plucked Andrew from his Estonian home and despatched him to Siberia and thence to Central Asia, Iran, Israel & the Palestinian Territories and eventually, after months of begging phone calls from him, back to Egypt.

For the purposes of this guide Andrew spent a further 12 months in Cairo during which time he also co-founded the *Cairo Times* newspaper. He has no idea what he's going to do next.

From the Author

In no particular order, Andrew would like to thank Andrew Hammond, Steve Negus, Ben Faulks and Samir Raafat for permission to recycle and steal outright from articles they wrote for the *Cairo Times*. Thanks also to Siona Jenkins for bailing me out of the Egyptian Museum, Stuart Kinloch for help in the bars and Golo for coffeeshops and conversation. Thanks also to Al Burnside whose enthusiasm for Cairo first got me hooked.

Most of all thank you to Gadi Farfour – co-researcher, manuscript assessor, map maker and my wife – for having the strength and patience to put up with a 24 hour author and his obsessions.

This Book

Some of the text in this book was adapted from Lonely Planet's *Egypt* guide (edition 4) which was written by Damien Simonis, Leanne Logan and Geert Cole. The Gods & Goddesses of Pharaonic Egypt section was taken from Christine Niven's Gods & Goddesses in Tomb & Temple Art, also in our *Egypt* guide.

From the Publisher

This first edition was edited and proofed by Michelle Glynn with assistance from Isabelle Young and Joyce Connolly. Geoff Stringer and Verity Campbell coordinated the design. The maps were drawn by Geoff with assistance from Paul Piaia. The cover was designed by Adam McCrow. Thanks to Dan Levin for creating the fonts, Quentin Frayne for organising the language section, Trudi Canavan and Golo for their terrific illustrations, Geoff Stringer for the drawings of the Egyptian Gods & Goddesses, and Leonie Mugavin for her tireless trawling of Melbourne's libraries and the Net. Finally, a special thanks also to Andrew and Gadi – for their boundless energy, enthusiasm and patience.

Warning & Request

Things change – prices go up, schedules change, good places go bad and bad places go bankrupt – nothing stays the same. So, if you find things better or worse, recently opened or long since closed, please tell us and help make the next edition even more accurate and useful.

We value all of the feedback we receive from travellers. Julie Young coordinates a small team who read and acknowledge every letter, postcard and email, and make sure that every bit of information that is sent in finds its way to the appropriate authors, editors and publishers.

Everyone who writes in to us will find their name in the next edition of the appropriate guide and will also receive a free subscription to our quarterly newsletter, *Planet Talk*. The very best contributions will be rewarded with a free copy of a Lonely Planet guide.

Excerpts from your correspondence may appear in new editions of this guide; in our newsletter, *Planet Talk*; or in updates on our Web site – so please let us know if you don't want your letter published or your name acknowledged.

Contents

Introduction

Encountering Cairo for the first time can turn out to be one of those life defining experiences. It's a city that people tend to react to, and react in fairly extreme ways. For some visitors the result of their encounter is a Dorothy in Oz sort of realisation that there's just 'no place like home'. If given a pair of red shoes, they would click their heels three times and be gone from Cairo forever. At the other extreme, there are just as many, if not more, visitors who revel in the fact that not only is Cairo unlike home, but it's unlike any other place on earth.

For my part, I'm a reveller. I first came to Cairo on holiday, filling in a month between jobs in London; in the end, it was three years

before I returned home. What ensnared and entranced me – and still does – was the sheer intensity of the city. As home to around 16 million Egyptians, Arabs, Africans and international hangers-on, and with one of the world's greatest densities of people, being in Cairo means submitting to an almost perpetual all-out assault on the senses. Some days the most unambitious stroll around town can leave you with the same sort of feeling you might get after a sadistically vigorous massage – tender, unsteady on your feet and stinkingly sweaty, but also strangely satisfied.

Cairo's like that, it is not a gentle city. It doesn't have graceful boulevards and cobbled squares and the kind of dolled-up, prettified buildings that cry out to be photographed and stuck in an album. It doesn't have the resources to spare to be picturesque. Buildings that in almost any other city would take pride of place, Cairo has in abundance, from 10th century mosques to pseudo-Hindu temples. Its old quarters have not been tamed and made tourist-friendly in the way that they have in places like Morocco or Jerusalem. They probably never will be for the simple reason that Cairo's medieval quarters still support a huge population that has nowhere else to go.

This lack of room to develop or expand constantly throws up startling juxtapositions. In one central Nile-side district, less than 500m from a new computer superstore, there are mud-brick houses where goats wander through living rooms and where water is available from spigots in the street.

Across town, a recently-completed funfair/restaurant complex has gone up on the fringes of a 1000-year-old cemetery, which is still in use with the dead vying for space with the living.

Cairenes see nothing strange in this. Possibly as a result of living in such close proximity to 4½ millennia of history (the Pyramids are visible from the upper storeys of buildings all over the city), they aren't driven by the western obsession to update and upgrade. The latest model Toyota is obliged to share lane space with a donkey and cart; you go to buy paper for your fax machine and the sales assistant tallies the bill on an abacus. Of course, a lack of money and opportunity may also have something to do with it, but Cairo has such an overwhelming sense of its own history that it can take or leave the twentieth century.

It is – if I can attempt to identify just one characteristic this pervasive sense of timelessness that really has me hooked. It's possible to move from the medieval backstreets of Islamic Cairo to the Pharaonic monumentalism of the Pyramids, take time out in a coffeehouse that looks completely identical to those portrayed in 19th century prints and then drink in a bar time-locked in the pre-Revolutionary days. And what really matters here is that none of these places feels 'historical', they all just feel like Cairo. That's to say, they're chaotic, noisy, totally unpredictable and seething with humanity.

Life is what this city is about and, to paraphrase a cliché, only if you're tired of it can you fail to see its charm.

Facts about Cairo

HISTORY

Cairo is not a Pharaonic city, though the presence of the Pyramids leads many to believe otherwise. At the time the Pyramids were being built the capital of ancient Egypt was Memphis, 22km south of the Giza Plateau. The site of modern-day Cairo was probably a royal estate at this time, a temporary encampment housing the hundreds of thousands of workers required to hack, smooth and haul the massive stone blocks that were piled up into the awesome forms they survive in today – the Pyramids of Giza.

Babylon: The Founding of Cairo

The era of the Pharaohs was brought to an end by the invasion of the Persians in 525 BC who, in turn, were swept aside by the Greeks. However, neither army chose to settle in the shadow of the Pyramids. It was left to the Romans to found the city that was to become Cairo.

Egypt was easily swallowed up as the unstoppable legions pushed the boundaries of Rome's empire ever further. The Romans established a fortress on the site of a Pharaonic river crossing 10km to the east of the Pyramids. Controlling the access to the upper Nile, the fortress of Babylon-in-Egypt, as it became known, grew to become a busy port and major frontier stronghold.

In order to impose their will on the native population the Romans set about eradicating the Egyptians' old Pharaonic-derived religion. This led many Egyptians to turn to the growing, alternative cult of Christianity. When Christianity was adopted as the official religion of the Roman Empire in 323 AD, Rome declared the Christianity of the Egyptians (see Copts under Religion later in this chapter) to be heretical and continued to persecute the local population. This oppressive state of affairs came to an abrupt end in 640 AD when a crusading army of Muslim Arabs arrived at the walls of Babylon riding under the flag of Islam.

Fustat: The First Islamic Capital

The besieged Romans surrendered, while the Egyptian peasants and townspeople welcomed the conquering Muslim Arabs as liberators. Under the command of their general Amr ibn al-As, the Islamic army chose not to occupy Babylon and instead set up their own tent city, Fustat, just to the north. To this day, Babylon, known now as Coptic Cairo, remains non-Muslim and is a tightly walled enclave of ancient Christianity and Judaism.

The centre of Fustat was a mosque (its direct descendant, the Mosque of Amr ibn al-As, still stands), around which the original tent city was rapidly replaced by mud-brick and wood. The population was increased by the arrival of more tribes from Arabia, and the new city prospered.

In 750 the ruling Arabian caliphs were superseded by a rival dynasty based in Iraq called the Abbasids. Abbasid control of Fustat and Egypt was maintained through a governor appointed by the caliph in Baghdad. One such governor was Ahmed ibn Tulun (835-84), the son of a former slave at the caliph's court. Once in Egypt Ibn Tulun quickly acquired so much wealth and such a huge entourage of soldiers and slaves of his own that he had to create a new mini-city just to the north of Fustat. His city was called Al-Qatai, meaning 'the districts', after the way it was divided into zones, with one area for soldiers, one for palace servants and so on. Ibn Tulun was a lavish builder and the crowning glory of his royal city was his mosque, which still stands today (more than a millennium later) and is one of the most striking of Cairo's Islamic monuments.

Ibn Tulun felt powerful enough to cut loose from his masters in Baghdad, keeping Egypt as his personal kingdom and handing over the succession to his son. In 905 the Abbasids decided enough was enough and took it back, devastating Al-Qatai in the process. However, Fustat continued to thrive as one of the richest components of the new Muslim world order; its wealth was based on Egypt's excessively rich soil and the taxes imposed on the heavy Nile traffic. Descriptions left by 10th century travellers portray Fustat as a cosmopolitan metropolis with public gardens, street lighting and buildings up to 14 storeys high. It was a glittering treasury and in August 969 the army of the Fatimids, an Islamic dynasty from North Africa, marched in from the west to claim it.

Al-Qahira: The City Victorious

As Amr ibn al-As, the Abbasids and Ibn Tulun had done before them, the Fatimids chose not to base their authority in the existing city but to occupy the territory to the north and create a new capital. The area for the new city, so the story goes, was pegged out, and labourers were waiting for a signal from the astrologers to begin digging. The signal was to be the ringing of bells attached to the ropes marking off the construction area, but a raven landed on the rope and set off the bells prematurely. As the planet Mars (Al-Qahir) was in the ascendant, the Fatimid caliph decided to call the city Al-Qahira (from which the word 'Cairo' is derived), which can also be understood as 'the Victorious'.

The city the Fatimids built formed the core of Cairo until the mid-19th century. It was originally a fortified, walled enclosure completely off limits to the citizens of Fustat. The division between those within the walls and those without was made even greater by the fact that the Fatimids were Shi'ias, a brand of Islam at odds with the orthodox Sunnism of the Egyptians (see the boxed text 'Shi'ia Head, Sunni Body' in the Things to See & Do chapter for more information).

The unhappy relationship between the Fatimid elite and the Egyptian population was not helped by the fact that the Fatimids produced a succession of caliphs all with varying degrees of insanity, the most infamous of whom was Al-Hakim – see the boxed text 'The Mad Caliph' in the Things to See & Do chapter. Al-Hakim's madness at one point led him to send in his troops to lay waste to Fustat, a move which almost ended in all-out civil war. In fact the former tent city was eventually destroyed by the Fatimids, but not until some 150 years after Al-Hakim's death.

In 1168 the Crusaders, having bloodily rampaged through Palestine, were advancing into Egypt. Fearing that Fustat was indefensible and would be quickly occupied by the Crusaders, from where they could comfortably lay siege to Al-Qahira, the Fatimids ordered Fustat evacuated and put to the torch. The magnificent city burnt for 54 days until virtually nothing remained. The Crusaders never attacked. They were driven off by the Seljuk Turks of Damascus to whom the Fatimids had appealed for help. The Seljuks were Sunni Muslims and once in Al-Qahira they went on to depose the Shi'ia dynasty they had come to the aid of and sent the Fatimids into exile. The gates of the walled royal city were opened up to allow the dispossessed citizens of Fustat inside, marking the beginning of a city called Cairo.

The restorer of Sunni rule and the new overlord of Cairo was Salah ad-Din Ayyub (known to the Crusaders, and later to the west, as Saladin), who established a new dynasty, the Ayyubids. A soldier foremost, Salah ad-Din erected a defensive wall enclosing Cairo and Fustat together (of which next to nothing remains), and established the Citadel that still dominates the city.

The Ayyubid line ran to only four rulers before a bizarre episode in 1250 involving Egypt's only female Islamic potentate (see the boxed text 'Shagaret ad-Durr' in the Things to See & Do chapter) resulted in the rise to power of the Mamluks.

The Mamluks: City of the 1001 Nights

The Mamluks were a Turkish slave-soldier class whose military service had been rewarded by Salah ad-Din with gifts of land. They were organised in a quasi-feudal manner, with groups of Mamluks each attached to their own lord or emir. The groups were maintained not by recruitment or breeding, but by the purchase of new young slaves. There was no system of hereditary lineage, instead it was rule by the strongest. Rare was the sultan who died of old age.

The Mamluk era is usually associated with extreme brutality and an excess of blood-letting but the Mamluks also endowed Cairo with the most exquisite architectural constructions. During their 267 year reign the city was the intellectual and cultural centre of the Islamic world. The contradictions in the make-up of the Mamluks are typified in the figure of Qaitbey, who was bought as a slave-boy by one sultan and witnessed the brief reigns of nine more before he himself clawed his way to the throne. As sultan he rapaciously taxed all his subjects and dealt out vicious punishments with his own hands, once tearing out the eyes and tongue of a court chemist who had failed to transform lead into gold. Yet Qaitbey marked his ruthless sultanship with some of Cairo's most beautiful monuments, notably his mosque which stands in the Northern Cemetery.

The money the Mamluks were spending came from trade. In Pharaonic times a canal existed that connected the Red Sea with the Nile. This had been reopened by Amr ibn al-As and by the time of the Mamluks the canal (which flowed right by the city walls along the route of the present day Sharia Port (Bur) Said) was a vital commercial route linking Europe with India and the Orient. In the 14th and 15th centuries, Cairo's Bab al-Hadid port (now the site of Midan Ramses) was one of the world's busiest, and the Mamluks, in partnership with Venice, virtually controlled east-west trade and grew fabulously rich off it.

A city of great wealth, filled with merchants from distant lands, laden with bazaars of exotic wares, ruled by cruel and fickle sultans – this was the city that inspired many of the tales that make up *The Thousand and One Nights* (see the boxed text 'City of the Thousand and One Nights' in the Things to See & Do chapter).

The end of these fabled days came in the closing years of the 15th century when Vasco da Gama discovered the sea route around the Cape of Good Hope, so freeing European merchants from the heavy taxes raked in by

Cairo and Venice on all goods shipped through them. At around the same time the Turks were emerging as a mighty new empire looking to unify the Muslim world, a goal which included the conquest of Egypt. In 1516, Sultan al-Ghouri and his Mamluk army met the Turks at Aleppo in Syria and were defeated. In January of the following year the Turkish Sultan Selim entered Cairo.

The Ottomans: The Provincialisation of Cairo

Cairo's days as a great imperial centre were at an end. Under the Ottomans it was reduced to the level of a provincial city. What trading revenues there were went back to Istanbul, as did the taxes that were squeezed from Egyptian population.

Although the Mamluk sultanate had been abolished, the Mamluks themselves lived on in the form of lords known as *beys* and maintained considerable power. Over time the Turkish hold on Egypt became weaker as the Turkish Empire went into decline. In 1796 one of the Mamluk beys was confident enough to take on the Turkish garrison in Cairo, defeat them and dispatch the Ottoman governor back to Istanbul. But the Mamluks' re-emergence was short-lived. Within two years they were unseated again, though not by the Turks but by a new force in Egypt – Europeans, in the form of Napoleon and the French army.

The French in Cairo

France was engaged in a war of the empires with Britain. One of the prizes of the fight was India. It was with his sights on India that Napoleon landed at Alexandria in 1798 and then marched on to Cairo where his trained musket-bearing army decimated the sword-wielding Mamluk cavalry at Imbaba. The diminutive general set up headquarters in a Mamluk palace on the edge of the Ezbekiyya lake with the expressed intention of exerting a benevolent rule. However, benevolent or not, this was an occupation and an occupation by non-Muslim foreigners at that. The Mamluks had fled but the citizens of Cairo resisted with open revolt. The revolt was suppressed but the population continued to openly oppose the French.

Sitting on a powder keg in Cairo with the British and Turks allying in Syria, Napoleon decided to cut his losses and get out. The general he left behind was murdered by the Egyptians and in 1801, with the British, the Turks and the Mamluks all gathered on the edges of Cairo, the remaining French forces readily agreed to an armistice and departed the way they had come, via Alexandria.

The Turks were reinstated in Cairo. Among their number was an officer named Mohammed Ali, an Albanian mercenary. Within five years of the departure of the French he had fought and intrigued his way to become the *pasha* of Egypt, nominally the vassal of Istanbul but in practice looking on Egypt, and Cairo, as his own.

Mohammed Ali: Cairo, City of the Orient

As long as the Mamluks were still around they posed a potential threat to Mohammed Ali's security. This was settled by the infamous slaughter that took place at the Citadel in 1811 – see the boxed text 'The Massacre of the Mamluks' in the Things to See & Do chapter. In the weeks that followed, a further 3500 Mamluks were murdered in Cairo bringing a 560 year chapter of the city's history to a bloody close.

Although Mohammed Ali's means of achieving his ends could be barbarous, his reign is pivotal in the history of Cairo as under his uncompromising rule the city underwent a transition from a medieval-style feudalism to something approaching industrialisation. Mohammed Ali is credited with introducing a public education system and with planting Egypt's fields with the valuable cash crop of cotton.

Mohammed Ali was said to have a mania for all things new and foreign; conversely, during his reign, a growing number of foreigners became ever more fascinated by Egypt and all things 'Oriental'. The 1820s, 30s and 40s saw Cairo visited by a stream of adventurers and intrepid early travellers, including Mark Twain, Gustave Flaubert, Florence Nightingale and Richard Burton, translator of *The Thousand and One Nights*, and artists like David Roberts and Edward

David Roberts

You might not know the name but stick around Cairo for any length of time and you'll certainly come across his work. One hundred and thirty years after his death, David Roberts is as ubiquitous as ever – his lithographs illustrate countless calendars and postcards and are reproduced in just about every book on Cairo, Egypt and the Holy Land, this one included.

A former scene painter for the Drury Lane theatre in London, Scottish-born Roberts travelled to Cairo in 1838. He spent less than five months in Egypt, but the sketches and notes he made then formed the basis for a vast body of work produced over the next 10 years and ensured him enduring fame and a fortune in his lifetime. Individually his lithographs are beautiful – intricately detailed and painstakingly accurate – but taken together they present a fantastic survey of Cairo at a time when the city remained, in appearance, very much unchanged since the rule of the Mamluks. ■

View of Bab Zuweyla from inside the city walls; painted by Roberts in 1838.

Shepheard's Hotel

If there was one institution that encapsulated the colonial iced tea and gin-sling lifestyle of Cairo under British rule it was Shepheard's Hotel, which in its day was the city's most famous landmark after the Pyramids.

The hotel was established in 1841 by Samuel Shepheard, a farmer's son from northern England, and occupied the site of Napoleon's former headquarters on the Ezbekiyya. It immediately became the base camp for all travellers in the Middle East and Africa, and provided the first offices for the fledgling company of Thomas Cook. Early guests included General Gordon before he set forth on his ill-fated mission to Khartoum, Stanley bound for Africa and his historic meeting with Livingstone, Sir Richard Burton after his pilgrimage to Mecca, and Rudyard Kipling en route between England and India.

As its reputation increased, the hotel expanded to include a fabulous Moorish Hall lit by a dome of coloured glass and a ballroom with lotus-topped pillars modelled on those at Karnak. Most famous of all was the street-side terrace crowded with wicker chairs and tables. This was the giddy centre of Cairo social life and during the war it became the favoured watering hole of the British officer classes.

When anti-British sentiments came to a head on Black Saturday in 1952, Shepheard's was one of the arsonists' first targets. The hotel was completely destroyed, an action which, as much as the coup that followed, delivered notice that the era of Cairo as a playground of the west was at an end. ∎

Lear. Their journals and lithographs were eagerly devoured by romantically inclined readers enraptured by accounts of temples in the sand, veiled harems and the bare-breasted women of the slave markets.

Ironically, it was the interests and influence of the Europeans that was very soon to completely change Cairo from a city of the east to one that looked almost exclusively to the west.

Ismailia: The New European Cairo

In 1848, the year before he died, Mohammed Ali was succeeded by his grandson Abbas, then by one of his own sons Said and then, in 1863, by Ismail, another grandson, who in his 16-year reign did more than anybody since the Mamluks to alter the appearance of Cairo.

It was Ismail who expanded the city from the Ezbekiyya lake, its westernmost edge for the previous 900 years, right up to the banks of the Nile – in effect establishing a new European-style Cairo beside the old Islamic one. It was also during his reign that the Suez Canal was completed. The canal's opening in 1869 brought Cairo to the attention of the whole world and attracted a guest list that

included every crowned head, president and prime minister of importance, all of whom were accommodated in newly constructed palaces and regal apartment buildings.

By this time Cairo was attracting ever-increasing numbers of foreign tourists, particularly with the advent of the railway connecting it to the Mediterranean port of Alexandria. By 1860 Thomas Cook had already begun leading organised tours to Cairo and Egypt, and new hotels ringed the Ezbekiyya area. The city rapidly gained a large foreign population (in 1872 there were 25,000 Europeans and Americans out of a total population of 300,000) who were involved in running businesses and conducting trade. Cairo almost had the character of a gold rush town.

The pickings were particularly rich for the European bankers who, with the connivance of their governments, bestowed lavish loans upon Ismail for his grandiose schemes. They advanced the kind of money Egypt could never conceivably repay, at insatiable rates of interest. In 1882, the British stepped in and announced that until Egypt could repay its debts, they were taking control.

The British in Cairo

The British allowed the heirs of Mohammed Ali to remain on the throne but all power was concentrated in the hands of the British Agent, the governor by another name. What Britain was interested in was reaping the profits from Egyptian cotton and ensuring the security of the Suez Canal, the passageway to British India.

The British often saw their role in Cairo as a stern sort of paternalism, acting for a country that couldn't look after itself. They introduced a form of Egyptian legislative assembly and improved public transport, and many local land owners benefited from the cotton trade and built fantastic villas in newly developed Garden City and Gezira, but again the bottom line was that it was occupation by military might.

Egypt's desire for self-determination was strengthened by the Allies' use of Cairo as a glorified barracks during WWI, even though Egypt was never itself a theatre of the war. Saad Zaghloul, the most brilliant of a newly emerging breed of young Egyptian politicians, spoke for his nation when he said, 'I have no quarrel with them personally ... but I want to see an independent Egypt'.

As a sop to nationalist sentiments the British granted Egypt its 'sovereignty' but this was very much an empty gesture – 'King' Fuad enjoyed little popularity among his people and the British kept tight hold of the reins.

More than that, they came in ever greater numbers with the outbreak of WWII. To the thousands of Allied troops posted in Cairo following Germany's invasion of North Africa, the city seemed like bliss. It was hot and luxurious, food and beer were in plentiful supply and there were many other welcome diversions from the war being fought out in the desert. Officers were billeted in apartments beside the Gezira Club or overlooking the Nile in Garden City and frequented Shepheard's terrace, Groppi's, the Turf Club and Madame Badia's Cabaret with its famed belly-dancers.

While many Egyptians were also enjoying the benefits of this the most glamorous of wars, particularly shopkeepers and businessmen, there was a vocal element among the locals who saw the Germans as potential liberators who would deliver them from British rule. Students held rallies in support of Rommel and in the Egyptian army a small cabal of officers, which included future presidents Nasser and Sadat, plotted to aid the German general's advance on their city.

There was a brief scare as Rommel pushed the Allied forces back almost to Alexandria, which had the British embassy and GHQ hurriedly burning documents in such quantity that the skies over Cairo turned dark

The Real English Patient

Anyone who is familiar with the book or film *The English Patient* may be intrigued to know that the character played by Ralph Fiennes – the 'English Patient' of the title – is not a fictional creation; neither was he English nor was he ever a patient crippled by burns and a broken heart.

Ladislaus 'László' Almásy was a Hungarian aristocrat who arrived in Cairo during the interwar years. There are still people around who remember him and claim he was a bit of an introvert who was very much overshadowed by his playboy brother Janós. László Almásy, however, was an explorer and a pilot, and he worked for the British-run Egyptian Desert Survey Department conducting aerial surveys. Flying alone in the Western Desert in his Gypsy Moth, László did make the discoveries attributed to him in the book and film.

When WWII broke out Almásy enlisted with the pro-German Hungarian air force and found himself attached to Rommel's Afrika Korps teaching desert survival. Famously, in 1942 Almásy led a German spy on a gruelling overland trek across the Western Desert to get him into Egypt undetected by the British.

Far from then returning to the desert to recover the dead body of Kristin Scott Thomas, slamming his aircraft into the deck and getting toasted, and then dying under the tearful gaze of Juliette Binoche, Almásy survived the war to die in Salzburg, Austria in 1951 following a protracted illness.

With thanks to Samir Raafat

with the ash, but the Germans never broke through. Instead, the British were to remain for almost 10 more years before a day of greater and fiercer flames was to drive them out for good.

Masr: Cairo Returns to the Egyptians

On Saturday 26 January 1952 – Black Saturday – European Cairo was set on fire. After years of demonstrations, strikes and riots against the continued presence of the British in Egypt, the British storming of a rebellious Egyptian police station in the Suez Canal zone provided the necessary spark to ignite the capital. Foreign-owned and foreigner-frequented shops and businesses all over town were targeted by mobs and set ablaze. All the landmarks of 80 years of British rule were reduced to charred ruins within the space of one day.

The British must have realised that as far as they were concerned Egypt was ungovernable, so when just a few weeks later a group of young army officers seized power in a coup it was accepted as a *fait accompli*. On 26 July 1952, the Egyptian puppet-king Farouk, descendant of the Albanian Mohammed Ali, departed Alexandria harbour aboard the royal yacht, leaving Egypt to be ruled by Egyptians for the first time since the Pharaohs.

Capital of the Arab World

As the leader of the revolutionary Free Officers, Colonel Gamal Abdel Nasser ascended to power and was confirmed as president by elections in 1956. His priority was domestic transformation – to create a situation whereby the Egyptians would be masters in their own land. To this end all the old feudal estates were broken up and the land was distributed among the *fellaheen*, Egypt's large and long put-upon agrarian workforce. While Cairo's huge foreign community was not forced to go, they nevertheless began to steadily decline in numbers.

Meanwhile, Cairo grew spectacularly in population and the urban planners struggled to keep pace. The west bank of the Nile was concreted over with new suburbs like Medinet Mohandiseen (Engineers' City) and Medinet Sahafayeen (Journalists' City). Expansion also took place to the north, most notably in the hideous form of Medinet Nasr (Victory City) named after Nasser's success in facing down the British, French and Israelis over the Suez Canal.

Nasser's skills as a tough negotiator, and his ability to stand up to the western powers earned him plaudits all over the developing world, and Nasser's Cairo came to be seen as the centre of a newly emerging Arab nationalism. Already, less than 30 years after his death in 1970, the Nasser years are viewed by a great many Egyptians as something of a lost golden era; the biggest cinema hit of 1997 was *Nasser '56*, a flattering biopic of the president's finest moment.

Cairo: The Surviving City

Local opinion regarding Sadat, Nasser's successor, is more divided. Egypt's second president initiated a complete about face, ditching the socialist idealisms of Nasser and instead wholeheartedly embracing capitalism. After a decade and a half of keeping a low profile the wealthy resurfaced and were joined by a large, new moneyed middle class grown rich on the back of a much-touted 'Open Door Policy'. The likes of Mohandiseen and Nasr City, originally conceived as Soviet-style workers' dormitories, became the addresses of choice for the new money and favoured locations for rashes of western fast-food outlets, boutiques and car showrooms.

More contentious was Sadat's willingness to talk peace with the Jewish state. This cost him his life when he was assassinated during a 1981 military parade by members of the Muslim Brotherhood – an uncompromising political organisation that aimed to establish an Islamic state in Egypt.

Leadership of the country since Sadat's assassination has been in the hands of Hosni Mubarak who inherited a whole host of problems, not least of which has been how to stay alive. (Returning to Cairo in 1996 I asked an Egyptian friend, 'So what's new?' 'Mubarak hasn't been shot at this month,' he replied.) Less flamboyant than Sadat and less charismatic than Nasser, Hosni Mubarak is often criticised as being both unimaginative and indecisive. Nevertheless, Cairo has seen significant, if agonisingly slow, improvements during his 16 years in power. The city has gained an underground metro system, there's an ongoing program of arterial road construction, new residential projects are springing up in the desert and a limited form of private enterprise is being encouraged.

The changes, however, are slow in coming and fall well short of keeping pace with the litany of woes (overcrowding, collapsing infrastructure, the widening poverty gap, unemployment and health-endangering pollution) afflicting the overstretched and greatly abused metropolis. The city's major source of revenue, its history – in the shape of the Pyramids, the antiquities of the Egyptian Museum and the Islamic monuments – are also under threat from pollutant-accelerated decay, neglect and downright bad management.

While Cairo has five millennia's worth of a glorious and rich history, as we approach the new millennium the future for the city looks far less grand.

GEOGRAPHY
Cairo sits on the Nile at the point at which the river fans out to become the fertile green Delta. The city covers some 214sq km, most of which is on the east bank. As with Egypt itself (where the country's population is strung out along the narrow stem of the Nile valley), Cairo clings to the river, stretching 40km from north to south. Its lateral spread east used to be constrained by the bare-rock Muqattam Hills, which give way to the Eastern Desert, but in recent years, population pressure has meant that the Muqattam have been leap-frogged, and the once-barren desert is now a vast and messy construction site for a series of overspill-soaking satellite cities (see the boxed text 'Desert Developments' under Ecology & Environment for more information).

Cairo's expansion on the west bank is much smaller. Here, if you stray more than a half-dozen kilometres from the Nile, the loamy valley soil gives way to the fine sand of the Western Desert. From the Pyramids, on the westernmost edge of Cairo, there is nothing but 600km of sand between the city and the Libyan border.

CLIMATE
Most of the year, except for the winter months of December, January and February, Cairo is hot and dry. In summer a punishing sun keeps temperatures up around 35 to 38°C (95 to 100°F), though a relatively low humidity generally makes the heat bearable. During the winter, daytime temperatures drop to a very comfortable 15 to 20°C (59 to 68°F). Jumpers or a light jacket are useful but a coat is not necessary. However, the evenings can be quite chilly in winter, with temperatures plummeting to as low as 8°C (47°F). This is made worse by the fact there is no such thing as central heating in Cairo apartments.

Rainfall is modest, about 25mm per year, occurring during January and February in an infrequent spattering of downpours.

Between March and April, Cairo is occasionally subject to the *khamseen*, a dry, hot and very dusty wind that blows in from the parched Western Desert at up to 150km per hour. The name comes from the Arabic word for 'fifty' and refers to the 50 days for which the winds are supposed to blow. In fact, during the khamseen period the storms rarely occur more than once a week and last for just a few hours at a time.

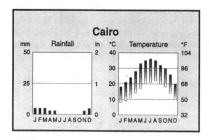

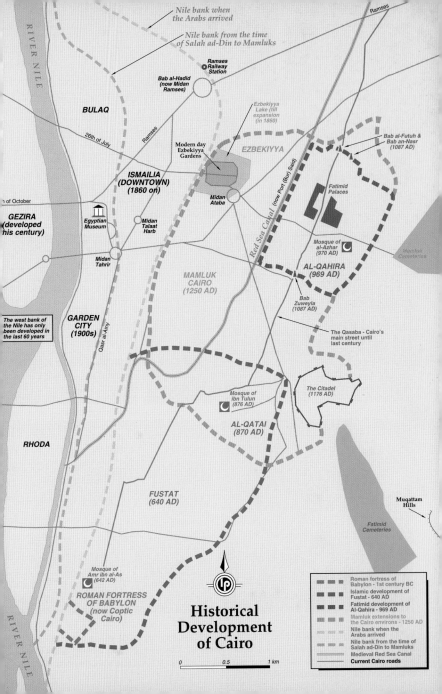

Nile bank when the Arabs arrived

Nile bank from the time of Salah ad-Din to Mamluks

Ramses

RIVER NILE

Ramses Railway Station

Bab al-Hadid (now Midan Ramses)

Ezbekiyya Lake (till expansion in 1860)

Bab al-Futuh & Bab an-Nasr (1087 AD)

BULAQ

26th of July

Ramses

EZBEKIYYA

Modern day Ezbekiyya Gardens

ISMAILIA (DOWNTOWN) (1860 on)

Fatimid Palaces

of October

Midan Ataba

Red Sea Canal (now Port (Bur) Said)

Mamluk Cemeteries

GEZIRA (developed his century)

Egyptian Museum

Midan Talaat Harb

Mosque of al-Azhar (970 AD)

Midan Tahrir

AL-QAHIRA (969 AD)

MAMLUK CAIRO (1250 AD)

Bab Zuweyla (1087 AD)

The west bank of the Nile has only been developed in the last 60 years

GARDEN CITY (1900s)

Qasr al-Ainy

The Qasaba - Cairo's main street until last century

The Citadel (1176 AD)

RHODA

Mosque of Ibn Tulun (876 AD)

AL-QATAI (870 AD)

Muqattam Hills

FUSTAT (640 AD)

Fatimid Cemeteries

Mosque of Amr ibn al-As (642 AD)

ROMAN FORTRESS OF BABYLON (now Coptic Cairo)

Historical Development of Cairo

RIVER NILE

0   0.5   1 km

Roman fortress of Babylon - 1st century BC

Islamic development of Fustat - 640 AD

Fatimid development of Al-Qahira - 969 AD

Mamluk extensions to the Cairo environs - 1250 AD

Nile bank when the Arabs arrived

Nile bank from the time of Salah ad-Din to Mamluks

Medieval Red Sea Canal

Current Cairo roads

EDDIE GERALD

EDDIE GERALD

EDDIE GERALD

BETHUNE CARMICHAEL

EDDIE GERALD

EDDIE GERALD

While Cairo is blessed with the Pyramids, the Pharaonic treasures of the Egyptian Museum and an embarrassing wealth of Islamic architecture, the city's main asset is its inhabitants who, despite challenging conditions, remain the most stubbornly cheerful and hospitable people imaginable.

ECOLOGY & ENVIRONMENT

There are no two ways about it, Cairo is bad for your health. Chief among the city's afflictions is air pollution, but water pollution, noise pollution, unsafe buildings and over-crowding are also seriously problematic issues. Caring about the environment is a luxury that traditionally few Cairenes have had time to indulge in, but this is now changing and in recent years an Egyptian Environmental Affairs Agency has been set up and new environment laws introduced. But while laws may be passed, little is done to implement and enforce them and the deterioration shows no sign of reversal.

Air Pollution

Cairo is the great upturned ashtray (a phrase coined by Tony Horwitz in his book *Baghdad Without a Map*), with an air so full of filth and ill health that breathing the atmosphere Downtown is said to be equivalent to smoking a packet of cigarettes a day. During summer, a few minutes on the streets of Central Cairo is enough to acquire a gritty coating that turns tissues black when wiped across perspiring foreheads. Over a million vehicles (most old and badly maintained) jam the city's roads, belching out clouds of noxious fumes. There is next to no control on vehicle emissions, and unleaded fuel has yet to catch on. Concrete factories on the edge of town spew dust into the air. The net result is that Cairo may well be the world's second most-polluted urban centre after Mexico City. The level of lead in the air is three to 20 times higher than internationally permissible levels (depending on which agency you ask), while the density of suspended solid particles (the main cause of respiratory problems) is between five and 10 times the recommended international level.

The government is finally sufficiently alarmed to do something about all this. As part of a 1994 environmental law factories are required to install filters (reportedly, few have so far done so); a pilot scheme has introduced compressed natural gas to power state-owned vehicles (so far limited to a small fleet of microbuses); and a US$200 million USAID-sponsored air improvement project has been launched. For the time being, however, residents of Cairo have to resign themselves to a pretty nasty habit of passive smoking.

Overcrowding

If the latest census results are accurate then Egypt's long-running family planning campaigns may be on the way to conquering the country's problem of uncontrolled population growth, particularly regarding Cairo.

Desert Developments

A scheme drawn up by the Ministry of Housing in the 1980s aimed to move almost two million people out of the capital by the year 2000 into a series of small satellite cities in the desert. Progress has been slow, with most Cairenes reluctant to relocate and leave behind family, friends and their neighbourhood. Some success was achieved with three larger 'cities' (6th of October, 10th of Ramadan and Sadat), all with their own supporting industries, but two dozen smaller dormitory 'communities' have languished in various states of non-completion. To date, the population of the new desert developments has possibly not yet reached six figures.

The master plan did receive an injection of urgency in the wake of the 1992 earthquake. Tracts of housing were quickly thrown up to accommodate some 20,000 Cairenes made homeless by the disaster. However, since that time, there has been a boom in land prices and a rethink on the part of the ministry – out goes public housing in favour of selling off desert land to the wealthy. So the residents of Qatamiyya, the earthquake victim housing project, now find themselves neighbours of Egypt's first world-class golf course, 'Qatamiyya Heights'. The problem is that the privileged few teeing off on the exquisitely manicured fairways are said to be none too keen on the view of the slum-like housing blocks downhill. And so it was, according to one daily Egyptian newspaper, that the housing minister in the summer of 1997 decreed that the 129 buildings were unsafe and had to be demolished, just seven years after they were built. ■

According to the statistics, Egypt's population growth rate has fallen from 2.8% a decade ago to the current 2.1%. On top of that, the census showed that the trend of urbanisation has been reversed, with fewer people migrating to the capital.

That said, around 16 million people still inhabit Cairo. By the government's own admission, parts of the city continue to house the densest number of people per kilometre anywhere in the world (it's for this reason that the south Cairo suburb of Dar as-Salaam is known locally as 'Little China'). The strain placed on the city's decaying infrastructure is enormous, particularly in what are termed the 'unplanned housing districts' – or, in less wilfully obscure words, slums. Some 20% of Cairenes live in slums with makeshift sewers that leak into the streets, no fresh water supply, no garbage collection, and the most rudimentary types of dwellings. Government plans to provide some alternative accommodation in the desert (see the boxed text 'Desert Developments' on the previous page) are proving less than successful and, despite the good news contained in the census results, current estimates still warn that by the year 2001 Egypt will need almost another million housing units.

GOVERNMENT & POLITICS

In terms of the state, Egypt and Cairo are virtually synonymous – in Arabic the traditional name for both is the same, *Masr*. In the minds of many – academics, business people, media people and politicians – little beyond the capital matters. While the Ministry of Tourism might ponder upon Upper Egypt and Sinai and the Ministry of Foreign Affairs may look to Paris or Washington, the gaze of government is fixed almost exclusively on the capital. While Cairo does have a governor (in fact it has three: one for Cairo, one for Giza, and one for Qalyubiyya, a grouping of the city's northern districts) all major initiatives and decisions concerning the city are dealt with at ministerial level.

The public interface with these unreachable, and very much unaccountable, holders of office is through the multi-layered complexity of Cairo's bureaucracy. If there is one unquestionable achievement of the Egyptian administration since 1952, when President Nasser guaranteed a job to each and every university graduate, it has been to raise the inanity of bureaucracy to the point of surrealism. No application or request may be accepted before it has been stamped four times, signed and countersigned at least the same number of times, passed by the desks of a half dozen individuals, and a certain amount of small bills have changed hands. For the average Cairene, whose interest in politics has been blunted by fraudulent elections and the marginalisation of opposition parties, bureaucracy *is* government.

ECONOMY

Until recently, the most widely quoted statistic about Cairo's economy was that the average government employee does just 27 minutes of work per day. These days the talk is of Egypt being one of the world's most attractive emerging markets, with great potential for fast growth. The change has been brought about by a seeming 'road to Damascus' type conversion at the highest levels. After decades of subsidising unproductive and over-staffed state-owned industries, the government has begun dismantling the Nasserist system of central planning, selling off businesses, and introducing packages of liberalising reforms to encourage foreign investment.

The new policies are already starting to pay off. More than US$500 million flowed into the Cairo stock exchange in 1996, while foreign investment increased by a factor of almost 150%. The new money is well in evidence: in spring 1997 Rolls Royce set up a showroom in Cairo, hot on the heels of Jaguar; a new Nile-side apartment block in Giza is offering three-bedroom units at a starting price of US$1.3 million; and a rash of US-style shopping malls is springing up around town filled with designer clothes stores, Belgian confectioners and sushi bars. This comes with its own problems. As part of the reform program the government is also committed to cutting subsidies on housing, food, electricity, and transport – the greater part of society is soon going to be wondering why the cost of their daily bread is rising while they're seeing more and more luxury cars on the roads. This isn't yet Brazil, but with the present absence of any real wealth redistribution Cairo is looking at a startling widening of the rich-poor divide.

See also the Doing Business section in the Facts for the Visitor chapter.

POPULATION & PEOPLE

Cairo is reckoned to be home to about 27% of the country's population; if the latest census statistics are accurate, this means that the city is heaving with some 16.5 million people (see the discussion about overcrowding under Ecology & Environment, earlier in this chapter). There are more Cairenes than there are Austrians, Belgians or Greeks. Each day this number is swollen by thousands of commuters from the Delta villages and towns arriving at Ramses railway station and the city's various bus stations.

The make-up of the city is predominantly working class. The typical Cairene male lives in the hemmed-in side streets of a suburb like Shubra or Dar as-Salaam, in a six floor concrete tenement with cracking walls and only intermittent water. If he's lucky he may own a small Fiat or Lada which will be 10 or more years old, otherwise he'll take the metro to work or, more likely, fight for a handhold on one of the city's sardine-can buses. He may well be a university graduate (about 40,000 people graduate each year), although that is no longer any guarantee of a job. Chances are he'll be one of the million-plus paper-pushing civil servants, earning a pittance to while away each day in an un-demanding job. This at least allows him to slip away early each afternoon to borrow his cousin's taxi for a few hours and bring in some much needed supplementary income.

His wife remains at home each day cooking, looking after the three or more children, and swapping visits with his mother, her mother and various family members.

The aspirations of this typical family are to move up the social scale. With no class system as such or aristocracy, movement upwards is completely dependent on money. In the 1970s Sadat's free market policies resulted in a lot of people becoming very rich. These people now form Cairo's middle classes. They largely inhabit the newer concrete districts of Mohandiseen, Doqqi and Nasser City, where they cruise the wide tree-lined avenues in Mercedes, Audis and BMWs, dropping off the kids (dressed in clothes bought in London last spring) at the club.

At the other end of the scale are the masses of fellaheen, who move to Cairo to escape the poverty of working the land. They end up living in 'unplanned housing', a rabble of shanty towns fringing the city. If they're lucky they manage to find employment as construction labourers or as *bawwabs*, doormen to middle-class apartment blocks.

Africans Cairo is the largest city on the African continent and is home to large numbers of Africans, particularly from Sudan and the Horn of Africa, but also from as far afield as Tanzania, Mali and Sierra Leone. Cairo's Al-Azhar university offers many scholarships to African Islamic countries and there are about 20,000 African students in Cairo. An even larger group are refugees or 'displaced persons'; these are people who left their homeland but in the eyes of the authorities don't meet refugee criteria.

The Sudanese community is by far the largest non-Egyptian group in Cairo. Estimates vary wildly but according to the Sudanese embassy the population is around 400,000. Many fled the fighting that still rages in the south of Sudan, but to date only 1500 Sudanese have been granted official refugee status.

For most Africans Cairo is not a comfortable home. Many find the society restrictive, they encounter racism and there is always the fear of deportation. Many Africans are in Cairo for economic reasons or because they have finished their studies and have decided to stay on (often in the hope of moving on to the west). The Egyptian government is not welcoming of these would-be immigrants and frequent sweeps are made hauling in truckloads of Africans to check their documentation.

Unsurprisingly, the Africans tend to stick together; they have their own social clubs and their own places to hang out in at night – the African discos offer some of the liveliest nightlife in Cairo (for more information see the Entertainment chapter).

Expatriates Continuing the tradition that began in the 19th century when Egypt was 'discovered' first by Europe then America, Cairo is home to around 50,000 western expatriates. Many work for nongovernmental organisations, in petroleum companies or as teachers. Cairo offers them a chance to live somewhere exotic but safe; a place where it's possible to jostle elbows and bargain in the bazaar, but then return home to snack on Twinkies and Oreos bought in the mini-market down the street.

The main expat neighbourhoods are chic Zamalek, leafy Maadi, and colonial-era Heliopolis. These are the places where you'll find the top restaurants, the trendiest bars, western-style supermarkets and the meeting places of groups like the Petroleum Wives and the Tuesday Knitters.

ARTS
Literature
Naguib Mahfouz is not just the most famous Egyptian writer of all time, he can also claim to have single-handedly shaped the nature of Arabic literature this century. Born in 1911 in Cairo's Islamic quarter (see the boxed text 'Mahfouz's Cairo' in the Things to See & Do chapter) Mahfouz began writing when he was 17. His first efforts were very much influenced by European models, but over the course of his 66 year writing career (brutally cut short: see the boxed text 'A Lesson To Salman Rushdie') he developed a voice that was uniquely of the Arab world and that drew its inspiration from the talk in the coffeehouses and the dialect and slang of Cairo's streets.

His masterpiece is usually considered to be *The Cairo Trilogy* (comprising *Palace Walk, Palace of Desire* and *Sugar Street)*, a generational saga of family life set in the districts of Mahfouz's youth. It was this work that sealed it for the Swedish Academy when they awarded him the Nobel Prize for Literature in 1988. Also well worth reading are *Midaq Alley* (one of his earliest and most popular works), a soap operatic portrayal of

---

A Lesson to Salman Rushdie
The Nobel Prize for Literature awarded to Naguib Mahfouz in 1988 for his lifetime's work precipitated the end of his writing career. The attendant publicity revived the long dormant issue of his novel *Children of the Alley* which upon its newspaper serialisation in 1959 had been condemned by religious authorities for its alleged allegorical depictions of Allah and his prophets. Four months after Mahfouz was thrust into the limelight by the Nobel committee, blind Sheikh Omar Abdel Rahman – currently imprisoned in the USA for his involvement in the World Trade Centre bombing – was widely reported as saying that if Mahfouz had been punished when he wrote *Children of the Alley*, then Salman Rushdie would never have dared write his novel *The Satanic Verses*.

For a small extremist minority this was as good as a *fatwa* against Mahfouz. On an October afternoon in 1994, as the writer was climbing into a friend's car outside his home, he was approached by a young man who drew a knife and stabbed his victim twice in the neck. Mahfouz miraculously survived but the attack left his right arm and hand paralysed and he can now write little more than his own name.

Non-Arabic readers, however, still have the pleasure of more Mahfouz to come. Only half of his 40 or so novels and short story collections have so far been translated into English. Many of the rest are scheduled to appear over the next few years as part of an ambitious publishing program shared between the American University in Cairo Press and Anchor/Doubleday in the USA. ■

life in a poor back-alley in Islamic Cairo, and *The Harafish*, which is perhaps the definitive Mahfouz book. *The Harafish* is another 'alley novel' but it was written much later in an episodic, almost folkloric style that owes much to the tradition of *The Thousand and One Nights*.

On the strength of what's available in English it's all too easy to view Cairo literature as beginning and ending with Mahfouz, but he's only the best known of a canon of respected writers, all of whom have been superseded by a newer, younger literati intent on making their own mark. Of Mahfouz's peers, only Gamal al-Ghitani has achieved anything in the way of widespread international acclaim with *Zayni Barakat*, a tale of intrigue in Mamluk-era Cairo, which was picked up in translation by major US and UK publishing houses. The late Yousef Idris, a writer of powerful short stories (*The Cheapest Nights* and *Rings of Burnished Brass*) is also worthy of much more attention, but at present he's published in English only by the AUC Press, a small Cairo-based academic publishing house.

Few of the younger generation of writers, despite much acclaim in Cairo's literary circles, have yet to make it into translation. However, one writer to watch out for is Ibrahim Abdel Meguid who US publishers Anchor/Doubleday are hoping might be the next Mahfouz, at least as far as sales are concerned. His book, *The Other Village*, is due to be released in an English-language translation in early 1998.

Ahdaf Soueif is something of an anomaly: an Egyptian writer more easily available in overseas editions than she is in Arabic. The reason for this is that although Soueif was born and educated in Cairo, she has always written in English and for a long time has lived in London. Her heavily autobiographical novel *In the Eye of the Sun* (yet to appear in Arabic) and her two short-story collections *Aisha* and *Sandpiper* flit between her grey, drizzly adopted English home and the close, muggy city of her birth. The predominant theme of much of her work is, unsurprisingly, the notion of foreignness.

Tackling Taboos

Egypt may be a male-dominated society, but its female writers are arguably enjoying more international success than their male counterparts. After Mahfouz, the country's best known writer abroad is Nawal al-Saadawi, whose most popular fictional work *Woman At Point Zero* has been published, at last count, in 28 languages. An outspoken critic on behalf of women, al-Saadawi is very much marginalised at home – her nonfiction book *The Hidden Face of Eve* which considers the role of women in the Arab world is banned in Egypt. In the early 1990s, at the height of the Islamist problem, Saadawi left Egypt in fear of her life after receiving death threats. She returned to Cairo in 1997. Her autobiography is due to be published in the USA in 1998.

Equally forthright and uncompromising is Salwa Bakr, another female writer who tackles taboo subjects like sexual prejudice and social inequality head on. Her only novel available in English, *The Golden Chariot*, tells the stories of a group of women prison inmates driven to transgress the law through poverty and oppression. It may sound a bit heavy but it's actually a thoroughly absorbing read with some heart-warming touches of humour.

Salwa Bakr is just one of eight contemporary Egyptian women writers collected in the short story anthology *My Grandmother's Cactus*, edited by Marilyn Booth and published in the UK by Quartet. ■

Painting

While Egypt has produced one or two outstanding painters, contemporary art is very much in the doldrums. The problem stems from the Egyptian art school system, where a student's ability to do well largely depends on their ability to emulate the artistic styles favoured or practised by their professors. Nepotism reigns over originality and as a result much of what finds its way into the galleries is of very dubious merit. Unsurprisingly, some of the most interesting work comes from artists with no formal training at all. Such artists are often shunned by the state-run galleries but there are several private exhibition spaces which are happy to show nonconformist work. Anyone seriously interested in contemporary art should visit the Mashrabia, Cairo-Berlin or Extra galleries (see the Activities section at the end of the Things to See & Do chapter).

Things have not always been so stagnant and it is worth paying a visit to the Museum of Modern Art in the Opera House grounds. In particular look out for the work of Abdel Hady al-Gazzar, a true one-off who painted Egypt as a kind of colourful but slightly freakish circus. The rich, warm portraits of Mahmoud Said, several of which hang in the museum, are also beautiful. For more information there's a fairly decent book by Lilliane Karnouk, *Modern Egyptian Art*, or pick up Fatma Ismail's *29 Artists in the Museum of Egyptian Modern Art* – both are available at the art museum and at the Mashrabia Gallery.

Music

Unlike literature and painting, which are take it or leave it affairs, there's no getting away from music in Cairo. Taking a taxi, shopping or just walking the streets; the routines of daily life are played out to a constant musical accompaniment blasted from wheezing and tinny cassette players. The music you hear can be broadly divided into two categories: classical and pop.

Classical There was a time when Cairo was the undisputed music capital of the Arab world, a city from where the likes of Umm Kolthum and Abdel Halim Hafez ruled the airwaves from Algeria to Iraq. Egypt's love affair with the singer Umm Kolthum was such that on the afternoon of the first Thursday of each month, streets would become deserted as the whole country sat beside its radios to listen to her regular live-broadcast performance. She had her male counterparts in Abdel Halim Hafez and Farid al-Atrash but they never attracted anything like the devotion accorded to 'the mother of Egypt'. When she died in 1975 her funeral was attended by a bevy of Arab leaders and

the streets of Cairo were filled with millions of mourners. Her appeal wasn't purely confined to Egypt and its neighbours; former Led Zeppelin vocalist Robert Plant was reported as saying that one of his lifetime ambitions was to reform the Middle Eastern Orchestra, Umm Kolthum's group of backing musicians.

The kind of orchestra in question is a curious cross-fertilisation of east and west, with the instruments familiar to western ears augmented by the *oud* (a type of lute), *nai* (reed pipe), *qanun* (zither) and *tabla* (a small hand-held drum).

Classical Arab music has become much less popular since the death of Umm Kolthum, which marked the end of what's popularly regarded as a golden era, but her songs are still ubiquitous on radio and TV, and an Umm Kolthum cassette remains an essential part of any taxi driver's equipment.

Umm Kolthum – whose voice would regularly bring Cairo to a standstill until her death in 1975. She lives on in taxis everywhere.

Pop Although to this day the likes of Umm Kolthum and Abdel Halim Hafez are still eulogised and revered, as Egypt experienced a population boom and the mean age decreased, a gap in popular culture developed which the memory of the greats couldn't fill. Enter Ahmed Adawiyya who did for Arabic music the same service that punk rendered in the west. Throwing off the traditional melodies and lyrical melodramas, Adawiyya's streetwise and, to some, politically subversive songs captured the spirit of the time and dominated popular culture throughout the entire 1970s.

Adawiyya set the blueprint for a new kind of music known as *al-jeel* (the generation), characterised by a clattering, hand-clapping rhythm overlaid with synthesised twirlings and a catchy, repetitive vocal (the word *habibi*, meaning 'my love' or 'my darling', often constitutes the bulk of the lyric). Adawiyya's legacy also spawned something called *shaabi* (popular), considered the real music of the working class quarters of Cairo. Shaabi is far cruder than al-jeel and its lyrics are often satirical or politically provocative. Shaabi artists rarely make it onto TV.

In recent years the Egyptians are being beaten at their own game and many of the current biggest selling artists come from Iraq, Syria or Lebanon. Of the home-grown talent, the top names (the industry is solo vocal artist oriented, there are no pop groups) are Hakim, Amr Diab and Mohammed Fuad, but selling half a million albums in Cairo doesn't necessarily mean that their tapes are accessible to unattuned western ears. Despite constant exposure in taxis, shops and on the street, Cairo pop is an acquired taste and one that few non-Arabs pick up. For a buyers' guide to Egyptian music, see the Shopping chapter.

Dance
There is strong evidence from sources such as tomb paintings that Egypt's tradition of formalised dancing goes back to the time of the Pharaohs. During medieval times dancing became institutionalised in the form of the *ghawazee*, a caste of dancers who travelled in groups and performed publicly or for hire. The female ghawazee, who according to 18th and 19th century descriptions danced in baggy trousers and loose shirts sometimes open to the navel, were also often prostitutes. Flaubert devotes a lot of space in his Egyptian diaries to his encounters with dancers. This was exactly the kind of exoticism travellers to the mystical east were hoping to discover, and it's possible that it was in response to European tastes that what we now call belly-dancing developed, along with its stage-showy Oriental trappings of diaphanous veils, sequined bras and exposed midriffs.

Belly-dancing began to gain credibility and popularity in Egypt with the advent of cinema, when the dancers were lifted out of nightclubs and put on the screen before mass audiences. The cinema imbued belly-dancing with glamour and made household names of a handful of dancers. It also started the modern phenomenon of the belly-dancer as a superstar who can command Hollywood-style fees for an appearance. Such is the present-day earning power of the top dancers that in 1997 a series of court cases was able to haul in E£900 million in back taxes from 12 of the country's top artists.

Despite the celebrity and wealth of some of its practitioners, belly-dancing is still not considered to be completely respectable, especially not by the Islamists. For a couple of years in the early 1990s, pressure was successfully exerted on the dancers to cover up their midriffs. However, as of our last visit, bellies are now bare again. The fact is that belly-dancing is the one native Egyptian art form to have been successfully exported worldwide, reaching nightschool classes and community centres where Tutankhamun has yet to be heard of.

For more on Egypt's present-day belly-dancing scene, see the Nightclubs section in the Entertainment chapter.

Away from the glitz of the professional scene, dance in Egypt survives at a grassroots level where it's known as *raqs sharqi* (eastern dancing). Visit the humblest of weddings and you'll witness the unmarried girls moving to the tabla beat, hands clasped above their heads and pelvises gyrating in a blatant bid to attract male attention and a possible future groom of their own.

Belly-dancing and raqs sharqi are exclusively female pursuits but there is also a male dance performed with wooden staves. It involves lots of stick twirling and mock fighting and comes across as very contrived, although the hotel nightclubs that present it in performances billed as 'folkloric dancing' insist that it's an authentic rural tradition.

Sufi Dancing In its true form this isn't dancing but a form of worship. The Sufis are adherents of a Muslim mystical order who seek to attain a trance-like state as a direct personal experience of God. One of the ways in which they do this is to spin around and around and around – hence the name we in the west know them by, the whirling dervishes. There's a Sufi troupe that performs regularly in Islamic Cairo – see the Entertainment chapter for details.

Film

In the halcyon years of the 1940s and 50s Cairo's film studios would be turning out over 100 movies annually, filling cinemas throughout the Arab world. These days, the average number of films made is around 20 a year. The chief reason for the decline, according to the producers, is excessive government taxation and restrictive censorship (asked what sort of things they censor one film industry figure replied, 'Sex, politics, religion ... that's all'), but at least one Cairo film critic has suggested that another reason might be that so much of what is made is trash. The ingredients of the typical Egyptian film are moronic slapstick humour, over-the-top acting and perhaps a little belly-dancing thrown in for spice. It's a

---

Cairo in the Movies

Partially set in Egypt *The English Patient*, which almost single-handedly swept the board at 1997's Oscar ceremony, put Cairo back up on the big screen again. Except it didn't, because the Egyptian locations were actually shot in Tunisia and, in the case of some interiors, in Venice. (Obstructive bureaucracy and extortionate taxes mitigated against shooting in Egypt itself.) Tunisia also doubled as a much less convincing Cairo in Spielberg's *The Raiders of the Lost Ark*.

A couple of American film crews have braved the bureaucratic hazards in recent years, notably for Spike Lee's *Malcolm X* (Denzel Washington's character patronises the natives before praying in Mohammed Ali's mosque), and to shoot Andie MacDowell and Liam Neeson in *Ruby Cairo*, a limp tale of a wife who, while clearing out her dead husband's bank accounts, discovers he's not dead at all. Much of the film takes place in Cairo, covering all the clichés – camels, Pyramids, moulids and feluccas – but the city does look wonderful.

When MacDowell does catch up with her husband, he's living in what is actually the Gayer-Anderson Museum (see the Things to See & Do chapter). A favoured film location, this house also turned up in the 1977 James Bond movie *The Spy Who Loved Me* – 007 gets to throw someone off its roof. Other Bond-visited locations include the neighbouring Ibn Tulun mosque and, of course, the Pyramids.

The beauty of the Pyramids for Hollywood is that they are a superb shorthand way of telegraphing 'Egypt', yet there's no need to send a crew all that way when a talented SFX department will do. For example, see *Stargate*, a recent sci-fi yarn which opens on the Giza Plateau (actually Arizona), or the 1996 box office smash *Independence Day* which has a 15km-diameter spaceship crash into the Pyramids.

Incidentally, having the country's best known antiquities smashed by extraterrestrial debris was fine by the Egyptians, the real threat of *Independence Day* came with its pro-Jewish overtones. Before it could be screened in Cairo several cuts had to be made to shed the scenes involving Torahs, skullcaps and any other overtly Jewish trappings. ■

formula Egyptian audiences find easy to resist and audience turnouts are invariably low.

There are exceptions. Adel Imam and Ahmed Zaki, the two main leading men of recent years, always pull in a good crowd, as does Yousra, who is widely regarded as a fairly classy actress (her 'quality' image ensured that she was paid a fortune to appear in a series of TV ads alongside Omar Sherif pushing ceramic tiling). For anyone who was wondering what happened to Sherif, he's making undistinguished films in Cairo.

The one director who stands apart from the mainstream detritus is Yousef Chahine. Born in 1926, he's directed 37 films to date in a career that defies classification. Accorded messiah-like status at home, he's been called Egypt's Fellini and he was also honoured at Cannes in 1997 with a lifetime achievement award. Chahine's films are also some of the very few Egyptian productions that are ever subtitled into English or French, and they regularly do the rounds of international film festivals. His most recent works are 1997's *Al-Masir* (Destiny) and from three years earlier *Al-Muhagir* (The Emigrant), effectively banned in Egypt because of Islamist claims that it portrays scenes from the life of the Prophet. Others to look out for are *Al-Widaa Bonaparte* (Adieu Bonaparte), a historical drama about the French occupation, and *Iskandariya Ley?* (Alexandria Why?), an autobiographical meditation on the Mediterranean city of his birth.

Architecture

Cairo contains the world's largest collection of medieval Islamic architecture, with more than 800 listed buildings, dating mainly from the 11th to the 16th centuries. The styles vary greatly depending on the period to which they belong but one frequently seen indigenous feature is the delicate wooden-lace screens that cover many windows, known as *mashrabiyya*. As will be frequently pointed out to anyone visiting any of Cairo's old houses, the mashrabiyya acts like an early form of tinted glass – a person at the window can see out without themselves being seen.

The windows of women's quarters were usually fitted out in this manner.

Traditional houses were typically built around an open courtyard off which was the main *qa'a*, or reception room, the most splendid room in the house, often with a small central fountain. You can see good examples of qa'as at the Beit as-Suhaymi and Gayer-Anderson Museum. An intricate system of light wells through the building ensured rooms received natural light while roofs were adorned with wooden right-angled triangle shaped wind-catchers, designed to funnel any breezes down into the building.

Much of this expertise in building for the climate was lost by the 19th century when Cairo experienced a great building boom at the instigation of Mohammed Ali (1805-48) and his grandson Ismail (1863-79). The subtleties of traditional masonry work were dispensed with in favour of heavy mouldings and rashes of cupolas and other imported decorations. Some of the results are clumsy and outright ugly, such as Mohammed Ali's mosque in the Citadel, while some achieve a sort of magnificence in their extravagance like the Sakakini Palace at Ghamra.

The process of Europeanisation continued during the era of British rule, leaving Cairo with a legacy of grand and fanciful apartment blocks and villas which embody a fusion of Continental styles – predominantly Art Nouveau and Deco – with Orientalist motifs. There were also some interesting experiments in creating a neo-Islamic architecture which was a pastiche of the Mamluk style: the Ministry of Waqf in Bab al-Luq and Ramses railway station are good examples.

Post-WWII, architecture has been disastrous. The advent of concrete has changed the face of the city. Only in the sphere of mosque construction has anything of beauty been created (the Al-Fath mosque on Midan Ramses, for example) and then only by the duplication of traditional models. A new school of Egyptian urban architecture has yet to emerge.

continued on page 30

Islamic Architecture

Cairo is one of the greatest repositories in the world of medieval Islamic architecture. Starting with the Mosque of Amr (642), the earliest existing Islamic structure in Cairo, it's possible to trace the development of Muslim architecture through more than 1000 years of history.

For the first 300 years or so (a period known as Early Islamic) there was no uniform style and the few buildings in Cairo that remain from this period vary in inspiration – the Mosque of ibn Tulun, for example, has its stylistic precedents in Iraq (see the Things to See & Do chapter for more information). A common architectural vocabulary only began to develop with the Fatimids who were the first to introduce the use of the dome and the keel arch, the pointed arch that has come to typify Islamic architecture. The Fatimids also introduced the use of heavy stone masonry, where previously mud-brick and stucco had been the main building

Highlights of Islamic Architecture

Early Islamic (640-969)	Mosque of ibn Tulun (pages 122-3)
Fatimid (969-1171)	Mosques of al-Aqmar (page 109) and al-Hakim (page 108), and the city gates of Bab al-Futuh, Bab an-Nasr (page 107-8) and Bab Zuweyla (page 114)
Ayyubid (1171-1250)	Citadel walls (page 117) and the Madrassa & Mausoleum of as-Salih Ayyub (page 111)
Mamluk (1250-1517)	Mosques of Sultan Hassan (pages 120-1) and Qaitbey (pages 124-5), and the Al-Ghouri complex (page 113)
Ottoman (1517-1798)	Mosques of Suleyman Pasha (page 120) and Sinan Pasha (page 100), and Beit as-Suhaymi (page 109)
Mohammed Ali (1805-49)	Mosque of Mohammed Ali (pages 118-19)
Modern (20th century)	Al-Fath Mosque (pages 99-100)

Mosque of Mohammed Ali, built between 1830 and 1848.

GLENN BEANLAND

materials. The Ayyubids did little to advance these building techniques, though Salah ad-Din made good use of stone in constructing the walls of Cairo's Citadel.

However, under the influence of the Mamluks, Islamic architecture quickly became very sophisticated and expressive. During their time in power, the Mamluks extended the existing repertoire of buildings to include not only mosques, walls and gates but also *madrassas, khanqahs* and mausoleum complexes. These buildings, especially in the latter part of the Mamluk era, are often characterised by the banding of red and white stonework (a technique known as *ablaq*) and by the elaborate stalactite carvings (*muqarnas*) and patterns around the windows and in the recessed portals. The Mamluks were also responsible for the transformation of the minaret from a squat, stubby, often square tower, into the slender cylindrical structure typical of Cairo.

The Mamluks were eventually defeated by the Ottoman Turks who ruled out of Istanbul and Cairo became a provincial capital. Most of the city's Ottoman buildings are therefore small practical structures like houses, *wikalas* and *sabil-kuttabs*; however, there is also a handful of mosques, instantly recognisable by their slim pencil-shaped minarets.

Anyone interested in knowing more about Cairo's Islamic architecture should pick up the excellent *Islamic Monuments in Cairo: A Practical Guide* or *An Introduction to the Islamic Architecture of Cairo*, both readily available in the city's bookshops.

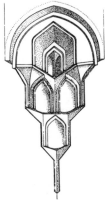

The stalactite-like stone carving known as muqarnas.

Glossary of Islamic Architecture

ablaq	banding of different coloured stone, typical of Mamluk building
bab	gate or door
beit	house; sometimes spelt 'bayt'
burg	tower
caravanserai	medieval merchants' inn
finial	the crowning part of a minaret
hammam	bathhouse
khan	another name for a caravanserai
khanqah	Sufi monastery
kufic	early style of Arabic script, very angular
iwan	vaulted hall, usually opening off the courtyard of a mosque or madrassa; sometimes spelt 'liwan'
madrassa	school where Islamic law was taught
maristan	hospital
mashhad	tomb or shrine
mashrabiyya	wooden lattice screen
mihrab	prayer niche indicating the direction of Mecca
minbar	pulpit
muqarnas	stalactite stonework, usually decorating entrance ways or windows
qa'a	reception room
qasr	palace; pronounced 'asr' with a glottal stop 'q'
sabil	fountain or public water dispensary
sabil-kuttab	combination of *sabil* with a Quranic school
takiyya	Turkish term for khanqah
wikala	another name for a caravanserai
zawiya	small school dedicated to the teachings of a particular sheikh

Minarets

Trite as it may sound, the over-employed description of Cairo as the 'City of 1000 Minarets' isn't a bad one. It's doubtful whether anyone knows exactly how many minarets Cairo does have but it would be a safe guess to say that the number is actually way in excess of 1000, no two of which are the same. That said, they do fall into some broad categories and it's useful to be able to recognise these as they instantly identify the period to which a building belongs.

The earliest surviving minarets, which are mainly from the Ayyubid and Fatimid periods, tended to have square bases and were often topped by a pepper-pot cap – the minaret on the Madrassa & Mausoleum of as-Salih Ayyub (1250) on Bayn al-Qasryn is a good example. These early minarets were also usually quite short and stubby, but this changed with the onset of the Mamluk period when minarets started to grow taller. Take a look at the minaret on the Madrassa & Mausoleum of Qalaun, across the street from As-Salih Ayyub, which was built 40 years later – it still has a square base but is much taller, with three tiers. The next significant development saw the abandonment of the square tower in favour of a wholly cylindrical structure; by the time the Madrassa & Mausoleum of Barquq (1386) went up 100m north of Qalaun this circular, three-tiered minaret had become standard. The most beautiful and graceful minarets of Cairo conform to this late-Mamluk model and it's still widely emulated today in the design of new mosques.

Left: Early Mamluk minaret from the Mosque of Beybars al-Jashankir (1307) with square base and pepperpot cap.

Middle: Lavishly decorated late Mamluk minaret from the Mosque of Amir Qurqumas (1506) with its characteristic three tiers.

Right: Ottoman pencil-minaret from the Mosque of Suleyman Pasha (1528) at the Citadel.

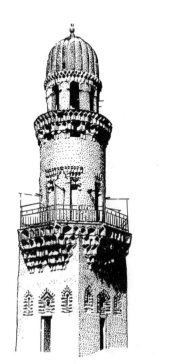

When the Ottoman Turks conquered Cairo in 1517 they brought with them their own architectural forms. Their architects favoured plain, slender minarets which, with their sharp pointed caps, look a bit like giant stone pencils. This remained the basic model right through until late last century – the Mosque of Mohammed Ali (completed in 1848) that dominates the city skyline has Ottoman-style minarets.

Domes

The dome first appeared during the Fatimid period and it remained plain and unadorned until about the middle of the Mamluk era when it began to receive its first tentative decoration in the form of zigzags. This decorative trend developed quickly as the stone masons progressed to using geometric star patterns, floral designs and, finally, a combination of the two. In the Northern Cemetery you can witness this development in the space of 400m – from the Khanqah-Mausoleum of ibn Barquq (1411) to the complex of Sultan Ashraf Barsbey (1432) and the final glory of the Mosque of Qaitbey (1474). The art of stone carving on domes died with the fall of the Mamluks in 1517.

Carved domes from the Northern Cemetery illustrating the three basic styles of decoration: zigzags, star and floral.

SOCIETY & CONDUCT

There's no simple definition of Cairo society. On the one hand there's traditional conservatism, reinforced by poverty, in which the diet is one of *fuul* (beans), *taamiyya* (deep-fried chickpea balls) and vegetables; women wear the long black, all-concealing *abeyyas* and men *galabeyyas*; cousins marry; going to Alexandria constitutes the trip of a lifetime; and all is 'God's will'. On the other hand, there are sections of society who order out from McDonald's; whose daughters wear little black slinky numbers and flirt outrageously; who think nothing of regular trips to the States; and who never set foot in a mosque until the day they're laid out in one.

While this latter group is definitely in the minority, due to their money and status they exert an influence on society vastly disproportionate to their numbers. Occasionally there is a backlash, as in 1997 when around 80 sons and daughters of the westernised elite were rounded up on charges of Satan worshipping. They were accused of drinking the blood of rats, digging up corpses and burning the Quran when in reality all they had done was listen to western music (the CDs confiscated included Guns 'n' Roses and Beethoven's 5th), dress like kids of the MTV generation (a black Bugs Bunny T-shirt was taken as evidence), and enjoy access to satellite TV and the Internet. Within two weeks they were all released without charges.

The bulk of the Cairo populace falls somewhere between these two extremes, with a pattern of life more like that described under Population & People earlier this chapter.

Attitudes to Women

Most Egyptian women don't wear veils but they are still, for the most part, quite restricted in what they can do with their lives. They do not have the same degree of freedom, if any at all, that western women enjoy. Egyptian men see this not as restraint and control, but as protection and security – many women see it that way too.

For many Egyptians, the role of a woman is specifically defined: she is mother and matron of the household, and it is this which the men seek to protect – they don't want their wives to have to work. Even if she can afford domestic help and doesn't do any household work herself, her husband's view is still that she should not have to work for a wage. It is *his* role to provide for the family.

Any Egyptian women wanting to go beyond the family roles allotted to them are going to have a hard time. On rare occasions outstanding and determined individuals – almost exclusively in the more moneyed classes – succeed in carving out a niche for themselves. The vast majority of women continue to be raised in and embrace the traditional roles. This is an important consideration – women take the division of roles as seriously as men. And the men are quick to assert that, within the family, women have far greater power than is at first apparent.

Premarital sex is a taboo subject in Egypt, although, as in any society that disapproves of what is considered promiscuous activity, it does happen. Nevertheless, it is still the exception rather than the rule – and that goes for men as well as women. The presence of foreign women presents, in the eyes of some Egyptian men, a chance to get around the local norms with greater ease. That this is even possible is heavily reinforced by distorted impressions gained from western TV and, it has to be said, the behaviour of some foreign women in Cairo.

The belief that western women are ready and willing to hop into bed with the nearest male has produced in some Egyptian men the belief that they are all candidates for immediate gratification by any western woman who walks down the street. At the very least, pinching bottoms, brushing breasts or making lewd suggestions seem to be considered by some to be a perfectly natural means of communication with an unknown foreign woman. Flashing and masturbating in front of the victim are not unknown, but serious physical harassment and rape are not significant threats.

For guidelines on dealing with Egyptian men, see Women Travellers in the Facts for the Visitor chapter.

Dos & Don'ts

Dress Although they are increasingly used to the antics of westerners, Cairenes have a different code of behaviour on many subjects and find many western ways at best curious and at worst offensive. Dress is the first obvious point, particularly with regard to women. The amount of harassment you get will be directly related to how you dress. Wearing short pants and a tight T-shirt is, in some eyes, confirmation of the worst views held of western women. Unless you want to attract wandering hands, or worse, cover up. Wear at least knee-length skirts or trousers and, in the more out-of-the-way or conservative places like Islamic Cairo, elbow-length shirts. Covering your hair is not necessary when visiting Cairo's mosques. And, don't think this goes for women alone. In places less used to tourists, the sight of a man in shorts and singlet is considered offensive. Count the number of Egyptian men in shorts.

Unfortunately, although dressing conservatively will definitely reduce the incidence of harassment, it by no means guarantees you'll be left alone.

Drink While alcohol is *haram* (forbidden) in the eyes of many Muslims, it is tolerated by most, drunk by a fair few, and quite freely available. That said, getting blasted is not a widespread national pastime. It is advisable not to go reeling around Cairo's streets otherwise you may end up cooling your heels in a police cell. We speak from experience.

RELIGION

About 90% of Cairo's population are Muslims; most of the rest are Coptic Christians. Although occassionally there are flare-ups in Upper Egypt between the followers of these two religions, in Cairo the two communities enjoy a more or less easy coexistence. Intermarrying between Christians and Muslims is forbidden.

Islam

Islam is the predominant religion of Cairo and Egypt. It shares its roots with two of the world's other major religions – Judaism and Christianity. Adam, Abraham (Ibrahim), Noah, Moses and Jesus are all accepted as Muslim prophets, although Jesus is not recognised as the son of God. Muslim teachings correspond closely to the Torah (the first five chapters of the Old Testament and the foundation of the Jewish religion) and the Gospels. However, the essence of Islam is the Quran (or Koran) and the Prophet Mohammed who was the last true prophet to deliver messages from Allah (God) to the people.

Islam was founded in the early 7th century by Mohammed, who was born around 570 AD in Mecca (now in Saudi Arabia). Mohammed received his first divine message at about the age of 40. The revelations continued for the rest of his life and were written down to form the holy Quran. To this day not one dot has been changed in the Quran, which is why foreign translations can never be definitive, only interpretative.

Mohammed's teachings were not an immediate success. He started preaching in 613, three years after the first revelation, but could only attract a few dozen followers. Having attacked the ways of Meccan life, especially the worship of a wealth of idols, he made many enemies. In 622 he and his followers retreated to Medina, an oasis town some 360km from Mecca. It is this *hejira*, or migration, that marks the start of the Muslim calendar.

Mohammed died in 632 but the new religion continued its rapid spread, reaching all of Arabia by 634 and Egypt in 642.

Islam means 'submission' and this principle is visible in the daily life of Muslims. The faith is expressed by observance of the five so-called pillars of Islam. Muslims must:

1. Publicly declare that 'there is no God but Allah and Mohammed is his Prophet'.
2. Pray five times a day: at sunrise, noon, midafternoon, sunset, and night.
3. Give *zakat*, alms, for the propagation of Islam and to help the needy.
4. Fast during daylight hours during the month of Ramadan.
5. Complete the *haj*, the pilgrimage to Mecca.

The first pillar is accomplished through prayer, which is the second pillar. Prayer is an essential part of the daily life of a believer. Five times a day the muezzins bellow out the call to prayer through speakers on top of the minarets. It is perfectly permissible to pray at home or elsewhere – only the noon prayer on Friday should be conducted in the mosque. It is preferred that women pray at home. (For information about Islamic holidays and festivals, see Public Holidays in the Facts for the Visitor chapter.)

The ultimate Islamic authority in Egypt is the Sheikh of Al-Azhar, a position currently held by Mohammed Sayyed Tantawi. It is the role of the supreme Sheikh to define the official Islamic line on any particular matter from organ donations to heavy-metal music.

Visiting Mosques Non-Muslims cannot visit mosques during prayer time but any other time is fine. Some mosques, specifically the mosques of Sayyida Zeinab and Al-Hussein, can't be visited at all by non-Muslims. If non-Muslims enter one of these mosques by mistake, they will probably be asked to leave.

You must dress modestly to visit a mosque. For men that means no shorts; for women that means no shorts, tight pants, shirts that aren't done up, or anything else that might be considered immodest. You must also either take off your shoes or use the shoe coverings that are available at most mosques for a few piastres.

Copts

Before the arrival of Islam, Christianity was the predominant religion in Egypt. St Mark, one of the 12 apostles of Jesus, began preaching Christianity in Egypt around 35 AD and although it didn't become the official religion of the country until the 4th century, Egypt was one of the first countries to embrace the new faith.

Egyptian Christians split from the orthodox church of the Eastern (or Byzantine) Empire, of which Egypt was then a part, after the main body of the church described Christ as both human and divine. Dioscurus, the

patriarch of Alexandria, refused to accept this description. He embraced the theory that Christ is totally absorbed by his divinity and that it is blasphemous to consider him human. Since that time, Egyptian Christians have been referred to as Coptic Christians. The term 'Copt' is derived from the Greek word *Aegyptios* (meaning Egyptian), which the Arabs transliterated and eventually shortened to Copt.

The Coptic Church is ruled by a patriarch (presently Pope Shenouda), other members of the religious hierarchy, and an ecclesiastical council of laypeople. It has a long history of monasticism and can justly claim that the first Christian monks, St Anthony and St Pachomius, were Copts. The Coptic language is still used in religious ceremonies, sometimes in conjunction with Arabic for the benefit of the congregation. It has its origins in a combination of Egyptian hieroglyphs and Ancient Greek. Today, the Coptic language is based on the Greek alphabet with an additional seven characters taken from hieroglyphs.

The Copts have long provided something of an educated elite in Egypt, filling many important government and bureaucratic posts. They have always been an economically powerful minority. In Cairo the Coptic community is concentrated particularly in the districts of Bulaq, Shubra and Al-Daher, east of Midan Ramses. Internationally, the most famous Copt today is the former United Nations secretary-general, Boutros Boutros Ghali.

LANGUAGE

Arabic is the official language of Egypt. However, the Arabic spoken on the streets differs greatly from the standard or classical Arabic written in newspapers, spoken on the radio or recited in prayers at the mosque.

Egyptian Arabic is basically a dialect of classical Arabic, but so different in many respects as to be virtually like another language. It is purely a spoken language and other than in some 'experimental' writing and systems devised for language learners, it has no written form.

Pronunciation

Pronunciation of Arabic can be somewhat tongue-tying for someone unfamiliar with the intonation and combination of sounds. Pronounce the transliterated words and phrases slowly and clearly.

The following guide should help, but it isn't complete because the myriad rules governing pronunciation and vowel use are too extensive to be covered here.

Vowels In Egyptian Arabic, five basic vowel sounds can be distinguished:

a   as in 'had'
e   as in 'bet'
i   as in 'hit'
o   as in 'hot'
u   as in 'book'

A macron ¯ over a vowel gives the vowel a long sound:

ā   as in 'father'
ē   as in 'ten', but lengthened
ī   as the 'e' in 'ear', only softer
ō   as in 'for'
ū   as the 'oo' in 'food'

Combinations Certain combinations of vowels with vowels or consonants form other vowel sounds:

aw   as the 'ow' in 'how'
ay   as the 'i' in 'high'
ei   as the 'a' in 'cake'

These last two are tricky, as one can slide into the other in certain words, depending on who is pronouncing them. Remember these rules are an outline and far from exhaustive.

Consonants Most of the consonants used in this section are the same as in English. However, a few of the consonant sounds need to be explained in greater detail.

'   glottal stop – the sound you hear between the vowels in the expression 'Oh oh!'. It is a closing of the glottis at the back of the throat so that the passage of air is momentarily halted.

gh   the 'rayn' – tighten the muscles at the back of the throat and growl this sound; like a French 'r'

'   the 'ayn' – gag muscles at the back of the throat as when vomiting; like the 'u' in 'hut' only closed. When this occurs before a vowel, the vowel is 'growled' from the back of the throat. If it's before a consonant or at the end of a word, it sounds like a glottal stop. The best way to learn this sound is to listen to a native speaker.

Other common consonant sounds include the following:

g   as in 'gain' (Egyptian Arabic is the only Arabic dialect with this sound – the others have a 'j' sound, as in 'John'. The Egyptians have in fact introduced an extra letter for the rare occasion when they need a 'j' sound, as in 'garage', which is pronounced as in English).
H   a strongly whispered 'h', almost like a sigh of relief
kh   a slightly gurgling sound, like 'ch' in the Scottish 'loch'
q   strong guttural 'k' sound. In Egyptian Arabic, often pronounced as a glottal stop. Often transcribed as 'k', though there is another letter in the Arabic alphabet which is the equivalent of 'k' (see Transliteration section).
r   a rolled 'r', as in Spanish 'para'
s   pronounced as in English 'sit', never as in 'wisdom'
sh   as in 'shelf'

Double Consonants In Arabic, double consonants are both pronounced. For example, the word *istanna*, which means 'wait', is pronounced 'istan-na'.

Transliteration

Transliteration from the Arabic script into English – or any other language for that matter – is at best an approximate science.

The presence of sounds unknown in European languages and the fact that the script is 'defective' (most vowels are not written) combine to make it nearly impossible to settle on one method of transliteration. A wide variety of spellings is therefore possible for words when they appear in Latin script – and that goes for place names and people's names as well. For this book, an attempt has been made to standardise some spellings of place names and the like. There is only one word for 'the' in Arabic: 'al'. (Before certain consonants, it is modified: in Arabic, Saladin's name is Salah ad-Din, meaning 'righteousness of the faith'; here 'al' has been modified to 'ad' before the 'd' of 'Din'.) Nevertheless, 'el' is often used. This has been left only in a few circumstances such as well known place names (El Alamein, Sharm el-Sheikh) or where locals have used it in, say, restaurant and hotel names. River-side boulevards in Nile cities are often called Corniche el-Nil (pronounced Corniche an-Nil).

Greetings & Civilities

Arabic is more formal than English, especially with greetings; thus even the simplest greetings, such as 'hello', vary according to when and how they are used. In addition, each greeting requires a certain response that varies according to whether it is said to a male (m), female (f) or group of people (grp).

Hello.	salām 'alēkum (lit. peace upon you)
And hello to you.	wa 'alēkum es salām (lit. and peace upon you)
Hello/Welcome.	ahlan wa sahlan
Hello. (in response)	ahlan bīk (to m)
	ahlan bīkī (to f)
	ahlan bīkum (to grp)

Pleased to meet you. (when first meeting)	tasharrafna (pol) fursa sa'īda (inf)
How are you?	izzayyak? (to m) izzayyik? (to f) izzayyukum? (to grp)
Fine. (lit. fine, thanks be to God)	kwayyis ilHamdu lillah (m) kwaysa ilHamdu lillah (f) kwaysīn ilHamdu lillah (grp)

(On their own, kwayyis, kwaysa and kwaysīn literally mean 'good' or 'fine', but they are rarely heard alone in response to 'How are you?')

Good morning.	sabāH al-khēr
Good morning. (in response)	sabāH an-nūr
Good evening.	misa' al-khēr
Good evening. (in response)	misa' an-nūr
Good night.	tisbaH 'ala khēr (to m) tisbaHī 'ala khēr (to f) tisbaHu 'ala khēr (to grp)
Good night. (in response; also used as 'Good afternoon' in the late afternoon)	wenta bikhēr (to m) wentī bikhēr (to f) wentū bikhēr (to grp)
Goodbye. (lit. go in safety)	ma'as salāma
Excuse me.	'an iznak, esmaHlī (to m) 'an iznik, esmaHīlī (to f) 'an iznukum, esmaHūlī (to grp)
Thank you.	shukran
Thank you very much.	shukran gazīlan
You are welcome.	'afwan
No thank you.	la' shukran
Sorry.	'assif

There are three ways to say 'Please', each of which is used somewhat differently:

When asking for something in a shop, say:
    min fadlak (to m)
    min fadlik (to f)
    min fadlukum (to grp)

Under similar, but more formal, circumstances (eg when trying to get a waiter's attention), say:
    law samaHt (to m)
    law samaHfi (to f)
    law samaHtu (to grp)

When offering something to someone, for example a chair or bus seat, or when inviting someone into your home or to join in a meal, say:
    itfaddal (to m)
    itfaddali (to f)
    itfaddalū (to grp)

Small Talk

My name is ...	*ismī ...*
What is your name?	*ismak ēh?* (to m)
	ismīk ēh? (to f)
I understand.	*ana fāhem* (to m)
	ana fāhema (to f)
I don't understand.	*ana mish fāhem* (to m)
	ana mish fāhema (to f)
Do you speak English?	*enta bititkallim inglīzī?* (to m)
	entī bititkallimī inglīzī? (to f)
Yes.	*aywa*
	na'am (more formal)
No.	*la'*

One of the most useful words to know is *imshī*, which means 'Go away'. Use this at the Pyramids or at other tourist sites when you are being besieged by children. Do not use it on adults; instead, just say, *la' shukran* (No thank you).

Accommodation

Where is the hotel ...?	*fein al-funduq ...?*
Can you show me the way to the hotel ...?	*mumkin tewarrīnī at-tarīq lil-funduq ...?*
I'd like to see the rooms.	*awiz ashūf al-owad*
May I see other rooms?	*mumkin ashūf owad tānī?*
How much is this room per night?	*kam ugrat al-odda bil-laila?*
Do you have any cheaper rooms?	*fī owad arkhas?*
That's too expensive.	*da ghālī 'awī*
This is fine.	*da kwayyis*
air-conditioning	*takyīf hawa*

Getting Around

Where is the ...?	*fein ...?*
airport	*matār*
bus stop	*maw'if al-otobīs*
bus station	*maHattat al-otobīs*
railway station	*maHattat al-'atr*
station	*al-maHatta*
ticket office	*maktab at-tazāker*
street	*shāri'*
city	*al-medīna*
village	*al-qarya*
How far is ...?	*kam kilo li ...?*
When does the ... leave/arrive?	*emta qiyam/ wusuul ...?*
bus	*al-otobīs*
train	*al-'atr*
boat	*al-markib*
Which bus goes to ...?	*otobīs nimra kam yerūH ...?*
Does this bus go to ...?	*al-otobīs da yerūH ...?*
How many buses per day go to ...?	*kam otobīs fil yōm yerūH ...?*
Please tell me when we arrive ...	*min fadlak, ullī emta Hanūsel ...*
I want to go to ...	*ana 'ayiz arūH ...*
What is the fare to ...?	*bikam at-tazkara li ...?*
Stop here, please.	*wa'if* (or *hassib*) *hena, min fadlak*
Please wait for me.	*mumkin testanani*
May I/we sit here?	*mumkin eglis/neglis hena?*

Where can I rent a bicycle?	*fein e'aggar 'agala?*
Wait!	*istanna!*
Where?	*fein?*
here	*hina*
there	*hinak*
left side	*'ala ash-shimāl*
this address	*al-'anwān da*
north	*shimāl*
south	*ganūb*
east	*shark*
west	*gharb*
bicycle	*'agala or bīsīklēta*
car	*sayyāra/'arabiyya*
boat	*markib*
ferry	*ma'adiya*
crowded	*zaHma*
camel	*gamal*
donkey	*Humār*
horse	*Husān*
ticket	*tazkara*

Around Town

Where is the ...?	*fein ...?*
bank	*al-bank*
barber	*al-Hallē'*
beach	*al-plā/ash-shaataq*
citadel	*al-'ala*
embassy	*as-sifāra*
market	*as-sūq*
monastery	*dēr*
mosque	*al-gāme'*
museum	*al-matHaf*
old city	*al-medīna; al-'adīma*
palace	*al-'asr*
police station	*al-bolīs*
post office	*al-bōsta/maktab al-barīd*
restaurant	*al-mat'am*
synagogue	*al-ma'bad al-yehūdī/al-kinees*
toilet (men)	*twalēt ar-igali*
toilet (women)	*twalēt al-Harīmī*
university	*al-gam'a*
zoo	*Hadīqat al-Haywān*

Money

pound	*guinay*
half pound (50 pt)	*nuss guinay*
quarter pound (25 pt)	*ruba' guinay*

I want to change ...	*ana 'ayiz asarraf ...*
money	*fulūs*
US$	*dolār amrikānī*
UK£	*guinay sterlīnī*
A$	*dolār ustrālī*
DM	*mārk almānī*
travellers cheques	*shīkāt siyaHiyya*

Shopping

Where can I buy ...?	*fein mumkin ashtirī ...?*
How much is this/that ...?	*bikam da ...?*
It costs too much.	*da ghālī 'awī*
Do you have?	*fī 'andak?*

Time & Dates

What time is it?	*sā'ah kam?*
When?	*emta?*
today	*el nharda*
tomorrow	*bokra*
yesterday	*imberrah*
early	*badrī*
late	*met'akhar*
daily	*kull yōm*
day	*yom*
week	*esbuwa*
month	*shaher*
year	*sana*

Numbers

Arabic numerals, unlike the written language, are read from left to right.

0	٠	*sifr, zero*
1	١	*wāHid*
2	٢	*itnein*
3	٣	*talāta*
4	٤	*arba'a*
5	٥	*khamsa*
6	٦	*sitta*
7	٧	*sab'a*
8	٨	*tamanya*
9	٩	*tis'a*
10	١٠	*'ashara*

11	١١	*Hidāshar*
12	١٢	*itnāshar*
13	١٣	*talattāshar*
14	١٤	*arba'tāshar*
15	١٥	*khamastāshar*
16	١٦	*sittāshar*
17	١٧	*saba'tāshar*
18	١٨	*tamantāshar*
19	١٩	*tisa'tāshar*
20	٢٠	*'ishrīn*
21	٢١	*wāHid wi 'ishrīn*
30	٣٠	*talatīn*
40	٤٠	*arba'īn*
50	٥٠	*khamsīn*
60	٦٠	*sittīn*
70	٧٠	*sab'īn*
80	٨٠	*tamanīn*
90	٩٠	*tis'īn*
100	١٠٠	*miyya*
1000	١٠٠٠	*'alf*

Ordinal Numbers

first	*'awwal*
second	*tānī*
third	*tālit*
fourth	*rābi'*
fifth	*khāmis*

Days of the Week

Sunday	*(yōm) al-aHadd*
Monday	*(yōm) al-itnīn*
Tuesday	*(yōm) at-talāt*
Wednesday	*(yōm) al-arba'a*
Thursday	*(yōm) al-khamīs*
Friday	*(yōm) al-gum'a*
Saturday	*(yōm) as-sabt*

Months of the Year

In Egypt the names of the months are virtually the same as their European counterparts and are easily recognisable.

January	*yanāyir*
February	*fibrāyir*
March	*māris*
April	*abrīl*
May	*māyu*
June	*yunyu*
July	*yulyu*
August	*aghustus*
September	*sibtimbir*
October	*'uktoobir*
November	*nufimbir*
December	*disimbir*

Health & Emergencies

I need a doctor.	*'awiz doktōr*
My friend is ill.	*sadīqi 'ayan*
I'm allergic to anti-biotics/penicillin.	*'andī Hasasiyya dodd el enītbiyotik/ el binisilīn*

I'm ...	*'indī ...*
asthmatic	*hasāsiyya fi sadri*
diabetic	*sukkar*
epileptic	*sar'*

antiseptic	*mutahhir*
aspirin	*asbirin*
Band-Aids	*blāstir*
condoms	*kabābīt*
diarrhoea	*is-hāl*
fever	*sukhūneya*
headache	*sudā'*
hospital	*mustashfa*
pharmacy	*agzakhana*
pregnant	*Hāmel*
prescription	*roshetta*
stomachache	*waga' fil batn*

Facts for the Visitor

WHEN TO GO

Climatically, Cairo has only two seasons: summer and 'not-summer' (see Climate in the Facts about Cairo chapter). Given the choice, you would be far better advised to visit during 'not-summer', a period which stretches roughly from September to April or May. January and February can be a little overcast with the occasional downpour but the months immediately either side are comfortably warm, with daytime temperatures leavened by breezes.

During summer the city is insufferably hot and grimy. There are very few places to take respite from the heat (shops and public buildings aren't usually air-conditioned) and you'll find yourself wanting to shower and change clothes at least twice daily. Cairenes who can afford to tend to sit out the summer up on the coast in Alexandria.

It's also worth considering the timing of the various Muslim festivals, in particular Ramadan (see Public Holidays later in this chapter) when for a whole month many businesses only work half-days, museums and tourist sites shut early, and many restaurants stay closed until sundown.

ORIENTATION

Finding your way about the vast sprawl of Cairo is, remarkably, not as difficult as it may first seem. Midan Tahrir is the centre. North-east of Tahrir is Downtown. Centred on Talaat Harb, Downtown is a noisy, busy commercial district, but under the dust and grime it's full of attractive turn-of-the-century architecture. There's a lot of cheap eating places and budget accommodation around here. Midan Ramses, location of the city's main railway station, marks the northernmost extent of Downtown. Beyond are the teeming working class suburbs of Shubra (the true soul of modern-day Cairo), Hadayek al-Koba and Abbassiyya. The latter leads on to Heliopolis, a one-time desert suburb with wonderfully fanciful architecture that has

now been swallowed up by the creeping metropolis. Cairo's airport lies on the north-eastern fringes of Heliopolis, some 22km from Downtown Cairo.

Heading east, Downtown ends at Midan Ataba which marks the abrupt beginning of what's broadly known as Islamic Cairo. This is a blanket term for districts that have existed since medieval times, a compress of narrow winding alleyways harbouring communities whose lives seem to have changed little in centuries. Eastwards, beyond Islamic Cairo, is a string of makeshift shanty towns that have grown up in the shadow of the Muqattam's rocky spurs to accommodate the floods of arrivals that have washed in over the decades from the surrounding countryside.

Immediately south of Midan Tahrir are the curving tree-lined streets of Garden City, prime embassy territory. Once past Garden City you are out of Central Cairo and into a vast area of ramshackle neighbourhoods loosely termed Old Cairo. Buried in here is the small tightly defined area of Coptic

---

Asking Your Way

Beware of asking directions from a Cairene. In their willingness to help out they will always oblige with instructions, even when they don't have the faintest idea where the place you're asking for is.

People tend to drop the word *sharia* (street) in speech and use only the street's name, for example ask for 'Talaat Harb' not 'Sharia Talaat Harb'. The same goes for *midan* (square) – people will generally just say 'Ataba' when they mean 'Midan Ataba'. The exceptions are something like Ramses, where there's a major sharia and midan of the same name and you'll have to specify which one you mean. If it's Ramses railway station you want, then ask for 'Mahattat Ramses'. ■

Cairo, a feature on many tourist agendas. Some 8km further south along the Corniche is Maadi, a very green, very suburban neighbourhood much beloved of American expats.

All of the districts described above are on the east bank of the Nile but Cairo sprawls across the river, alighting on two sizeable islands on the way. The more central of these, connected directly to Downtown by three bridges, is known as Gezira. It has traditionally been a retreat of the Egyptian upper classes and is still home to the city's largest, greenest and most exclusive club and to an opera house which has a strict tie-and-jacket policy. The northern half of Gezira is an affluent, leafy suburb called Zamalek, historically favoured by the city's European residents. The southern island is known as Rhoda but, again, its northern part goes by a different name, in this case Manial, home to Cairo University's medical faculty and a former royal palace (now a museum).

The west bank is less historical and much more residential. The primary districts, north to south are Mohandiseen, Agouza, Doqqi and Giza, all of which are heavy on concrete and light on charm. Giza covers by far the largest area of the four, stretching some 20km west either side of one long, straight road that ends at the foot of the Pyramids.

MAPS

Maps of Cairo are readily available in the city's better bookshops, though few of them are any good. Falk produces a detailed map of Cairo (1:13,000) but you have to appreciate the map's style of unravelling – you either like it or you hate it. It costs about E£24 in Cairo bookshops. The map you'll see around most (it has a very dated photo of the Cairo Tower on the cover) is the *Cairo Tourist Map* (1:12,500) produced by Lehnert & Landrock, which sells for around E£8. This is a terrible map, which is very hard to read. Probably the best of a bad bunch is the *City Map of Cairo* (1:25,000) which, despite the small scale, is clear and it has larger scale inserts of Downtown, Heliopolis and Maadi. It's conveniently pocket-sized and cheap at E£5.

If you're spending a long time in Cairo you may find the *Cairo A-Z* helpful, although its 150 pages make it very bulky and quite heavy. It sells for about E£40. There's a slimmer (32 pages), handier booklet, *Cairo Maps*, produced by the AUC Press (E£20) but, as is the problem with atlases and A-Zs, it fails to give any sense of how the place fits together as a whole.

TOURIST OFFICES
Local Tourist Offices

The head office of the Egyptian Tourist Authority (ETA) (☎ 391 3454) is at 5 Adly, three blocks east of Talaat Harb, Downtown (Map 4). The staff are usually helpful and if they can't assist they will call someone who can. The office is open daily from 8 am to 8 pm (from 9 am to 5 pm during Ramadan).

Cairo international airport's new Terminal II has a tourist office (☎ 291 4255) just after customs control. It should be open 24 hours, but don't bank on it.

There's also a tourist office (☎ 383 8823) at the Pyramids; it's opposite the entrance to the Mena House hotel. It's officially open from 8 am to 5 pm, but the staff admitted to us that you're unlikely to find anyone around before 9 am. There are other small offices at the Manial Palace and at the railway station.

The tourist police are on the 1st floor in the alley just to the left of the tourist office on Adly.

Tourist Friends Association

This is an organisation set up to introduce visitors to Egyptians, most of whom are students looking to improve their English. They organise discos and social activities where you make your own contacts and take it from there. The head office (☎ 392 2036) is on the 9th floor at 33 Qasr el-Nil, Downtown.

Tourist Offices Abroad

Australia
   Press & Information Bureau of the Arab Republic of Egypt, 1 Darwin Ave, Yarralumla, Canberra 2600 (☎ (02) 6273 4260; fax 6273 4629)

Canada
> Egyptian Tourist Authority, Suite 250, 1253 Mc-Gill College Ave, Montreal, Quebec H3B 2Y5 (☎ (514) 861-4420; fax 861-8071)

France
> Bureau de Tourisme, Ambassade de la RAE, 90 Ave des Champs-Élysées, Paris (☎ 01 45 62 94 42; fax 01 42 89 34 81)

Germany
> Aegyptisches Fremdenverkehrsamt, 64A Kaiserstrasse, 60329 Frankfurt am Main (☎ (69) 25 23 19; fax 23 98 76)

Japan
> Cultural Tourist Promotion Office of Egypt, Akasaka 2-Chome Annex, 2F. 19-18 Akasaka 2-Chome, Minato-Ku-Tokyo (☎ (3) 3589-0653; fax 3589-1372)

UK
> Egyptian Tourist Authority, 3rd floor West, Egyptian House, 170 Piccadilly, London W1V 9DD (☎ (0171) 493 5282; fax 408 0295)

USA
> Egyptian Tourist Authority, 630 5th Ave, Suite 1706, New York, NY 10111 (☎ (212) 332-2570; fax 956-6439)
>
> Egyptian Tourist Authority, Suite 215, 83 Wilshire Boulevard, Wilshire San Vincente Plaza, Beverly Hills, CA 90211 (☎ (213) 781-7676; fax 653-8961)
>
> Egyptian Tourist Authority, 645 North Michigan Ave, Suite 829, Chicago, IL 60611 (☎ (312) 280-4666; fax 280-4788)

DOCUMENTS
Visas

All foreigners entering Egypt, except nationals of Malta and Arab countries, must obtain visas from Egyptian consulates overseas or at the airport upon arrival. As a general rule, it is cheaper and much less fuss to get your visa at Cairo airport, where the whole process takes only a few minutes – Thomas Cook or one of the other 24-hour exchange booths you pass just before passport control will sell you the stamps that make up the visa, and no photo is required.

Elsewhere, processing of visa applications varies. In the USA and the UK, processing takes about 24 to 48 hours if you drop your application off in person, or anything from 10 days to six weeks if you mail it.

The single entry visa is valid for three months and entitles the holder to stay in Egypt for one month. Multiple-entry visas (for three visits) are also available for a little extra money (but not at the airport); these are valid for six months but they still only entitle the bearer to a total of one month in the country.

The Dreaded Mogamma

It is totally befitting that the building that dominates Midan Tahrir, Cairo's main square, is a monstrous 14 storey monument to bureaucracy. The Mogamma, Cairo's Central Government Complex, houses 18,000 bureaucrats from 14 ministries and 65 other government departments, all of whom are seemingly devoted to making life just that little bit more difficult. Add to this some 50,000 visitors each day, condemned to wait and queue and wait some more, and more time must be wasted in the Mogamma than in any other place on earth.

The business of visa extensions and residence permits is dealt with on the 1st floor – foreigners generally only have to spiral up one flight of the huge stairwell, down which, rumour has it, more than one despairing individual has flung themselves to their death. Things are marginally better these days. The requirement that all new arrivals must register has been lifted, and visa extensions, which used to involve a run around between up to half a dozen windows and at least one return visit, are now usually dealt with in under an hour.

Still, the Mogamma is a place to be approached with trepidation, for Egyptians every bit as much as for foreigners. In *Irhab wa Kebab* (Terrorists and Kebab), a big hit film of 1992, a group of hapless working-class Cairenes become so frustrated by their Mogamma experiences that they grab the guards' rifles and take the place over. They issue demands for a change in the system but eventually agree to surrender in exchange for a plate of skewered grilled meat.

The Mogamma's hours of business are from 8 am to 2 pm Sunday to Thursday. Go first thing to avoid the crowds. ■

Costs vary depending on your nationality and the country where you apply. For example, a single entry tourist visa costs most western applicants the equivalent of UK£15 (about US$22) in the UK. (Purchased at the airport a single entry visa costs UK£10 or US$15.)

Visa Extensions
A six month extension, called a 'tourism residence visa' costs E£12.10; a one year extension is E£38.10. You get them from the Mogamma; you need one photograph and a great deal of patience (see the boxed text 'The Dreaded Mogamma'). Go to window 42 to fill in a form (E£8). At window 24 everything is processed, and at window 28 you pick up your passport, after paying the balance.

Re-Entry Visas If you do not have a multiple entry visa, it is possible to get a re-entry visa that is valid to the expiry date of your visa and any extensions. Again, it involves a trip to the Mogamma. Start at window 42 and pay for the appropriate form (65 pt). Fill it in and go to windows 16 or 17. It will take about an hour to process. Single/multiple re-entry visas cost E£10/14.

Note There is a two week grace period beyond the expiry date of your visa. In other words, a one month stay is to all intents and purposes six weeks. If you stay beyond that, a fine of E£60 is imposed on exit or on applying for a new extension. If you are caught at the airport in this situation, you may well have to kiss your flight goodbye.

Photocopies
It's a good idea to make photocopies of all vital documents – such as the data pages of your passport, your birth certificate, credit cards, airline tickets, the serial numbers of your travellers cheques and other travel documents – and keep them separate from your real documents. Add to this an emergency stash of about US$50. Also leave copies of all these things with someone at home.

Travel Insurance
However you're travelling, it's worth taking out travel insurance. Work out what you need and consult your travel agent for the most appropriate policy. You may not want to insure that grotty old army surplus backpack, but everyone should be covered for the worst possible case: an accident, for example, that will require hospital treatment and a flight home. Check out the details. In most cases you need to pay extra to cover yourself for 'dangerous sports' such as diving. Also, you often need to pay a surcharge for expensive camera equipment and the like.

It's a good idea to make a copy of your policy in case the original gets lost. If you are planning to travel for a long time, the insurance may seem very expensive – but if you can't afford it, you certainly won't be able to afford to deal with a medical emergency overseas.

Driving Licence & Permits
If you plan to drive in Cairo, you should obtain an international driving permit from your local automobile association before you leave home – you'll need a passport photo and a valid licence. For information about driving in Cairo, see the Getting Around chapter.

Hostel Card
You don't need to be a Hostelling International (HI) member to stay at Cairo's sole HI hostel but they do charge a few pounds less if you have a card. Membership cards are available at the Egyptian Youth Hostels Association office in Garden City (see the Places to Stay chapter for details).

Student Cards
For years, it has been notoriously easy to get a legitimate International Student Identification Card (ISIC) in Cairo. At the time of writing they were available from two places – the Medical Scientific Centre (MSC) and the Faculty of Engineering at Cairo University. These locations are prone to change so ask around before you set off.

The MSC (☎ 363 8815) is at 103 Sharia al-Manial on Rhoda Island and is open daily, except Friday, from 8 am to 8 pm. Cards are issued in a matter of minutes and cost E£20; no proof is required but you'll need a passport photo (preferably colour).

Finding the office at the Faculty of Engineering on Sharia Gamiat al-Qahira in Giza is more difficult and cards issued from here are more expensive – E£30 for foreigners studying outside Egypt and E£21 for those studying in Cairo. The tiny office is next to the (empty) swimming pool at the rear of the grounds – ask any of the Egyptian students to point the way. The office is open from 9.30 am to 1.30 pm Saturday to Thursday, and from 10 am to noon on Friday.

Given the benefits, it is well worth having a student card as it entitles you to a 50% discount on admission to almost all of the antiquities and museums, as well as significant reductions on train travel.

EMBASSIES
Egyptian Embassies Abroad
Australia
  Embassy: 1 Darwin Ave, Yarralumla, Canberra, ACT 2600 (☎ (02) 6273 4437/8)
  Consulates: 9th floor, 124 Exhibition St, Melbourne, Vic 3000 (☎ (03) 9654 8869/634)
  112 Glenmore Rd, Paddington, Sydney NSW 2021 (☎ (02) 9332 3388/3177/3199)
Belgium
  44 Ave Léon Herrera, 1180 Brussels (☎ (2) 345 50 15)
Canada
  Embassy: 454 Laurier Ave East, Ottawa, Ontario K1N 6R3 (☎ (613) 234-4931/35/58)
  Consulate: 1 Place Sainte Marie, 2617 Montreal, Quebec H3B 4S3 (☎ (514) 866-8455)
Denmark
  Kristianiagade 19, 2100 Copenhagen (☎ 35 43 70 70/71 52)
France
  Embassy: 56 Ave d'Iena, 75116 Paris (☎ 01 53 67 88 30; fax 01 47 23 06 43)
  Consulates: 58 Ave Foch, 75116 Paris (☎ 01 45 00 49 52/69 23)
  166 Ave d'Hambourg, 13008 Marseilles (☎ 04 91 25 04 04)
Germany
  Embassy: Kronprinzenstrasse 2, Bad Godesberg, 53173 Bonn (☎ (228) 9 56 83 11/2/3)
  Embassy branch: Waldstrasse 15, 13156 Berlin (☎ (30) 4 77 10 48)
  Consulate: Eysseneckstrasse 34, 60322 Frankfurt am Main (☎ (69) 59 05 57/8)

Israel
  Embassy: 54 Basel, Tel Aviv (☎ (3) 546 4151/2)
  Consulate: 68 Afraty St, Bna Betkha, Eilat (☎ (7) 597 6115)
Japan
  4-5, 1 Chome, Aobadai, Meguro-Ku, Tokyo 153 (☎ (3) 3770-8022)
Jordan
  3rd floor Oman, Mt Oman (☎ (9626) 641 7705)
Netherlands
  Badhuisweg 92, 2587 CL, Scheveningen (☎ (70) 354 2000)
Sweden
  Strandvagen 35, Stockholm (☎ (8) 660 3145, 662 9603/87)
Tunisia
  Ave Mohammed V, Cite Montplaisir, Tunis (☎ (1) 791 181)
Turkey
  Embassy: Ataturk Bulvari 126, Kavaklidere, Ankara 06800 (☎ (312) 468 4647)
  Consulate: Cevdet Pasa Caddesi 173, Bebek, Istanbul 26087 (☎ (212) 165 2440, 163 6038)
UK
  Embassy: 26 South St, Mayfair, London W1Y 6DD (☎ (0171) 499 2401)
  Consulate: 2 Lowndes St, London SW1 (☎ (0171) 235 9777/19)
USA
  Embassy: 3521 International Court NW, Washington DC 20008 (☎ (202) 232-5400, 224-5131)
  Consulates: 1110 2nd Ave, New York, NY 10022 (☎ (212) 759-7120/1/2)
  3001 Pacific Ave, San Francisco, CA 94115 (☎ (415) 346-9700/2)
  1990 Post Oak Blvd – Suite 2180, Houston, TX 77056 (☎ (713) 961-4915/6)
  500 N Michigan Ave – Suite 1900, Chicago, IL 60611 (☎ (312) 828-9162/4/7)

Foreign Embassies in Egypt
Most embassies and consulates are closed on Friday and Saturday. Working hours tend to be from around 8.30 am to 3 pm.

Australia
  World Trade Centre, 11th floor, 1191 Corniche el-Nil, Bulaq (Map 3; ☎ 575 0444; fax 578 1638)
Belgium
  20 Kamel ash-Shennawi, Garden City (Map 7; ☎ 354 7494/5; fax 354 3147)
Canada
  5 Midan al-Saraya al-Kubra, Garden City (Map 7; ☎ 354 3110; fax 356 3548)
Cyprus
  23A Ismail Mohammed, Zamalek (Map 3; ☎ 341 1288/0327; fax 341 5299)

Denmark
    12 Hassan Sabry, Zamalek (Map 3; ☎ 340
    7411/2502; fax 341 1780)
France
    29 Sharia al-Giza, Giza (Map 10; ☎ 570 3916/20;
    fax 571 0276)
    Consulate: 5 Sharia Fadl (off Talaat Harb),
    Downtown (Map 8; ☎ 393 4645/4316; fax 393
    4922)
Germany
    8 Hassan Sabry, Zamalek (Map 3; ☎ 341 0015;
    fax 341 0530)
Israel
    6 Ibn el-Malek, Giza (Map 7; ☎ 361 0528/45)
Japan
    Cairo Centre building, 2 Abdel Kader Hamza,
    Garden City (Map 7; ☎ 355 3962; fax 356 3540)
Jordan
    6 Gohainy, Doqqi (Map 7; ☎ 348 5566; fax 360
    1027). The embassy is two blocks west of the
    Cairo Sheraton.
Libya
    7 El-Salah Ayyoub (Map 3; ☎ 340 8219; fax 341
    4615)
Netherlands
    18 Hassan Sabry, Zamalek (Map 3; ☎ 340 1936;
    fax 341 5249)
New Zealand
    New Zealand's affairs are handled by the UK
    Embassy.
South Africa
    18th floor, Nile Tower, 21-23 Sharia al-Giza,
    Giza (Map 10; ☎ 571 7234; fax 571 7241)
Sudan
    3 Ibrahimy, Garden City (Map 7; ☎ 354 5043; fax
    354 2693)
    Consulate: 1 Mohammed Fahmy as-Said, Gar-
    den City (☎ 354 9661)
Syria
    18 Abdel Rahim Sabry, Doqqi (Map 6; ☎ 337
    7020; fax 335 8232)
UK
    7 Ahmed Ragheb, Garden City (Map 7; ☎ 354
    0852/59; fax 355 1235)
USA
    3 Lazoughli, Garden City (Map 7; ☎ 355 7371;
    fax 357 3200)

CUSTOMS

A grand total of E£1000 can be imported into
or exported out of the country. If you have
more than this on leaving the country, there
is a slim chance you might have the excess
confiscated. There are no restrictions on the
import of foreign currencies, although you are
supposed to declare all you have brought in

when you enter. You are not supposed to take
out more than you brought in and declared.

Sometimes the 'Customs Declaration
Form D' is given to arriving tourists to fill
out. You are supposed to list all cameras,
jewellery, cash, travellers cheques and electronics (personal stereos, computers, radios,
VCRs etc). No one ever seems to be asked
for this form on departure, and few tourists
are given it on arrival. Travellers are, however, regularly asked to declare and register
their video cameras.

Be aware that if you are bringing in elec-
tronic goods such as computers, videos,
televisions or ghetto blasters, you may be
charged tax on them. Alternatively, they will
be written into your passport and must accompany you out of the country again. It's a
good idea to keep them buried out of sight in
your luggage, if possible.

The duty-free limit on arrival is 1L of
alcohol, 1L of perfume, 200 cigarettes and
25 cigars. On top of that, you can buy another
4L of alcohol plus four cartons of cigarettes
at the airport duty-free shop. Alternatively,
you can take advantage of your allowance
(slightly reduced) at one of the duty-free
shops in Central Cairo any time within 30
days of your arrival – see the Shopping chapter for more information.

MONEY
Cash
There seems little point in buying Egyptian
currency before you leave home. Aside from
the fact that importing more than E£1000
is illegal (even if they don't seem to check
what you're carrying), you may well lose
out. Thomas Cook in London was quoting a
rate 10% inferior to that available in Cairo at
the time of writing.

Most hard foreign currencies, cash or
travellers cheques, can be readily changed in
Cairo, although US dollars, UK sterling and
Deutschmarks are always the safest bet.
Avoid bringing US$100 bills; there has been
a problem with counterfeits in recent years
and many banks and exchange offices are
still reluctant to take them.

FACTS FOR THE VISITOR

Travellers Cheques

There is no problem cashing most well known brands of travellers cheques at Cairo's major banks – go to Banque Masr or the National Bank of Egypt in one of the five-star hotels. Eurocheques can also be cashed at these places – you need your Eurocheque card and passport.

Cheques issued on post office accounts (common in Europe) or cards linked to such accounts cannot be used in Egypt. Banks sometimes have a small handling charge on travellers cheques, usually about 50 pt, plus E£2 to E£3 for stamps. Always ask about commission as it can vary.

American Express travellers cheques can be cashed at one of their offices, all of which are open daily from 8.30 am to 5 pm, closed Friday. These include:

Downtown
    15 Qasr el-Nil, between Midan Tahrir and Midan Talaat Harb (☎ 574 7991; fax 574 7997)
    Nile Hilton (☎ 578 5001/2)
Giza
    Nile Tower, 21-23 Sharia al-Giza (☎ 570 3411)
Heliopolis
    72 Omar ibn al-Khattab (☎ 418 2144)

Similarly, Thomas Cook has several offices at which their cheques may be cashed; all are open from 8 am to 5 pm seven days a week.

Downtown
    17 Mahmoud Bassiouni (☎ 574 3955; fax 762 750)
Maadi
    88 Road 9 (☎ 351 1438; fax 350 2651)
Mohandiseen
    9/10 Sharia 26th of July (☎ 346 7187; fax 303 4530)
Heliopolis
    7 Baghdad (☎ 417 3511/12/13)

ATMs

ATMs have only recently made their appearance in Cairo. There are two sorts: those belonging to Banque Masr and those belonging to the Egyptian British Bank (EBB). If you have your PIN number then Banque Masr machines will dispense cash on Visa and MasterCard and any Cirrus or Plus compatible bits of plastic. In Central Cairo, machines are located at Banque Masr branches on Talaat Harb (on the 1st floor of the concrete tower block just south of the midan), on Qasr al-Ainy (200m south of Midan Tahrir), and on Mohammed Farid (just south of the junction with Qasr el-Nil). Egyptian British Bank machines respond to Visa, Midland Bank and Plus, as well as EBB's own cashpoint cards; they're located in the foyers of the Cairo Marriott, Nile Hilton and Semiramis hotels, at the main entrance to the Bustan shopping centre on Sharia Bustan, Downtown, at the British Council in Agouza, and at the EBB on Abu al-Feda in Zamalek. The machines are all accessible 24 hours a day.

Credit Cards

American Express, Visa and MasterCard are becoming ever more useful in Cairo and are now accepted quite widely in shops and restaurants. Make sure you retain any receipts to check later against your statements as there have been several recent cases of shop owners adding extra noughts – it's a stupid and easily detectable crime, but the swindlers are playing on the fact that they will only be found out once the victim has returned home and is thousands of miles from Cairo.

Visa and MasterCard can be used for cash advances at Banque Masr and the National Bank of Egypt, as well as at Thomas Cook offices (see the Travellers Cheques section for addresses). Banque Masr does not generally charge commission for cash advances, but does set a limit of E£1500.

In case of lost cards phone: American Express ☎ 570 3411; MasterCard and Visa ☎ 357 1148/9.

International Transfers

Western Union, the international money transfer specialists, operate jointly in Egypt with Masr America International Bank and IBA business centres. For details call their hotline ☎ 357 1375/85.

Affiliated offices that only receive are at:

1079 Corniche el-Nil, Garden City (☎ 357 1375)
24 Syria, Mohandiseen (☎ 331 3500)
Midan al-Mahkama, Heliopolis (☎ 246 4197)

These offices are open Saturday to Thursday from 9 am to 9 pm; Friday from 10 am to 6 pm.

Affiliated offices that only send are at:

19 Qasr el-Nil, Downtown (☎ 393 4906)
8 Ibrahim Naguib, Garden City (☎ 55 7071)
8 Boutros Ghali, Heliopolis (☎ 258 8649)

The opening hours for these offices are the same as those of the banks.

It is also possible to have money wired from home through American Express. This service operates through most of its branches (see the Travellers Cheques section for the addresses), and can be used by anyone, regardless of whether you have one of their cards or not. The charge for this service is about US$80 per US$1000, payable in the country from which the money is sent.

Currency

The official currency of Egypt is the pound (E£). In Arabic it is called a *guinay*. A pound is subdivided into 100 piastres (pt). The Arabic word for piastre is *irsh*. Notes come in denominations of 25 pt, 50 pt, E£1, E£5, E£10, E£20, E£50 and E£100.

Many of the notes in circulation are unbelievably filthy or are held together by yellowing bits of Sellotape – if you are presented with such a specimen don't take it as you will have trouble passing it on. Instead, demand money that's in better condition.

Coins are in denominations of 5, 10, 20 and 25 pt.

Prices can be written in E£ or pt. For example, E£3.35 can also be written as 335 pt.

There is a shortage of small change in Egypt. The 25 and 50 pt notes, which are useful for tipping, local transport and avoiding being given the wrong change, are not always easy to come by – they should be hoarded. Sometimes you're offered change in the form of boxes of matches, sweets, aspirins and the like, but more often than not the sum will be rounded up; an E£8.50 bill will become E£10 if you don't have exactly E£8.50 to hand over.

Currency Exchange

The Egyptian pound was partly floated in 1987 and, to the surprise of many, it has remained fairly steady since late 1990.

Exchange rates for a range of foreign currencies were as follows at the time of writing. Check with your bank if you want to know the latest rates.

Australia	A$1	=	E£2.26
Canada	C$1	=	E£2.38
France	F10	=	E£5.74
Germany	DM1	=	E£1.92
Israel	NIS	=	E£1.00
Japan	Y100	=	E£2.61
Jordan	JD1	=	E£4.80
UK	UK£1	=	E£5.63
USA	US$1	=	E£3.40

Changing Money

Money can be officially changed at American Express and Thomas Cook offices, commercial banks, foreign exchange (forex) bureaus and some hotels. Note that rates can vary quite a bit between banks though the variations on the US dollar seem to be minimal. Hotels sometimes charge higher commissions than the other institutions. The forex bureaus often offer slightly better rates than the banks for cash, but sometimes don't accept travellers cheques. Make sure you have your passport with you, as you'll nearly always need it.

Excess Egyptian pounds can be changed back into hard currency at the end of your stay.

Banking hours are from 8 or 8.30 am to 2 pm from Sunday to Thursday. Banque Masr at the Nile Hilton hotel and in the narrow street between the Semiramis and Helnan Shepheard's hotels is open 24 hours, and there are 24-hour banking services at Terminal II at the airport.

Black Market

The black market for hard currency is negligible and few travellers can be bothered hunting it out for the fraction of the difference it makes.

Costs

By international standards Cairo is still fairly cheap. It is quite possible to get by on US$15 a day or maybe less if you're willing to stick to hostels or cheap hotels (E£5 to E£10), eat the staple snacks of fuul or taamiyya, and limit yourself to one historic site per day. At the other end of the scale, Cairo has plenty of accommodation choices where you can pay US$150 or more for a room, and some of the better restaurants will set you back US$20 a head or more.

However, if you stay in a modest hotel and have a room with a fan and private bathroom, eat in regular restaurants, with the occasional splurge, and aim to see a couple of sites each day, you'll be looking at between US$30 and US$50 a day.

To give some indication of daily costs, a fuul or taamiyya sandwich costs about 35 pt (around US$0.10), while a Big Mac goes for E£5 (US$1.70). A meal in a cheap restaurant will set you back around E£10 (US$3) but if you prefer to go a little upmarket you can eat very well for E£20 to E£30 (US$7 to US$10). A cup of coffee is anything between 50 pt and E£2 (US$0.17 to US$0.66), a beer retails for around E£6 (US$2), and a bottle of mineral water is E£1.50 (US$0.50).

Taxi rides around town are on average E£2 to E£3.50 a trip.

A major expense is the entry fees to tourist

Backhand Economy – The Art of Baksheesh

Tipping in Egypt is called *baksheesh*, although it is more than just a reward for having rendered a service. Salaries and wages in Egypt are much lower than in western countries, so baksheesh is regarded as an often essential means of supplementing income. To cleaners in a one or two star hotel who might earn only about E£150 per month, the accumulated daily E£1 tips given by guests can constitute the mainstay of their salary.

For western travellers who are not used to continual tipping, demands for baksheesh for doing anything from opening doors to pointing out the obvious in museums can be quite irritating. But it is the accepted way in Egypt. Don't be intimidated into paying baksheesh when you don't think it is warranted. But remember, more things warrant baksheesh here than anywhere in the west.

In hotels and restaurants a 12% service charge is included at the bottom of the bill, but the money goes into the till; it's necessary therefore to leave an additional tip for the waiter. Services such as opening a door or carrying your bags warrant 25 or 50 pt. A guard who shows you something off the beaten track at an ancient site should receive about E£1. Baksheesh is not necessary when asking for directions.

Baksheesh, by the way, is not a custom exclusively reserved for foreigners. Egyptians likewise have to pay baksheesh all day long – to park their cars, receive their mail, ensure they get fresh produce at the grocers, or be shown to their seat at the cinema. So endemic is the practice, particularly in the civil service, that one economist suggested setting up a 'National Baksheesh Fund' to formalise what he estimates to be an E£5 billion-a-year black economy in tipping.

One last tip: carry lots of small change with you, but keep it separate from bigger bills so that baksheesh demands don't increase when they see that you could potentially afford more. ∎

sites. Foreigners are seen as dollars on legs so places where they flock tend to be pricey. A complete visit to the Pyramids will set you back E£80 (US$27) in admission charges, and if you want to see the mummies at the Egyptian Museum, you're looking at a combined fee of E£60 (US$20).

Note A service charge of 12% is applied in restaurants and hotels to which a 5 to 7% sales tax is added. In other words, the price you are quoted at a hotel or read on a menu could be almost 20% higher when it comes to paying the bill.

Bargaining

Bargaining is part of everyday life in Cairo and almost everything is open to haggling, from hotel rooms to the price of a packet of imported Marlboros. Even in shops when prices are clearly marked, many Cairenes will still try to shave something of the bill. One Irish friend in Cairo would buy his air tickets home by placing his cash on the counter saying, 'It's two hundred short but take it or leave it' – the cashier would invariably take it. Of course, when buying in the souqs like Khan al-Khalili, bargaining is unavoidable unless you are willing to pay well over the odds. See the Shopping chapter for a few hints on how to go about it.

DOING BUSINESS

It will be some time yet before the power breakfast catches on in Cairo. And the idea of log-jamming several appointments into one clock-beating afternoon is unlikely ever to take off. Set a meeting for two and it's likely to be closer to three when your appointment shows. Then allow another half hour or so for tea or *haga saa* (something cold) and a great deal of informal pleasantries, and you're rolling on for four before the business of the fast-fading day can be broached. Try to speed up the languorous pace and you stand to cause offence and the seeds of non-cooperation are sown.

Cultural considerations such as the above mean that doing business in Cairo is next to impossible without the aid of Egyptian

experience. On a practical level, the laws governing business are changing constantly and a definitive ruling often seems hard to come by. Regulations always seem open to the widest interpretation. To help know what has to be done, and then how it can be circumvented, to know who must be tipped and how much, and what papers to sign and the quickest route from desk A to desk B, you must have a consultant or adviser. Preferably one with good contacts.

Where you find your magic worker is another question altogether. Start with the chambers of commerce listed below. There are also a couple of specialist English-language business monthlies on the newsstands, *Al-Wekallah* and *Business Today*, both of which carry directory sections. You could also try to get hold of the superior *Business Monthly* which is distributed free by the American Chamber of Commerce – try the commercial section of your embassy. There's a commercial library at the USAID office (☎ 354 8211) in the Cairo Centre building, at 106 Qasr al-Ainy, which is open to the public.

Chambers of Commerce

American Chamber of Commerce in Egypt
Suite 1541, Cairo Marriott, Zamalek (Map 3; ☎ 340 8888 ext 1541; fax 340 9482)
British Egyptian Business Association
Suite 9, Nile Hilton, Midan Tahrir (Map 7; ☎ 579 1660; fax 579 1665)
Cairo Chamber of Commerce
4 Midan Falaki, Bab al-Luq, Central Cairo (Map 8; ☎ 355 8261; fax 356 3603)
Club d'Affaires Franco-Egyptien
Meridien Le-Caire, Manial (Map 7; ☎ 362 1717; fax 362 1927)
Egyptian-American Businessmen's Association
Nile Tower, 21-23 Sharia Giza, Giza (Map 10; ☎ 737 258)
Trade Development Centre
Nile Tower, 21-23 Sharia Giza, Giza (Map 10; ☎ 570 2586; fax 570 2565)

POST & COMMUNICATIONS
Post

Cairo's main post office (GPO) on Midan Ataba is open from 7 am to 7 pm, seven days a week (be wary on Friday and public holidays). The poste restante is through the last door down the side street to the right of the main entrance, opposite the EMS office, and is open from 8 am to 6 pm (Friday and holidays from 10 am until noon). Mail is held for three weeks.

There are also post office branches in the grounds of the Egyptian Museum, at Ramses station, and on Shagaret ad-Durr and also Sharia Brazil in Zamalek. Branch post offices are generally open from 8.30 am to 3 pm daily except Friday.

Postcards and letters up to 15g cost 80 pt to most countries and take four or five days to get to Europe and a week to 10 days to the USA.

Receiving Mail Letters usually take a week to arrive from Europe, and a week to 10 days from the USA or Australia. Mail can be received at American Express offices or at the poste restante. American Express offices are the better option and you don't need to have an American Express card or travellers cheques to use the mail pick-up service. Have mail sent to its office at 15 Qasr el-Nil, Cairo. Take your passport when you go to pick it up.

If you receive a package, you'll get a card (written in Arabic) directing you to some far-flung corner of the city to collect it. Take your passport, money and patience.

Packages To send a package abroad, you must go to the Post Traffic Centre near Ramses railway station. It is open daily except Friday from 8.30 am to 3 pm. Set aside at least half an hour for this process and bring your passport. You'll need to go to the first big room to the left on the 2nd floor. At the counter get form No 13 (E£5), have the parcel weighed and pay for it. Customs will probably want to have a look at it. After it has been inspected, someone will wrap it for you (E£1.50 per metre of paper used plus E£1.60 for sealing).

Courier Services It is possible to send a letter of up to 100g for E£37 by Express Mail Service (EMS); delivery takes two or three days depending on the destination. Letters of up to 500g cost E£44. The main office (☎ 393 9796) is opposite the GPO's poste restante (open from 8 am to 7 pm daily except Friday).

In addition to EMS, Cairo also has a full complement of international courier services on offer:

DHL
  Head office: Al-Mona Towers, 16 Sharia Libnan, Mohandiseen (☎ 302 9801)
  20 Gamal ad-Din Abu al-Mahasin, Garden City (☎ 355 7118)
  34 Abdel Khalek Sarwat, Downtown (☎ 393 8988)
  35 Ismail Ramzy, Heliopolis (☎ 246 0324)
Federal Express
  1079 Corniche el-Nil, Garden City (☎ 357 1300)
  24 Syria, Mohandiseen (☎ 331 3500)
  67 Hegaz, Heliopolis (☎ 246 4197)
TNT Skypak
  33 Sharia Doqqi, Doqqi (☎ 348 8204)

Telephone

In Central Cairo there are telephone offices (known as *centrales*) on the north side of Midan Tahrir, on Adly two blocks east of Talaat Harb, on Alfy, and in Bab al-Luq on Mohammed Mahmoud in the Telecommunications building. These main telephone offices are open 24 hours while branch offices (located all over the city) are open from 8 am to 10 pm.

To make an international call use one of the bright orange card phones in the telephone offices. A phone card, bought from the desk, costs E£15 (135 units) or E£30 (210 units). Alternatively, you can book a call at the desk which must be paid for in advance (there is a three minute minimum). The operator directs you to a booth when a connection is made. Note that Egyptian minutes seem to be shorter than the norm.

According to *Cairo: A Practical Guide* (see Guidebooks & Reference under Books later in this chapter) Egypt ranks among the five most expensive countries in the world for international calls. There are different rates for day (8 am to 7.59 pm) and night (8 pm to 7.59 am) calls. For example, a three

The Nile continues to be the lifeblood of Cairo: serving as a busy transport artery for river buses and barges; providing a living for fishermen and felucca captains; even acting as a home for the city's many houseboat dwellers. Its banks are also popular recreation spaces as shown here at Gezira (bottom).

EDDIE GERALD

EDDIE GERALD

The cliché is that Cairo is a city where the ancient meets the modern, but it would be more true to say that it's a place where the ancient meets the slightly less old.

Phonophobia

This is not offered as a pre-emptive excuse, but it is tough to get phone numbers in Cairo. According to a report in a local paper, in one year alone the phone numbers in a certain part of the city were changed three times. Even more astounding is that the subscribers weren't even always informed that they were getting new numbers. There's also a certain random element in making connections – just because you've dialled the right number does not mean you're going to end up on the right line.

If you are sure that the number we have listed is inaccurate, then you could always try dialling ☎ 140 for directory inquiries, but even if you can get through – if the lines aren't busy and if they decide to pick up the phone – there's still no guarantee that you'll be given the right number. ■

minute call to the USA costs E£21/11 at the day/night rates respectively; it costs E£27/23.50 to Australia and E£18.50/12.80 to the UK and Europe .

International calls can also be made from most of the big hotels but at a considerable premium.

Local calls are best made from shops or kiosks which have phones for public use; they charge 50 pt per call.

International Calling Cards These can be used at five-star hotels: AT&T ☎ 510 0200; MCI ☎ 355 5770; Sprint ☎ 356 4777.

Fax & Telegraph

Faxes can be sent to/from the telephone offices on Adly (fax 393 3909 – the fax office is to the right of the main office and up the stairs), on Midan Tahrir (fax 578 0979) and also on Alfy (fax 589 7662). You can also send and receive faxes from the EMS office (fax 393 4807) near the GPO. Sending a fax costs E£14 per page to the UK and USA, and E£20 to Australia; receiving a fax message costs E£6 at a telephone office or E£5.50 at an EMS office.

Alternatively, you can receive (but not send) faxes at American Express (fax 574 7997) at 15 Qasr el-Nil (there's no charge).

Telegrams in English or French can be sent from the telephone and telegraph offices in Central Cairo. The rates to the UK, USA and Europe are 67 pt per word and to Australia 84 pt per word. Each word in an address is also counted. Major hotels also offer this service but rates vary.

Email

Email can be sent and received from several cybercafes that are run by InternetEgypt. The centre of operations (☎ 356 2882) is up on the 6th floor at 2 Midan Simon Bolivar (above the Alexandria Kuwait Bank), to the south of the Mogamma building. Setting up a mailing account costs E£75 for three months and the use of the computers costs E£6 per half-hour. The centre is open from 9 am to 10 pm daily except Fridays when its hours are 3 to 10 pm.

Other InternetEgypt cybercafes are in: Mohandiseen (☎ 305 0493), on a side street off Gamiat ad-Dowal al-Arabiyya between McDonald's and Arby's; the basement of the Nile Hilton Shopping Mall (☎ 578 0666, ext 758); the basement of the Maadi Grand Mall (☎ 518 4223); and Heliopolis (☎ 453 2077) at the Pasta Fresca Restaurant, opposite the gates of Merryland on Sharia Hegaz.

To its credit, Egypt does not as yet impose any form of censorship on the Net.

Service Providers InternetEgypt (address and ☎ above) is one of the better service providers in that subscribers usually get through the first time and the company offers some technical support. Costs are E£50 for 10 hours usage per month or E£100 for 25 hours usage per month. Set-up and registration is E£100. At the time of writing about eight other providers exist but of these the only ones that come recommended are Intouch (☎ 337 6407) at 3 Mossadeq, Doqqi and Egypt Online (☎ 395 4111) at 34 Adly, Downtown. Fees are all roughly similar to those charged by InternetEgypt.

Cairo Online

Entering the word 'Cairo' into one of the many Net search engines will result in several thousand links, offering everything from current prayer times to current theories on who built the Pyramids. Narrowing the field down a little, these are some of our recommendations:

http://www.lonelyplanet.com
This is the Lonely Planet site home page. Follow the links to the travel reports for the latest updates on Cairo and Egypt.

http://pharos.bu.edu/Egypt/Home.html
This is the Egypt World Wide Web index with hundreds of links broken down into categories including Egyptology, travel, media and cooking. This is *the* place to start surfing.

http://pharos.bu.edu/Egypt/Cairo/home
Billing itself as *The Cairo Guide*, this has information similar to that contained in this book. If the site is updated regularly, it may be useful.

http://interoz.com/Egypt
The official site of the Egyptian Ministry of Tourism. It has pretty standard stuff like travel tips and travel news updates but also has more interesting features such as the virtual dive centre with plenty of graphics and descriptions of wreck dive sites.

http://www.presidency.gov.eg
Egypt's presidential Web site offers a photo tour of the Abdin Palace, biographies of former rulers and a fairly fleshless biography of the current incumbent.

http://www.metimes.com
The online edition of the weekly *Middle East Times*. Includes all the articles the censors wouldn't allow into the print edition. No fee.

http://www.egypttoday.com
The online edition of the monthly *Egypt Today* magazine; the complete text minus the photos. There's also access to previous issues dating back to January 1996.

http://watt.seas.Virginia.EDU/aoa5v
Exodus Egypt, an online magazine and database including some interesting photo features and daily updated news from Cairo, translated from the local press.

http://www.mt.net/watcher/pyramid.html
Just one of the many, many sites devoted to pyramidology. One of the more wacky and technically adept examples, this is run by the Watcher Ministries who believe that angels built the Pyramids and Sphinx – and a parallel city on Mars.

http://www.egy.com
Excellent site containing a catalogue of authoritative and entertaining articles on the local history of Cairo. ■

BOOKS

Most of the titles given below can be picked up in Cairo's bookshops (see the Shopping chapter for information), which are great in their coverage of matters relating to Egypt and the Middle East, but not so comprehensive on other topics.

Most books are published in different editions by different publishers in different countries. As a result, a book might be a hardcover rarity in one country while it's readily available in paperback in another. Fortunately, bookshops and libraries search by title or author, so your local bookshop or library is the best place to go if you want advice on the availability of the following recommendations.

For books written by Egyptian authors, see Literature in the Arts section in the Facts about Cairo chapter.

Lonely Planet

If you want to see more of the area around Cairo, Lonely Planet also publishes a guide to Egypt, an *Egypt travel atlas* and an *Egyptian Arabic phrasebook* to help you get around. For more information about travel throughout the Middle Eastern region as a whole, see Lonely Planet's *Middle East on a shoestring*.

Guidebooks & Reference

What promises to be the definitive book on Cairo was in production at the time of writing. It's tentatively titled *Cairo: The City Victorious* and the author is Max Rodenbeck, an American journalist who is Cairo born and bred. It should be available from a major US and UK publishing house by the time you read this.

In the meantime Insight Guide's *Cairo*

contains some informative and entertaining essays on the city and its inhabitants written by long-term residents. The photography is excellent too.

Cairo: A Practical Guide, published by the American University in Cairo (AUC) Press, is aimed at people setting up home in the city and focuses on matters such as finding a flat and a school for the kids; it has a very useful directory. The AUC also publishes several guides to more specific areas of the city such as Khan al-Khalili, Islamic Monuments and Saqqara and Memphis. These titles are stocked by most of Cairo's bookshops.

As if the Real Story isn't Enough: Cairo in Fiction

With a vivid history stretching back some 5000 years encompassing Pyramid builders (human or otherwise), Hammer horror caliphs, the enchantments of *The Thousand and One Nights*, colonial high jinks and romance, and the modern-day tinderbox that is the Middle East, it is little wonder that Cairo has provided a perfect backdrop for the imaginings of writers.

In *Leo the African* author Amin Maalouf has his eponymous hero visit a superbly evoked Ottoman-era Cairo where he gets caught up in the tumultuous events of the day – the result is a piece of historical fiction that reads like a thriller. The *Arabian Nightmare* by Robert Irwin is a hallucinogenic tale of Mamluk-era Cairo which veers heavily toward the genre of fantasy.

The Snake-Catcher's Daughter by Michael Pearce is part of a series of lightweight mystery novels featuring the Mamur Zapt, a police inspector in 19th century Cairo. It reads a bit like Tintin but without the pictures.

Real life adventure inspired *The Key to Rebecca* by British thriller-writer Ken Follett. It's a heavily fictionalised version of the story of the German spy John Eppler who was smuggled into Egypt during WWII to pass on information to Rommel about British troop movements. Eppler shacked up on a Nile houseboat with a well-known Egyptian belly-dancer who was used as bait for British officers bearing promising-looking attaché cases. Fact is well and truly jettisoned towards the end but the book is entertaining reading. The man who guided Eppler into Egypt was a Hungarian named László Almásy, immortalised as *The English Patient* in the book by Michael Ondaatje – see the boxed text 'The Real English Patient' in the Facts about Cairo chapter.

The Eppler episode was also the inspiration for *City of Gold* by Len Deighton, which scores highly for its meticulously researched portrayal of wartime Cairo. The city during the war also serves as the setting for Olivia Manning's brain-numbing *The Levant Trilogy*, though it's very much pushed into the background by the trials and traumas of the dislikeable bunch of expats that form the core of the work. More expats in distress feature in *Moon Tiger* by Penelope Lively, again with wartime Cairo for added colour.

A Woman of Cairo by Noel Barber is one of those historical novels of breathtaking sweep in which dynasties crash and fall about a pair of star-crossed lovers. King Farouk, Nasser and Sadat all get walk-on parts in this tale of two neighbouring families, one British and one Egyptian, in the run-up to the revolution.

For a real flight of fantasy, *The Name of the Beast* by Daniel Easterman is near unbeatable – to wit, the leader of a bunch of Islamists turns out to be the anti-Christ and the Pyramids are dismantled to build a wall around the borders of Egypt. It's great fun but it would have worked far better as a video game. ■

Travel

The 19th century saw the publication of a steady stream of books about western travellers' adventures in Cairo and Egypt, a few of which are currently available in modern editions. *Flaubert in Egypt* reprints extracts from diaries Flaubert kept when he visited the country for a few months in 1849. The Pyramids receive short shrift with Flaubert who preferred to focus on his exploits in the bathhouses and bordellos. Six years earlier another French eccentric, Gerard de Nerval, most noted for taking his pet lobster for walks around Paris, set out for the east. The resulting book *Journey to the Orient* is a fantastical work with de Nerval departing from the norms of travel writing to indulge in the retelling and embellishing of some fairly surreal tales concerning the mad caliph Hakim and Solomon and Sheba.

Far more sober is *Eothen* by Alexander Kingslake, an account of a journey undertaken in 1830 from Constantinople to Egypt; at the time Kingslake visited Cairo the city was suffering one of its periodic plagues.

More recent efforts are thinner on the ground and far more conventional. *Beyond the Pyramids* by Douglas Kennedy is a fairly patchy account of the author's exploration of Egypt in the mid-1980s – the Cairo chapter is one of the book's weaker sections. Possibly some of the best recent writing on Cairo appears in a book called *Baghdad Without a Map* by Tony Horwitz, a novice freelance journalist chasing stories around the Middle East. Horwitz was based in Cairo and his descriptions of the city, its characters and its chaos are memorable and entertaining and ring true.

History

For entertainment value as well as elucidation, *Great Cairo: Mother of the World* by Desmond Stewart, published by the AUC Press, is hard to beat. It's a fairly slim volume covering 55 centuries of history so a lot of condensing goes on, but where Stewart doesn't spare is in the wonderful descriptions of Cairo's various diabolical rulers.

The Arabian Nights: A Companion by Robert Irwin traces the origins of the legendary cycle of stories woven by Sheherezade. Medieval Cairo features as a source of many of the tales and the descriptions of the city's lowlife types and their scams make fascinating reading.

Egypt's Belle Epoque by Trevor Le Gassick and *Lifting the Veil* by Anthony Sattin both deal with Egypt – but largely Cairo – during the period of British rule, while *Cairo During the War* by Artemis Cooper focuses on six years in the life of the city during WWII. But what years they were – the guest book for Cairo at this time would have read like a who's who of international high society, celebrity and royalty.

NEWSPAPERS & MAGAZINES

Although the venerable state-owned *Al-Ahram* remains the best known of Egypt's national Arabic-language newspapers, its journalism is very stilted and conservative in comparison to some of the newer publications such as the progressive business-focused *Al-Alam al-Yom* and the Egyptian edition of the Arab world daily *Al-Hayat*.

The *Egyptian Gazette* is Egypt's awful daily English-language newspaper. It serves largely as a press puff for the office of the president, although it also offers great entertainment for lovers of typos and seriously screwed-up headlines. The Saturday issue is called the *Egyptian Mail*. The French-language equivalents are the daily *Le Progrès Égyptien* and Sunday's *Progrès Dimanche*.

Al-Ahram Weekly and *Middle East Times* (*MET*) both appear every Thursday and do a much better job of keeping English-readers informed of what's going on. Of the two, the *MET* is more readable but the overly academic *Weekly* does benefit from good comprehensive listings covering cinema, theatre, classical music, the arts and lectures. *Al-Ahram* also puts out a weekly French edition, *Hebdo*.

Egypt Today, an ad-saturated, general interest glossy, also has excellent listings but its monthly schedule means that in notoriously unpredictable Cairo much of the information has a certain hypothetical quality.

Egypt Today also has two monthly sister publications: *Sports & Fitness* and *Business Today*.

An extremely broad range of western newspapers and magazines are sold at hotel bookshops and street side newsstands (see the Shopping chapter for information about the best locations). Papers are just a day old and monthly magazines usually make it over within a week of their home publication dates, but expect to pay up to twice the cover price.

RADIO & TV

Despite a firm state stranglehold, Egyptian TV is booming. In the last few years the traditional three channels have been supplemented by half a dozen or more, as throughout the country every governorate gets in on the act with their own station. There's little for non-Arabic speakers, apart from the occasional old American movie (the Saturday night cine club on Channel One sometimes screens the odd good one) and a nightly English-language news bulletin on Channel Two at 8 pm. Nile TV, which is based in Cairo, broadcasts news and current affairs exclusively in English and French from 7 am each day until past midnight.

Satellite has made a big splash in Cairo (check the number of dishes on the skyline), as has cable to a lesser extent. Many hotels have satellite TV, even some of those towards the lower end. MTV seems to be a staple at many of the city's fast-food joints. Sports fans without access to satellite or cable should check Harry's Pub at the Cairo Marriott where the management usually oblige by tuning in to major fixtures and bouts.

Radio-wise, FM95 broadcasts news in English on 557 kHz at 7.30 am and 2.30 and 8 pm daily. This is the European-language station and, in addition to English-language programs, it has programs in French, German, Italian, and Greek. BBC and Voice of America (VOA) broadcasts can be picked up on medium wave at various times of the morning and evening. The BBC can be heard on both 639 kHz and 1320 kHz, and VOA on 1290 kHz.

Check the *Egyptian Gazette* for the day's TV (both local and satellite) and radio program information. There are a couple of special monthly program-listing magazines for satellite and cable.

PHOTOGRAPHY & VIDEO
Film & Processing

Film generally costs as much as, if not more than, it does in the west; for example, Kodacolor 100/200 (36 exposures) costs about E£22, while for Kodachrome 100 slide film, you'll pay E£24 (36 exposures). If you buy film in Cairo, check the expiry dates and don't buy from anywhere that stores the film in direct sunlight.

Colour print processing costs from E£2 to E£4 depending on whether it's a one hour or overnight service, plus from 50 pt to 135 pt per print depending on print size. B&W processing is not recommended, but colour processing is usually adequate for nonprofessional purposes. There are plenty of labs Downtown and in Zamalek. One Downtown place we recommend – for both quality and price – is the Photo Centre (Map 8; ☎ 392 0031) on the 1st floor at 3 Sharia Mahrani, a backstreet off Sherifeen, which itself is a side street off Qasr el-Nil. Also Downtown, there's a Kodak shop on Adly between Sherif and Mohammed Farid, and in Zamalek there's another Kodak on Sharia 26th of July and an Agfa outlet at 22 Hassan Sabry.

If you need professional processing, the place to go is Antar Photostores (Map 8; ☎ 354 0786) at 180 Sharia Tahrir, just east of Midan Falaki, Bab al-Luq.

There are numerous places to have passport photos done. The cheapest option is to ask one of the photographers in front of the Mogamma. They will use an antique box camera to copy your passport photo or any other photo and make four copies (B&W only and often a bit out of focus) for E£4. For colour shots done quickly, your cheapest bet is the instant photo booth (E£6 for four photos) near the ticket windows in Sadat metro station under Midan Tahrir.

Video

Outrageous fees have been introduced for the use of videos at Cairo's prime tourist sites – quite often up to 10 times as much as you pay for admission. Fees of E£100 are becoming standard fare, and at the Manial Palace Museum the charge is E£150.

Restrictions

There are several places that are definite no nos when it comes to taking photos – these include the parliament building, the presidential palace in Heliopolis, the Abdin Palace in Central Cairo and any embassies or ministries – beyond that it's more difficult to predict what you can and cannot point a camera at. A photographer friend had her film confiscated for shooting pictures of public telephones, while another spent a day held at a police station for inadvertently snapping a factory. Always be careful when taking photos of anything other than tourist sites, especially things like bridges, railway stations, anything military, airports and other public works.

Egyptians are also sensitive about the negative aspects of their country. It is not uncommon for someone to yell at you when you're trying to take photos of things like a crowded bus, a dilapidated building or a donkey cart full of garbage. Be sure to exercise discretion.

TIME

Egypt is two hours ahead of GMT/UTC and daylight saving time is observed (it begins on 1 May and ends on 30 September). So, without allowing for variations due to daylight saving, when it is noon in Cairo it's 10 am in London, 5 am in New York and Montreal, 2 am in Los Angeles, 1 pm in Moscow and 7 pm in Melbourne and Sydney.

ELECTRICITY

Electric current is 220V AC, 50 Hz. Wall sockets are the round, two-pin European type, though for some strange reason the socket holes are often too narrow to accept European plugs. Bring adapter plugs (although they can be bought at Sunny's supermarket in Zamalek) and transformers if necessary; travel-size transformers are difficult to obtain in Egypt.

LAUNDRY

There are no self-service laundries that we know of but most hotels, even those at the very bottom end of the scale, can arrange to have your washing done. The other option is to find your local *makwagee*, the 'hole-in-the-wall' laundryman who will wash and iron your clothes by hand for about E£1 or E£1.50 per item.

WEIGHTS & MEASURES

Egypt is on the metric system.

HEALTH

Before travelling, it's a good idea to ensure that your tetanus, diphtheria and polio vaccinations are up to date. Discuss your requirements with your doctor. Other diseases you should consider having vaccinations against before you leave are typhoid and hepatitis A, which are food-borne diseases, and hepatitis B, which is transmitted through sexual activity and blood. If you are coming from a yellow fever infected area (most of subSaharan Africa and parts of South America) you'll need a yellow fever vaccination certificate. There is no risk of yellow fever in Egypt.

Schistosomiasis (or bilharzia), a potentially serious disease carried in fresh water by minute worms, is prevalent in the Nile Delta area and in the Nile Valley. Do not drink, wash, paddle or even stand in water that may be affected and do not swim in the Nile. Seek medical attention if you think you may have been exposed to the disease.

Cairo is not in a malarial zone but there is a risk of malaria in the Al-Fayoum area from June to October. If you intend to travel to this region you should consider taking antimalarials. Other insect-borne diseases, such as dengue fever, typhus, filariasis and West Nile fever, occur along the Nile but the risk to travellers is small. It is wise, however, to take steps to avoid insect bites.

The main concern in Cairo for most of

the year is the heat. Drink plenty of fluids to prevent dehydration. Avoid sunburn by using sunscreen and wearing a hat, and protect your eyes with good quality sunglasses. Dehydration and salt deficiency can cause heat exhaustion. Take time to acclimatise to the high temperatures, drink sufficient liquids and do not do anything too physically demanding. Salt deficiency is characterised by fatigue, lethargy, headaches, giddiness and muscle cramps; salt tablets may help, but adding extra salt to your food is better.

Food & Water

On first sight, Cairo seems a nightmare city for the health conscious: air pollution; street vendors displaying their wares amid clouds of carbon monoxide; leaking sewer systems; and dirt everywhere. However, things are nowhere near as bad as they might seem. For a start, US embassy tests on Cairo's tap water have confirmed it to be fine – the funny taste is due to its high chlorine content, which makes it a great antiseptic for washing fruit and vegetables in.

If you are in Cairo on a short-term stay, doctors recommend sticking to mineral water as it takes a while for digestive systems to adapt to even minor changes in water content. For similar reasons, it's almost inevitable that any newcomer to Cairo will go down with travellers' diarrhoea or, as it's more commonly known, the 'Pharaoh's revenge'. If – or more likely, when – you get it, drink plenty of water. This will prevent you from becoming dehydrated. In severe cases, a rehydrating solution is preferable to replace minerals and salt lost. Commercially available oral rehydration salts such as Rehydran are very useful; add them to purified or bottled water and keep drinking small amounts often.

Health conscious folk might like to check out the Sekem Health Store (Map 3; ☎ 342 4979) at 6 Ahmed Sabry in Zamalek. It stocks organic fruit and vegetables, additive-free jams and honey, herbs and pulses, as well as a range of herbal and homeopathic teas. It's open daily from 8 am to 9 pm. There

are also Sekem stores in Heliopolis and Maadi.

Hospitals

Many of Cairo's hospitals suffer from antiquated equipment and a cavalier attitude to hygiene but there are several exceptions:

Cairo Medical Centre
    Midan Roxy, Heliopolis (☎ 258 0566/1003)
Anglo-American Hospital
    Sharia Hadayek al-Zuhreya, to the west of the Cairo Tower, Gezira (Map 7; ☎ 340 6162/3/4/5)
Masr International Hospital
    12 Sharia al-Saraya, near Midan Fini, Doqqi (Map 7; ☎ 360 8261)
As-Salam International Hospital
    Corniche el-Nil, Maadi (☎ 363 8050)
    3 Syria, Mohandiseen (Map 2; ☎ 302 9091/2/3)

Both the Doqqi and Maadi hospitals have 24-hour facilities.

Doctors & Dentists

It's best to inquire at your embassy for the latest list of recommended doctors and dentists. The UK and US embassies also have health units that can direct people with special problems, or who need immediate care, to suitable physicians.

It may also be worth contacting SOS Assistance, especially if you are considering a long stay in Egypt. This organisation can be contacted care of Cairoscan (☎ 360 0965), 35 Suleyman Abaza, Mohandiseen. Its policy offers full medical cover in case of emergency, including a flight out to the country of your choice under the SOS MEDEVAC scheme. Contact SOS Assistance for more information.

Pharmacies

There's no shortage of pharmacies in Cairo, and almost anything can be obtained without a prescription. A few 24-hour pharmacies worth noting are Isaaf (Map 4; ☎ 574 3369) on the corner of sharias Ramses and 26th of July, Downtown, the Zamalek Pharmacy (Map 3; ☎ 341 6424) at 3 Shagaret ad-Durr, Zamalek, and Al-Ezaby (☎ 418 0838) at 1 Ahmed Tayseer, up in Heliopolis.

Vaccination Centre

The International Vaccination Centre is in the former Hotel Continental-Savoy on Sharia al-Gomhuriyya facing the Ezbekiyya Gardens; it's on the right at the back of the lobby. Vaccinations against cholera and yellow fever are available from the centre for E£1.50 each, and you are given the standard yellow International Certificate of Vaccination card free. The centre is open daily from 10 am to 1 pm and 6 to 7 pm (closed Friday evening). It's advisable to bring your own needles.

Emergency

Some important numbers in Cairo are:

Ambulance
  Cairo Ambulance Service (☎ 123 or ☎ 770 123/ 230)
  Giza (☎ 720 385)
  Heliopolis (☎ 244 4327)
  Maadi (☎ 350 2873)
Police
  Central (☎ 13)
  Emergency (☎ 122 or ☎ 900 112)
  Tourist Police (☎ 126)
Fire
  All districts (☎ 125 or ☎ 391 0115)

TOILETS

There are very few public toilets in Cairo – Midan Falaki and Midan Abdel Moniem Riad, behind the Egyptian Museum, are the only places we've seen them. The best idea is to make use of the facilities offered by the five-star hotels and fast-food chains. Keep a mental map in your head of the location of all the various Hiltons, Sheratons, McDonald's and KFCs and you'll be fine.

WOMEN TRAVELLERS

Egyptians are conservative, especially in matters concerning sex and women – Egyptian women that is, not foreign women. See Attitudes to Women under Society & Conduct in the Facts about Cairo chapter.

An entire book could be written from the comments and stories of women travellers about their adventures and misadventures in Cairo. Most of the incidents are nonthreatening nuisances, in the same way a fly buzzing in your ear is a nuisance: you can swat him away and keep him at a distance, but he's always out there buzzing around.

There are a number of things that you can do to lessen the harassment although nothing you can do short of wearing a full Saudi-style chador is ever going to completely leave you free of unwanted attention:

- Dress modestly – no shorts, short skirts, bikini tops or low cut dresses. See Dos & Don'ts in Facts about Cairo for more information.
- Wear a wedding band. Generally, Egyptian men seem to have more respect for a married woman.
- If you are unmarried but travelling in male company, say you are married rather than girlfriend/ boyfriend or just friends.
- Avoid direct eye contact with an Egyptian man unless you know him well; dark sunglasses may help.
- Don't respond to any obnoxious comments from a man – act as if you didn't hear them.
- Be careful in crowds and other situations where you are crammed between people, as it is not unusual for crude things to happen to you from behind.
- Don't sit in the front seat of taxis unless the driver is a woman.
- On public transport, sit next to a woman if possible or, even better, on the Cairo metro take the first compartment, which is reserved for women only.
- Be very careful about behaving in a flirtatious or suggestive manner, it could create more problems than you ever imagined.
- If you need help for any reason (directions etc), ask a woman first.
- Be wary when horse or camel riding, especially at touristy places. It's not unknown for a guy to ride close to you and grab your horse, among other things. Riding in front of a man on a camel is simply asking for trouble.

GAY & LESBIAN TRAVELLERS

Homosexuality among males in Egypt is no more or less prevalent than elsewhere in the world. It is, however, relatively clandestine. No man will attest to being gay as Egyptians in general perceive gay men to be weak and feminine.

There is no mention in the law of sexual behaviour between consenting adults of the same sex being a criminal offence, however, discretion is advisable.

There are no national support groups or

gay information lines but there are a few places that are recognised gay hang-outs. Chief of these is Casanova's disco at the Burg Hotel on Gezira. The Taverne du Champs de Mars and Jackie's Disco, both in the Nile Hilton Hotel, are also popular with gays.

DISABLED TRAVELLERS

Cairo is tough on travellers with a mobility problem: pavements are crowded and uneven; kerbs are high and frequent; ramps are few; public facilities don't necessarily have lifts; and gaining entrance to some of the sites is all but impossible due to their narrow entrances and steep stairs.

If you have a physical disability, you should get in touch with your national support organisation (preferably the travel officer if there is one) before you leave.

You may also like to contact ETAMS (☎ 575 4721; fax 575 4191) at 13 Qasr el-Nil, Central Cairo. This tour company specialises in custom-made tours, accommodation and sightseeing in specially equipped buses for disabled individuals and groups, and it also has information on hotels that have facilities for the disabled.

SENIOR TRAVELLERS

Unlike in many western countries, there are no discounts on things like public transport and museum admission fees for senior travellers in Egypt.

If you plan to stay in cheap hotels, you'll need to be fit enough to cope with numerous flights of stairs. Many tombs are also accessed by stairs, some of which are steep. The corridors inside tombs are sometimes very low, forcing you to bend over double; some people find this, coupled with the heat and dim lights inside the tombs, quite claustrophobic.

CAIRO FOR CHILDREN

For an Egyptian, the answer to keeping the kids happy is to take them to the club (see the Entertainment chapter). However, if you don't have membership granting access to one of these precious swathes of green and you don't want to stump up for the day fee,

there are several other things to do. Although very pricey, Dr Ragab's Pharaonic Village (see the Things to See & Do chapter) is usually a big hit with kids of all ages; it's fairly educational too and takes up most of a day. Cairo Zoo is good in that it's one of the few zoos where children get to feed the animals – the keepers sell the appropriate foodstuffs. If you are going to the zoo, a fun way of getting there is by river bus, departing from Maspero in front of the TV & Radio building (see the Getting Around chapter for more details).

In Zamalek there's the Fish Garden – never mind that half the fish in question are floating belly-up at the top of the aquariums, as the grottoes are great for hide-and-seek and there are some good, tiring grassy hillocks to run up and roll down. On the fringes of Islamic Cairo is the unusual Sayyida Zeinab Cultural Park (Map 8; ☎ 391 5220) a 20 acre garden specially landscaped for children. It contains a small mock village and has plenty of other structures for children to clamber over and run around. There are also occasional music and drama activities. Entrance is free but two passport photos are required for an ID card. The park is on Sharia Qadry, the street that leads from Sharia Port Said (Bur Said) to the Ibn Tulun mosque.

If you have the benefit of a car, there are two water parks on the outskirts of the city. Crazy Water has half a dozen or more water slides, a wave pool, a kiddies pool, and a playground area with sand, slides and tunnels. Admission is E£15, or E£12 for small fry. It's open daily 10 am to 10 pm. To get there, drive 15km from the intersection of the Giza road and Cairo-Alexandria road, then turn left on the route to 6th of October City. Aquapark (☎ 477 088/99) is newer, with presumably much the same facilities, and is 32km out on the Ismailia road.

For toyshops, Cairo's best is reputedly Toys & Joys which occupies two floors at 3 Mossadeq in Doqqi. It's open 10 am to 10 pm daily except Sunday.

If you're looking for somewhere children-friendly to dine out, then Andrea's, the open-air chicken restaurant out near the

Pyramids, is great. The kids can roam around the garden, and there's a big climbing frame and sometimes a guy giving donkey rides too. Children also seem to enjoy the Downtown Felfela – the tree-trunk tables are fun and the caged birds and turtle-filled aquariums provide plenty of distraction. (The Maadi Felfela, which is on the Corniche, has trampolines.) Other options are the food court in the basement of the Nile Hilton Shopping Mall, which has a kid's playroom, and the Mohandiseen Gamiat ad-Dowal al-Arabiyya branch of McDonald's which has a play area. See the Places to Eat chapter for further details.

USEFUL ORGANISATIONS

The following organisations might be of interest to anyone in Cairo for an extended stay:

British Community Association (BCA)
> 2 Abdel Rahman al-Rifai, Mohandiseen (☎ 348 1358)
> 18 Road 10, Maadi (☎ 353 8677)
> 11 Mohammed Yousef al-Qady, Heliopolis (☎ 417 9775)
> A social group for British citizens resident in Egypt that organises frequent get-togethers, talks and functions.

Community Services Association (CSA)
> 4 Road 21, Maadi (☎ 350 5285)
> Helps newcomers orient themselves. Also offers a library, holds talks and organises trips.

Egypt Exploration Society
> At the British Council, 192 Sharia el-Nil, Agouza (☎ 301 0319)
> Organises lectures and arranges good guided archaeological tours.

Middle East Wives
> Contact Carole Addas (☎ 418 3091)
> A friendship society for non-Arab women married to Egyptian/Arab men.

LIBRARIES

For English-readers the best libraries are at the British Council and American Cultural Centre (see the American Studies Library in the Cultural Centres section following). Otherwise, the best public library is the new and very grand Greater Cairo Library (Map 3; ☎ 341 2280) housed in a villa at 15 Mohammed Mazhar, Zamalek. It's stocked with a fantastic collection of art, science and other reference books (this library does not lend any of its books), mainly in English, and it also has a selection of newspapers and magazines for browsing. Opening hours are from 9 am to 7 pm daily except Monday (10 am to 8 pm during summer). The Mubarak Library (☎ 336 0291) beside 70 Sharia el-Nil in Giza also has a large collection of English, French and German-language titles, with more fiction than at the Greater Cairo Library, but borrowers must have maintained residence in Cairo for at least three years. It's open from 9 am to 7 pm daily except Tuesday.

CAMPUSES

For details about the American University in Cairo and some Egyptian universities, see the Courses section in the Things to See & Do chapter.

CULTURAL CENTRES

Bring your passport along as many cultural centres require some ID before they'll allow you to enter.

France
> 1 Madrassat al-Huquq al-Fransiyya, Mounira (Map 8; ☎ 355 3725). This newly renovated institute is at the southern end of Sharia Falaki, just east of Garden City. It's open Sunday to Thursday from 9 am to 9 pm.
> 27 Sharia Sabri Abu Alam, Midan Ismailia, Heliopolis (☎ 414 4824)
> Both centres regularly put on films, lectures and exhibitions, have libraries open to the public (call to check hours, as they are liable to frequent change) and get news and views from the French-speaking world via the satellite TV station TV-5. The institute at Mounira also runs French and Arabic language courses.

Germany
> Goethe Institut, 5 Bustan, Downtown (Map 8; ☎ 575 9877). Situated to the north of Midan Tahrir, this centre presents seminars and lectures in German on Egyptology and other topics. There are also performances by visiting music groups and special art exhibits and film screenings. The library has over 15,000 titles mainly in German. It's open Monday to Thursday from 1 to 7 pm and Friday from 8 am to noon.

Italy
>   Italian Cultural Institute, 3 Sheikh Marsafy, Zamalek (Map 3; ☎ 340 8791). The centre puts on films, organises lectures and has a library. It also hosts a great many art exhibitions.

Netherlands
>   Netherlands Cultural Institute, 1 Mahmoud Azmy, Zamalek (Map 3; ☎ 340 0076). Hosts art exhibitions and is well known in the Cairo expatriate community for its weekly lectures, delivered on a wide variety of topics and usually in English.

UK
>   British Council, 192 Sharia el-Nil, Agouza (Map 2; ☎ 345 3281). The Council has a library which carries most of the major UK daily and weekly newspapers and has more than 55,000 books and 90 periodicals. The reading rooms are open Monday to Thursday from 9 am to 2 pm and from 3 to 8 pm, Friday and Saturday from 9 am to 3 pm only and closed on Sunday. Library membership costs E£25, or nonmembers can browse for 20 minutes only (never enforced) free of charge.

USA
>   American Studies Library, 5 Latin America, Garden City (Map 7; ☎ 357 3133). Part of the embassy complex, this cultural centre has a library with more than 200 periodicals and 10,000 books, and is where you can watch daily broadcasts of *CBS Evening News with Dan Rather* Monday to Friday from 1 to 1.30 pm. The reading rooms are open from 10 am to 7 pm on Monday and Wednesday, and from 10 am to 4 pm the rest of the week; they are closed on Saturday and US and Egyptian holidays. Admission to the reading rooms is free.

DANGERS & ANNOYANCES

The amount of violent crime in Cairo is almost negligible compared with most western countries. (Crimes of passion are another thing. The *Egyptian Gazette* carries a column called 'Red Handed' which most days is filled with tales of murderous wives, revengeful jilted lovers, and assorted cases of fratricide, patricide and matricide. It makes fascinating reading.) Most visitors and residents would agree that Cairo is one of the world's safest cities, one in which pedestrians can walk abroad in almost any part of town at any hour of the day or night. Unfortunately, the hassle factor often means that this isn't quite the case for an unaccompanied foreign woman – see Women Travellers earlier in this chapter.

Pickpocketing

While theft is not a major problem – Lonely Planet has received very few stories of outright theft in Cairo – pickpocketing is. The metro and the buses running from Midan Tahrir to the Pyramids seem to be the main risk zones. Be careful about carrying money and valuables in a day-pack or handbag as a common technique is for the pickpocket to use a razor to stealthily slice them open. Moneybelts and pouches around your neck are the safest ways to carry your cash.

Terrorism

Despite an uncompromising government campaign to stamp out the extremist Islamist elements who consider tourists a fair target, terrorism remains a fact of life in Cairo. Eighteen Greeks were gunned down outside their hotel in April 1996 and nine German tourists were killed outside the Egyptian Museum as recently as September 1997. The likelihood of further attacks at some point in the future remains. Expect frequent security checks at government buildings, offices, hotels and tourist sights and keep abreast of regional and local news as this can signal changes in the security situation.

LEGAL MATTERS

Egyptian penalties for smuggling, dealing and even possessing drugs are high (the death penalty can be invoked).

Foreign travellers are subject to Egyptian laws – you'll get no special consideration just because you're not Egyptian. If arrested, you have the right to immediately telephone your embassy.

BUSINESS HOURS

Most government offices operate from about 8 am to 2 pm Sunday to Thursday, with Friday and Saturday being the official weekend. Shops generally have different hours at different times of the year. In summer most shops are open from 9 or 10 am through to 9 or 10 pm or even later. Winter hours are from 10 am to 6 pm. Hours during Ramadan are from 9.30 am to 3.30 pm and from 8 pm to midnight. Closing day can be either Friday, Saturday or Sunday. Generally, much of Downtown is closed Friday, while places like Heliopolis and Zamalek, heavily frequented by foreigners, are quieter on Sundays. There are no real hard and fast rules.

For banking business hours see the Changing Money section earlier this chapter.

PUBLIC HOLIDAYS

Egypt's holidays and festivals are primarily Islamic or Coptic religious celebrations, although there are a few secular public holidays as follows:

New Year's Day
   1 January
Sinai Liberation Day
   25 April
May Day
   1 May
Revolution Day
   23 July (Anniversary of the 1952 Revolution)
National Day
   6 October

Islamic Holidays

Although not official government holidays, the whole city closes down on the Prophet's birthday (Moulid an-Nabi) and for the duration of the two *eid* feasts.

Because the Islamic, or Hejira (meaning 'flight', as in the flight of Mohammed from Mecca to Medina in 622 AD) calendar is 11 days shorter than the Gregorian (western) calendar, Islamic holidays fall 11 days earlier each year. The 11 day rule is not entirely strict – the holidays can fall from 10 to 12 days earlier. The precise dates are known only shortly before they fall as they are dependent upon the sighting of the moon. See the Islamic Holidays table for the approximate dates for the next few years.

Ramadan Ramadan is the ninth month of the Muslim calendar, when all believers fast during the day. Pious Muslims do not allow *anything* to pass their lips in daylight hours. Although many Muslims do not follow the injunctions to the letter, most conform to some extent. However, the impact of the fasting is often lessened by a shift in waking hours – many only get up in the afternoon when there are just a few hours of fasting left to observe. They then feast through the night until sunrise. The combination of abstinence and lack of sleep mean that tempers are often short during Ramadan.

Although there are no public holidays until the feast at the end of the month, it is difficult to get anything done because of erratic hours. Almost everything closes in the afternoon or has shorter daytime hours; this does not apply to businesses that cater mostly to foreign tourists, but some restaurants and hotels may be closed for the entire month. It is considered impolite for non-Muslims to eat or drink in public during fasting hours.

The evening meal during Ramadan, called *iftar* (breaking the fast), is always a bit of a celebration. In some parts of town tables are laid out in the street as charitable acts by the wealthy to provide food for the less fortunate. The well-off themselves often have

Table of Holidays

Hejira Year	New Year	Prophet's Birthday	Ramadan Begins	Eid al-Fitr	Eid al-Adha
1418	09.05.97	17.07.97	31.12.97	29.01.98	08.04.98
1419	28.04.98	06.07.98	19.12.98	18.01.99	28.03.99
1420	17.04.99	26.06.99	09.12.99	08.01.00	16.03.00
1421	06.04.00	14.06.00	27.11.00	27.12.00	06.03.01
1422	26.03.01	03.06.01	16.11.01	16.12.01	23.02.02

iftar at the bigger restaurants. Midan Hussein is a great, if crowded, place to be at this time and the entertainment there goes on throughout the night until sunrise.

Other Islamic Holidays Following is a list of the other main Muslim holidays:

Ras as-Sana
    Islamic New Year
Moulid an-Nabi
    Birthday of the Prophet Mohammed. The streets of Cairo are a feast of lights and food on this day.
Eid al-Fitr
    The end of Ramadan fasting is marked by three days of feasting. Many people head off out of town and Cairo is extremely quiet.
Eid al-Adha (Bairam)
    The 'great feast' held 70 days after the end of Ramadan. Also the time for Muslims to fulfil the fifth pillar of Islam, the pilgrimage to Mecca.

Getting the Goat

Feasts, particularly the annual Eid al-Adha and Eid al-Fitr, are celebrated by the slaughter of sheep, goats and, less commonly, cows, the meat of which is meant to be shared with those who can't afford an animal of their own to kill and consume. It's a tradition common throughout the Muslim world.

In Cairo, police have their hands full trying to manage the chaos caused by the introduction of hundreds of thousands of sheep into the city's households over the feast. In the weeks leading up to the feast the streets become filled with temporary holding pens, while from balconies above the plaintive bleating of tightly tethered animals can be heard at all hours.

And then one morning you wake up and the farmyard sounds are gone. Instead, on the rooftop opposite, and in the backstreets of most neighbourhoods, are large pools of blood.

But the feasters don't have it all their own way. Every year local newspapers report at least one ovine-induced fatality. In 1997, according to a local press report, a sheep about to be sacrificed for the feast of Eid al-Adha rushed its executioner who lost his footing and fell to his death from a fourth storey balcony. ∎

Coptic Holidays

These are a mixture of religious and commemorative holidays. Curiously, although less than 10% of Cairo's population is Coptic Christian, on holidays like Christmas and Sham an-Nessim the rest of the city seems to undergo a quick conversion, and they all shut up shop for the day too.

Christmas
    7 January (Copts go to midnight mass)
Epiphany
    19 January (Celebrating the baptism of Jesus)
Annunciation
    23 March
Easter
    This is the most important date in the Coptic calendar. It's preceded by 55 days of fasting, and is celebrated on different dates each year.
Sham an-Nessim
    A special Coptic holiday with Pharaonic origins, it literally means 'the smell of a fresh wind'. It falls on the first Monday after the Coptic Easter and is celebrated by all Egyptians, with family picnics and outings.

SPECIAL EVENTS
Arabic Music Festival

Held in early November this is a 10 day festival of classical, traditional and orchestral Arabic music held at the Opera House. Programs are usually in Arabic only but the tourist office should have details.

Book Fair

Held every January at the Cairo Exhibition Grounds, this is one of the major events on the Cairo cultural calendar. It draws in massive crowds, most of whom are there for a day out rather than because of any literary leanings. Far more burgers, soft drinks and balloons are sold than books.

Cairo International Film Festival

Held in early December every year, this 14 day festival gives Cairenes the chance to watch a vast range of recent films from all over the world. The main attraction however, is that the films are all supposedly uncensored. Anything that sounds like it might contain scenes of exposed flesh sells out immediately, despite the fact that ticket

The Moulid

Literally meaning 'birth', a moulid celebrates the birthday of a local saint or holy person. Although the biggest moulid of all is held in the Delta town of Tanta, Cairo's moulids are often riotous affairs, with hundreds of thousands of people coming from far and wide to take part in a frenzy of celebrations ranging from fasting and feasting to prayer and performing *zikrs*.

A zikr (remembrance) is the communal recitation of the name of Allah in a bid to reach enlightenment. More often than not it's performed by a group of Sufi believers, known as *mugzzabin* (meaning 'those drawn in'), and can either be a very restrained event or one charged with energy. In the former, mugzzabin stand in straight lines and sway from side to side to the rhythm of clapping. As the clapping gains momentum, the zikr reaches its peak and the mugzzabin, having attained oneness with Allah, awake sweating and blinking from their trance-like state. Other zikrs are formidable endurance tests where troupes of musicians perform for hours in the company of ecstatic dancers.

Moulids generally take place around the tomb of the venerated saint and the whole scene usually resembles a fair. Those from out of town set up camp in the streets close to the saint's tomb. Children's rides, sideshows and food stalls are erected, and *tartours* (cone-shaped hats) and *fenous* (lanterns) are made and sold to passers-by. Much of this infrastructure is provided by 'professional' moulid people who spend their lives going from one moulid to another. Most moulids last for about a week, and climax with the *leila kebira* (the big night).

For visitors, the hardest part about attending a moulid is ascertaining dates. Events are tied to either the Islamic or Gregorian calendars, and dates can be different each year. Also, you'll need to be prepared for immense crowds (hold onto your valuables or, better still, leave them behind) and women should be escorted by a man.

Cairo hosts three of the country's biggest moulids: the Moulid an-Nabi; the Moulid of Sayyida Zeinab and the Moulid of al-Hussein. You'll need to ask a local for the exact dates in any particular year. ■

---

prices are twice those charged any other time of the year. The local press carries details of the screenings.

Experimental Theatre Festival

Held each September over 10 days, this theatre festival brings to Egypt a vast selection (40 at the last outing) of international theatre troupes. Directors have complained in the past that government censorship effectively prevents any 'experimentation' in the performances but nevertheless the festival represents almost the only time each year that it's worth turning out for the theatre in Cairo.

Pharaohs' Rally

This is a 4WD race through the desert beginning and ending at the Pyramids. It is held each October and attracts competitors from all over the world.

WORK

More than 40,000 foreigners live and work in Egypt. That figure alone should give you some idea of the immense presence foreign companies have in the country. Although most of these people were sent to Cairo by their company at home, there are plenty who came to Egypt for reasons other than work – often as tourists – and picked up employment while there. The kind of jobs that come up out of the blue vary widely but the kind of areas in which people often find work are photography, design, teaching, journalism and tourism. Knowing some Arabic is a definite advantage. Once you have an employer, securing a work permit should not be difficult, although many stay on for years without ever getting such a document.

For job notices check the small ads in the monthly *Egypt Today* and weekly *Middle East Times* and on the notice board at Sunny's supermarket in Zamalek.

Teaching English

There are many opportunities for teaching English as a second language. Internationally accredited schools (such as the British Council or International House affiliates) pay better and are usually better equipped. The down side is that you will need a qualification. The RSA Teaching English as a Foreign Language (TEFL) Certificate is the minimum requirement. If you have that and some experience, try the British Council (Map 2; ☎ 345 3281) at 192 Sharia el-Nil, the Centre for Adult & Continuing Education (Map 8; ☎ 354 2964) at the American University in Cairo, or the International Language Institute (ILI) (Map 12; ☎ 291 9295; fax 418 7275) at 2 Mohammed Bayoumi, in Heliopolis. Full-time teachers (100 hours per month) at the ILI earn a monthly wage of approximately E£2500. The British Council pays higher rates but only UK citizens can get full-year contract packages there, though other nationals often work part time.

If you have no qualification or experience, you could try some of the schools in Cairo and Alexandria that are listed in *Egypt Today*. Some of them are what the trade knows as 'cowboy outfits' – you work hard for little return and often with only minimal interest taken in the progress of students. Check with recognised institutions such as the American University in Cairo and British Council for advice.

The British Council and the ILI run TEFL certificate and diploma courses throughout the year.

Getting There & Away

AIR

Cairo international airport is 22km to the north-east of Central Cairo. There are two terminals about 3km apart. The newer terminal, Terminal II, services most international airlines; Terminal I is mainly used by Egypt-Air (domestic and international flights). For flight information call: Terminal I ☎ 244 8977; Terminal II ☎ 291 4255. For details of getting to and from the airport, see the Getting Around chapter.

Air fares for travelling to Egypt vary considerably according to the season, with the most expensive time of the year being around Christmas.

The USA & Canada

The *New York Times*, the *LA Times*, the *Chicago Tribune* and the *San Francisco Examiner* all produce weekly travel sections in which you'll find any number of travel

agents' ads. Council Travel (☎ (800) 226-8624) and STA Travel (☎ (800) 777-0112) have offices in major cities nationwide.

The magazine *Travel Unlimited* (PO Box 1058, Allston, Mass 02134) publishes details of the cheapest air fares and courier possibilities for destinations all over the world from the USA.

In Canada, Travel CUTS has offices in all major cities. The *Toronto Globe & Mail* and the *Vancouver Sun* carry travel agents' ads. The magazine *Great Expeditions* (PO Box 8000-411, Abbotsford, BC V2S 6H1) is useful.

The cheapest way to get from the USA or Canada to the Middle East and Africa is usually a return flight to London and a bucket-shop deal from there.

A round-the-world (RTW) ticket including a stopover in Cairo is a possibility. Check the travel sections of Sunday newspapers for the latest deals.

EgyptAir flies from New York and Los Angeles to Cairo. The cheapest advance purchase tickets are for a minimum stay of seven days and a maximum stay of two months. Regular fares from New York and Los Angeles are approximately US$1155/1687 one way/return and US$1838/2055 one way/return, respectively. EgyptAir has no connections to Canada.

Lufthansa has connections to Cairo via Frankfurt from many cities in the USA. Advance purchase fares are available. From Los Angeles, the return fare is US$2055 and entails a minimum stay of seven days and a maximum of two months. A one-way ticket is US$1838. From New York, it costs US$1555 and US$1013, respectively.

TWA and Pakistan International Airlines also fly between New York and Cairo.

Australia & New Zealand

STA and Flight Centres International are major dealers in cheap air fares from Australia and New Zealand. Check the travel

EDDIE GERALD

EDDIE GERALD

The details (portraits of Bill Clinton and Hosni Mubarak and crates of Sprite) date the photos to the 1980s or 90s, but for the most part, much of Cairo manages to keep the late 20th century at bay.

PATRICK HORTON

EDDIE GERALD

Starting at the medieval city gate of Bab an-Nasr (top), a walk through the winding streets of Islamic Cairo provides the opportunity to barter in the markets of Sugar Street (bottom), a street made famous by the writing of Naguib Mahfouz.

agents' ads in the Yellow Pages and ring around.

A one-way/return EgyptAir flight between Cairo and Sydney costs around A\$1129/1659 (January to May and September to November) or A\$1189/1759 (August and December). RTW fares with a stopover in Cairo start from A\$2399 but vary according to season. Gulf Air, Emirates Airlines, Singapore Airlines and Olympic Airways also fly between Australia and Cairo.

The UK

At the time of writing, the cheapest Cairo deal is a 12 month open return with Olympic Airways for approximately UK£240. Best bets for this are Trailfinders (☎ (0171) 938 3366) and STA Travel (☎ (0171) 937 9962), who have several branches in the UK. Check the listings in magazines such as *Time Out* and *TNT* and the ads in the Sunday papers and *Exchange & Mart* for alternative companies. Also look out for the free magazines that are widely available in London – start by looking outside the main railway and underground stations.

Most British travel agents are registered with ABTA (Association of British Travel Agents). If you have paid for your flight with an ABTA-registered agent who then goes out of business, ABTA will guarantee a refund or an alternative. Unregistered bucket shops are riskier but sometimes cheaper.

Continental Europe

Lufthansa and its charter subsidiary Condor offer some of the most frequent connections, with flights to and from Egypt. Austrian Airlines also has some good deals as does MALEV-Hungarian Airlines.

In Munich, a great source of both travel information and travel gear is Travel Overland (☎ (89) 27 27 61 00; fax 2 71 97 45) at Zentrale Schwabing, Barerstrasse 73, 80799 München. As well as producing a comprehensive travel equipment catalogue, it runs an 'Expedition Service' which has current flight information. In Berlin, Kilroy (☎ (30) 3 10 00 40), at Hardenbergstrasse 9, near Berlin Zoo (with five branches around the city), is a popular travel agency. In Hannover, Explorer at Röseler Strasse 1, 30159 Hannover (☎ (0511) 3 07 71 00; fax 32 55 14) has been recommended.

In Amsterdam some of the best fares are offered by the student travel agency NBBS Reiswinkels (☎ (20) 624 09 89). It has seven branches throughout the city, with fares comparable to those of London bucket shops. NBBS Reiswinkels has branches in Brussels, Belgium, as well.

Paris seems to abound with Egypt and desert specialists. Voyageurs au Proche Orient et Dans Les Pays Arabes (☎ 01 42 86 17 19) at 55 rue Sainte-Anne, 75002 Paris, has a return flight on EgyptAir for 2775FF.

Middle East

Air Sinai and El Al Israel Airlines regularly fly between Cairo and Tel Aviv for about E£473 (US\$141) one way or E£946 (US\$282) return (valid for one month). There are daily flights with Royal Jordanian Airlines and EgyptAir between Cairo and Amman, but there is no discounting. Amman to Cairo is JD86 (US\$124) one way and JD173 (US\$248) return. Going the other way, the fare is E£411 (US\$124) one way and E£822 (US\$248) return. There are no student reductions.

Africa

Sudan Airways and EgyptAir both have two flights a week between Cairo and Khartoum. The 2½ hour flight costs E£1118 (US\$336) one way or E£1387 (US\$416) return (valid for one month). Sudan Airways also has a youth fare (for those under 25 years) which costs E£849 one way or E£1565 return (open for one year). However, one-way tickets will not be sold unless you can show a ticket from Sudan to your home country, and no ticket will be issued until you've got your Sudanese visa.

Other than the above, there is nothing cheap about air travel in Africa. About the best you can do to Nairobi is E£1930 (US\$578) one way with Kenyan Airways. A return ticket, valid for two months, costs E£2756 (US\$826). The flight to Addis Ababa in Ethiopia is E£1577 (US\$472) one way and E£2259 (US$677) return with Ethiopian Airlines. However, one-way tickets can only be purchased if you can show a credit card or travellers cheques to cover the cost of a return ticket.

Asia

Bangkok and Singapore are Asia's main centres for bucket shops and they also have direct flights and transfers to Cairo. Manila and Kuala Lumpur also have a fair number of flights but are not as good for buying cheap tickets. Tokyo has very few flights and is a hopeless place to find discounts. STA Travel has branches in Bangkok (☎ (02) 233-2582), Singapore (☎ (65) 734-5681), Kuala Lumpur (☎ (03) 248-9800) and Tokyo (☎ (03) 5391-2922). Also worth trying are Council Travel who have offices in Tokyo (☎ (03) 3581-5517), Singapore (☎ (65) 738-7066) and Bangkok (☎ (02) 282-7705).

As an example of costs, Kuwait Airways and EgyptAir both offer good deals on flights between Singapore and Cairo. A one-way/return fare on Kuwait Airways costs around US$405/639; a similar flight on EgyptAir costs US$513/806.

Within Egypt

EgyptAir (see the Airline Offices section following for Cairo office addresses) is not one of the world's better airlines. Its flights are often delayed without explanation, the inflight service is lousy, and to top it all, it is extremely expensive (though not for Egyptians and residence permit holders, who only pay a third of the foreigners' fare). Domestically, it flies between Cairo and Alexandria (US$120); Sharm el-Sheikh (US$277); Hurghada (US$264); Luxor (US$243); Aswan (US$336); and Abu Simbel (US$477). All fares are for the round trip for foreigners.

Buying Tickets in Egypt Air tickets bought in Egypt are subject to some hefty government taxes, which makes them extremely expensive. Always fly in on a return ticket. If you do have to buy a ticket in Cairo, see the Travel Agents section later in this chapter for addresses.

Airline Offices All of the offices are Downtown (Maps 4 & 8) unless otherwise stated. Opening hours are generally 8 or 9 am until 3.30 or 4.30 pm. Most are closed Friday and sometimes Saturday too.

Note It is essential that you reconfirm any flights out of Cairo, even to domestic destinations, as overbooking and cancellations are not uncommon.

Air France
    2 Midan Talaat Harb (☎ 575 8899)
Air India
    1 Talaat Harb (☎ 392 2592)
Air Malta
    2 Talaat Harb (☎ 574 9360, 390 7045)
Air Sinai
    Nile Hilton (☎ 760 948, 772 949)
Alitalia
    Nile Hilton (☎ 578 5823/4)
Austrian Airlines
    22 Qasr el-Nil (☎ 392 1522)
British Airways
    1 Bustan, Midan Tahrir (☎ 578 0743)
Cyprus Airways
    16 Adly (☎ 390 8099)
Czech Airlines
    9 Talaat Harb (☎ 393 0395)
EgyptAir
    Nile Hilton (☎ 765 200)
    Midan Opera (☎ 391 4501)
    6 Adly (☎ 390 0999); open until 8 pm
    9 Talaat Harb (☎ 393 2836); open until 8 pm
    22 Ibrahim Laqqany, Heliopolis (☎ 290 8453)
El Al Israel Airlines
    5 Makrizy, Zamalek (☎ 341 1795)
Ethiopian Airlines
    Nile Hilton (☎ 574 0911)
Gulf Air
    21 Mahmoud Bassiouni (☎ 574 3336)
Japan Airlines (JAL)
    Nile Hilton (☎ 574 7233)
Kenya Airways
    Nile Hilton (☎ 762 494)
KLM-Royal Dutch Airlines
    11 Qasr el-Nil (☎ 574 7004)
Lufthansa Airlines
    6 Sheikh Marsafi, Zamalek (☎ 339 8339)
MALEV-Hungarian Airlines
    12 Talaat Harb (☎ 574 4959, 573 3898)
Middle East Airlines (MEA)
    12 Qasr el-Nil (☎ 574 3100); closed Sunday
Olympic Airways
    23 Qasr el-Nil (☎ 393 1318)
Royal Jordanian
    6 Qasr el-Nil (☎ 575 0875/0905)

Scandinavian Airlines System (SAS)
  2 Champollion, Midan Tahrir (☎ 575 3627);
  closed Saturday and Sunday
Singapore Airlines (SIA)
  Nile Hilton (☎ 575 0276)
Sudan Airways
  1 Bustan, Midan Tahrir (☎ 578 7398); open until
  7 pm
Swissair
  22 Qasr el-Nil (☎ 393 7955)
TWA (Trans World Airlines)
  1 Qasr el-Nil (☎ 574 9904)
Tunis Air
  14 Talaat Harb (☎ 575 3971)
Turkish Airlines
  3 Midan Mustafa Kamel (☎ 390 8960/1)
Yemenia Airlines
  10 Talaat Harb, Evergreen Building (☎ 574
  0711)

BUS

Israel & Palestinian Territories

There is a bus service every day except Saturday from Central Cairo to Tel Aviv and Jerusalem. The service is split between two companies: Masr Travel (☎ 393 0168) at 7 Talaat Harb, Downtown and Travco (☎ 340 4493) at 13 Mahmoud Azmy, Zamalek. Tickets can also be bought from many of the travel agencies on Midan Tahrir and Talaat Harb. The bus departs from the Cairo Sheraton at 5.30 am and takes 10 hours, travelling via the border point of Rafah on the southern edge of the Gaza Strip. A one-way ticket is E£100; the round trip costs E£150. Alternatively, you can catch a local bus to Rafah and make your own way onwards from the Israeli side; note, however, that there is only one bus a day (at 3 pm) from the border to Jerusalem or Tel Aviv.

Another possible route is to catch a bus to Taba in Sinai. These depart twice daily from the Sinai bus station in Abbassiyya and a one way ticket is E£66. At Taba you can walk across the border into Israel and take a taxi to Eilat from where there are buses onward to Jerusalem and Tel Aviv. Doing it this way will take about 18 hours nonstop and it works out more expensive than going on the scheduled bus through Rafah.

Jordan & the Gulf

It is possible to book a combined bus and ferry ticket from Cairo that goes via Nuweiba to Aqaba in Jordan at Midan Ulali (near Midan Ramses) or Midan Abdel Moniem Riad stations (Map 4), but the bus for the Cairo to Nuweiba leg leaves from the Sinai bus station in Abbassiyya.

To Saudi Arabia and other Gulf destinations, tickets must be bought at the Sinai bus station itself.

Libya

The East Delta Bus Company runs a daily service to Benghazi from Midan Ulali (you can also book the ticket at the Midan Abdel Moniem Riad office). The bus leaves at 9 am and takes about 20 hours. On Monday and Thursday the bus continues for another 16 hours to Tripoli. Make sure you have a visa. Superjet also runs a bus to Benghazi and Tripoli which departs at 7.30 am from Midan Abdel Moniem Riad.

Cheaper tickets are available with the Hebton bus company at 305 Sharia Shubra, Midan al-Khalifawi, Shubra, or at its office on Midan Ataba.

Internal

Cairo has five long-distance bus stations. The main one is on Midan Abdel Moniem Riad (Map 7; near the Ramses Hilton in Central Cairo). The other four are: the station on Midan Ulali, the Ahmed Helmy bus station (behind Ramses railway station), the Upper Egypt Bus Company station at 45 Sharia al-Azhar (a few blocks east of Midan Ataba) and Abbassiyya station (about a kilometre from Midan Abbassiyya), which is commonly known as the Sinai station.

From Midan Abdel Moniem Riad, luxury buses leave for Alexandria, the Delta, Marsa Matruh, Hurghada, Sharm el-Sheikh, Luxor and Aswan. It's also the departure point for ordinary buses to the Cairo satellite towns of the 6th of October and 10th of Ramadan. Also from here you can book tickets to destinations as far afield as Tunis, Istanbul, Damascus, Amman and cities throughout Saudi Arabia and the Gulf. All these services involve transfers to national carriers.

Alexandria & the Mediterranean Coast
Superjet's mega-comfy buses will whisk you from Midan Abdel Moniem Riad to Alexandria in about 2½ hours. There are departures every half an hour, starting at 5 am and continuing through until 9 or 10 pm. Superjet also has a daily bus to Marsa Matruh plus, in summer only, two extra services at 7 and 8 am.

West Delta Bus Company buses also depart from Midan Abdel Moniem Riad. It has two types of services running to Alexandria: luxury buses (with video, air-con and toilet) and ordinary buses which are half the price but, depending on how clapped out they are, take longer. Buses leave at 5.30, 6, 6.30 and 7 am and then hourly until midnight. There's a daily West Delta bus to Marsa Matruh at 8.45 am which operates year-round. In summer, there are six extra luxury buses to Marsa Matruh; five in the morning (the first one is at 7.15 am) and one in the afternoon. In addition there's a no-frills bus at 8.30 am.

The Nile Delta, Suez Canal & Red Sea Coast The East Delta Bus Company's white and yellow-green striped buses leave from Midan Ulali (near Midan Ramses) for Mansura and Damietta. Tickets can be bought from the Delta zone booth. From the Canal zone booth around the corner there are buses to Port Said (hourly), Ismailia (about every 45 minutes) and also to Suez (about every 30 minutes). Port Said is also served by Superjet buses, of which there are nine a day, departing from a small office on Sharia Ramses about 300m north of Midan Ramses.

The Upper Egypt Bus Company runs luxury buses from Midan Abdel Moniem Riad to Hurghada six times daily. The 10.30 pm bus goes on to Quseir. The Upper Egypt Bus Co's ordinary buses to Red Sea coast destinations depart from the Ahmed Helmy bus station, behind Ramses station; there are five services daily to Hurghada and two to both Port Safaga and Quseir.

Superjet also has a bus to Hurghada departing from Midan Abdel Moniem Riad.

Upper Egypt The Upper Egypt Bus Company has a luxury bus from Midan Abdel Moniem Riad to Luxor each evening at 9.15 pm and to Aswan at 5 pm.

Sinai Nearly all East Delta Company buses to the Sinai leave from the Sinai bus station in Abbassiyya. There are six buses a day to Sharm el-Sheikh; the 7 am and 4 and 9.45 pm buses continue on to Dahab (nine hours). The 9 am bus to Nuweiba (nine hours) goes via St Catherine's (7½ hours), and the 7 and 9 pm services go on to Taba. Ticket prices vary with the service and time of day.

Buses to Al-Arish and Rafah leave from Midan Ulali but also pick up at the Sinai bus station. There are buses to Al-Arish (five hours) at 7.30 and 8.30 am, noon and 4 pm. Buses to Rafah (six hours) leave at 7.30 and 8.30 am.

The Western Oases Buses travel daily to the Western Desert Oases in the New Valley (Al-Wadi al-Gedid) from a small Upper Egypt Bus Company station at 45 Sharia al-Azhar, a few blocks east of Midan Ataba – look out for the small white on green sign. All buses stop near Midan Giza – at the 6th of October City minibus stop where the overpass forks and Pyramids Rd begins – to take on additional passengers. However if you want to be sure of a place it's best to reserve tickets 24 hours in advance and catch the bus from the main station.

There are no direct buses from the bus station to Siwa – you must first get a bus to Alexandria or Marsa Matruh and then another from there.

Al-Fayoum Buses for Al-Fayoum (E£3, two hours) leave from the Ahmed Helmy station and a separate station to the east of Midan Giza. To find this station, continue past the minibus stop near Midan Giza until you reach Sharia Sudan. The bus lot is to the east of the railway line.

TRAIN
There are no international rail links and the only lines are internal.

Ramses station (Mahattat Ramses), on Midan Ramses (Map 4), is Cairo's main railway station. There is a tourist office with tourist police just inside the main entrance on the left; it is open from 8 am to 8 pm. Note also that among the phones, farther inside on the left, are a few card phones. In a secondary entrance to the right is a small post office and, next to it, the left-luggage area (marked 'cloak room') which is open 24 hours every day; the service costs E£1 per piece.

For travel information phone ☎ 147 or ☎ 575 3555.

Wagons-Lits

The wagons-lits office (☎ 574 9474; fax 574 9074) at Ramses station is in a separate building south of the car park on the left side of the main building; it's open from 9 am to 4 pm (Friday until 2 pm). Follow the blue on yellow signs which read 'Res. Office'. The spacious office is on the 1st floor. There is now only one train a day which travels to Luxor and Aswan. For either destination it costs E£451 one way in 1st class, E£293 in 2nd class, and includes all meals. There is no student reduction. In the high season (from about October to April) it is best to book two or three days in advance.

Tickets for this train can also be booked at the office at the Helnan Shepheard Hotel on the Corniche south of Midan Tahrir.

Southern Destinations

The overnight trains to Luxor and Aswan are the ones generally taken by foreigners. They are among the best trains in Egypt. Even for sit-up tickets you'll need to book at least a day, and probably two days, in advance.

There are five express overnight trains from Cairo to Luxor and Aswan, however, foreigners are only allowed to travel on two of them.

First, 2nd and 3rd class tickets for destinations south of Cairo are bought along platform 11. There are eight windows and each one deals with specific trains. The destinations and train numbers are written up in Arabic on the windows, although the system does not seem to be rigorously applied.

The 1st/2nd class air-con fare from Cairo to Luxor (about 10 hours) is E£48/28 and the student fare is E£28/22. These fares are excluding meals. The trip to Aswan (about 15 hours) is E£60/34 in 1st/2nd class.

Northern Destinations

For both 1st and 2nd class air-con tickets to Alexandria, Marsa Matruh and the Nile Delta, head for the windows directly in front of you when you come in the main entrance of Ramses station, past the tourist office and the telephones. For 2nd class ordinary tickets, walk past the 1st class ticket windows outside and across to the next office.

The best trains running between Cairo and Alexandria are the Turbos. They make only one stop, at Sidi Gaber station in Alexandria, and take two hours. Second class in this train is about as good as 1st class in most others. Turbo Nos 905, 917 and 927 leave Cairo at 9 am and 2 and 7 pm, respectively. Turbos are more expensive than other trains and the student discount is not much. Tickets for 1st/2nd class air-con cost E£22/17.

Other direct trains leave at 9 am and 3, 6 and 10.30 pm. They're the same price as the Turbos and take roughly the same time.

Other trains, known as the 'French-line' services, take at least 2¾ hours (often longer) and call at Benha, Tanta and Damanhur on the way.

Eastern Destinations

Four trains make the trip from Cairo to Port Said (four hours), stopping en route at Zagazig, Ismailia and Qantara.

SERVICE TAXI

Cairo's service taxis depart from various places around the city. By Ramses station, they stretch around from the Midan Ulali bus station up to the railway station. They depart for Mansura, Qantara, Damietta (Ras al-Bar), Alexandria (E£8 to E£10), Suez (E£5), Ismailia (E£5), Port Said (E£8), Al-Arish (E£12, five hours) and Rafah (E£15, six hours). Fares are determined by the distance travelled, so keep an eye out for what others pay to get an idea of the set price.

Service taxis for Alexandria also leave from in front of Ramses station and the Nile Hilton. Taxis for destinations in and around Al-Fayoum (E£4) leave from the Al-Fayoum bus stop near Midan Giza. The service-taxi station at Midan Ahmed Helmy covers the Delta area.

Service taxis are usually Peugeot 504s but sometimes they are microbuses (private minibuses).

TRAVEL AGENTS

The area around Midan Tahrir is teeming with travel agencies. Although it is no London bucket shop scene, you should hunt around, but don't expect huge differences in prices or amazing deals.

De Castro Tours (Map 8; ☎ 574 3144), at 12 Talaat Harb, is fairly reliable. It offers a wide range of flights, many with considerable student discounts. Just down the road at No 10 is Norma Tours (☎ 760 007), which touts itself as being a cheap air-fare specialist.

One of the best and most reputable agencies in town, though it's way down in Maadi, is Egypt Panorama Tours (☎ 350 5880; fax 351 1199; email ept@intouch.com) at 4 Road 79 (it's right outside the Al-Maadi metro station). They're good on cheap air fares and trips and tours within Egypt and around the Mediterranean region. If you don't want to make the trip, you can always make bookings over the phone (the staff speak excellent English); payment is collected when the tickets are couriered to you.

Avoid Metro Travel and Wonder Travel, as well as the touts from these agencies who hang around Midan Talaat Harb.

The official Egyptian government travel agency, Masr Travel (☎ 393 0010; fax 392 4440), has its head office at 1 Talaat Harb, but it handles mainly administrative matters. For general information or bus tickets go to the office (Map 8; ☎ 393 0168) at 7 Talaat Harb.

DEPARTURE TAXES

There is no departure tax if you are leaving Cairo via air, but if you are travelling overland to Israel you will have to pay around E£17 at the border.

Getting Around

Overcrowded buses and minibuses are the most common form of transport for the majority of Cairenes, but for anyone who favours breathing, taxis are the only option. By western standards they are very cheap and there's never one far away. The only time when taxis aren't the best bet – they become too expensive – is if you are travelling a fair distance, say north to Heliopolis or south down to Maadi. In such cases, two cheaper alternatives are the partially underground metro or the tram.

It's also wise to avoid taking taxis between about 2.30 and 4 pm (that's always supposing that you can find one free at this time of day) as this is when everyone slinks off home for the day and the roads are even more congested than usual.

THE AIRPORT
Taxi

Cairo's airport is not the easiest of airports to get away from. Although there are bus services they are far from obvious and you may well just decide to grab a taxi. If you do, then the going rate is around E£25 to E£30 for Central Cairo. If you take one of the large 'official' airport taxis the fixed rate will be double that. It's generally better to get out of the arrivals hall and away from all the touts before starting to bargain with anyone. Walking away often tends to bring the price down. Triple check the agreed fare, as there is an irritating tendency for drivers to nod at what you say and hit you with an out-of-the-world fare later on.

In the traffic-free early hours of the morning (when so many flights seem to arrive) the journey to Central Cairo takes less than half an hour; at other, busier times of the day it takes 45 minutes to an hour.

Bus

Don't believe anyone who tells you that there is no bus to the city centre. In fact there are quite a few buses and minibuses to various points in Cairo from the older Terminal I and several pass by the newer Terminal II first.

At Terminal II, buses stop on the ground level between the arrival and departure halls. They serve as a shuttle to Terminal I, where buses stop in front of the obelisk across the parking lot from the main building. Here you have a wider choice of buses and minibuses into the city centre (25 to 50 pt). There are at least hourly buses to Midan Tahrir (No 422) for 25 pt, to Midan Giza (No 949) via Midan Ramses and Midan Tahrir, and to Midan Ataba (No 948). Bus No 400 (25 pt) and minibus No 27 (50 pt) depart frequently round the clock. The journey to Midan Tahrir takes at least an hour; longer if it's peak hour.

Going to the airport, you can take bus No 400 from the bus station on Midan Abdel Moniem Riad (just north of the Egyptian Museum), or minibus No 27 from the stands in front of the Nile Hilton.

BUS & MINIBUS

Taking a bus in Cairo is an experience all of its own. First, there's getting on. Cairenes stampede buses, charging the entrance before the thing has even slowed down. Hand-to-hand combat ensues as they run alongside the bus trying to leap aboard. If

Travelling Salesmen
Buses and trams idling at terminals are the perfect pitch for street vendors. Men and young boys wander up and down the aisle with boxes of sweets, hair brushes, toiletries, cards with Quranic verses etc. The usual sales method is to drop one of whatever it is into the lap of each passenger. If this happens to you, don't bother protesting or trying to give it back – just before the bus or tram departs, the vendor returns along the aisle collecting up all his goods and the money from anyone who decides to buy. ■

you wait for it to stop, the pushing and shoving to get on is even worse. Often several passengers don't quite manage to get on and they make their journey hanging off the back doorway, clinging perilously to the frame or to someone with a firmer hold.

The scene inside the bus in this case usually resembles a Guinness World Record attempt on the greatest number of people in a fixed space. There are times when, crammed up the back with exhaust fumes billowing around you and ever more people squeezing on, asphyxiation seems perilously close. At some point during the trip, a man will somehow manage to squeeze his way through to sell you your ticket, which is usually 25 pt.

Just as the bus doesn't always stop to let people on, it frequently does little more than slow down to let passengers off. In this case you stand in the doorway, wait for the opportune moment and launch yourself into the road.

Taking a minibus is an easier option. Passengers are not allowed to stand (although this rule is frequently overlooked), and each minibus leaves as soon as every seat is taken. It costs 25 to 50 pt (depending on your destination) for a seat.

Microbus

Increasingly, Cairenes are using private microbuses (as opposed to the public minibuses) to get around. Destinations are not marked in any language, so they are hard to use, except for those travelling to the Pyramids from in front of the Nile Hilton for 50 pt. If you do want to catch one around town, it's best to position yourself at a large intersection at the start of the road you want to go along. When a microbus passes, yell out your destination; if it's going in the right direction, the driver will stop.

Bus Stations & Routes

Cairo's main bus station (for local buses only) is directly in front of the Nile Hilton on Midan Tahrir. From here, buses leave for just about everywhere in the city. This is also where the minibus station is. Minibuses

adorned by orange and white stripes (sometimes a black and red one) run from this and other stops to places like Giza and the Pyramids, the Citadel (ask for 'Al-Qalaa'), the City of the Dead, Maadi, and Doqqi and Mohandiseen in the west of the city.

Note that although the area in front of the Nile Hilton is the main station, many buses passing *through* Midan Tahrir from other parts of the city don't actually stop there. Instead, a lot of buses heading out to Zamalek, Doqqi and beyond slow down to set down and pick up passengers on Sharia Tahrir as they pass between the Nile Hilton and the Mogamma.

There are other local bus stations worth noting. The station on Midan Abdel Moniem Riad, just north of the Egyptian Museum, has buses to Abbassiyya and the airport. Midan Ataba, which is just east of the Ezbekiyya Gardens, has plenty of buses going out to the Citadel.

The local bus station at Giza has buses to the Pyramids, the airport and the Citadel. Next to it is a microbus stand, where you can catch a microbus to the Pyramids for 25 pt.

Following is a list of some of the bus numbers and their destinations. Route numbers are usually indicated in Arabic numerals (sometimes in English also) on small signs behind the windscreen and on painted signs on the side of the bus. A word of caution – sometimes route numbers change, even while the route itself stays the same. Cairenes say this is little more than a ruse to put up fares – new route number, higher fare. Also, some buses to the airport occasionally have fares higher than 25 pt.

Note that some of the information in the tables that follow overlaps for ease of use.

To/From Midan Tahrir – Nile Hilton station

No 422	Midan Tahrir – Midan Roxy (Heliopolis) – Terminals I & II (airport)
Minibus No 27	Midan Tahrir – Heliopolis – Terminals I & II (airport)
Minibus Nos 30	Midan Tahrir – Abbassiyya (Sinai) bus station
Minibus No 2	Midan Tahrir – Midan Ahmed Helmy – Shubra

Minibus No 38	Midan Tahrir – Sharia Port Said (Bur Said) – Midan al-Amiriyya
Minibus No 54	Midan Tahrir – Sayyida Zeinab – Citadel
Minibus No 83	Midan Tahrir – Pyramids
Minibus No 52	Midan Tahrir – Maadi
No 16	Midan Tahrir – Galaa Bridge – Agouza
No 99	Midan Tahrir – Agouza – Midan Libnan
No 815	Midan Tahrir – Al-Azhar & Khan al-Khalili
Minibus No 77	Midan Tahrir – Al-Azhar & Khan al-Khalili
No 913	Midan Tahrir – Pyramids

To/From Midan Abdel Moniem Riad

No 400	Midan Abdel Moniem Riad – Heliopolis – Terminal I (airport)
No 300	Midan Abdel Moniem Riad – Abbassiyya – Ain Shams
Minibus No 35	Midan Abdel Moniem Riad – Abbassiyya
Minibus No 24	Midan Abdel Moniem Riad – Midan Roxy (Heliopolis)

To/From Midan Ataba

No 99	Midan Ataba – Midan Libnan
No 904	Ad-Darasa (City of the Dead) – Midan Ataba – Midan Tahrir – Pyramids
No 404	Midan Ataba – Citadel – Midan Tahrir
No 951	Midan Ataba – Citadel
No 57	Midan Ataba – Citadel
No 65	Midan Ataba – Khan al-Khalili
No 48	Midan Ataba – Zamalek
No 930	Midan Ataba – Qanater
No 948	Midan Ataba – airport
Minibus No 84	Midan Ataba – zoo – Midan Giza

To/From Ramses Station

No 812	Ramses station – Midan Giza
No 804	Ramses station – Midan Tahrir – Pyramids
No 174	Ramses station – Citadel
No 210	Ramses station – Qanater
Minibus No 63	Ramses station – Al-Azhar
No 65	Ramses station – Midan Ataba – Khan al-Khalili
Minibus No 72	Ramses station – Midan Libnan

To/From Midan Giza

No 3	Midan Giza – Pyramids
No 812	Midan Giza – Ramses station
No 116	Midan Giza – Kerdassa
No 929	Midan Giza – Midan Tahrir
No 949	Midan Giza – Midan Ramses – Terminals I & II (airport)

To/From Zamalek

No 13	Midan Falaki – Midan Tahrir – Zamalek
Minibus No 48	Midan Ataba – Zamalek
Minibus No 49	Midan Falaki – Midan Tahrir – Zamalek
Minibus No 47	Midan Ramses – Zamalek

To/From the Pyramids

No 904	Ad-Darasa (City of the Dead) – Midan Ataba – Midan Tahrir – Pyramids
No 905	Citadel – Midan Tahrir – Qasr al-Ainy – Manial – Pyramids
No 3	Midan Giza – Pyramids
No 804	Ramses station – Citadel – Midan Tahrir – Manial – Pyramids
Minibus No 82	Midan Tahrir – Manial – Giza – Pyramids
Minibus No 83	Midan Tahrir – Doqqi – Pyramids

To/From the Citadel

No 173	Midan Falaki – Citadel
No 174	Ramses station – Citadel
No 905	Citadel – Manial – Giza – Pyramids
No 404	Midan Ataba – Citadel – Midan Tahrir
No 951	Midan Ataba – Citadel
No 57	Midan Ataba – Citadel
Minibus No 54	Midan Tahrir – Citadel

TRAM

Most of Cairo's trams (known to Cairenes, confusingly, as 'metros') have been phased out. The remaining lines that are of use are those which connect Central Cairo to Heliopolis. Three of the original lines still run in the north-east of town, coming from Nouzha, Mirghani and Abdel Aziz Fahmy, and merge around Midan Roxy in Heliopolis. From here they all follow the same line down to Midan Ramses and then down to the terminus on Sharia Galaa, just north of Midan Abdel Moniem Riad. These trams are supposed to have colour-coded direction boards – Nouzha (red), Mirghani (green) and Abdel

BETHUNE CARMICHAEL

When catching a tram from Midan Ramses, make sure you're there early to get a seat.

Aziz Fahmy (yellow) – but these are often not displayed.

There are several other lines, such as one from Matariyya (north-west of Heliopolis) which runs along Sharia Port Said next to the Museum of Islamic Art and one from Midan Triomphe in Heliopolis to Ad-Darasa next to the Northern Cemetery.

The trams are as cheap, and often as crowded, as the buses. It costs 25 pt from Midan Ramses to Midan Roxy and takes 20 to 30 minutes depending on whether it's peak hour or not.

METRO

The Metro system is startlingly efficient, and the stations are cleaner than any other public places in Cairo. It's also extremely inexpensive and, outside rush hours, not too crowded. At the time of writing there are two lines in operation with a third due to start up soon. The main line, with 33 stations, stretches for 43km from the southern suburb of Helwan passing through Maadi, Old Cairo, Midan Tahrir and Midan Ramses and then on up to Al-Marg, near Heliopolis. The second line connects Shubra with Midan Ramses. By 1998 this line should extend under the Nile to Doqqi, and by the end of the century it's planned to reach Giza. Metro stations are easily identified by signs with a big red 'M' in a blue star.

It costs 30 pt to ride up to nine stops; 50 pt for up to 16 stops; 70 pt for up to 22 stops; E£1 for up to 28 stops; and E£1.20 to ride the length of the line. The service starts at about 5 am and closes around 11.30 pm.

Men should note that the first carriage is reserved for women only. Women who want to ride in this carriage should make sure they're standing at the right place on the platform (near where the front part of the train will stop) as the trains don't hang around in the station for long.

CAR

Driving in Cairo is not for the faint-hearted. It's like the chariot race in Ben Hur only with Fiats. The roads are always crowded; rush hour begins at about 8 am each morning and doesn't slack off until about midnight. Lane markings are ignored as Cairo drivers treat other vehicles like obstacles on a slalom, and a favourite manoeuvre is to suddenly sweep across multiple lanes of traffic to make a turn on the opposite side of the carriageway. Brakes are scorned in favour of the horn (see the boxed text 'City Chorus'). Traffic lights are discretionary unless enforced by a policeman, who is equally likely to wave you through on a red light and halt you on green. Driving at night is particularly hazardous as headlights are reserved exclusively for flashing oncoming vehicles.

The wonder is that the roads aren't strewn with shattered glass and crumpled bits of bodywork. But in fact there are very few accidents (outside the city it's a different story – the Cairo-Alexandria road is one of the world's deadliest highways). Cairo drivers have their own road rules, they look out for each other and they are extremely tolerant of the type of driving that anywhere else would spark an epidemic of road-rage. Things only tend to go awry when an inexperienced driver is thrown into the mix – something anyone considering driving here should bear in mind.

Rental

If you are crazy enough to want to battle the traffic in Cairo, there are a number of car

CRXXXXXXXXXXXXX

City Chorus

Brakes are for sissies, real men use horns. Rather than slow down, drivers beep their horns furiously to signal to the car ahead to get out of the way or to alert pedestrians that they intend to run a red light. It's almost like dialogue: *barp, barp* move over, I'm coming through; *beep* sure; *barp* thanks. With some drivers the use of the horn is incessant, like a nervous tick. A friend of ours had a taxi driver pull over and suggest she find another cab, explaining that he couldn't go on because his horn wasn't working.

However, now Cairo drivers are to be penalised for their volubility as the government is going to clamp down on unnecessary use of car horns. They aim to reduce noise pollution by introducing fines of E£100 for unnecessary horn use and may also introduce devices that silence the horn after a short beep. Anyone looking to make a quick buck in Cairo in the coming years ought to open a shop selling brake pads. ■

CRXXXXXXXXXXXXX

rental agencies in the city, including the 'big three' – Avis, Hertz and Budget.

You need to be over the age of 25 and have an international driving permit; the rental agencies don't care whether you have a permit or not and will rent you the car regardless but you can be liable to cop a heavy fine if you're caught driving without one.

As an indication of prices, for a small car like a Suzuki Swift you'll be looking at about US$40 per day, plus up to US$0.20 for each extra kilometre. A Toyota Corolla is about US$56 to US$60 per day, plus around US$0.25 per kilometre. Remember that a 10 to 17% tax will be added to your bill. It's usually possible to pay with travellers cheques or by credit card.

Avis
16 Mamal as-Sukkar, Garden City (☎ 354 7400; fax 356 2464)
Meridien Le-Caire (☎ 989 400)
Nile Hilton (☎ 766 432)
Cairo international airport (☎ 291 4288 – ask for Avis)

Heliopolis Sheraton (☎ 291 0223)
Meridien Heliopolis (☎ 290 5055)
Budget Rent-a-Car
5 Makrizy, Zamalek (head office) (☎ 340 0070; fax 341 3790)
Cairo Marriott (☎ 340 6667)
Cairo international airport (☎ 265 2395)
Europcar
27 Libnan, Mohandiseen (☎ 347 4712/3; fax 303 6123)
Cairo international airport (☎ 291 4288 – ask for Europcar)
Hertz
195 Sharia 26th of July, Mohandiseen (☎ 303 4241; fax 347 4172)
Ramses Hilton (☎ 574 4400)
Semiramis Intercontinental (☎ 354 3239; fax 356 3020)
Cairo international airport (☎ 291 4288 – ask for Hertz)
J Car
33 Missaha, Doqqi (☎ 335 0521; fax 360 3255)
Cairo international airport (☎ 291 4288 – ask for J Car)
Thrifty
1 Al-Entesar, Heliopolis (☎ & fax 266 3313)
Cairo international airport (☎ 265 2620)

TAXI

If the distance you want to travel is too far to walk, then a taxi is the most convenient way to get around Cairo. Stand at the side of the road, stick your hand out and shout your destination at any black and white cab that looks to be passing in the right direction. It doesn't matter if there is already someone inside, as taxis are shared. When a taxi stops restate where you want to go and if the driver's amenable hop in. Do not talk money. The etiquette is that you get in knowing what to pay and when you arrive you get out and hand the money through the window. If a driver suspects that you don't know what the correct fare is then you're fair game for fleecing.

As a rough guide, the cost of a taxi from Downtown to Khan al-Khalili should be around E£3; from Downtown to Zamalek, E£3; from Midan Tahrir to Midan Ramses, E£2; from Midan Tahrir to the Citadel, E£4; from Midan Tahrir to the Pyramids, E£15; from Downtown to Heliopolis, E£10; and from Downtown to Cairo international airport, E£20.

GETTING AROUND

Taxi!

Taxis are at once a blessing and a curse. They're a remarkably convenient and easily affordable way of getting around the city, but they can also be a frequent source of unpleasantness, particularly when it comes to paying the fare. The problem comes with the unmetered system of payment, which almost always guarantees discontent. Passengers frequently feel they've been taken advantage of (which they often have been), while drivers are occasionally genuinely aggrieved by what they see as underpayment. So why don't the drivers use the meter? Because they are all calibrated for a time when petrol was ludicrously cheap. This is no longer the case and any driver relying on his meter would now be out of pocket every time he came to fill up.

Taxi driving is far from being a lucrative profession. Of the 60,000 plus taxis on the road it would be a safe bet to assume none of the drivers are yet millionaires. Average earnings after fuel has been paid for are about E£8 per hour. Consider too, that many drivers don't even own their car and have to hand over part of their earnings as 'rent'. Which isn't to say that next time you flag a taxi for a short hop across town and the driver hisses 'Ten bounds' that you should smile and say 'okay', but maybe you can see that from a certain point of view, it was worth their while trying. ■

Often a driver will demand more money, sometimes yelling. Don't be intimidated and don't be drawn into an arguement. As long as you know you are not underpaying (and the fares listed on the previous page are generous) just walk away. He's playing on the fact that you are a *khwaga* (foreigner) and don't know any better.

It also sometimes happens that as soon as you're in the taxi the driver names a fare, invariably one that is ridiculously high. In this case, simply tell him what you are prepared to pay and demand to be let out if he does not accept.

The big Peugeot 504 taxis, sometimes marked 'special', charge more than other taxis. The advantage of these taxis is that you can get a group together and commandeer one for a long trip.

HANTOUR

These horse-drawn carriages and their insistent drivers hang around on the Corniche near Helnan Shepheard's hotel and on Gezira near the Cairo Tower. They aren't a feasible means of getting around the city and are there for pleasure rides.

RIVER BUS

The river bus terminal is at Maspero, on the Corniche in front of the big round Radio & Television building (see Map 3). From here, boats depart daily every 15 minutes or so from 6.30 am for University, a landing over on the Giza side of the river just north of the Kubri al-Gamaa (University Bridge; Map 7). Every second boat continues south stopping at Manial, Rhoda, Giza and Masr al-Qadima (Old Cairo). The last stop is convenient for Coptic Cairo. The complete trip takes 50 minutes and the fare is 25 pt.

Immediately south of the river bus terminal at Maspero is the departure point for boats to Qanater – see the Excursions chapter.

ORGANISED TOURS

Some of the budget hotels in Central Cairo arrange tours to various places around the city such as the Giza and Saqqara pyramids and Memphis. The price is usually about

E£20 and includes transport only – there's no guide and admission fees are extra. The stories about these trips have often been negative, so forewarned is forearmed. The Hotel Select (Map 4; ☎ 393 3707), at 19 Adly, Downtown, is one of the many places offering trips.

Better still, arrange to go with Salah Mohammed Abdel Hafez (☎ 298 0650; email samo@intouch.com). This genial chap organises a full day excursion to the places mentioned earlier, as well as to the Wissa Wassef Art Centre at Harraniyya, for E£18 (lunch and admission fees are extra). If you're staying at one of the city centre hotels, he'll pick you up at around 9 am. You'll need to arrange the tour at least one day in advance – leave a message on the answering machine if he's not there and mention Lonely Planet. If you book a tour with him via email before you arrive in Cairo, he will also offer you a free transfer from the airport to the Downtown area.

A third option is to go through a travel agency like Masr Travel. It does daily sightseeing tours in winter, less often in summer. Half-day tours to the Pyramids, Sphinx and Citadel cost US$30; the day trip for US$40 also includes Memphis, Saqqara and lunch. American Express offers a variety of tours (usually three hours) for US$20 taking in destinations like the Egyptian Museum and Coptic Cairo, the Pyramids, Islamic Cairo or Saqqara.

Tours to the Birqash camel market are organised by the Sun Hotel (Map 8; ☎ 578 1786) at 2 Talaat Harb, while a full day tour taking in Harraniyya, Memphis, Saqqara and the Pyramids (E£15, transport only but not a bad deal) is run by the Hotel Select.

Things to See & Do

Cairo is a densely cluttered heap of old and new neighbourhoods – as if all the villages that might have dotted Egypt had it not been desert have instead been thrown together in one spot. Each of these neighbourhoods has its own history, character and traditions that define the people who live there.

CAIRO HIGHLIGHTS

No poll was taken and no opinions were canvassed – the following list is completely subjective and in no particular order.

- **The Pyramids at Dawn** With hawkers and camel owners in your face, it's hard to be awed by the world's greatest ancient wonders, but at dawn it's different – you have them to yourself. (See page 136)
- **Fishawi's at 2 am** Any time of day is fine at Cairo's oldest coffeehouse but after midnight the visitors are gone and the place returns to the locals. (See page 105)
- **Sunset Felucca Rides** Drift on the Nile and watch the sun sink behind the Cairo skyline. (See page 145)
- **Tutankhamun at the Egyptian Museum** Although badly displayed, Tutankhamun's treasures are still some of the most magnificent objects held by any museum in the world. (See page 84)
- **Atop the Minarets at Bab Zuweyla** Lots of Cairo's minarets are climbable, but for peering into the heart of the medieval city the best view is from either of the two towers atop Bab Zuweyla. (See page 114)
- **Early Morning at the Hanging Church** One of the most serene and understatedly attractive sites in Cairo, best visited early in the morning before the coach parties arrive. (See page 129)
- **Evening Drinks at the Mena House** You don't have to be staying at Cairo's most famous hotel to sit beside the pool sipping something cool and gazing on the floodlit Pyramids rising beyond the palm trees. (See page 155)
- **Islamic Cairo** See the separate Highlights on page 101.

Central Cairo

There is no accepted notion of Central Cairo as such, but for the purposes of this book we define it as the area bound by the Nile to the west and Sharia Port Said (Bur Said) to the east, and stretching from Midan Ramses in the north down to the bottom of Garden City in the south. The epicentre of this area – Cairo's Times or Trafalgar Square – is Midan Tahrir.

MIDAN TAHRIR (Maps 7 & 8)

As a starting point for getting to know Cairo, there's nowhere better than Midan Tahrir (Liberation Square). It's a public transport terminus from where you can set out for most parts of the city – although much of what's worth seeing can easily be reached on foot from here. More importantly, it's one of the few places that isn't tightly hemmed in by buildings or wrapped around by flyovers, enabling the Cairo novice to stand back, look around and orient themselves.

One of the best buildings to use as a location aid is the **Nile Hilton**, a blue and white slab which stands between Midan Tahrir and the Nile. It was the first modern hotel to be built in Cairo (in 1959), and it replaced the Qasr el-Nil British army barracks – regarded by the soldiers who bunked there in WWII as the most bug-ridden barracks in the world – that had formerly stood on the site. Attached to the Hilton is a greenhouse-like shopping mall with a quiet cafe on the 1st floor – it's air-conditioned, and is a good place to go to escape the heat. Immediately south is the drab and very unprepossessing **Arab League Building**, gathering place of the leaders of the Arab world, or at least those who can be persuaded to attend.

To the east of the hotel is a chaotic and fume-shrouded local bus and minibus station. You have to wonder about the wisdom

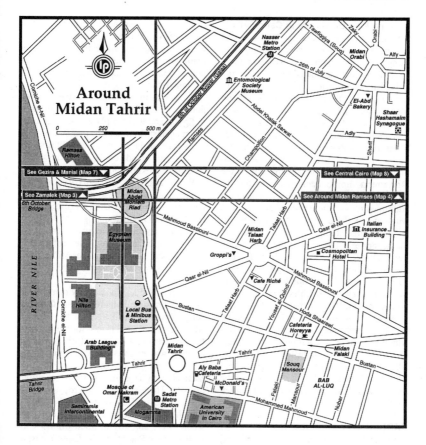

Around Midan Tahrir

0   250   500 m

of its position – not only do the Hilton's five-star residents have to risk being flattened or choked every time they leave the hotel, but the exhaust emissions also endanger the precious Pharaonic antiquities in the garden of the **Egyptian Museum** (see page 82), the pink building immediately north of the station.

Across the midan (square), the sweep of buildings topped by neon hoardings are home to several major airlines, some tourist agencies, a telephone office and a few cafes. The cafe with the whitewashed brick facade was bombed by militant Islamists in 1993.

The buildings break for Sharia Talaat Harb, which is Cairo's main Downtown thoroughfare, and for Sharia Tahrir, which leads into Bab al-Luq. Fifty metres south of the Sharia Tahrir corner is the **Aly Baba Cafeteria** which, until the 1994 knife attack that almost killed him, was a regular morning stop-off for Nobel Prize-winning author Naguib Mahfouz. It serves chilled Stella beer and the tables beside the window on the upper floor are a good place to watch the goings-on outside.

A little further south, over Sharia Mohammed Mahmoud, is the neo-Islamic facade of

THINGS TO SEE & DO

the **American University in Cairo** (AUC), the university of choice for the sons and daughters of Cairo's moneyed classes. The campus has an attractive courtyard, and it is possible to visit the bookshop or one of the university's galleries. You must present some form of ID. Entrance is via the gate on Mohammed Mahmoud, opposite the enterprisingly sited McDonald's.

It's a pretty sure thing that few graduates of the AUC will ever have to resort to employment in the monolithic white structure on the south side of the square. This is the **Mogamma**, home each working day to thousands of underpaid bureaucrats and the additional tens of thousands of unfortunates who have to chase around its corridors collecting forms, stamps and signatures. (See the boxed text 'The Dreaded Mogamma' in the Facts for the Visitor chapter.) The mosque adjacent to the Mogamma is the modern **Mosque of Omar Makram**, where the funerary receptions for deceased politicians and VIPs are held.

West of the mosque is **Tahrir Bridge**, formerly known as the Qasr el-Nil Bridge, which is flanked at each end by two great bronze lions. The bridge leads over to the island of Gezira, where the Opera House and the Cairo Tower can be found. South of the mosque is Midan Simon Bolivar and Garden City.

GARDEN CITY & MANIAL (Map 7)

If you read Olivia Manning's *Levant Trilogy*, a saga of British expat experiences in wartime Cairo, then all life seems to revolve around Garden City. And for many at that time it did. Garden City was Cairo's English suburb. Occupying a plot of agricultural land between two palaces (Qasr al-Ainy to the south, now replaced by a hospital, and Ismail's Qasr al-Dubara to the north where the Mogamma now stands), the district was developed in the early years of this century along the lines of an English garden suburb. Its curving tree-lined streets were intended to create an air of tranquillity, while the proximity of the **British Embassy** no doubt provided a reassuring veneer of security. The

embassy, which anchors the north-western corner of Garden City, originally had grounds which stretched down to the Nile but the bottom portion of the lawns was lopped off in the 1950s when Nasser had the Corniche ploughed through.

As well as the embassy, Garden City was home to the headquarters of the British Army in Egypt, and was the place where the campaign against Rommel was planned. Known to its staff of the time as **Grey Pillars**, this building still stands on the corner of sharias Al-Saraya al-Kubra and Al-Birgas.

While many of Garden City's elegant villas have fallen prey to quick-buck developers (including 13 Ibrahim Naguib, wartime residence of Olivia Manning) and the 1990s traffic has invaded the narrow avenues, the surviving architecture and the profusion of palm, rubber and mango trees still gives a sense of how things might have been 50 years ago.

On its east side, Garden City comes to an uncompromising halt at **Sharia Qasr al-Ainy** (Street of the Palace of the Spring), which takes its name from a former Mamluk palace. During the early 19th century a hospital was established within the palace which, in the 1980s, gave way to the new Qasr al-Ainy Hospital that now occupies the site. There's little of interest along the street, but east of its southern end is the old slaughterhouse district of Zein al-Abdin where there are several good offal restaurants (see the Places to Eat chapter); east of its northern end is where several ministries cluster, near the **People's Assembly** (Maglis ash-Shab), the Egyptian parliament building. Do not try taking photographs anywhere around here. A few blocks east of the People's Assembly building is the presidential palace of Abdin, while to its north is Bab al-Luq.

Manial & The Palace Museum

Manial is the name for the northern end of Rhoda, the southern of Cairo's two inhabited Nile islands. It's separated by just a narrow channel of water, the Sayalit al-Rhoda, from the southern end of Garden City. It's largely a middle-class residential district, but it's also home to one of Cairo's most eccentric tourist sites, the Manial Palace Museum.

The palace was built in the early part of this century as a residence for Prince Mohammed Ali Tawfiq, the uncle of King Farouk. Apparently the prince couldn't decide which architectural style he preferred, so he went for the lot – Ottoman, Moorish, Persian, Syrian and European rococo are represented by each of the five main buildings. In fact, the first of them, the **Reception Palace** (which you enter on your right just inside the main entrance on Sharia al-Saray – you have to buy a ticket first at a booth further inside the grounds) is a mishmash of several architectural styles.

After you enter the palace grounds, walk along the path on the right to the **Mosque of Mohammed Ali** and the **Hunting Museum** of the royal family. The hunting museum was added to the complex in 1962 to house King Farouk's huge collection of stuffed trophies. This is not a place for animal lovers.

Return to the path leading from the palace entrance and follow it to the other buildings. One of the highlights is the **Residence Palace**, where each room is ornately decorated with hand-painted geometric shapes. Several of the doors are inlaid with carved pieces of ivory, and the windows feature intricate mashrabiyya screens.

The largest building contains Mohammed Ali's collection of manuscripts, clothing, silver objects, furniture, writing implements and other items dating from medieval times to the 19th century. A self-appointed guide likes to show you around this part of the museum, object by object. If you don't want his services let him know.

The palace is open daily from 9 am to 4 pm, and admission is E£5 (E£2.50 for students). Photography permits are E£10; video shooting costs E£150.

The easiest way to get here from Midan Tahrir is to head down the Corniche and take the third bridge you come to – it's a very pleasant 20 minute walk. Alternatively, a taxi from Tahrir (ask simply for Al-Manial) should cost no more than E£2.

BAB AL-LUQ & ABDIN (Map 8)

Immediately east of Midan Tahrir, is the small district of Bab al-Luq, centred on **Midan Falaki**. Named after Mahmoud al-Falaki Bey, designer of Ismail's new Cairo (see Downtown later in this chapter for more information), this square has a couple of beautiful late-19th century buildings in its north-east corner but attention is distracted from them by the busy bus station and pedestrian walkways.

On the north side of the square is the **Cafeteria Horeyya**, a high-ceilinged coffeehouse with tall windows that dates back to 1936. It's one of the few venues for Cairo's chess players and is also unique (for a coffeehouse) in that it serves alcohol. South of the square is the **Souq Mansour**, a covered market of vegetable, meat and fish stalls – and a big favourite with the city's cats. The streets either side of the souq, sharias Mansour and Falaki, are filled with cheap kushari, pizza and kebab joints (for more information about these restaurants see the Places to Eat chapter).

On the south side of Mansour is one of Cairo's last remaining open-air cinemas, the **Cinema Rio**. At the time of writing it had been closed for three months because of a murder that took place in the stalls. Note the old painted Stella ad up on the side of the building to the left of the cinema, evidence of the more liberal and relaxed times of Egypt's past.

As you move east from Midan Falaki, Sharia Bustan empties into **Midan al-Gomhuriyya** (Square of the Republic), a sparse empty plaza skirted by speeding traffic. The one time of the year that it livens up is during Ramadan, when a makeshift canteen fills the square by doling out free food each evening at *iftar*. For the rest of the year, the only notable activity in this square focuses on the building with the Toytown tower on the midan's north side – the **Cairo Governorate**. The great building over to the east, which dominates the square, is the Abdin Palace, former residence of the rulers of Egypt.

continued on page 95

Egyptian Museum

More than 100,000 relics and antiquities from almost every period of ancient Egyptian history are housed in the Egyptian Museum (known simply as *Al-Mathaf*, 'the museum'). To put that in perspective, if you spent only one minute at each exhibit it would take more than nine months to see everything.

This collection was first gathered under one roof in Bulaq in 1858 by Auguste Mariette, a French archaeologist who had excavated in Upper Egypt. It was moved to its present purpose-built neoclassical home in 1902. Since then the number of exhibits has completely outgrown the available space and the place is virtually bursting at the seams. A persistent urban legend in Cairo has it that the building's basement is piled so high with uncatalogued artefacts that archaeologists will have to excavate its contents when a long-promised new museum is eventually built.

Beyond arranging the exhibits chronologically from the Old Kingdom to the Roman Empire, little has been done to present them in any sort of context or to highlight pieces of particular significance or beauty. Labelling is poor or nonexistent, while the manner of display – mostly old wood and glass cases with no direct lighting – is hardly the last word in modern museum techniques. But this is starting – slowly – to change. Following a sensational attempted robbery in 1996, Egypt's authorities belatedly realised that the outmoded security system (basically barred windows and a dog making the rounds after closing) was insufficient protection for the museum's priceless contents, and new security and lighting

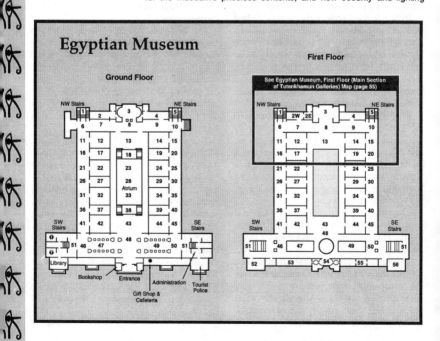

systems are currently being installed. Still, the museum's eccentricity is part of its charm and accidentally stumbling across treasures in its sometimes musty rooms is half the fun.

Admission to the museum is E£20 (E£10 for students). Access to the recently reopened Royal Mummy Room costs an additional E£40 (E£20 for students); tickets for this must be bought on the 1st floor at the entrance to the room. The museum (☎ 575 4319) opens daily at 9 am and closes at 4.45 pm. On Friday it closes between noon and 2 pm in summer and between 11.30 am and 1.30 pm in winter. If you're visiting on Friday morning, note that you can't get back in with the same ticket in the afternoon. Also, remember that the Royal Mummy Room and Room 53 both close at 4.15 pm. Permission to use cameras (without flash) costs E£10; otherwise cameras must be left at the entrance. Use of a video camera costs E£100. There are official guides who will take you around for about E£40 per hour.

ADAM MCCROW

The current neoclassical sandstone museum building was designed in 1895 by the French architect Marcel Durgnon.

Books

To help you negotiate this fascinating but overwhelming storehouse of history, we recommend using any of the following guides which can all be purchased at the museum:

- *A Guide to the Egyptian Museum* – a 300 page list of the museum's artefacts for E£10. It's organised by catalogue number rather than by room, with very little description on each item but it is being updated and may improve with the next edition.
- *The Blue Guide* at E£151 – a costlier alternative to the above-mentioned guide but it describes the museum room by room in excellent detail.
- *The Egyptian Museum Cairo – Official Catalogue* – slightly cheaper (E£100) than the *Blue Guide* and also a good reference source.
- *Egyptian Museum Cairo* (E£60) by Dr Edouard Lambelet – published in English, French and German. It has a fairly extensive and generously illustrated description of the main objects of interest, identified by room and catalogue numbers, although it doesn't have a map of the museum.
- *The Egypt of the Pharaohs at the Cairo Museum* (E£85) by Jean-Pierre Corteggiani – less well-ordered than Lamberlet's guide; it's put out by the French publishers Hachette.
- *Royal Mummies in the Egyptian Museum* (E£35) by Salima Ikram and Adian Dodson – a new book that is worth buying for its explanation of the mummification process as well as its descriptions of the bandaged, desiccated royals themselves.

Highlights of the Egyptian Museum

For those people who do not have nine months to see everything in the museum, the following is our list of the top ten must-see exhibits (described in more detail on pages 84 to 88):

1 Tutankhamun Galleries
2 Royal Mummy Room
3 Akhenaten Room
4 Graeco-Roman Mummies
5 Middle Kingdom Models
6 Old Kingdom Rooms
7 Pharaonic Technology
8 Yuya & Thuyu Rooms
9 Jewellery Rooms
10 Animal Mummies

1. Tutankhamun Galleries

Without doubt, the exhibit that outshines everything else in the museum is the treasure of the young and comparatively insignificant New Kingdom Pharaoh Tutankhamun.

The tomb and treasures of this king, who ruled for only nine years during the 14th century BC, were discovered in 1922 by English archaeologist Howard Carter. Its well-hidden location in the Valley of the Kings, below the much grander but ransacked tomb of Ramses VI, had prevented tomb robbers and, later, archaeologists from finding it earlier. The incredible contents of his rather modest tomb can only make you wonder about the fabulous wealth looted from the tombs of Pharaohs far greater than Tutankhamun.

The king's decaying mummified body, the outer of three mummiform coffins and the huge stone sarcophagus are all that remain in his tomb. The rest of his funerary treasures, about 1700 items, are spread throughout a number of rooms on the 1st floor of the museum. Note that most of the 'rooms' are in fact sections of the museum's north and east-wing corridors and room numbers are not displayed, which makes it hard sometimes to find what you're looking for. The rooms and the best relics are:

Left: An elaborate pectoral made of gold, silver, semi-precious stones and glass was found in the linen wrappings on Tutankhamun's mummy.

Right: Tutankhamun's life-size gold mask – it protected the head of the mummy.

Room 3: Gold is the glittering attraction of this room, which features an astounding collection of jewellery, including the 143 amulets and pieces of jewellery found among the wrappings on the king's body and a pair of gold sandals which were on the feet of the mummy. The centrepiece of the room is Tutankhamun's legendary and exquisite mask of beaten gold inlaid with lapis lazuli and other gems.

Rooms 7 & 8: These rooms house the four huge gilded wooden shrines that fitted inside each other and held the gold sarcophagus of Tutankhamun at their centre.

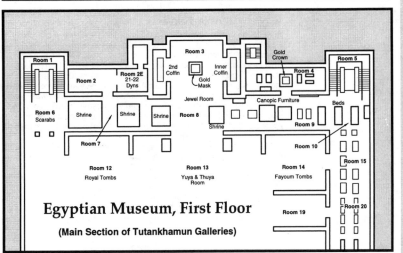

Room 3
Gold Crown
Room 1
Room 5
2nd Coffin
Inner Coffin
Room 2E 21-22 Dyns
Room 4
Room 2
Gold Mask
Jewel Room
Canopic Furniture
Beds
Room 6 Scarabs
Shrine
Shrine
Shrine
Room 8
Shrine
Room 9
Room 7
Room 10
Room 15
Room 12
Royal Tombs
Room 13
Yuya & Thuya Room
Room 14
Fayoum Tombs
Room 20

Egyptian Museum, First Floor

(Main Section of Tutankhamun Galleries)

Room 19

Room 9: This room is dominated by the chest filled with four translucent alabaster Canopic jars, each shaped like a goddess, which once contained the viscera of the young Pharaoh.

Room 10: Tutankhamun's bed befits a Pharaoh; it is covered with sheet gold, with string stretched across a frame that represents Hathor. The elongated cows wearing sun discs between their horns were used as the supports. This bed is accompanied by two more modest beds (to be found in Room 9) featuring hippos and lions.

Room 15: Beautifully rigged model ships, to be used by the Pharaoh on his voyage through the afterworld, are found here. Also, almost unnoticed against the back wall is a small, beautifully rendered plaster head of the boy-king emerging from a lotus flower.

Room 20: Here you can see some exquisite alabaster jars, caskets and boxes, including a chalice in which a small light has been inserted to demonstrate the delicacy of its translucent artwork.

Room 35: The highlight of this room is Tutankhamun's wooden throne. Covered with sheet gold and silver and encrusted with gems and glass, the wooden throne has winged cobras and lions' heads on the arms and the back; it is decorated with the famous scene of Tutankhamun's queen placing her hand on his shoulder under the rays of the sun, or Aten – a hangover from his predecessor, Akhenaten. Here, too, is a beautifully carved wooden clothes chest.

Rooms 40 & 45: Exhibits in these rooms include a board game (Room 45, case 189) with ivory playing pieces that resembles checkers or draughts and a statue of Anubis, the dog who was the god of mummification, sitting on a chest of gilded, inlaid wood.

2. Royal Mummy Room

After being hidden behind closed doors for 15 years, a selection of Egypt's ancient rulers is again on public display. Opened in 1995, the Royal Mummy Room (No 56 on the 1st floor) houses the bodies of 11 of Egypt's most illustrious kings and queens from the 18th to 21st dynasties, who ruled Egypt between 1552 and 1069 BC. They include Ramses II, his father Seti I, Tuthmosis II and Queen Meret Amun (wife of Amenhotep I).

In 1981, the room housing the royal mummies (27 in total) was closed to the public as President Sadat thought it disrespectful to the dead (he had just berated the Iranians for displaying the charred bodies of eight Americans killed during the hostage crisis). The remaining 16 mummies are still under lock and key in Room 52.

The 11 mummies moved to Room 56 now lie in individual glass showcases (kept at a constant temperature of 22°C) in a sombre, dimly lit environment reminiscent of a tomb. Talking above a hushed whisper is not permitted (although irreverent tour groups often need to be reminded of this) and, for this reason, tour guides are not allowed in, making it one of the most peaceful havens in the museum.

For more information on the mummies, there's a booklet on sale at the ticket counter for E£3 or see the book – *Royal Mummies in the Egyptian Museum*.

3. Akhenaten Room

Those interested in the Pharaoh who set up Ancient Egypt's first and last monotheistic faith should head for Room 3 on the ground floor. A quick glance around the room is enough to see that artistic styles changed almost as drastically as the state religion during Akhenaten's 15-year tenure (which ended with the accession of Tutankhamun). There are four massive statues which have strangely bulbous bellies, hips and thighs; heads are elongated and lips are thick and sensuous. Also worth a look, for their unusual informality, are stelae of the king and queen playing with their children. In the adjoining Room 8, a model house from this period gives an idea of what the homes of Egypt's rich and famous were like some 3300 years ago.

This broken sandstone bust of Akhenaten (Amenophis IV) was found in Karnak at the temple of Aten. Akhenaten's abandonment of the traditional gods and priesthood in favour of the worship of Aten, god of the sun disk, was not looked on favourably by the priests at Thebes and Karnak. After his death they regained their religious control and did their best to obliterate all record of Akhenaten and his religion.

4. Graeco-Roman Mummies

Room 14 on the 1st floor contains a small sample (over 1000 have been discovered) of the stunning portraits found on Graeco-Roman period mummies. These images, whose large watchful eyes seem to follow you around the room, were painted onto wooden panels that were then placed over the mummy's embalmed face – some were even painted directly onto the shrouds themselves. As few other painted portraits from the Graeco-Roman era have survived, this collection is unique for both the number of its paintings and the high quality of its images.

Although the cases are barely lit and are piled with dust, the beautiful and hauntingly realistic faces that stare out from behind the glass bring the personalities of their long-dead owners to life in a way that the stylised elegance of most ancient Egyptian art somehow can't. Peer through the gloom in the case to the right of the entrance and see the portrait of the little girl still affixed to her tiny mummified remains.

Most these portraits were discovered at Hawara and Er-Rubayat in the the Al-Fayoum Oasis, just west of Cairo, but a substantial portion have come from the Nile Valley at sites such as Saqqara and Thebes.

5. Middle Kingdom Models

For a great look at daily life almost 4000 years ago, head to Room 27 on the 1st floor. The lifelike models here were mostly found in the tomb of Meket-Re, a Middle Kingdom notable in Thebes. They include fishing boats (complete with fish in the nets) a slaughterhouse, a carpentry workshop, a loom and a model of Meket-Re's house (with figs on the trees and painted columns). Most spectacular is the 1.5m wide scene of Meket-Re sitting with four scribes and various other hangers-on counting cattle. Plaster model slaves hold the animals by miniature ropes as they pass by the shaded dais on which the boss sits.

6. Old Kingdom Rooms

Some of the best objects in the museum are also the oldest. In the centre of Room 42 on the ground floor is a diorite statue of Chephren, builder of the second largest pyramid at Giza. Even in smooth black stone he is a commanding presence. Slightly to the left in front of the Pharaoh is the wooden statue of Ka-Aper. Carved out of a single piece of sycamore (except for the arms) with inlaid alabaster and rock-crystal eyes he is spookily lifelike. When they dug up Ka-Aper, local workmen named him Sheikh el-Balad, or 'headman', because he so resembled their own village chief.

Room 32 is dominated by two beautiful statues of the Old Kingdom couple, Rahotep and Nofret. Almost life-sized with well-preserved painted surfaces, the simple lines of the limestone sculpture make them seem almost contemporary, despite being around for a staggering 4000 years. Another highlight in here is the slightly bizarre tableau of the chief dwarf Seneb and his family. He is sitting cross-legged in an effort to disguise his short legs and his children have been strategically placed where an ordinary man's legs would be. His (non-dwarf) wife has her arms protectively around his shoulders. In front are miniature offering jars that were found with the statue.

In the glass case on the right-hand side of the entrance to Room 32, you get a glimpse of how ancient Egyptians actually looked. The death masks here were found at Giza and Saqqara, although they look like they were made yesterday.

7. Pharaonic Technology

For gadget buffs, the rarely visited Room 34 on the 1st floor is definitely worth a look. Everyday objects that helped support Ancient Egypt's great leap out of prehistory are on show in surprisingly well-ordered cases. Everything from combs and mirrors to fishing tackle, ploughs, hoes (that look exactly like the ones still used by Egypt's fellaheen today), serious-looking blades and razors can be found here. Hunting paraphernalia includes Pharaonic boomerangs which were apparently used for killing birds.

8. Yuya and Thuyu Rooms

If the Tutankhamun galleries are too clogged with tour groups, or you want to see how a royal relative was buried, check out Gallery 13, adjoining the atrium on the first floor. Yuya and Thuyu were the parents of New Kingdom Queen Tyi and their tomb in the Valley of the Kings was found virtually intact at the beginning of this century. Some of the hundreds of beautiful objects found there include inlaid boxes, gold coffins, inlaid sarcophagi, beds, sandals, a chariot and other necessities for life in the hereafter.

9. Jewellery Rooms

An impressive amount of high-tech security equipment has been in-stalled for the transformation of 1st-floor rooms 2E and 4 into the museum's new jewellery galleries. Due to open in early 1998, this will be the place to see the best of the museum's glittering collection of Pharaonic and Graeco-Roman baubles. Room 2E will house gold and silver encrusted amulets, daggers, bracelets, collars – you name it – from intact New Kingdom tombs found in the Delta site of Tanis. Room 4 will include, among many other treasures, death masks, crowns, necklaces and silver model boats from the Middle Kingdom and Graeco-Roman periods.

10. Animal Mummies

Before the rise of Pharaonic dynasties in Egypt, animal cults proliferated and the results can be seen in the battered and dust-covered little mummified cats, dogs, birds, rams and jackals in Room 53. More of these bizarre little trussed-up packages can be seen just outside in Room 54, where the better preserved remains of a mummified falcon, a fish, a cat, an ibis, a monkey and a tiny crocodile are on show.

Throughout Egypt falcons were worshipped as representations of Ra (and sometimes Horus), and were used in temple rites and rituals. When they died they were mummified and buried in small clay coffins.

Gods & Goddesses of Pharaonic Egypt

Ancient Egypt produced a wealth of gods and goddesses, animal deities and magical practices that has both captured the modern imagination and defied attempts to create for it neat and tidy categories. Describing the gods, goddesses and belief systems of Ancient Egypt is a tricky business. First is the sheer amount of time to consider – its history spanned some 3000 years. Next is the proliferation of local deities and the tendency over time for some of these to assume the characteristics of others. Then there are the deities' various manifestations; one god could take many forms. At least four cosmogonies provide slightly different explanations of how the world began. In addition, there are a number of myths (for example, the struggle between the brothers Horus and Seth for control of the world) which may well echo an even more distant past and the struggle between Upper and Lower Egypt for supremacy.

Following are brief descriptions of some of the major gods and goddesses represented in the reliefs and carvings in the Egyptian Museum. The emphasis is on 'some'. If you are interested in delving deeper into the subject, there are many books that can enlighten. They include: *Egyptian Religion* by S Merenz (translated by A Keep); *Egyptian Mythology* by Veronica Ions; *Reading Egyptian Art* by RH Wilkinson; *Atlas of Ancient Egypt* by John Baines & Jaromir Malek; and *A Dictionary of Egyptian Gods and Goddesses* by George Hart.

Aker
An earth-god who watched over the western and eastern gates of the underworld *(duat)*. Shown with a lion's head or with two human heads facing opposite directions.

Amun (Amen)
The hidden one. Amun is portrayed as a man with blue-coloured flesh. He is sometimes depicted with ram's horns (the ram being one of his sacred animals, along with the goose), but more often he is shown wearing a crown topped with two tall plumes and holding a crook and a flail (symbols of sovereignty).

Amun was initially a minor deity in Thebes, but during the Middle Kingdom began to eclipse and assimilate other gods, such as the Theban god of war, Montu, and the fertility-god Min. In the New Kingdom Amun became associated with the sun-god Ra. As Amun-Ra he was regarded as King of the Gods and father of the Pharaoh, and so he remained for almost the entire Pharaonic period.

Amun (Amen)

Anubis
God of cemeteries and of embalming, and patron of embalmers. Anubis is depicted as a man with a canine head, or as a reclining dog, often thought to be a jackal. His coat is black, and it is suggested this represents the discolouration of the corpse after it has been treated with natron (a mineral of hydrated sodium carbonate) and other substances during mummification. It could also be symbolic of renewed life, a reference to the rich, dark Nile silt vital for crops.

In the *Book of the Dead* Anubis, in the presence of 42 assessor gods, weighs the deceased's heart (regarded as the centre of the intellect and emotions) against the feather of truth (the symbol of Maat, goddess of truth, justice and cosmic order).

Anubis

Apis
Sacred bull and herald of Ptah, god of Memphis. According to the Greek writer Herodotus, an Apis calf was singled out for deification because of

its special markings. It had to be black with a white diamond on its forehead and have double hairs on its tail, carry the image of a crescent moon on its right flank and the mark of a scarab on its tongue. The Apis bull is depicted with a sun disc between its horns and, on its back, the protective wings of the vulture-goddess Nekhbet.

When an Apis bull died it was mummified (some of the alabaster tables used for the purpose can still be seen at Memphis) and buried at Saqqara.

Apophis
Snake god. Embodiment of darkness, symbolic of chaos and enemy of the sun-god Ra. As Ra enters and leaves the underworld in his solar boat, he is attacked by Apophis, who is in turn beheaded (some versions of the legend say by Bastet, others, Seth), his blood staining the morning and evening skies as the struggle is endlessly repeated.

Aten (Aton)
An aspect of the sun-god Ra. The sun at noon. Aten is depicted as a disc from which rays extend ending in outstretched hands. Those pointing towards the king or queen clutch ankhs (the hieroglyph for life). At the base of the disc is the uraeus (a symbol of sovereignty).

Atum
Creator god of Heliopolis and identified from earliest times with the sun-god Ra (generally an aged aspect of the sun; the setting sun). Atum embodies the notion of completeness and is generally depicted as a man wearing the crowns of both Upper and Lower Egypt. Atum was said to have arisen from Nun (chaos or primordial ocean) and to have formed from himself both men and gods. According to the Heliopolitan cosmology (which eventually became the most widely accepted), Atum created the sky deities Shu (air) and Tefnut (moisture). They in turn produced Geb (earth god) and Nut (sky goddess). From them came Osiris, Seth, Isis and Nephthys. The entire 'family' is often referred to as the divine ennead (nine).

Bastet

Bastet
Cat goddess and daughter of sun-god Ra. Her cult centred on Bubastis in the north-east Delta. Bastet could be ferocious, associated as she was with the sun's vengeance, but she was more usually regarded as a friendly deity and associated with joy.

Bes
Despite his grotesque appearance, dwarfish, bandy-legged Bes was a benign character fond of music and dancing. He protected women in childbirth by frightening away evil spirits (see Taweret later) and watched over newborns.

Geb
Earth-god Geb was married to his sister, the sky-goddess Nut. He is usually depicted as a reclining man. According to legend, Geb divided Egypt in two, giving one son, Horus, the lower half and another son, Seth, the upper.

Bes

Hapy
Hapy symbolised the Nile's annual flood. He appears as a man and, as he embodies fertility and abundance, often possesses female breasts and a rounded abdomen, and wears aquatic plants on his head.

Hathor

Hathor, daughter of the sun-god Ra, was goddess of joy and love. She also protected women and travellers, although one myth depicts her as very violent, wishing to destroy humankind. She is often represented as a cow, or as a woman with cow's ears or horns between which sits a sun disc.

Horus

Sky god and Lower Egyptian counterpart of Seth. Horus came to be acknowledged as the son of Osiris and Isis. He sometimes appears as a hawk, but is more often depicted in the form of a man with a hawk's head.

Hathor

Isis

Isis, sister/wife of Osiris, mother goddess and (as mother of Horus) symbolic mother of the king, possessed great magical powers. Isis is depicted as a woman wearing either a throne on her head or a sun disc flanked with cow's horns. Sometimes she appears (along with her sister Nephthys) as a kite, mourning the dead.

She used her magical powers to restore Osiris to life and to protect the young Horus. Those seeking protection or healing for children therefore appealed to her for assistance.

Khepri

The rising sun. Khepri was regarded as self-created and depicted as a scarab beetle, whose habit of rolling balls of dirt over the ground could be viewed as analogous to the divine task of pushing the sun disc up from the underworld to begin its journey across the sky. Hence the symbol of daily resurrection when incorporated into funerary jewellery. Small stone or faience scarabs were made in their thousands as amulets and stamp seals.

Khons

Moon-god Khons (wanderer or traveller) is depicted as a man (sometimes with a hawk's head), wearing a crown topped with a crescent moon cradling a full moon. As the son of Amun and Mut, he also appears wearing the lock of youth.

Horus

Isis

Khepri

Khons

Maat

Personification of cosmic order (truth, justice, harmony). Maat is depicted as a woman wearing an ostrich feather on her head, although sometimes she is symbolised solely by the feather (she is represented as such during the weighing of the heart ceremony).

Maat

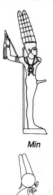

Min

Meretseger

Cobra goddess. Her name means 'she who loves silence'. She is represented as a coiled cobra or with a snake's body and a woman's head.

Min

Fertility god and protector of mining areas in the Eastern Desert. Min is generally depicted wrapped in mummy bandages, standing with his right arm extended and bent upwards at the elbow. In his left hand he clutches a royal flail. He wears a crown that is topped with two tall plumes.

Montu

Falcon-headed Theban god of war. He is depicted wearing a sun disc on his head with two tall plumes.

Mut

A symbolic mother of the king, Amun's consort and Thebes' principal goddess. She appears as a slender woman wearing a vulture-shaped headdress. Sometimes she appears with the head of a lion.

Montu

Neith

An ancient deity associated with hunting or war and creator goddess of Sais, capital of Egypt around 700 BC. She appears as a woman wearing the red crown of Lower Egypt.

Nekhbet

Vulture goddess of Nekheb (el-Kab). Nekhbet appears as a vulture clutching the symbol for eternity in her talons. She is often included in the Pharaoh's crown (as the wadjet), and represents Upper Egypt.

Mut

Neith

Nephthys

Daughter of Geb and Nut. Mother of Anubis. On her head Nephthys wears hieroglyphs symbolising her name, which is 'lady of the mansion'. In the form of a kite she stands guard over the deceased.

Nun

Represents the primordial, chaotic waters from which arose the first god.

Nut

Sky goddess and both sister and wife of the earth-god Geb. Mother of Osiris, Isis, Seth and Nephthys. She usually appears as a woman, but sometimes as a cow, and is often depicted stretched across the ceilings of tombs, swallowing the sun and creating the night.

Above: Nephthys Left: Nut, Geb and Shu are often depicted together. The sky goddess, Nut, is supported by Shu, god of air and light, who separates her from the reclining earth god Geb.

Osiris

God of the underworld and of fertility. He generally appears in mummy wrappings holding the crook and flail (representing kingship) and wearing a conical headdress that includes a pair of ram's horns and a tall plume. He is the brother of Isis and father of Horus.

Ptah

Anthropomorphic creator god of Memphis. Ptah was also regarded as a skilled artisan and leader of craftsmen. He appears wearing a tight cap on his shaven head and he carries a sceptre (*was*) on which are the emblems of power, life and stability. Ptah is sometimes linked with the solar-god Sokar.

Osiris

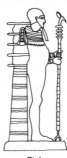

Ptah

Ra

Sun god and creator god of Heliopolis. Ra takes many forms (for example, as Khepri, Aten), and other deities also merge with him, enhancing their own powers (for example, Amun-Ra). He is generally shown as a man with a falcon's head upon which rests a sun disc. The ancient Egyptians believed that Ra traversed the sky in a solar boat, rising from the underworld in the east and re-entering it in the land of the dead in the west.

Ra

Renenutet

Cobra goddess and protector of the Pharaoh. She appears on the king's headdress in the form of a rearing cobra (uraeus).

Sekhmet

Lion goddess and daughter of sun-god Ra. Sekhmet's name means 'powerful' and she represents the burning heat of the sun. According to legend, the sun-god Ra sent Sekhmet (his 'eye') to punish an irreverent humankind.

Sekhmet

Selket

Represented as a woman with a scorpion on her head, Selket is associated with funerary rites and helps protect the dead.

Seth

Worshipped from very early times. Upper Egyptian counterpart to Horus. Seth is often seen as synonymous with evil. His birth was indeed violent (he wrenched himself apart from Nut, his mother) and one of ancient Egypt's most enduring legends relates his ferocious fights with his brother, Osiris, who he eventually murders. God of chaotic forces (and associated with wind, rain, storms and thunder), Seth has some redeeming features. For example, sitting in the prow of Ra's solar boat, he spears the evil snake Apophis as the boat begins its entry from the western horizon into the underworld.

Seth

Shu

God of air and light, Shu supported the heavens. He is depicted as a kneeling man bearing the sky-goddess Nut in his upraised arms, separating her from the earth-god Geb.

Sobek

Crocodile deity and symbol of royal power.

Taweret

Like Bes, Taweret protected women in childbirth, her eccentric appearance (hippo head, lion legs and arms, crocodile tail and pendulous breasts) supposedly scaring off evil forces.

Thoth

God of writing and counting, and patron of scribes. Thoth was worshipped in the form of a baboon or an ibis. He is usually depicted during the weighing of the heart ceremony as poised to record the results before the assessor gods.

Sobek

Thoth

continued from page 81

Abdin Palace

As part of his plan for creating a new, European Cairo, Ismail thought it befitting that Egypt's seat of power be moved out of its traditional medieval stronghold at the Citadel. He ordered the construction of several palaces dotted around his new capital, chief of which was Abdin. Designed by a French architect, Rosseau, the palace was started in 1863 and completed – 500 rooms later – in 1874. Abdin served as the sometime residence of Ismail and his successors through to Farouk. Following the abolition of the monarchy it became the presidential palace. The presidents have since moved out (Mubarak prefers the Uruba Palace up in Heliopolis) and Abdin today houses the Ministry of Culture and National Guidance.

Behind the pastiche Italianate facade are reputedly some fine staterooms and gardens but the palace is not open to the public. The best you can do is a virtual tour on any computer hooked up to the Web – see the boxed text 'Egypt Online' in the Facts for the Visitor chapter.

The **Abdin quarter**, south and east of the palace, once an area of prosperity, is now quite run down and is sliding towards the level of its poor neighbour Sayyida Zeinab (see Islamic Cairo later in this chapter for more information about Sayyida Zeinab).

DOWNTOWN (Maps 3, 4, 7 & 8)

Downtown (Al-Balad) can be roughly defined as the area contained within the triangle of Midan Tahrir, Midan Ramses and Midan Ataba (see Maps 4 & 8). This area is the unmistakable commercial heart of Cairo with streets packed with glitzy shops and above them a beehive of countless thousands of small, dusty businesses. The buildings sag under the weight of peeling signboards and fading placards and the streets have a typically Egyptian time-worn appearance, which is mildly misleading when you consider that up until 130 years ago there were no buildings here at all.

Before the 1860s the city extended west

only as far as the Ezbekiyya, or what is Midan Opera. The site of Downtown was then a swampy plain subject to the annual flooding of the Nile. In 1863, when the French-educated Ismail came to power, he was determined to upgrade the image of his capital which he believed could only be done by dismissing what had gone before and starting afresh with a new model. For 10 years the former marsh became one vast building site for a new, western-style Cairo to be known as 'Ismailia'.

The khedive's inspiration was the Paris of Haussmann, a city of wide, leafy avenues and elegant squares. Stand at one of Downtown's busy midans today and you can still get a sense of the designs of Ismail's chief city planner, Mahmoud al-Falaki Bey. Banks, businesses and rich land owners were offered incentives to build and so they did, employing architects brought in from Italy, France, Belgium and Germany.

The grand architecture remains but the character of the area has changed considerably from its cosmopolitan, cafe-society heyday. The money has fled to newer, more chic suburbs, abandoning Ismail's city to the swarming poorer classes. Modern-day Downtown boasts few sights as such but there is great entertainment to be had window-shopping and crowd-watching.

Midan Tahrir to Midan Talaat Harb

Sharias Talaat Harb and Qasr el-Nil are Downtown Cairo's two main shop-filled streets. They both run north-east from Midan Tahrir and intersect at **Midan Talaat Harb**, formerly Midan Suleyman Pasha – named after a French colonel who trained Mohammed Ali's armies. His statue was removed to the Citadel (where it stands in a courtyard of the Military Museum) after the Revolution and replaced by the current, tarboosh-wearing figure of Mr Harb, founder of the National Bank. The European influence, however, remains visible in **Groppi's** (see the boxed text over the page) and in architectural details like the typically French mansard roof on the Abu Dhabi Bank building (on the midan at the corner of Talaat Harb and Qasr el-Nil).

Midan Talaat Harb is also the place to pick up international newspapers, at the stand outside Groppi's or, if you are an Arabic reader, to go book shopping – Madbouli's on the north side of the midan is one of Cairo's oldest and most respected booksellers. Just to the south, on Sharia Talaat Harb, the **Cafe Riché** was a traditional hang-out for Egyptian writers and intellectuals. It has been closed since the late 1980s but is rumoured to be reopening any time soon. In the meantime, the writers and poets have moved down the little alley beside the Riché to the Zahret al-Bustan coffeehouse. Right around the corner from the Riché on Sharia Hoda Shaarawi (named for one of Egypt's first women's rights

campaigners) is **Felfela**, a restaurant which, after the Pyramids and Egyptian Museum, seems to be a must on every tourist's itinerary (see the Places to Eat chapter for more information).

North of Midan Talaat Harb

North of the midan, the two main streets are largely devoted to shoe shops that are filled with some of the tackiest footwear imaginable. Qasr el-Nil is redeemed by some particularly fine architecture, notably the **Italian Insurance building** at the corner with Sharia Sherif and the **Cosmopolitan Hotel**, hidden away just a block to the south of Qasr el-Nil, and recently restored to its full Art Deco splendour.

Talaat Harb has the **Cinema Metro building**, a great 1930s movie palace which when it opened (with *Gone With The Wind*) also had a Ford showroom and a diner. That diner is now the Excelsior restaurant; the food isn't so great these days but they serve cold Stella beer and the view from its large windows is usually every bit as entertaining as whatever piece of Hollywood junk is being screened next door.

One block east of the Excelsior along Sharia Adly, the strange movie-set temple is the **Shaar Hashamaim Synagogue**, the most visible testament to Cairo's once thriving Jewish community (see the boxed text 'The Jews of Cairo' later in this chapter). The synagogue can be visited on Saturday, the Jewish holy day of *shabbat*, when it's opened up on the off chance there'll be somebody coming by to pray. Another block east, past the impressive brick-red **Davies Bryan Building** (a pre-Revolution, Welsh-owned department store that specialised in 'helmets, puggarees, mosquito nets and cholera belts') on the corner with Sharia Mohammed Farid, is the entrance to **Groppi's garden terrace**. It's still open for business but there's little custom these days.

Back on Mohammed Farid, heading south, beyond the elegant little midan named for nationalist politician Mustafa Kamel, is the **1920 Bank Masr building**, a wonderful bit of neo-Islamism by French architect Antoine

---

Groppi's of Cairo

Groppi's is conspicuously empty these days. Perhaps it's the fact that a cup of tea costs four times as much here as anywhere else. But there was a time when that wouldn't have mattered, when Groppi's was the most celebrated patisserie and tearoom this side of the Mediterranean. From its opening in the 1920s it was the most fashionable place to be seen in, and attendance at Groppi's society functions and nonstop concert dances was *de rigueur* for Cairo's smart set.

In addition to the tearoom on the midan there was the equally popular Groppi's Garden, a big favourite with British officers and soldiers during the two world wars. English author Penelope Lively was a child in Cairo in the late 1930s and in her book *Oleander, Jacaranda* she remembers Groppi's as a place where you could sit at marble-topped tables in a garden that contained a vine-covered pergola and have tea and cakes. The garden also features prominently in Olivia Manning's *Levant Trilogy*.

Both Groppi's establishments survive today in much reduced forms. The beautiful Italian mosaic entrance to the Midan Talaat Harb patisserie is about the only sparkle that remains, while the 'sumptuous' cakes and confectionery remembered by Penelope Lively – once made to order for the royalty of Egypt and Great Britain – have become third-rate and virtually inedible. ■

Three highlights of the city's 800 or so listed Islamic monuments: the Mosque of ibn Tulun (top); the Mosque-Madrassa of Sultan Hassan (middle); and the Al-Muayyad mosque seen from Bab Zuweyla (bottom).

ADAM MCCROW

EDDIE GERALD

BETHUNE CARMICHAEL

KRISTIE BURNS

ADAM MCCROW

It's usually Cairo's skyline assemblage of domes and minarets that wows visitors and gets the cameras clicking, but when you get up closer, you see that the greater beauty is in the subtle variety and intricate detailing.

Lasciac (who also was responsible for Qasr el-Nil's Italian Insurance building). Opposite the bank is **St Joseph's Church**, a huge Italianate structure painted in bands of buff and maroon. Dating from 1904, this is the home of Cairo's Catholic community and services are still held here daily.

Sharia 26th of July & North

Sharia 26th of July (referred to by Cairenes simply as *sita wa'shreen*) is one of Cairo's major arteries, beginning at Ezbekiyya and cutting west across Downtown, through Bulaq, across Zamalek and on into Mohandiseen. It was previously known as Sharia Fuad I in honour of the father of King Farouk but after the hapless regent was forced to step down, the boulevard was renamed to mark the date of his abdication. As Sharia Fuad I it was considered to be Cairo's Oxford St, its

Champs-Élysées, and was home to several grand department stores, such as Cicurel and Chemla, where uniformed Albanian doormen held the doors open for baggage-laden ladies. A few of the names remain, but the businesses were nationalised in the early 1960s and the glamour and grace was dispelled. The biggest store on the street is now the kitsch-filled, state-owned Omar Effendi, the Kmart of Egypt.

The major attraction of Sharia 26th of July as far as Cairenes are concerned is the **El-Abd Bakery** on the corner with Sherif. It sells the best cakes, sticky sweets and pastries in town, and is thronged from early morning until midnight. (There's another branch on Talaat Harb.) Smoke-filled **Sharia Ezbekiyya** one block north is *the* street for kebabs, while newly pedestrianised **Sharia Alfy** is Downtown's nightlife centre with several seedy bars, a couple of belly-dancing

---

The Ezbekiyya

Today it resembles little more than a bomb site, but for more than 500 years the Ezbekiyya was a glittering place of entertainment. The district takes its name from the Mamluk Emir Ezbek who built a palace on the shore of what was then a small lake outside the walls of Al-Qahira. It was a place where Cairenes went to relax after Friday prayers. The lake's surface was covered with yellow water lilies, and pleasure boats which were illuminated by lanterns at night. Other palaces followed and during the Ottoman era the shores of the Ezbekiyya became a classy residential neighbourhood favoured by wealthy merchants and the city's elite. When Napoleon Bonaparte took Egypt in 1798, he commandeered the grandest of the palaces, that of Mohammed Bey al-Alfy, as his residence. However, he considered the Ezbekiyya lake to be a health hazard and had it filled in. Napoleon's artillery also destroyed many of the palaces while quelling revolts.

Mohammed Ali later transformed the Ezbekiyya into a sycamore park which the Khedive Ismail later had relaid by a former gardener to the city of Paris. With lawns and grottoes and paths lit by tulip-shaped gas lamps, the Ezbekiyya became the centre of the city's social life. The best cafes and restaurants were here, and strollers and diners were entertained by military bands and open-air theatre. The streets bordering the gardens were where the new European-style hotels chose to locate themselves – the most famous of all, Shepheard's (see the boxed text 'Shepheard's Hotel' in the Facts about Cairo chapter), occupied the site on which the Palace of Alfy Bey once stood.

The Black Saturday riots in 1952, in which Shepheard's was burnt to the ground, presaged the beginning of the end. The gardens were torn through the middle by the extension of Sharia 26th of July, while ugly, concrete public sector buildings made further encroachments into the former green spaces. These days the gardens are little more than a traffic island to the north of Midan Opera, and fencing now keeps people out of what remains. But in keeping the grass safe the authorities have created an out-of-view area which was recently the site of two highly publicised rape attacks. Ezbekiyya has become a place that half the population shuns. The glitter has well and truly gone. ∎

joints (see the Entertainment chapter) and a good 24 hour eating place in the Akher Saa (see the Places to Eat chapter).

The nearby **Tawfiqiyya souq** stays busy into the early hours too. It's a colourful fruit and vegetable market with several cheap eating places and a couple of good coffeehouses in the surrounding alleyways (see the Places to Eat and Entertainment chapters).

Just south of where 26th of July and Sharia Ramses intersect, at 14 Ramses, is the **Entomological Society Museum** housing an excellent and well preserved collection of birds and insects. It's open from 9 am to 1 pm Saturday to Thursday and from 6 to 9 pm on Saturday, Monday and Wednesday; it's closed all day Friday.

MIDAN OPERA (Maps 4 & 8)

The opera house that bequeathed its name to this Central Cairo square was burnt to the ground in 1971. In its place now stands a multistorey car park. That the opera house was burnt so completely was due to its wooden construction, a result of the rush to have it completed in time for the celebrations surrounding the opening of the Suez Canal in November 1869. It was inaugurated with a performance of Verdi's *Rigoletto* – not *Aida* which Ismail had commissioned from the composer for the occasion but which wouldn't be ready for another two years. At this time, Midan Opera was the grandest of Cairo's squares; as well as the Italianate opera house on the east side, the Ezbekiyya Gardens (see the boxed text on the previous page) were to the north, Madame Badia's casino was to the south, and the Continental-Savoy hotel was to the west. Only the once world-renowned **Continental-Savoy** remains. It's derelict these days, but you can still push open the main door and enter the dust-filled foyer. The Pharaonic ballroom, former venue for high-society fancy-dress balls, is off to the left but everywhere else is padlocked and sealed with a patina of grime.

Ibrahim Pasha, father of Ismail, still sits astride his horse at the centre of the midan but he's looking increasingly uncomfortable.

MIDAN ATABA (Maps 4 & 8)

Midan Ataba is the chaotic transition zone where 'European' Cairo runs up against Islamic Cairo. At the point where many roads converge, it is choked by the surrounding bus and minibus stations. On the south face of the square is the quaint central **fire station** and next door is the domed **Central Post Office** with an attractive courtyard interior. On the 1st floor is the **Post Office Museum** with a vast collection of commemorative stamps and displays on the history of Egypt's postal service. It's open daily, except Friday, from 9 am to 1 pm; admission is free.

Ataba is one big bazaar, with all its corners filled with traders and hawkers. In the southwest, by the post office, cards and stationary fill the space under the flyover, while east of the fire station Sharia Abdel Aziz is the place for electronics. Immediately behind the ornate building with the green painted shutters on the east face is the **meat market**, fascinating but not for the squeamish, while just to the north stalls of cheap clothing mark the beginning of **Sharia Muski** the long market street that leads into Khan al-Khalili. The building with the globe on top supported by four Herculean figures is the former **Tiring department store**, now gutted and inhabited by squatters.

Ataba to Ramses

On the north side of Ataba, hidden behind a high, pink curving wall is the **National Theatre**, beyond which is the concrete crate that is a multistorey car park and bus station. Beyond this is **Midan Khazindar**, the address for several 19th century hotels, including the Du Nil where Gustave Flaubert stayed for a few weeks in 1849. In the 19th century, Khazindar lay at the north-east corner of the Ezbekiyya and was the centre of the foreign quarter. Although severely battered and bedraggled, the architecture is still suggestive of colonial splendour – look around for the lettering marking out the former Hotel New Eden. Still intact and splendid is **Sednaoui**, one of Cairo's famed department stores. Now state-owned and full of tat, the three-storey glass atrium interior nevertheless remains glorious.

Running north from Khazindar, arcing its way over 1.5km up to Midan Ramses, is **Sharia Clot Bey** (see Map 4) named for a French physician Antoine Clot who introduced western ideas of public health into Mohammed Ali's Egypt. Ironically, by WWI this street had become the heart of Cairo's red-light district. Known as the Birka, after the Wagh al-Birkat, a street running parallel to Clot Bey, it was a quarter of brothels, peep-shows and pornographic cabarets. In 1941, with Cairo full of Allied troops, no less than seven venereal disease centres had to be set up in the city to deal with the fall out from the Birka.

These days Clot Bey is a shabby but charming street with stone arcades over the pavements sheltering dozens of sepia-toned coffeehouses and eating places. It has been renamed Sharia Khulud but for most people it's still Clot Bey.

MIDAN RAMSES (Map 4)

The northern gateway into Central Cairo, Midan Ramses is a byword for bedlam. The city's main north-south access collides with flyovers and numerous arterial roads to swamp the square with an unchoreographed slew of minibuses, buses, taxis and cars. Commuters swarm from the minibus ranks while the main railway station disgorges carriage loads of passengers, adding to the melee. Hundreds of street vendors take advantage of the pedestrian crush to hawk their shabby goods.

It has been busy here since ancient times when the Nile flowed farther to the east and this was the site of a Pharaonic port. Much later Salah ad-Din built an iron gate here which gave the area its name – Bab al-Hadid. The gate came down in 1854 when the railway arrived and the Bab al-Hadid station went up in its place. In 1955 a Pharaonic era **colossus of Ramses II** discovered near Giza was re-erected in front of the station (see the boxed text 'Ramses II to Go'), which henceforth became known as Ramses station (Mahattat Ramses).

The station building comprises an attractive marriage of Islamic styles and industrial age engineering. At its eastern end it houses the **Egyptian National Railways Museum**, which has a beautiful collection of old locomotives including one built in 1862 for Princess Eugenie on the occasion of the opening of the Suez Canal. The museum (☎ 763 793) is open daily, except Monday, from 8.30 am to 1 pm. Admission is E£1.50; E£3 on Friday and holidays.

On the south side of the midan is Cairo's pre-eminent orientation aid, the **Al-Fath**

Ramses II to Go

It must have seemed like a good idea at the time. When a colossus of Ramses II was unearthed at the village of Mit Rahina near Giza in the 1950s, the new revolutionary leadership thought that it would make the perfect adornment for the broad plaza in front of Cairo's main railway station. Forty years on, the 11m-high Pharaoh has become lost among the square's ever-increasing clutter of pedestrian walkways and concrete flyovers. More worrisome is the serious deterioration threatened by the exhaust emissions and vibrations from the thousands of cars that rumble by the statue each day.

In summer 1997 it was finally decided that, for his own good, Ramses would have to go. Several sites were considered, including a spot beside the Pyramids, but it's most likely that he'll go back to his place of discovery, Mit Rahina, to take pride of place in a new open-air archaeological museum. ■

EDDIE GERALD

Statue of Ramses II – soon to move to more salubrious surroundings in Mit Rahina.

Mosque. Completed in the early 1990s the mosque's minaret is visible from just about anywhere in Central and Islamic Cairo. Just east of the mosque, where Sharia al-Gomhuriyya joins Ramses is the ornate **Sabil of Umm Mohammed Ali** built by an Italian architect in 1870. *Al-Ahram*, the most important paper in Egypt and the Arab world in general, was founded in this building by a bunch of Lebanese journalists in the late 19th century.

Sakakini Palace

Second only to the Baron's Palace in Heliopolis, the Sakakini Palace (see Map 5) is one of Cairo's greatest architectural follies. It was built in 1897 by Count Sakakini Pasha who, legend has it, from humble origins hit on the path to fame and wealth by exporting a camel caravan of cats to the rat-infested canal then under construction at Suez.

His palace is sited at the junction where eight roadways meet, which gives rise to its circular plan. From its base the building rises up like a great rococo wedding cake adorned with frilly buttresses, domes and steeples. The decoration also includes some 300 gargoyles, busts and statues. Unfortunately, after years of service as a rarely visited Museum of Hygiene, the building is woefully neglected and in a terrible state of repair. It's now closed to the public but worth a visit for the exterior alone.

To get to Sakakini take the metro or tram one stop north from Midan Ramses to Ghamra; the palace is about 300m south of the station, and is visible from Sharia Ramses.

BULAQ (Maps 3 & 4)

Up until the middle of the 19th century Bulaq was a small port on the banks of the Nile; Cairo, which it served, was several miles away over the fields. Before the advent of air travel this was where tourists to Egypt arrived, brought down by boat from Alexandria. After stepping ashore on 26 November 1849, Florence Nightingale recorded that she needed a servant to keep at bay all the hawkers – a situation familiar to anyone arriving nowadays at Cairo International Airport. She writes of then being 'driven up the great valley of acacias from Boulak to the Ezbekeeyah.'

The acacias, needless to say, are long gone. These days Bulaq sprawls inland from the river as far as Sharia Galaa, Cairo's newspaper district, where the Arab world's most famous newspaper *Al-Ahram* now has its offices. South to north, Bulaq stretches from Sharia 26th of July to Midan Ramses in a tangle of narrow alleyways. The most interesting part is the oldest section (see Map 3), which is closest to the Nile. The **Abu al-Ela Mosque** was built in 1485, centuries before the 26th of July flyover which now passes its door. The mosque gave its name to an attractive turn-of-the-century iron bridge which stood beside the present bridge until it was removed in 1997. Directly north of the Abu al-Ela Mosque (head in beside the orange house with the *mashrabiyya* windows), the Bulaq alleyways are filled with a **used car parts market** which quickly switches over to wholesale cloth and cheap clothing.

These ramshackle backstreets house dozens of old medieval structures but few are obvious. At the Qadi Yahia mosque (which dates from 1448), identifiable by its half minaret, take a left and then resume walking north to reach the beautiful **Mosque of Sinan Pasha**. Built in 1571 by Egypt's Ottoman viceroy, the mosque is arcaded on three sides leading into a small overgrown garden. If the caretaker is around it may be possible to climb the stairs up to the gallery which goes around the inside of the dome to get a better look at the intricate coloured glass windows.

Over the mosque loom the twin towers of the National Bank. Located on the Corniche the bank is part of a scheme to gentrify the Nile-side fringes of Bulaq. Just a little way north is the **World Trade Centre** which offers office space to international corporations, high finance merchants, and the Australian embassy. The lower floors are taken up with an exclusive shopping centre.

Islamic Cairo

Islamic Cairo (see Maps 6, 8 & 9) is almost another city altogether, distinct from its 20th century incarnation to the west. Like Alice passing through her looking glass, as the visitor heads east from Midan Ataba all the familiar trappings of the modern world drop away to be replaced by chaos and curiosities of a completely different nature.

Lying to the east of Central Cairo this is the old medieval metropolis, stretching from the northern walls and gates of Al-Qahira down to Fustat in the south, the site of the first Islamic city (see History in the Facts about Cairo chapter). Unchanged over the centuries to an astonishing degree, Islamic Cairo's neighbourhoods are full of twisting alleyways so narrow that the houses seem to touch at the top. Splendid mosques and crushes of medieval facades hedge in rutted streets on which little Suzuki vans compete for the right of way with donkeys and carts, and merchants with impossibly laden barrows. The sweet, pungent aromas of turmeric, basil and cumin mix with the odours of livestock and petrol. It's a maze-like area that is completely disorientating in that the casual visitor easily loses not just any sense of direction but also any sense of time.

The term Islamic Cairo, by the way, is a bit of a misnomer – the area is no more or less Islamic than any other part of the city – but maybe the profusion of minarets and domes on the skyline give the impression of piety.

Visiting Islamic Cairo

Islamic Cairo is a fairly daunting area with few obvious routes and focal points and, as a result, some extremely impressive monuments and atmospheric districts receive far fewer visitors than they deserve. We have broken it down into eight sections, each one of which makes for a half-day's outing:

Anyone wanting to know more about Islamic Cairo should pick up *Islamic Monuments in Cairo – A Practical Guide* published by the AUC Press (E£40). This guide contains 300-plus pages of history and descriptions of all the monuments in Islamic Cairo. The Society

THINGS TO SEE & DO

City of the Thousand and One Nights

Ever since the first English and French translations appeared in the 19th century, the tales contained in *The Thousand and One Nights* (in Arabic, *Alf Layla wa Layla*) have influenced the way in which the west imagines the east. CNN footage and daily reports of the latest Middle Eastern terrorist activities and politicking now provide an effective counter to most people's Orientalist fantasies; however, the exploits of Aladdin and Sinbad, replete with thieves and evil viziers, caves of gold, djinns and bazaars, continue to enrapture the young.

Cairo has a strong claim to being the city of the Thousand and One Nights. Although Sheherezade and her nightly stories have their origins in pre-Islamic Persia, successive storytellers over the ages have added new exploits, relocated the action and generally reshaped the material to suit their audience. In the version passed down to this day, the adventures, enchantments and lowlife goings on described in *The Nights* take place in the semi-fabled Baghdad of Harun ar-Rashid and in the Cairo of the Mamluks.

Anyone reading one of the more comprehensive editions of *The Nights* can locate the action for themselves, as the authors have provided a wealth of topographical detail. We're told that Marouf the Cobbler, who features in a cycle of tales, lives on Darb al-Ahmar, and there are numerous mentions of places like Bab Zuweyla and Bayn al-Qasryn, along with descriptions of the things that go on there. And if the physical sites are still there to be seen, you only have to fall into conversation with a local to learn that even in this day there's no shortage of hidden treasures, wicked robbers and evil djinns. In Islamic Cairo the Thousand and One Nights are far from being at an end. ■

for the Preservation of the Architectural Resources of Egypt (SPARE) puts out four semi-pictorial maps that are also excellent tools for exploration. The book and the maps are available from most Cairo bookshops.

Appropriate dress is necessary for visiting this part of Cairo – legs and shoulders should be decently covered, otherwise custodians may baulk at allowing you inside mosques. Shoes have to be taken off before entering prayer halls so it might be wise to come in footwear that can be easily slipped off and on, but it should also be robust enough for rutted and rubble-strewn alleyways.

Carry lots of small change. You'll need it for tipping guardians and caretakers who will expect baksheesh for unlocking the doors to minarets or switching on lights so that you can see what you've just paid admission to come in and look at.

Also note that any given opening times should be interpreted as a rough guide only; caretakers are usually around from 9 am until early evening but they follow their own whims. Additionally, most mosques are closed to visitors during prayer times.

AL-AZHAR & KHAN AL-KHALILI (Map 9)

By far the best place to start becoming acquainted with Islamic Cairo is the area around the great bazaar, Khan al-Khalili. It's a place that panders to preconceptions – this is what everybody always imagines the 'east' to be like. It's also very accessible; to walk from Midan Ataba in Downtown, straight along Sharia al-Azhar, takes about 20 to 30 minutes (or you could brave Muski – see the Sharia Muski section later) or it's a short taxi ride. Ask for 'Al-Hussein'. The fare should be no more than E£3 from Talaat Harb. Get out at the Al-Azhar mosque where a pedestrian subway burrows under the busy road to surface just off Midan Hussein. The Khan is straight ahead. Although most people are in a rush to dive, or at least dip a tentative foot, into the teeming passageways of the bazaar, it is certainly worth taking time out first to visit what is one of Cairo's most famous mosques, that of Al-Azhar.

Al-Azhar Mosque & University

The oldest university in the world, and one of the first mosques in Cairo, Al-Azhar was

THINGS TO SEE & DO

built in 970 AD as the centrepiece of Fatimid Cairo. It continues to play a dominant role in Egyptian theological life to this day, with the Sheikh of al-Azhar being the country's ultimate religious authority. Students, however, are no longer taught in the mosque's courtyard, they attend one of Al-Azhar's nine campuses around the country.

Architecturally the mosque is a mixture of styles, the result of frequent enlargements over its 1000 year history. The central courtyard is the earliest part, while from south to north, the three minarets date from the 14th, 15th and 16th centuries; the last (with the double finial) was added by Sultan al-Ghouri whose own mosque stands about 200m to the west (see the Al-Azhar to the Citadel section later in this chapter).

At the time of writing the mosque was closed for renovation, but it is scheduled to reopen some time before the end of 1997. When it is open, you will not be allowed to enter if you have bare legs and women must cover their heads with the scarves provided.

Ottoman Houses

Leaving the mosque and turning left and then left again brings you into an alley squeezed

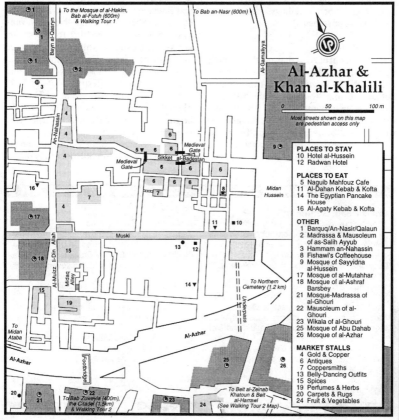

Al-Azhar & Khan al-Khalili

0   50   100 m

Most streets shown on this map are pedestrian access only

PLACES TO STAY
10 Hotel al-Hussein
12 Radwan Hotel

PLACES TO EAT
5   Naguib Mahfouz Cafe
11 Al-Dahan Kebab & Kofta
14 The Egyptian Pancake House
16 Al-Agaty Kebab & Kofta

OTHER
1   Barquq/An-Nasir/Qalaun
2   Madrassa & Mausoleum of as-Salih Ayyub
3   Hammam an-Nahassin
8   Fishawi's Coffeehouse
9   Mosque of Sayyidna al-Hussein
17 Mosque of al-Mutahhar
18 Mosque of al-Ashraf Barsbey
21 Mosque-Madrassa of al-Ghouri
22 Mausoleum of al-Ghouri
23 Wikala of al-Ghouri
25 Mosque of Abu Dahab
26 Mosque of al-Azhar

MARKET STALLS
4   Gold & Copper
6   Antiques
7   Coppersmiths
13 Belly-Dancing Outfits
15 Spices
19 Perfumes & Herbs
20 Carpets & Rugs
24 Fruit & Vegetables

THINGS TO SEE & DO

between the southern wall of Al-Azhar and a row of tiny shops housed in the vaults of a 15th century merchants' building. You also pass a great water dispenser crowned with an elaborate tin-plate model of a mosque. At what first appears to be the end of the alley, the road doglegs; the building it jogs around is **Beit al-Zeinab Khatoun** (House of Zeinab Khatoun), a restored Ottoman-era house that now serves as a cultural centre and sometime gallery.

Facing this, across the small garden, is **Beit al-Harrawi**, another fine piece of 18th century vernacular architecture. It's very sparse inside with no furnishing and little ornamentation but there's some fine mashrabiyya and wooden ceilings. Admission is E£10 (E£5 for students).

Wikala of al-Ghouri

Coming left out of Al-Azhar and then turning right, past the fruit and vegetable market, you reach the *wikala*, or *caravanserai*, of Sultan al-Ghouri (built in 1505), a kind of medieval merchants' hostel. The traders slept in the upper rooms while their animals were stabled below. The ground floor also had storage areas and business was carried out in the courtyard around the fountain. The

gates of the wikala were locked at night to protect the merchandise. In Ottoman times Cairo had over 360 wikalas but now less than 20 remain, of which this is in by far the best condition.

The courtyard now serves as a theatre and concert hall. The former stables are artists' ateliers, and one houses a small permanent exhibition of peasant and Bedouin crafts. The wikala (☎ 511 0472) is open from 8 am to midnight daily. The entrance fee is E£6.

Midan Hussein

This was one of the main squares of medieval Cairo, stretching between the two highly venerated mosques of Al-Azhar to the south and Sayyidna al-Hussein to the north. The four-lane Sharia al-Azhar that now runs through it has done nothing for the space, but Midan Hussein is still considered to be the heart of Islamic Cairo, particularly at feast times, on Ramadan evenings, and during the *moulids* (festivals) of An-Nabi Mohammed and especially Al-Hussein. Then the square is filled with vast crowds, bright lights and loud music, and the partying goes on until early the next morning.

On the northern side of Midan Hussein the **Mosque of Sayyidna al-Hussein** is one of

---

Shi'ia Head, Sunni Body

The Mosque of Sayyidna al-Hussein is one of two mosques in Cairo considered too sacred to allow non-Muslims to enter (the other is Sayyida Zeinab). It reputedly contains one of the most holy relics of Islam: the head of Al-Hussein, grandson of the Prophet. This was brought here in a green silk bag in 1153 (almost 500 years after his death) out of reach of the Crusaders who were busy desecrating Islamic sites in Palestine. The head is not on view but is buried several metres beneath a shrine.

Al-Hussein was killed by the Umayyad clan who had assumed control of the caliphate after the Prophet Mohammed had died without naming a successor. Ali, the husband of Mohammed's daughter Fatima, put himself forward as the natural successor, claiming the right by marriage. Passed over, he took up arms against the Umayyads, but was assassinated. His son Al-Hussein then led a revolt but was killed at the battle of Kerbala.

The schism is perpetuated in Islam today. The followers of Al-Hussein and Ali became the Shi'ia, who refuse to acknowledge as caliph anyone but descendants of Mohammed. Those who believe that the true line of succession went via the Umayyads are known as Sunnis; Sunnis constitute 90% of all Muslims.

Despite being a Shi'ia martyr, Al-Hussein was a blood relative of the Prophet and as such is regarded as a popular saint in Egypt. ■

THINGS TO SEE & DO

the most sacred places of Muslim worship in Cairo – see the boxed text 'Shi'ia Head, Sunni Body'. The current building, which dates from about 1870, replaces an earlier 12th century mosque. Age isn't everything though, and the Al-Hussein mosque attracts some 2000 worshippers a day and up to 10,000 for Friday prayers – including the president on Islamic holy days. The mosque can only be viewed from the outside by non-Muslims.

Khan al-Khalili

Jaundiced travellers have been known to glibly dismiss Khan al-Khalili as a tourist trap, and it's true that the tour bus-pleasing, travellers cheque-pulling element is well and truly present. But that's just a veneer and the grain of this bazaar, perhaps the Middle East's largest, runs much deeper. Generations of Cairenes have lived their lives in these narrow, canvas covered alleys, doing their crafts, dyeing, carving and sewing. The buying and selling did not begin with the arrival of the first tour group.

Khan al-Khalili began as a single caravanserai built in 1382 by Garkas al-Khalili, who was Sultan Barquq's master of horses. It was rebuilt by Al-Ghouri some 130-odd years later on a much grander scale and it's his two huge carved **stone gates** that can be seen in the part of the bazaar called the Badestan. It was Khalili's name, however, that stuck.

Today the Khan is an immense conglomeration of markets and shops (many of which are closed on Sunday). Within the labyrinth of squeezed shop fronts you'll find everything from glassware, leather goods and brasswork to books of magic spells and prayer beads – as well, of course, as plenty of stuffed camels and alabaster pyramids. The clumsy 'Hey mister, look for free' touts aside, the merchants of Khan al-Khalili are some of the greatest salespeople and smooth talkers you will ever meet. Almost anything can be bought in the Khan, and if one merchant doesn't have what you're looking for, then he'll find somebody who does. For more details about bargaining and what can be bought where, see the Shopping chapter.

There are few specific things to see in the Khan but a stop off at **Fishawi's** coffeehouse is a must. Hung with huge ornately framed mirrors and packed day and night, it's been open 24 hours a day for the last 200 years. Entertainment comes in the form of roaming salesmen, women and children who hawk wallets, cigarette lighters in the form of pistols, canes with carved tops, sheesha-style cigarette holders, and packet after packet after packet of Kleenex tissues. It's easily found; it fills a narrow alleyway with rickety tables and chairs just one block in off Midan Hussein. If you are the outgoing type, then at the Hussein end of Sharia Muski are the shops selling belly-dancers' outfits; for a thoroughly aromatic experience head for the spice area, which is around Sharia al-Muizz li-Din Allah, next to the Al-Ashraf Barsbey mosque.

Sharia Muski

Sharia Muski is a congested market street that runs parallel to Sharia al-Azhar from Midan Hussein all the way to Midan Ataba on the edge of Downtown. It is less overtly Oriental than Khan al-Khalili but all the more vivid and boisterous for it. The goods on sale range from plastic furniture and party toys on a little midan 200m beyond the Barsbey mosque junction, to items like wedding dresses and great mounds of bucket-sized bras at the western end.

The chants of the hawkers are fun, often sung to popular tunes, and many shops have their young male staff and friends stand outside hollering discounted prices at the press of shoppers struggling by.

To walk from Ataba to Hussein, or vice versa, takes about 20 to 30 minutes depending on how ruthless you are with your elbows.

NORTH OF KHAN AL-KHALILI (Map 5)

Al-Qahira was the walled royal enclave outside which sprawled the poorer quarters and cemeteries of medieval Cairo. It was relatively modest in size, covering about 1sq km

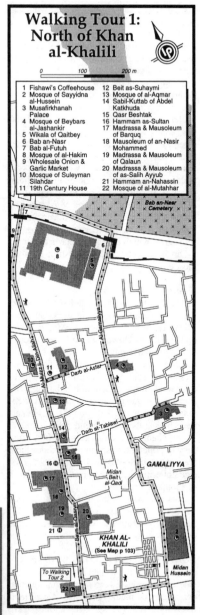

Walking Tour 1: North of Khan al-Khalili

0   100   200 m

1 Fishawi's Coffeehouse
2 Mosque of Sayyidna al-Hussein
3 Musafirkhanah Palace
4 Mosque of Beybars al-Jashankir
5 Wikala of Qaitbey
6 Bab an-Nasr
7 Bab al-Futuh
8 Mosque of al-Hakim
9 Wholesale Onion & Garlic Market
10 Mosque of Suleyman Silahdar
11 19th Century House
12 Beit as-Suhaymi
13 Mosque of al-Aqmar
14 Sabil-Kuttab of Abdel Katkhuda
15 Qasr Beshtak
16 Hammam as-Sultan
17 Madrassa & Mausoleum of Barquq
18 Mausoleum of an-Nasir Mohammed
19 Madrassa & Mausoleum of Qalaun
20 Madrassa & Mausoleum of as-Salih Ayyub
21 Hammam an-Nahassin
22 Mosque of al-Mutahhar

and accessed by some 60 gates of various sizes and importance. Today, only three of these gates remain: two are in the north – Bab an-Nasr and Bab al-Futuh – and one, Bab Zuweyla, is in the south. The Al-Futuh and Zuweyla gates, which lie about 1.5km apart, were connected by a main north-south artery generally known as the Qasaba, or high street, but with many other names for specific stretches. Earlier this century the axis of this old quarter was changed when Sharia al-Azhar was ploughed through, creating a new major east-west route where previously there had been none.

For the purposes of exploration, medieval Al-Qahira neatly divides up into north of Sharia al-Azhar and south of Al-Azhar (see Al-Azhar to the Citadel later in this chapter).

The district to the north of Al-Azhar and Khan al-Khalili is called **Gamaliyya**. It's where Nobel-laureate Naguib Mahfouz grew up and it forms the backdrop for many of his novels and stories (see the boxed text 'Mahfouz's Cairo'). The narrow street running up the western side of the Sayyidna al-Hussein mosque is Sharia al-Gamaliyya, the second most important of Al-Qahira's thoroughfares. Beyond the mosque it twists and jogs a little but carries on heading essentially north. At the first small mosque encountered on the right, turn right and then follow the alley (called Darb at-Tablawi) around to a restored stone wall. This is the wall of the Musafirkhanah Palace; the entrance is through an unimposing, un-marked doorway down the side.

Musafirkhanah Palace

This is a sprawling Ottoman palace, the name of which loosely translates as 'travellers' caravanserai'. It was built over a period of nine years (1779-88) by a wealthy merchant from Al-Fayoum but is better known for its later owner, Ibrahim Pasha, whose son Ismail, the future khedive and Suez Canal builder, was born here in 1829.

The central attraction is what is claimed to be the biggest mashrabiyya in the world, jutting out from the *haramlik* (women's quarters) – supported, note, by a Roman column

Mahfouz's Cairo

Naguib Mahfouz was born in Gamaliyya in the heart of Islamic Cairo and though his family moved away to Abbassiyya when he was just 12 years old, in his writing he never left. He grew up in a short alleyway called Darb Qirmiz, just off the north-east corner of Midan Beit al-Qadi, and went to an elementary school behind the Mosque of Sayyidna al-Hussein. Those first dozen years provided the images and impressions that were to supply the background for much of the Nobel laureate's writing.

Golo

One of his earliest books, yet to be translated into English, was called *Khan al-Khalili*, followed a few years later by *Midaq Alley* which focuses on the lives of the people who inhabit a small cul-de-sac within the bazaar. Midaq Alley (Zuqaq al-Midaq) exists and a film of the same name was shot there. To get to Midaq Alley from the junction of Al-Muizz li-Din and Muski, walk south towards Sharia al-Azhar then take the first left into Sharia as-Sanadqiya – Midaq Alley is the first on the left with a short flight of stairs leading up to three stubby dead ends. The street sign is kept in a coffeehouse at the foot of the steps and is produced only on payment of baksheesh.

Similarly, all the events in Mahfouz's *Cairo Trilogy* are rooted in geographical fact and the three separate titles are the names of streets in the area: *Palace Walk* (*Bayn al-Qasryn*), is a part of Al-Muizz li-Din; *Sugar Street* (*Sharia Sukariyya*) is near Bab Zuweyla; and *Palace of Desire* (*Qasr al-Shuq*) lies just east of Sharia al-Gamaliyya.

But while the names may stay the same, in some ways Mahfouz's stories have dated. The mix of upper, middle and working classes that he describes cohabiting these neighbourhoods is a thing of the past. History and place have lost out to lousy plumbing and lack of amenities. Everyone who can afford to has moved out, including Mahfouz – while Gamaliyya might hold the Nobel laureate's heart his body prefers the comforts of the modern Nile-side suburb of Agouza. ■

---

filched from Alexandria – above a courtyard and garden where the royal family enjoyed dancing and festivities. The male equivalent of the haramlik, the *salamlik*, is the first main room in the building to the left when you enter. You can also see a couple of private bath and sauna rooms – the coloured glass in the roof is original, as is most of the stained glass and the exquisite, carved mahogany used in the ceilings. Admission is E£6 and opening hours are flexible.

Back on Sharia al-Gamaliyya

Al-Gamaliyya continues north, impeded in parts by forests of crude wooden scaffolding shoring up damage inflicted by the 1992 earthquake (see the boxed text 'Scaffolding of Hosni Mubarak' on page 110). There are clusters of medieval wikalas, schools and mosques along the way but in an area of such historical wealth none of them are special. On the left, just before the street exits through the gate of Bab an-Nasr, is the **Wikala of Qaitbey** dating from 1481. It's now a workshop and tenement but in the early 1990s it briefly reverted to mercantile use when it became Liam Neeson's storage depot for the Hollywood film *Ruby Cairo*.

Bab an-Nasr & Bab al-Futuh

The square-towered Bab an-Nasr (Gate of Victory) and the rounded Bab al-Futuh (Gate of Conquests) were built in 1087, along with the stretch of fortified wall between. Walk along the outside and you'll see what a hugely imposing bit of military architecture the whole thing is – though it has never been put to the test as Cairo has never been besieged. The interior of the gates can be visited via the roof of the Mosque of al-Hakim.

Once on the roof bear left to Bab al-Futuh first. You can still see the shafts that allowed boiling oil to be poured on the heads of invaders below, but were probably only ever used for dumping litter. Look for the carving above one of the doorways which reads 'Tour Lascalle', which is a remnant of when Napoleon's troops of occupation were garrisoned here. Continue beyond the tower to the westernmost bastion where you'll find a descending staircase. On the wall as you go down are carved bullocks and Pharaonic figures, evidence that some of the stone for these fortifications was pinched from Memphis. At the bottom of the stairs underneath a window is a partially eroded hippo. The archway to the left here leads into a 200m-long interior passageway with a vaulted ceiling so high that patrolling soldiers could pass through on horseback. Only arrow slits of sunlight pierce the gloom and it would be wise to bring along a torch. There's enough light to see that the first arrow slit on the left is partially composed of Pharaonic stone.

At one point a locked gate means you have to climb back up and continue on to Bab an-Nasr along the ramparts. From here you overlook the former Bab an-Nasr cemetery, nowadays almost completely overbuilt with houses. Somewhere in there, now lost, is the final resting place of Johann Ludwig Burckhardt, the 19th century explorer who rediscovered Petra and the temple of Ramses II at Abu Simbel. Notice that Bab an-Nasr is also scratched with a Napoleonic name, 'Tour Milhaud'.

Admission to the gates is E£6. You may be asked for E£12 – E£6 for the Hakim mosque, E£6 for the gates – but if you've no interest in exploring the mosque (it can be seen quite well from up on the roof) just say 'Al-Abwab bas' and pay E£6 only.

Mosque of al-Hakim

Completed in 1010, the haunting mosque of the notorious Al-Hakim (see the boxed text 'The Mad Caliph') has rarely been used as a place of worship; instead, it was a prison in which Crusaders were held captive; Salah ad-Din stabled his horses here; Napoleon used it as a warehouse; and Nasser made it a boys' school. Most fittingly of all, it also served for a time as a madhouse.

In 1980, in exchange for a large donation made to the Egyptian antiquities people, the mosque was handed over to the Bohras, an Ismaili Shi'ia sect from India. Their treatment of the mosque – adding chandeliers and other fixtures that are out of keeping with local traditions – has outraged purists. Admission is E£6.

Sharia al-Muizz li-Din Allah

Al-Muizz li-Din (as it's often shortened to) is the name for the part of the Qasaba that runs all the way from Bab al-Futuh down to Bab Zuweyla, the southern gate. It takes its name from the conquering Fatimid caliph. In medieval times this was the route along which parades of pilgrims marched on their return from Mecca. Despite the best part of a thousand years in service as the city's main axis, Al-Muizz li-Din today remains narrow to the point that the attempted passage of one car can cause untold chaos and pedestrian congestion.

As late as the mid-19th century, the portion of Al-Muizz li-Din outside Al-Hakim's mosque was a slave market; these days, when they're in season, it's a garlic and onion market with sacks of the two piled high on the pavements. Heading south, the produce gives way to a variety of small places selling the metalworked accoutrements for coffeehouses and fuul vendors – sheeshas, braziers and big, pear-shaped cooking pots. On the right, after about 200m, is the **Mosque of Suleyman Silahdar**, built comparatively late in 1839 during the reign of Mohammed Ali and distinguished by its drainpipe-thin minaret. Reflecting the pasha's wider aims of grafting European ideas onto those of traditional Egypt,

The Mad Caliph

Al-Hakim bi-Amr Allah (he who rules by God's command) was only 11 years old when his father died and he became ruler of Egypt. His tutor nicknamed him 'Little Lizard' because of his frightening looks and behaviour – Hakim later had the tutor murdered. During his 24 year reign those nearest to him went in constant fear for their lives. A general buoyed up with confidence after defeating a marauding army on Egypt's borders entered the royal apartments unannounced to find a bloodied Hakim standing over a disembowelled page boy. The general was beheaded.

Hakim did, however, take a great interest in the affairs of his people and disregarded pomp and ceremony to patrol the city's streets on his donkey, called Moon. He would often receive petitions from his subjects, though it was a risky thing for anybody to approach the Caliph – if he found the complaint tiresome it would be the petitioner who suffered. Hakim was particularly irked by dishonest merchants and any found guilty of cheating their customers would be sodomised by a large black servant who accompanied him for this purpose. Neither was Hakim too keen on dogs – he had them all slaughtered – or women, who he forbade to be seen abroad on the city streets, a decree that lasted seven and a half years. He also placed a ban on the manufacture of women's shoes to make sure they stayed indoors.

The citizens of Cairo dealt with their ruler's caprices with equanimity – until he had himself proclaimed divine. When three of his disciples entered the Mosque of Amr for Friday prayers and attempted to substitute Hakim's name for Allah during worship, they were immediately killed by the outraged congregation. Hakim's response was to order his troops to raze and loot his own city.

Shortly after this, on one of his solitary nocturnal jaunts on Moon up into the Muqattam Hills, Hakim disappeared. His body was never found. To one of his followers, a man called Al-Darizy, this was proof of Hakim's divine nature and he went on to preach in Syria, founding a sect that continues to this day – the Druze. ■

the mosque mixes a Mamluk-style facade with rococo and baroque forms.

Over the street from the mosque is a 19th century house occupying a corner site; turn left here onto Sharia Darb al-Asfar and walk along to No 19, Beit as-Suhaymi.

Beit as-Suhaymi

Built in the 16th and 17th centuries, this is Cairo's finest Ottoman house. With few exceptions, restoration has left many of Cairo's historic houses completely soulless and feeling like reproductions rather than the real thing. In contrast, Beit as-Suhaymi has always had something of a Marie Celeste quality to it, as if its former owner might turn up at any moment. Unfortunately, at the time of going to press the restorers were in residence and Beit as-Suhaymi was closed for repairs; it is expected to remain so until 1999. Fingers crossed that it comes out unscathed.

Mosque of al-Aqmar

Back on Al-Muizz li-Din, just 50m south of the junction with Darb al-Asfar, is the petite Al-Aqmar (the Moonlit) mosque. Built in 1125 by one of the last Fatimid caliphs, it's important in terms of Cairo's architectural development because it's the oldest stone-facaded mosque in Egypt. Here, for the first time, appear several features that were to become part of the mosque builders' essential vocabulary – the stalactite carving, for instance, and the ribbing in the hooded arch. Note that at the time it was built the mosque was at street level.

Sabil-Kuttab of Abdel Katkhuda

A *sabil* is a fountain or tap from which passers-by can take a drink; a *kuttab* is a Quranic school. So, a *sabil-kuttab* provides the two things commended by the Prophet: water for the thirsty and spiritual enlightenment for the ignorant. The building of a sabil-kuttab was a popular way for wealthy people to atone for their sins. This particular example, imposingly placed at a point where Al-Muizz li-Din splits, was built in 1744 by a Mamluk emir well known for his debauched behaviour. It has some nice ceramic work inside which can't be seen from the street but if you linger the *bawwab* (doorman) may come along with the door key.

Qasr Beshtak

The second door along on the side street south of Abdel-Katkhuda's sabil-kuttab

belongs to the formerly splendid 14th century Beshtak Palace of which only a small part remains. Emir Beshtak was a very wealthy man who was married to the daughter of Sultan an-Nasir. When he built this palace it had five storeys, each with running water. Climb up on to the roof for a beautiful view south along Al-Muizz li-Din.

Barquq/An-Nasir/Qalaun

The part of Al-Muizz li-Din immediately south of the Katkhuda sabil-kuttab is known

---

Scaffolding of Hosni Mubarak

During the period of research for this book it seemed like most of Islamic Cairo was 'out of order'. The mosques of Al-Azhar and Al-Ghouri, the Mausoleum of Qalaun, and Beit as-Suhaymi – some of Cairo's finest medieval monuments – were all closed until further notice. Try again next year. Ostensibly the reason is the earthquake of 1992.

That the 1992 earthquake did untold damage is unquestionable. The Musafirkhanah Palace was split vertically down the middle leaving the rear half threatening to topple backwards any day now, and more than one mosque lost its minaret. But this natural disaster has been aided and abetted by human negligence and error. Damage at the Al-Ghouri mosque, for example, wouldn't have been half as bad if shopkeepers hadn't been enlarging their storage space by digging up its foundations.

Since then, to say that the repair work has been slow stretches the bounds of understatement. Five years on and 'emergency' scaffolding still props up much of Islamic Cairo. Some of these makeshift structures are impressive in themselves – towers of spindly beams bound together by rope. In fact it's been suggested that as it's all more than half a decade old now, perhaps the scaffolding should be granted permanent status and added to the list of the city's historic monuments.

With thanks to Max Rodenbeck

---

as Bayn al-Qasryn. It means 'between the palaces', a reference to two great royal complexes that flanked the street here during the Fatimid era. The palaces fell into ruin following the fall of the Fatimids but Bayn al-Qasryn remained the most important public space in medieval Cairo – it was a great marketplace filled with entertainers and stalls serving food, off which ran dozens of alleys containing more specialised markets wholly devoted to knives, books or candles. As such, the area remained a favourite building place for subsequent rulers whose monuments rose out of the rubble of the former palaces. Today, three great abutting Mamluk complexes line the west of the street, providing one of Cairo's most impressive assemblies of minarets, domes and towering facades. Entrance to each of these complexes is E£6; E£3 for students.

Northernmost of the three is the **Madrassa & Mausoleum of Barquq**. Barquq, whose name in Arabic means 'plum', seized power in 1382 as Egypt was reeling from plague and famine. His madrassa was completed four years later. It is entered through the bold black and white marble portal which leads into a vaulted passageway. To the right, the inner court has a colourful ceiling supported by four Pharaonic columns made of porphyry that were quarried from near the Red Sea coast. Although this is called the Mausoleum of Barquq, it's actually his daughter who is buried here in the splendid domed tomb chamber; the sultan himself rests in the Northern Cemetery (see the Khanqah-Mausoleum of ibn Barquq in the Northern Cemetery section later in this chapter).

South of the Barquq complex is the Kufic-banded facade belonging to the **Mausoleum of an-Nasir Mohammed** (1304). The Gothic doorway was taken from a church in Acre (now Akko, Israel) when An-Nasir and his Mamluk army ended Crusader domination there in 1290. More foreign influence is discernible in the fine stucco on the minaret which is North African in style. Buried in the mausoleum (on the right as you enter but usually kept locked) is An-Nasir's favourite

son – the sultan himself is buried next door in the mausoleum of *his* father, Qalaun.

If you are only going to visit one of the three complexes, make it the **Madrassa & Mausoleum of Qalaun**. The earliest of the trio, the Qalaun complex was completed in just 13 months in 1279; as well as the mausoleum and madrassa it also includes a *maristan*, or hospital. The Arab traveller and historian Ibn Battuta who visited Cairo in 1325 recorded that Qalaun's hospital contained 'an innumerable quantity of appliances and medicaments'. Incredibly, a clinic still occupies a part of the original building, maintaining a tradition of more than 700 years of medical care. It's reached by going down the alley at the south of the complex.

The madrassa and mausoleum are reached through the main door. The mausoleum, on the right, is a particularly beautiful assemblage of mashrabiyya, inlaid stone and stucco patterned with stars and floral motifs, all lit by stained glass windows. It's usually possible to climb Qalaun's minaret. Unfortunately, once again, at the time of writing the complex was closed for renovation.

Madrassa & Mausoleum of as-Salih Ayyub

Opposite Qalaun is a protruding sabil-kuttab which belongs to the Madrassa & Mausoleum of as-Salih Ayyub, built by the last sultan of Salah ad-Din's Ayyubid dynasty. As-Salih Ayyub died before his complex was finished, so it was completed (in 1250) by his wife, Shagaret ad-Durr, who seized power for herself to become one of Egypt's few female rulers (see the boxed text 'Shagaret ad-Durr' on page 124).

Back to Town

Want to buy a minaret top? South of As-Salih Ayyub's complex the monuments give way to a ramshackle string of shops filled with pots and pans and crescent-shaped finials, which is why this area is popularly known as Sharia an-Nahassin or the Coppersmiths' Street. After a short stretch, copper gives way to gold signifying that you have re-entered the precincts of Khan al-Khalili. At the junction with Muski, beside the two mosques, left leads to Midan Hussein, and right leads to Midan Ataba and Downtown (30 minutes walk away); straight ahead is Sharia al-Azhar, the best place to find a taxi.

AL-AZHAR TO THE CITADEL (Map 9)

South of Sharia al-Azhar, Al-Muizz li-Din continues as a busy market street (souq) running down to the twin-minareted gate of Bab Zuweyla. It's a leisurely 15 minute walk. From the gate there are then two possible routes to the Citadel – east along Darb al-Ahmar or south through the Street of the Tentmakers (Sharia al-Khayamiyya). Either way it takes about another 20 minutes of uninterrupted walking to reach the Citadel, where you can then take refreshments, enjoy the view, and exert yourself with a little more sightseeing before picking up a taxi at Midan Salah ad-Din to take you back to town. Alternatively, turning right outside Bab Zuweyla will take you the short distance to the Museum of Islamic Art.

To get to the start of this walk at the junction of Sharia al-Azhar and Al-Muizz li-Din ask for 'Al-Hussein' and get out of the taxi when you reach the green footbridge.

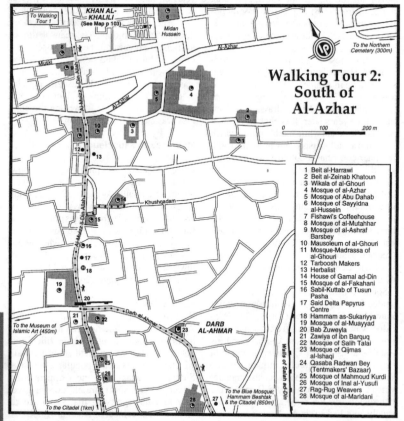

Walking Tour 2: South of Al-Azhar

0   100   200 m

1 Beit al-Harrawi
2 Beit al-Zeinab Khatoun
3 Wikala of al-Ghouri
4 Mosque of al-Azhar
5 Mosque of Abu Dahab
6 Mosque of Sayyidna al-Hussein
7 Fishawi's Coffeehouse
8 Mosque of al-Mutahhar
9 Mosque of al-Ashraf Barsbey
10 Mausoleum of al-Ghouri
11 Mosque-Madrassa of al-Ghouri
12 Tarboosh Makers
13 Herbalist
14 House of Gamal ad-Din
15 Mosque of al-Fakahani
16 Sabil-Kuttab of Tusun Pasha
17 Said Delta Papyrus Centre
18 Hammam as-Sukariyya
19 Mosque of al-Muayyad
20 Bab Zuweyla
21 Zawiya of ibn Barquq
22 Mosque of Salih Talai
23 Mosque of Qijmas al-Ishaqi
24 Qasaba Radwan Bey (Tentmakers' Bazaar)
25 Mosque of Mahmoud Kurdi
26 Mosque of Inal al-Yusufi
27 Rag-Rug Weavers
28 Mosque of al-Maridani

Al-Ghouri Complex

The grand pair of black and white buildings (dating from 1505; sometimes referred to as Al-Ghouriyya) facing each other across the market street are an exquisite monument to the end of the Mamluk era. Qansuh al-Ghouri, the penultimate Mamluk sultan, ruled for 16 years before being slain in battle with the Ottoman Turks in Syria at the age of 78. His head was sent to Constantinople and his body was never recovered. Al-Ghouri's mausoleum instead contains the body of Tumanbey, his successor, who was defeated by the conquering Turks and then hanged at Bab Zuweyla.

The building on the west with its red-chequered chimney-pot minaret is the mosque-madrassa complex; on the east is the mausoleum. You can see the base from which a dome that collapsed in 1860 originally rose. Part of the mausoleum now serves as a youth and cultural centre, and a theatre (☎ 510 0823) where twice-weekly performances of Sufi dancing are held – see the Entertainment chapter for details.

Gamal al-Ghitani's excellent novel *Zayni Barakat* is set during the last days of Al-Ghouri. David Roberts (see the boxed text 'David Roberts' in the Facts about Cairo chapter) also made a drawing of the Ghouriyya in 1839 – much reproduced since – which shows a wooden canopy between the two buildings forming a covered market.

Souq

The area around the Ghouriyya used to be known as the Silk Market and was where carpets were sold. Although they're no longer made of silk, the passageways behind Al-Ghouri's mosque-madrassa (slip down the side or enter from Sharia al-Azhar) are still filled with carpet sellers. The main street, Al-Muizz li-Din, is now a busy souq given over to household goods, cloth and cheap clothing, particularly gaudy *galabeyyas* (the full- length robe worn by men). Though just as colourful, with plenty of street food vendors, it is far less touristy than the Khan al-Khalili.

On the right, less than 50m south of the

David Roberts' 1839 painting of the covered silk market in Al-Ghouriyya.

Ghouriyya are two of Cairo's last tarboosh (fez) makers. You can watch them moulding the hats on their heavy brass presses. Once worn by every *effendi* (gentleman) the tarbooshes are mainly bought now by hotels and theatre troupes. They sell for E£5 to E£30. Further along, on the opposite side of the street, is a herbalist whose shop front is hung with bunches of dried hedgehogs. There's a small wizened alligator too. All this stuff is used in the preparation of healing compounds – but quite how, we've no idea.

House of Gamal ad-Din

This restored 16th century house is the former home of a rich gold merchant. It now houses a department of the Supreme Council of Antiquities, but entry to the public is still permitted. Enter through the mammoth-sized wooden door and continue into the fountain courtyard, then call out for the guard, who will show you around. Don't miss the beautiful mashrabiyya and stained-glass windows of the 'business room'. The house is open from 9 am to 5 pm, and admission is E£3 (E£1.50 for students). To get here from Sharia al-Muizz li-Din Allah take the side street that is on the left just before the crumbling Mosque of al-Fakahani. Follow this street round and then take the first right into Sharia Khushqadam; the house is No 6.

Mosque of al-Muayyad

Al-Muayyad was a great intriguer, for which he was arrested and thrown into a lice-infested prison which stood on this site. While incarcerated he vowed that one day he would replace the prison with a 'saintly place'. On coming to power he did just that. His mosque, a typically monumental Mamluk work, was completed in 1422. The great bronze doorway that you see originally belonged to the Mosque-Madrassa of Sultan Hassan. The entrance leads into the mausoleum where Al- Muayyad and his son lie in two cenotaphs; beyond that is the mosque itself, an extremely tranquil place with the prayer hall opening on to a large tree-filled garden courtyard. In the far corner of the prayer hall is a small door leading to the mosque's two minarets which sit on top of the Bab Zuweyla (added 330 years after the gate was built – how on earth did the master masons know that the gate could take the extra weight?). The view from the top of the minarets is about the best in Cairo, offering a panorama of rooftops used as chicken runs, goat pens, pigeon lofts, rubbish dumps and even workshops.

The entrance fee to the mosque is E£6 (E£1.50 for students) but the caretaker will probably insist on baksheesh to open the door up to the minarets.

Immediately across from the entrance to the mosque is a mashrabiyya-fronted wikala and beside that a door which leads into the Hammam as-Sukariyya, a public bath. The narrow alley beside this is Sharia Sukariyya, or Sugar Street, from which the second novel in Naguib Mahfouz's *Cairo Trilogy* takes its name (see the boxed text 'Mahfouz's Cairo' earlier in this chapter).

Bab Zuweyla

Built at the same time as the northern gates, Bab Zuweyla is the only remaining southern gate of the old medieval city of Al-Qahira. Until the late 19th century it was still closed each evening. The area in front of the gate was one of the main public gathering places in Mamluk times. It was also the site of executions, which were a highly popular form of street theatre. A particularly vicious bunch, the Mamluks used to execute victims by publicly sawing them in half or crucifying them on the great gates. The last Mamluk sultan, Tumanbey, was spared this indignity. He was sentenced to be hanged from the gate's vaulted ceiling; however, it took three attempts to kill him – the rope snapped the first two times. After the massacre at the Citadel (see the boxed text 'The Massacre of the Mamluks' on page 119) the heads of the 500 slain Mamluks were exhibited in front of the gate on spikes.

The gate gained a slightly better reputation in the 19th century when it became associated with Metwalli, a local saint who lived nearby. People in need of healing or divine intercession would leave a lock of hair or piece of clothing nailed to the gate in the hope of his attention. It's a practice continued to this day – look carefully and you will see fresh nails hammered into the great wooden doors.

Around Bab Zuweyla

Immediately in front of the gate are several Islamic monuments, including the tiny **Zawiya of ibn Barquq** (1408; a *zawiya* is small school dedicated to a particular sheikh – in this case Ibn Barquq) which has some beautiful but barely discernible marble work adorning its facade and, across the street, the freestanding **Mosque of Salih Talai** (1160). The mosque was built over a lower storey of shops the rent from which paid for its upkeep, but the ground has risen since that time and today the shops are 3m below street level. For many years the mosque was flooded but the American Research Centre has been busy with restoration work and it's starting to look pretty good.

THINGS TO SEE & DO

From here the routes south and east continue on to the Citadel (see the Street of the Tentmakers and the Darb al-Ahmar sections following), while west is the Museum of Islamic Art.

To the Museum of Islamic Art

Sharia Ahmed Mahir, which runs west from Bab Zuweyla, is lined with shops selling striped cotton and canvas, and tin-plate workshops turning out ducting, funnels,

Museum of Islamic Art

Overshadowed by the Pharaonic crowd-pulling power of the Egyptian Museum, this museum, which has one of the world's finest collections of Islamic applied art, receives little attention.

It has to be said though, it doesn't do itself any favours. Labelling is often completely inadequate ('Statue in the shape of a lion painted blue' reads the printed card beside a statue of a lion painted blue) and there's a definite warehouse quality to the place. Do a few walks though Islamic Cairo before coming here and visit a few mosques; that way you'll be able to supply the context required to better appreciate some of the museum's undeniably fine pieces.

Entrance is through the garden door off Sharia Port Said. This brings you into the central hall containing some of the most beautiful exhibits so we suggest you immediately turn right, saving the best for later. Rooms 8 and 9 contain woodwork, including some nice coffered ceilings; Room 11 is metalwork and Room 12 contains Mamluk weaponry. Room 13 is for 'masterpieces'. Beyond are the rooms (14-16) given over to ceramics. There is no tradition of glazed tile making in Egypt so most of what's on display comes from Iran. The cone-topped fireplace in Room 16, however, is from Turkey.

Museum of Islamic Art

Push on through Rooms 21 (glass) and 20 (Ottoman era) to Room 19 which contains a small collection of illuminated manuscripts and fantastically ornate Qurans formerly owned by King Farouk. From here make your way back to Rooms 4 and 4B, which are divided by a row of carved Mamluk columns. The museum's centrepiece is in 4B: an Ottoman fountain combined with some beautiful mashrabiyya and a carved wooden ceiling. There's another more elaborate sunken fountain in Room 5 which dates from the time of the Mamluks. The upstairs rooms containing textiles and carpets from Iran and Central Asia were closed for renovations (they have been for at least two years now) at the time of going to press.

The museum (☎ 390 9930) is open daily from 9 am to 4 pm but is closed on Friday from 11.30 am to 1.30 pm. Admission is E£16, or E£8 for students.

Getting There & Away The museum is about a 1km walk from Midan Ataba, straight down Sharia Mohammed Ali (also called Sharia al-Qalaa). Midan Tahrir is 1.5km west along Sharia Sami al-Barudi and its continuations. Alternatively, a taxi back Downtown should cost no more than E£3. ■

THINGS TO SEE & DO

scuttles and cages. In the run-up to Ramadan they also make *fanous*, the special ornate lanterns that are hung in most streets and households for the month of fasting. It's a great time to wander down here because the whole street is lit up like a fairy grotto. The street finishes at Midan Bab al-Khalq (Bab al-Khalq is the name of this district), also known as Midan Ahmed Mahir – the Museum of Islamic Art is across the road.

Street of the Tentmakers

This part of the Qasaba – the high street of medieval Al-Qahira – is known as Sharia al-Khayamiyya, or the Street of the Tentmakers. It is Cairo's only remaining covered market, built in 1650 by Radwan Bey, the commander in charge of the annual pilgrimage to Mecca. It takes its name from the artisans who traditionally worked here producing the brightly printed fabrics formerly used to adorn caravans but nowadays used to form the ceremonial tents that are set up for funerals, wakes, weddings and feasts. There's also a lot of appliqué work done here – wall panels, cushion coverings etc – for more information see the Shopping chapter.

Continuing south beyond the covered market, Sharia al-Khayamiyya runs for just over half a kilometre before intercepting Sharia Mohammed Ali; a left turn from this point will take you to the great mosque of Sultan Hassan and to the Citadel. However, rather than follow this route, we suggest that you backtrack from the Tentmakers' market and follow Darb al-Ahmar.

Darb al-Ahmar

This district, which takes its name from its main street, Darb al-Ahmar or the 'Red Road', was the heart of 14th and 15th century Cairo. During these centuries Cairo had a population of about a quarter of a million, most of whom lived outside the city walls in tightly packed residential districts like this where over half the narrow and twisting streets ended in cul-de-sacs. As the walled inner city of Al-Qahira was completely built up, patrons of new mosques, grand palaces and religious institutions were forced to build outside the city gates and most of the structures around here date from the late Mamluk era.

Mosque of Qijmas al-Ishaqi

Qijmas was master of the sultan's horses and took charge of the annual pilgrimage to Mecca. His mosque (1481) is one of the best examples of architecture from the late Mamluk period. The plain exterior of the building is quite deceptive, as inside there are beautiful stained glass windows, inlaid marble floors and stucco walls. The floor in the eastern *iwan* (vaulted hall) is particularly fine although it's usually covered by prayer mats – ask the caretaker to lift them. Note that, as at the Salih Talai mosque, there are workshops sunk below street level, although in this case they're still in use. There's no admission fee here but you'll be expected to offer a few pounds in baksheesh – E£3 should be enough.

Mosque of al-Maridani

Built in 1339, this mosque is one of the oldest buildings in the area. Several styles of architecture were used in its construction: eight granite columns were taken from a Pharaonic monument; the arches were made from Roman, Christian and Islamic designs; and the Ottomans added a fountain and wooden housing. There are several other decorative details inside. The lack of visitors, the trees in the courtyard and the attractive mashrabiyya screening make it a peaceful place to stop at. There is no official entry ticket but, as at the Qijmas al-Ishaqi mosque, someone will probably expect baksheesh.

Back on Darb al-Ahmar, known as Sharia at-Tabana at this point, across from the mosque is a small carpet-weaving workshop. As it's open to the street, you can see the great wooden loom inside on which they weave rag-rugs from colourful off-cuts. They weave to specification: choose your colour and name the size. It's about E£8 for something 1m by 1.5m. A little further on, where the road splits, is a small, friendly open-air coffeehouse (Map 9). It's a good place to take a break with an iced *limoon*.

The Hammam

At one time there were, reputedly, more baths in Cairo than there were in Rome. Islamic rites place a premium on cleanliness and many mosques and madrassas were built with baths attached. However, contrary to their pious origins, Cairo's hammams have a centuries-old reputation for offering more than just a steam and a scrub-down; Gustave Flaubert's diaries explicitly relate his experiences in a Cairo bathhouse, though, it should be noted, they fell way below his expectations.

The decline of the baths as a social institution began in the 18th century when running water became available in private homes, but to this day the water supply remains erratic in parts of town and a number of hammams are still in regular use. They are uniformly decrepit, having had no money spent on their upkeep for decades, but they are also fascinating underground warrens of steamy little stone-walled rooms, some of which have domed ceilings inlaid with coloured glass.

One of the best to visit is the **Hammam Beshtak** on Souq as-Silah (see Map 9) which has an impressive central hall with stone columns and a now dry central fountain flanked by raised marble platforms on which steamed customers would have once reclined. It remains a working bath with some of the inner chambers kept heated and suitably humid. It's open daily from 11 am to 5 pm for women only and from 7 pm onwards for men and costs E£10. A massage is E£15.

There are also two working hammams on Bayn al-Qasryn: **Hammam an-Nahassin**, a men-only hammam just off to the side from the hospital part of the Qalaun complex; and **Hammam as-Sultan**, just north of the Mausoleum of Barquq, opposite a shop signposted 'Saad al-Khawanky'. ■

The Blue Mosque

More correctly known as the Mosque of Aqsunqur, this building gets its more popular name from the combination of blue-grey marble on the exterior and the flowery tiling on the interior. The tiles, imported from Syria, were added in 1652 by a Turkish governor, Ibrahim Agha, but the original and much plainer structure dates from 1347. The minaret affords an excellent view of the Citadel, while over to the east, just behind the mosque, you can see the remains of Salah ad-Din's city walls, now largely covered with rubbish and the detritus of collapsed buildings. Admission to the mosque costs E£6.

From this mosque it's about another 400m up the slightly inclining street – here known as Sharia Bab al-Wazir – to the Citadel.

THE CITADEL (Map 9)

Sprawling over a limestone spur on the eastern edge of the city the Citadel (Al-Qalaa) was home to Egypt's rulers for some 700 years. Their legacy is a collection of three very different mosques, several palaces housing some fairly indifferent museums,

and some impressive fortifications offering superb panoramas of the city.

Salah ad-Din began building the Citadel in 1176 to fortify the city against the threat of the Crusaders, who were rampaging through Palestine. His son Al-Kamil subsequently strengthened the fortifications by enlarging some of the existing towers and adding new ones. Following the overthrow of Salah ad-Din's Ayyubid dynasty, the Mamluks took over the Citadel, adding sumptuous palaces and harems, and extending the walls south to embrace a royal polo field and a stockade where 2000 cattle were kept.

Under the Ottomans (1517-1798) the fortress was extended westwards and a new main gate, the Bab al-Azab, was added, but the Mamluk palaces were allowed to deteriorate. Even so, when Napoleon's French expedition took control of the Citadel in 1798, the emperor's savants regarded these buildings as some of the finest Islamic monuments in Cairo. Which didn't stop Mohammed Ali, who rose to power when the French left, demolishing them. The only Mamluk structure left standing was one

THINGS TO SEE & DO

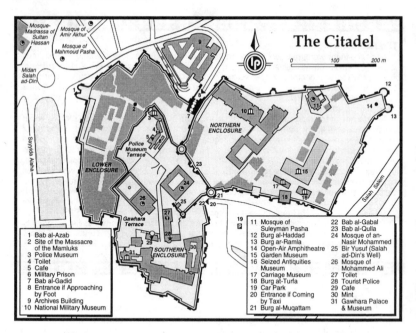

The Citadel

1	Bab al-Azab	11	Mosque of
2	Site of the Massacre		Suleyman Pasha
	of the Mamluks	12	Burg al-Haddad
3	Police Museum	13	Burg ar-Ramla
4	Toilet	14	Open-Air Amphitheatre
5	Cafe	15	Garden Museum
6	Military Prison	16	Seized Antiquities
7	Bab al-Gadid		Museum
8	Entrance if Approaching	17	Carriage Museum
	by Foot	18	Burg at-Turfa
9	Archives Building	19	Car Park
10	National Military Museum	20	Entrance if Coming
			by Taxi
		21	Burg al-Muqattam
22	Bab al-Gabal		
23	Bab al-Qulla		
24	Mosque of an-		
	Nasir Mohammed		
25	Bir Yusuf (Salah		
	ad-Din's Well)		
26	Mosque of		
	Mohammed Ali		
27	Toilet		
28	Tourist Police		
29	Cafe		
30	Mint		
31	Gawhara Palace		
	& Museum		

mosque, which was used as a stable. He completely remodelled the rest of the Citadel and crowned it with the Turkish-style mosque that currently dominates Cairo's eastern skyline.

After Mohammed Ali's grandson and heir Ismail moved the royal presence out of the Citadel, it was used as a military garrison. The British Army was barracked here in WWII to be replaced by Egyptian soldiers after 1952. The soldiers still have a small foothold but the Citadel has now almost entirely been given over to the tourists.

Anyone interested in knowing more should pick up William Lyster's *The Citadel – A Guide* or a map called *The Citadel to Ibn Tulun* published by SPARE; both are widely available in Cairo's bookshops.

The Citadel is divided into the Lower, Southern and Northern enclosures. Entrance is either from the midan below the Citadel – in which case walk up the hill with the walls on your right and loop around to the Bab al-Gadid (New Gate) – or from the car park at the back, which is where taxis often drop people off, and into the southern enclosure via the Bab al-Gabal (Gate of the Mountain).

The Citadel is open daily from 8 am to 5 pm (winter) or 6 pm (summer), but the museums close at 4.30 pm. Admission is E£20.

Lower Enclosure

Entered through the tunnel of the Bab al-Gadid (built by Mohammed Ali), the Lower Enclosure is closed to the public who are supposed to proceed straight ahead, through a second gate into the Southern Enclosure. Off to the right, down the slope and round the corner is a gully-like road with sheer rock sides – this is the site of Mohammed Ali's infamous massacre of the Mamluks (see the boxed text on the facing page).

Southern Enclosure

This is the main tourist area, presided over by the **Mosque of Mohammed Ali**. Mod-

The Massacre of the Mamluks

In addition to effacing almost all of the Mamluk structures from the Citadel, Mohammed Ali also had a damn good try at effacing the Mamluks themselves.

On 1 March 1811 he invited 500 Mamluk leaders to attend a grand day of feasting and revelry at the Citadel in honour of his son's imminent departure for Mecca. When the feasting was over, the Mamluks mounted their lavishly decorated horses and were led in procession down a narrow high-sided defile (below the Police Museum) towards the Bab al-Azab. But as they approached the Bab, the great gates swung closed before them. Gunfire rained down from above. After the scything fusillades, Mohammed Ali's soldiers waded in with swords and axes to finish the job. Not one Mamluk escaped alive. The Citadel 'looked like a slaughterhouse' according to a contemporary account.

There is a popular legend that tells of how one Mamluk survived by jumping his horse over the Citadel walls, but in fact the character in question saved his life by not turning up for the feast that bloody day. ■

elled along classic Turkish lines, this mosque took 18 years to build (1830-48) and then the domes had to be demolished and rebuilt later. It's a building that has never found much favour with those who have written about Cairo and has been variously described as being unimaginative, lacking in grace and resembling a great toad. In 1873 Amelia Edwards, author of *A Thousand Miles up the Nile*, noted that the interior was carpeted and 'hung with innumerable cut-glass chandeliers so that it looks like a huge vulgar dining room from which the furniture has been cleared out for dancing.' Oblivious to the criticism, the mosque's patron Mohammed Ali lies in the marble tomb on the right as you enter. Note the chintzy clock in the central courtyard; this was a gift from King Louis-Philippe of France (in thanks for the Pharaonic obelisk that adorns the Place de la Concorde in Paris) that was damaged on delivery and has yet to be repaired.

Dwarfed by the ungainly bulk of Mohammed Ali's mosque, the **Mosque of an-Nasir Mohammed** (1318) is the Citadel's sole surviving Mamluk structure. The interior is a little sparse because the Ottoman sultan Selim I had it stripped of its marble, but the twisted finials of the minarets are interesting in that they are covered with glazed tiles – something rarely seen in Egyptian mosques. The artisan responsible was from Tabriz (now in north-western Iran) which attests to the close commercial links between Persia and Mamluk Egypt. There's an admission fee of E£6.

Facing the entrance of the An-Nasir Mohammed mosque is a mock Gothic gateway leading out onto a terrace that has superb **views** across Islamic Cairo to the tower blocks of Downtown and, on a clear day, the Pyramids at Giza. The **Police Museum**, at the northern end of the terrace, has an intriguing Assassination Room, with text and photos telling the stories of the shooting of British sirdar (commander in chief of the Egyptian Army) Sir Lee Stack and the attempt on President Nasser's life. Curiously, the somewhat more successful assassination of Sadat fails to get a mention.

South of Mohammed Ali's mosque is another terrace with good views; this terrace leads to the disappointing **Gawhara Palace & Museum**. The Gawhara (or Jewel) was where Mohammed Ali resided and received guests, and its rooms have been reconstructed and filled with costumed dummies in a lacklustre attempt to evoke 19th century court life.

Northern Enclosure

Entrance to the Northern Enclosure is through the 16th century Bab al-Qulla, which faces the side of the An-Nasir Mohammed mosque. This brings you through into a large area of lawn which, at its centre, contains a replica of the equine statue of Ibrahim that stands in Midan Opera. Beyond the statue and the motley assortment of tanks and planes remaindered from the Arab-Israeli wars is Mohammed Ali's one-time Harem Palace, now the **National Military**

Museum. It's largely devoted to displays of ceremonial garb, but on the top floor is an excellent scale model of the Citadel.

East of the lawns a narrow road leads to a further part of the enclosure for which there's a separate E£20 admission charge. There's little to justify the extra money. The **Carriage Museum** contains a small collection of 19th century horse-drawn carriages which might occupy 10 minutes of your time, while one building east is the pointless **Seized Antiquities Museum** (signposted in Arabic only) which houses a random and unconnected assortment of sarcophagi, jewellery, icons, and other antiquities confiscated from would-be smugglers.

For devotees of Islamic architecture, it may be worth paying the extra charge to visit the **Mosque of Suleyman Pasha** (1528), a beautiful little Ottoman-era structure topped by a cluster of domes. The painted woodwork inside has been lovingly restored over the past few years by a local art student. From a point just behind the mosque it may still be possible to get up onto the wall ramparts and walk east towards the **Burg al-Haddad** (Blacksmith's Tower). If the way is now blocked, walk across the new, hideous, and completely useless, concrete 'amphitheatre' (this is the reason you have to pay that extra E£20) towards the tower and its companion, the **Burg ar-Ramla** (Sand Tower). These are two of Salah ad-Din's towers that were subsequently enlarged by his son Al-Kamil; they can be entered at ground level. Although we don't say that it is officially permitted, it is still physically possible to walk either through the walls or along the ramparts right around to the **Burg at-Turfa** (Masterpiece Tower).

Getting to/from the Citadel

It is a good 3km walk from Downtown to the Citadel. From Midan Ataba go straight down Sharia Mohammed Ali, while from Midan Tahrir the best route is via Midan Falaki to Midan Bab al-Khalq and then down Mohammed Ali. Either way, it's at least a 45 minute walk. Bus No 174 from Midan Ramses passes through Midan Salah ad-Din in front of the Citadel as does bus No 173 which

starts and terminates at Midan Falaki. Bus No 905 operates between the Citadel and the Pyramids. Bus No 404 leaves from Midan Ataba passes the Citadel and goes on to Midan Tahrir. Bus Nos 57 and 951 go to Midan Ataba and the No 54 minibus travels to Midan Tahrir.

AROUND THE CITADEL (Maps 8 & 9)

Anyone visiting the Citadel should also make time for the Mosque-Madrassa of Sultan Hassan, one of Cairo's most awesome pieces of monumental medieval Islamic architecture. The backstreets around this area are also filled with many smaller monuments which, while not justifying a trip on their own, make worthwhile detours. For instance, anyone walking to/from the Citadel along Sharia Mohammed Ali is strongly advised to swing by the Madrassa of Sunqur Sadi (mentioned later in this section) and it's also worth halting at the Sabil-Kuttab of Qaitbey to take a look at the intricate marble inlay.

The scruffy area that lies between the Citadel and the Sultan Hassan mosque, which these days is called Midan Salah ad-Din (or sometimes Midan al-Qalaa – which is awkward to pronounce as the 'q' isn't sounded), used to be called Midan ar-Ramla, the Sandy Square, and was a parade and polo ground in the time of the Mamluks.

Mosque-Madrassa of Sultan Hassan

Experts and interested amateurs alike rate this enormous mosque-madrassa as the finest piece of early Mamluk architecture in Cairo. Sultan Hassan took the throne in 1347, the same year that Cairo was decimated by the Black Death. Up to 10,000 people were reckoned to be dying each day. The money left behind by the rich went into the coffers of the sultan and with it he undertook the building of his mosque-madrassa. Even so, it nearly bankrupted the state. It took seven years to complete (1356-63) but the unfortunate sultan was murdered in 1362 and never saw it finished.

Planned as a mosque and madrassa, each of the four iwans surrounding the central court was a classroom devoted to one of the four main schools of Sunni Islam. Long chains which once held oil lamps still hang from the ceilings. At the rear of the eastern iwan is an especially beautiful *mihrab* (niche indicating the direction of Mecca) which is flanked by stolen Crusader columns; to the right is the bronze door which leads through to the sultan's mausoleum.

Notice that the minarets are of unequal height. The southernmost of the two is the second highest in Cairo (68m), after that of the new Al-Fath Mosque near Ramses station, and it was originally matched by a twin, but that collapsed in 1659 and was replaced by the one you see today.

Try to visit this place in the morning when the sun lights up the mausoleum portion of the mosque; the effect is quite eerie. The mosque is open daily from 8 am to 5 pm (6 pm in summer). Entrance is E£12 and the ticket office is at the rear of the mosque.

Mosque of ar-Rifai

This 19th century imitation of a Mamluk-style mosque is separated by a narrow alleyway from Sultan Hassan. The dowager princess Khushyar, mother of the khedive Ismail, had the mosque built in 1869 (although it was not completed until 1912) to serve as a tomb for herself, her descendants and future khedives. Members of modern Egypt's royal family, including Ismail and King Farouk, are buried here – as is the Shah of Iran. The shah sought asylum in Egypt in 1979 and, after his death in 1980, his casket was paraded through the streets of Cairo from the Abdin Palace to the mosque with his family, President Sadat and Richard Nixon leading the cortege.

The Mamluk-inspired motifs that decorate the interior were designed by European architect Max Herz who also designed the Museum of Islamic Art and the synagogue on Sharia Adly, Downtown. Opening hours and tickets prices are the same as for the Mosque-Madrassa of Sultan Hassan. Baksheesh is required to view the tombs of the royals, which lie off to the left of the entrance.

Other Mosques on Midan Salah ad-Din

Directly in front of the Ar-Rifai mosque is the **Mosque of Amir Akhur** a building of the late Mamluk era, as is signified by the heavy use of *ablaq* (banding of different coloured stone) and the double finial on the minaret – and the date above the doorway. There are good photographic opportunities of the Sultan Hassan and Ar-Rifai mosques from its minaret. Directly behind, down the little alley beside the mosque, is an **18th century house** that was lived in by the internationally renowned architect – and favourite of Britain's Prince Charles – Hassan Fathy. He died in the early 1990s and ever since there has been talk of turning the house into a memorial to his life and work, but nothing has happened to date.

The little mosque closest to the middle of the midan is the Ottoman **Mosque of Mahmoud Pasha** (1567). Although it has the typically Mamluk striped stonework, it also has a giveaway Turkish-style pencil minaret.

Madrassa of Sunqur Sadi

Also known locally as Hassan Sadaqa (after a local sheikh), this 1321 complex has some wonderful carved stucco (easily visible from the street) decorating its minaret and dome. In the 19th century, an order of Mevlevi dervishes (known as whirling dervishes in the west) extended the madrassa to include a hostel and theatre in which to perform their zikr (the dancing, chanting and swaying carried out to achieve oneness with God). Although the madrassa is in a terrible state, with its foundations being undermined by rising ground water, the dervish theatre has been restored by an Italian team. Go through the door on the right of the facade which leads into a small courtyard garden; there is always someone around who will open up the theatre for some baksheesh. From the theatre floor you can see down into the madrassa to the tomb of Hassan Sadaqa.

The madrassa is on Sharia Suyufiya: from the back of Sultan Hassan walk north along Sharia Mohammed Ali and take the first left, then left again at the T-junction.

Sharia Saliba

The Citadel has always contained a jail or two but as you can't have emaciated inmates upsetting the tourists, these days the prison is outside the walls in the triangular white building on the south-west corner of Midan Salah ad-Din. It's necessary to pass by the row of barred windows to enter Sharia Saliba which (under the name Abdel Meguid) runs up to Midan Sayyida Zeinab, passing another of Cairo's must-see monuments on the way – the Mosque of ibn Tulun.

Just past the prison, on the left, is the 15th century **Sabil-Kuttab of Qaitbey**. It's in poor condition but under all the grime it's still possible to make out the intricate inlaid marble decoration on the western facade. A short distance further to the west the street passes between the two sentinels – **Mosque of Sheikhu** on the right and the **Khanqah of Sheikhu** on the left. These buildings date from 1349 and 1355, respectively, and despite being in very bad shape, they are both still in use. Beyond the Sheikhu complex Saliba intersects with Sharia Suyufiya; turning right will take you up to the Madrassa of Sunqur Sadi and then on to Sharia Mohammed Ali, while continuing straight along Saliba brings you after a further 200m to the huge Ibn Tulun mosque.

SAYYIDA ZEINAB & IBN TULUN (Map 8)

The district of Sayyida Zeinab (St Zeinab), centred on the midan of the same name, commemorates the sister of the Prophet's grandson Hussein who, legend has it, was with him at the battle of Kerbala when he fell. She's buried in the **Mosque of Sayyida Zeinab** which in its present incarnation dates from 1885. Non-Muslims are not allowed inside.

On the north side of the midan, across from the Sayyida Zeinab mosque, is the garish **Sabil-Kuttab of Sultan Mustafa**, an Ottoman building that makes much use of coloured marble. If you take the side street squeezed down the west side of this building, you pass a good late-night kebab place; turn left here and follow the street around to the right, then take another right through an arch,

which brings you to **Beit as-Sennari**. This 18th century house was one of two requisitioned by Napoleon in 1798 for his Institut de l'Egypte, an academic centre composed of 100 scientists, scholars and artists brought to make the first European study of Egypt, which was later published as the *Description de l'Egypte*. Beit as-Sennari housed the artists and painters – their work can be seen in a recently reprinted edition of the *Description* published internationally by Taschen. At the time of writing the house was undergoing restoration (under the direction of the French) but by now it should have reopened as an arts and crafts centre.

Mosque of ibn Tulun

The best way to reach this mosque, possibly *the* most impressive medieval monument in Cairo (especially when taken in tandem with the Gayer-Anderson House next door), is to take a taxi to Midan Sayyida Zeinab and from there walk north-east along Port Said (Bur Said) for about 200m then turn right down Sharia Qadry. This way your first sight of Ibn Tulun will be of the great spiralling minaret looming up above a rabble of housing at the head of the street. Bear left at the junction, with the 14th century Mosque of Sarghatmish on your right, and then follow the rucked, unsurfaced road up to the right. This takes you along one of the mosque's outer walls topped with unique paper-doll cut-out crenellations – the entrance is through the last of the six great gates, made large enough to admit mounted riders.

Ibn Tulun was sent to rule Cairo in the 9th century by the Abbasid caliph of Baghdad. He had the mosque built between 876 and 879, making it the city's oldest intact functioning Islamic monument. It's quite unlike any other mosque in Cairo mainly because the inspiration is almost wholly Iraqi – the closest thing to it are the ancient mosques of Samarra.

To his original Iraqi model, Ibn Tulun added some innovations of his own. According to architectural historians this is the first structure to use the pointed arch – a good 200 years before Christianity adopted it for the

European Gothic arch. Constructed entirely of mud-brick and timber, the mosque covers six and a half acres in area, large enough for the whole community to gather in for Friday prayers. Although the mosque is still in use, these days the congregation is much more modest and is usually accommodated in just the south-eastern arcaded sanctuary. Notice the wooden band inscribed with Quranic verses that runs just under the ceiling – it goes all the way around the mosque and is 2km in length.

After wandering around the massive courtyard, you should climb the spiral minaret – reached from the outer, moat-like courtyard which, although originally created to keep the secular city at a distance, was at one time filled with shops and stalls. The top of the minaret is the best place to appreciate the grandeur and geometric simplicity of the mosque, and the views of the Citadel to the east and Cairo in general are magnificent.

Opening hours for the mosque and minaret are from 8 am to 6 pm; admission is E£6, plus baksheesh for slippers to put over your shoes in the mosque (unless you just want to take your shoes off).

Gayer-Anderson Museum
Another must-see, this museum is almost an annexe of the Ibn Tulun mosque, and can be reached from the outer court through a gateway to the south of the main entrance.

Also sometimes called Beit al-Kretliya (House of the Cretan Woman), the museum is actually two 16th century houses joined together. It gets its current name from a British major, John Gayer-Anderson, who restored and furnished the houses between 1935 and 1942.

The attraction of the museum is not the exhibits themselves but the houses, their puzzle of rooms and the décor. There's a Persian room with exquisite tiling and a Damascus room with its walls and ceiling patterned with lacquer and gold. There's also an enchanting mashrabiyya gallery that looks down upon Cairo's most magnificent *qa'a* (reception room) with a central marble fountain, decorated ceiling beams and carpet

covered alcoves. It is a complete Orientalist fantasy – which is why it provided such a suitable set for a James Bond rendezvous (see the boxed text 'Cairo in the Movies' in the Facts about Cairo chapter).

There are some great legends connected with the house, particularly concerning the well around which it was built (it's still there under an arch in the far right-hand side of the courtyard). This well is said to give access to the underground palaces of Sultan al-Watawit, ruler of the bats and king of the djinn.

Hours are 8 am to 4 pm daily, but the museum closes from noon to 1 pm on Friday. Admission is E£16, or E£8 for students. Those with a camera/video must pay another E£10/25.

On leaving Ibn Tulun and the Gayer-Anderson, immediately across the street is the Khan Misr Touloun, a good handicrafts emporium – see the Arts & Crafts section in the Shopping chapter for more information. You can turn left and retrace your steps back to Midan Sayyida Zeinab (it's actually quicker to stick on Sharia Abdel Meguid rather than go via Qadry), or turn right, then left at the T-junction, then right again onto Sharia al-Khalifa where, after about 300m, you will come to the Mausoleum of Shagaret ad-Durr on the left.

Mausoleum of Shagaret ad-Durr
Built in 1250, this is a small simple tomb, surrounded by garbage, which has Byzantine glass mosaics gracing its prayer niche. The most interesting thing about this place, however, is the story of the woman whose remains are entombed here (see the boxed text 'Shagaret ad-Durr' over the page).

About 100m south of the mausoleum a street branches off to the east; this leads to the **Mosque of Sayyida Aisha**, built in 1762 and pictured on the 25 pt note, which stands just off Sharia Salah Salem, the highway that connects the Corniche with Heliopolis. Running alongside Salah Salem is the **Aqueduct of an-Nasir Mohammed** built in the 14th century to supply the Citadel with water pumped from the Nile. Unused for centuries,

Shagaret ad-Durr

Shagaret ad-Durr, whose name means Tree of Pearls, was a slave of Turkish origin who managed, albeit briefly, to become the only female Muslim sovereign in Egyptian history in 1250 AD. Her husband Salih Ayyub, the last ruler of the Ayyubid dynasty, died of cancer while the Frankish soldiers of the 7th Crusade were occupying Damietta in the Nile Delta and getting ready to move on Cairo. Ayyub's son was off fighting in Iraq, and so in order to preserve the throne for him Shagaret ad-Durr hid Ayyub's corpse and for three months managed to pretend that Ayyub was still alive and passing on orders to his generals through her. When the son returned to receive his inheritance, he was assassinated by a rival for the throne. Shagaret ad-Durr herself then assumed the throne.

To forestall Islamic prejudice against the idea of a woman ruler, she married her Mamluk lover Aybek, the leader of her slave warriors, and ruled through him. Looking for a way to strengthen his own position, her husband decided on a strategic second marriage to the daughter of a powerful Syrian. Shagaret ad-Durr put an end to that by having him murdered in his bath. She offered to marry the new chief Mamluk but, probably wisely, he had her imprisoned instead. The son of Aybek by a former marriage became the next sultan and, as a suitable punishment, he handed Shagaret ad-Durr over to his mother who had her beaten to death with wooden bath-clogs. Her bloody corpse was thrown over the Citadel walls as food for the dogs and what they left was collected up and entombed in the small mausoleum Shagaret ad-Durr had built for herself during her brief 80 day reign. ■

the aqueduct is still largely intact and if you follow it west you'll hit the Nile opposite Manial, just south of the Qasr al-Ainy Hospital. East of Salah Salem is the Southern Cemetery.

NORTHERN CEMETERY (Maps 1 & 9)

The Northern Cemetery is one half of a vast necropolis inhabited by hundreds of thousands of Cairenes, both dead and alive, and is popularly known as the City of the Dead. It began as an area of desert outside the city walls which offered the Mamluk sultans and emirs the unlimited building space denied them in the already densely packed city.

The vast mausoleum complexes they built were more than just tombs, they were also meant as places for entertaining. This is part of an Egyptian tradition which has its roots in Pharaonic times – holiday picnicking among the graves. Even the humblest of family tombs were designed to include a room where visitors could stay overnight. Naturally, the city's homeless took to squatting in the tombs – not a new phenomenon, this has been going on since the 14th century – leading to the situation today where the living and dead coexist comfortably side by side. In some tomb-houses cenotaphs serve as tables and washing is strung between headstones. The municipality has run in water, gas and electricity, and there's a local police station and even a post office. On Fridays and holidays visitors flock here to picnic and pay their respects to the dead.

The easiest way to get to the Northern Cemetery is to walk east along Sharia al-Azhar from Hussein. As you breast the top of the hill bear right, under the overpass and straight on along the dusty road between the tombs. Follow this road to the left then right. You'll pass by a large crumbling domed tomb off to your left and then about 100m beyond a narrow lane goes off to the left passing under a stone archway. This stone archway is the gate to the former compound of Qaitbey whose splendid mosque is immediately ahead.

Mosque of Qaitbey

Completed in 1474 and rated as one of the most exquisite buildings in Cairo, Qaitbey's mosque is the one that is featured on the E£1 note.

Sultan Qaitbey, a prolific builder, was the last Mamluk leader with any real power in Egypt. He ruled for 28 years and, though he was as ruthless as the Mamluk sultans before him, he had a reputation for fairness. He was also something of an aesthete.

The interior of his mosque has four iwans around a central court that is suffused with light from large, lattice-screened windows. It's one of the most pleasant places in Cairo to sit a while and relax. The adjacent tomb chamber contains the cenotaphs of Qaitbey and his two sisters, as well as two stones which supposedly bear the footprints of the Prophet. The true glory, however, is above in the interlaced star and floral carving adorning the stone dome, which in its intricacy and delicacy was never surpassed here in Cairo or anywhere else in the Islamic world – climb the minaret for the best view. Admission is E£6 (E£3 for students).

From Qaitbey cross the square and continue north. The cemetery has an almost village-like feel with small stores and street sellers, and sandy paths pecked by chickens and nosed around by goats. After about 250m the street widens out and on the left a stone wall encloses a large area of rubble-strewn ground that was formerly the complex of Sultan Ashraf Barsbey.

Complex of Sultan Ashraf Barsbey

This grouping originally combined a khanqah, two sabils, two zawiyas and a hostel. The hostel is the long, partially built facade before the Khanqah of Barsbey, the only remaining complete structure, which was finished in 1432. Though not as sophisticated as the one topping Qaitbey, the dome here is carved with a beautiful star pattern. Inside, there is some fine marble flooring and a beautiful *minbar* (pulpit) inlaid with ivory. Look for the guard or have one of the children in the area find him – he'll let you in for baksheesh. The khanqah is generally open from 9 am to 5 pm.

The two small mausoleums to the north of the khanqah are put to excellent use as goalposts by the local boys.

Khanqah-Mausoleum of ibn Barquq

Ibn means 'son of', and this is the mausoleum of Farag, son of Barquq, whose great madrassa & mausoleum stands on Bayn al-Qasryn at the heart of Islamic Cairo. Barquq's tomb is in the small mausoleum to the north of the complex. Completed in 1411, the khanqah is an imposing fortress-like building with high, sheer facades, and twin minarets and domes. If you go through into the interior courtyard you can see the small monastic cells off the arcades. There's a tomb chamber under each dome, one for the women, one for the men. Both ceilings have been repainted in recent years and look great. It's also possible to get up onto the roof and climb the minarets. The area of surrounding greenery is a cemetery for some of the many Egyptians killed in the 1967 Arab-Israeli war. The khanqah is open from 8 am to 5 pm; admission is E£6.

Back to Hussein

North of Ibn Barquq are two large adjacent complexes, the **Mosque of Amir Qurqumas** (1507) and the **Khanqah of Sultan Inal** (1456), both of which have been the subject of extensive restoration work by a Polish team and neither of which at present are accessible to the public.

Rather than just retracing your steps, to get back to Hussein from Ibn Barquq, walk straight ahead from the entrance, passing the post office on your left, until you come to a small, elongated mausoleum; turn left immediately after this and a walk of a straight kilometre will bring you back to the road leading to the underpass.

SOUTHERN CEMETERY (Map 1)

The Northern and Southern cemeteries are two completely separate entities which developed at different times and are physically divided by the rocky outcrop on which the Citadel is built. The Southern Cemetery is the older of the two, with its beginnings in the Fatimid era – a time before the grand tradition of funerary architecture had taken hold. It's also less accessible (see Map 1) and doesn't contain as much to see, neither does

THINGS TO SEE & DO

it possess the almost rural charm that makes the Northern Cemetery such a pleasure to explore. However, if you have the time, then it is worth taking the trouble to visit the Mausoleum of Imam ash-Shafi, one of Cairo's most venerated shrines.

On Friday morning from about 6 to 11 am the Southern Cemetery is host to a sprawling **animal and bric-a-brac market**. It's mainly birds that are on sale – budgerigars, cockatiels, canaries and finches – but there are also tortoises, guinea pigs, dogs and snakes. For anybody who actually cares about animals it's a grim place. To get there, head south from the Citadel along the main Maadi highway; the market is off to your right after about a kilometre.

Mausoleum of Imam ash-Shafi

Imam ash-Shafi, a descendant of an uncle of the Prophet, was the founder of the Shafiite sect, one of the four major schools of Sunni Islam. Regarded as one of the great Muslim saints, he died in 820 AD. In the 12th century Salah ad-Din founded the first mausoleum on the site of the Imam's grave. The complex has been added to over the centuries – the neighbouring mosque dates from 1891 – but the teak cenotaph in the tomb is original. Around this cenotaph visiting pilgrims circumambulate, while tearful black-robed women are often pressed against the lattice screen whispering implorations to the long-dead sheikh.

Non-Muslims are permitted to enter (men and women through separate doorways) and there is no admission fee, but baksheesh will be requested.

The mausoleum is 2km south of Midan Salah ad-Din. To get there, walk south along Sharia Sayyida Aisha to Salah Salem. Across the junction a dusty road continues and almost immediately forks – take the right-hand branch and the mausoleum is about 1km farther on, easily identifiable by its domed lead roof, topped by a small copper boat.

Haush al-Basha

Right behind Imam ash-Shafi is the Haush al-Basha complex, constructed by Mohammed Ali in 1820 as his family mausoleum – though he had himself buried in his mosque at the Citadel. From outside it's drab, dull and seriously dilapidated but inside it's a riot. 'All the tombs of Mohammed Ali's family are in deplorable taste – rococo, Canova, Europo-Oriental, appointed and festooned like cabarets, with little ballroom chandeliers', wrote Gustave Flaubert who visited in December 1849. The chandeliers are gone but the ceilings are still painted like circus tents, while the cenotaphs still look as though they've been decorated by kids in time for Christmas.

To get to the Haush al-Basha take the first left after leaving the Imam ash-Shafi compound and then left again at the junction and it's 50m ahead on the left. Admission is E£10.

Old Cairo

Broadly speaking, Old Cairo (known in Egyptian as Masr al-Qadima, with a glottal stop 'q') incorporates the whole area south of Garden City and Sayyida Zeinab down to the quarter known to foreigners as Coptic Cairo (see Map 11). Most people visiting this area head straight to the latter, from where it is possible to explore sights further to the north-east, such as the Mosque of Amr ibn al-As and the archaeological site of ancient Fustat. The Early Islamic-era Nilometer on the island of Rhoda is also best visited from Coptic Cairo.

This is a very traditional part of Cairo and the appropriate dress is essential. Visitors of either sex wearing shorts or having bare shoulders will not be allowed into churches or mosques.

Getting There & Away

By far the easiest way of getting down to Old Cairo is by metro: Mari Girgis station is right outside the Coptic compound. The ride costs 30 pt from Midan Tahrir and the trains run every few minutes. There are buses running between Tahrir and Old Cairo but they are

Old Cairo Walking Tour

There is a good circular tour that can be made of Old Cairo which will take about three to four hours depending on the length of time spent at the various sites. Start by taking either the metro or the river bus down to **Coptic Cairo** where we recommend you visit the Coptic Museum, the Hanging Church, the Church of St Sergius and the Ben Ezra Synagogue. From Ben Ezra walk out of the rear entrance of the compound and turn left; this will take you to Sharia Ain as-Sirah, the road running alongside Fustat. If you want to visit the archaeological site turn right, otherwise head left, passing by all the shanty pottery workshops, and turn right at the junction and head for the **Mosque of Amr ibn al-As**.

If you have already visited any of Cairo's other large congregational mosques like Ibn Tulun, Al-Hakim or Al-Azhar, then the Mosque of Amr is totally missable. Continue along the main road past Amr and take the next left, Sharia Ali Salem. About 100m along on the right is a small wooden doorway that leads to a narrow cobbled alley; down this alley is the **Monastery of St Mercurius**. The monastery is dedicated to a martyred Roman legionary, and its walled compound contains three churches, the oldest of which is the Church of St Mercurius which in its present form dates back to 1176. Attached to the church is a crypt where the 14th century ascetic St Barsum the Naked lived with a snake.

The metro line runs beside the monastery – follow this south to the first footbridge. Cross over the footbridge and continue south on the other side of the tracks, taking the first right and then the second left. This should bring you into a large square at the centre of which, in a bedraggled garden, is a beautiful little structure of brick and cast iron – the **Tomb of Suleyman al-Faransawi**. Suleyman 'the Frenchman' was born Joseph Seves in Lyon. He fought in Napoleon's army but after the collapse of the republic he came to Egypt where he led Mohammed Ali's army against the Sultan in Constantinople and became one of the most powerful men in Egypt. The area surrounding the tomb, now occupied by shops and houses, was once the site of Suleyman's palace and gardens. All that remains is the tomb. Designed by Carl von Diebitsch, the German architect responsible for the ornate iron arcades at the Cairo Marriott, Al-Faransawi's final resting place is today badly neglected and stands in desperate need of restoration.

From the tomb you can see the Nile two blocks to the west. The bridge over to Rhoda and the **Nilometer** is just a short walk away or you can backtrack to the metro line and push through the market down to the Mari Girgis station less than half a kilometre away. ■

incredibly crowded. However, the bus trip back to Tahrir isn't as bad as you can get on at the terminal, beside the Amr ibn al-As mosque, before the bus has had a chance to fill up.

The slow way, but the most pleasant if you have the time, is to get a river bus from the Maspero terminal near the Radio & Television building, just north of the Ramses Hilton. Check it's going to Masr al-Qadima as not all do (see the Getting Around chapter for route details). The ride takes about 50 minutes and costs 25 pt. The last boat back to Maspero leaves at 4.15 pm. From the landing at Old Cairo cross the Corniche and head down the street with the Marlboro-emblazoned shop on the corner; at the end of the street turn left and walk straight along Athar an-Nabi for about 250m until you come to the footbridge over the metro line.

COPTIC CAIRO (Map 11)

Coptic Cairo is the heartland of Egypt's Christian community, as well as being the oldest part of modern-day Cairo. Seemingly oblivious to the growth and chaos which it has spawned, the tightly walled enclave remains a haven of tranquillity and peace.

Archaeologists claim that there was a small Nile-side settlement on this site as far back as the 6th century BC on which the Romans later established a fortress, called Babylon-in-Egypt, early in the 2nd century AD. The name Babylon is most likely a

THINGS TO SEE & DO

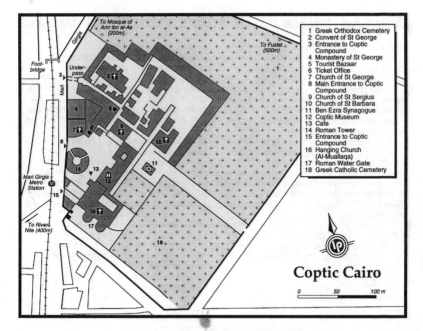

1 Greek Orthodox Cemetery
2 Convent of St George
3 Entrance to Coptic
   Compound
4 Monastery of St George
5 Tourist Bazaar
6 Ticket Office
7 Church of St George
8 Main Entrance to Coptic
   Compound
9 Church of St Sergius
10 Church of St Barbara
11 Ben Ezra Synagogue
12 Coptic Museum
13 Cafe
14 Roman Tower
15 Entrance to Coptic
   Compound
16 Hanging Church
   (Al-Muallaqa)
17 Roman Water Gate
18 Greek Catholic Cemetery

Coptic Cairo

0   50   100 m

Roman corruption of Per-hapi-en-on – Estate of the Nile god at On – a Pharaonic name for what was the former port for On (ancient Heliopolis).

Predating the arrival of Islam in Egypt, Babylon has always been a stronghold of Christianity – see the History section in the Facts about Cairo chapter. At one time there were more than 20 churches clustered within less than a square kilometre, although the number is down to only five today. They are linked by narrow cobbled alleyways that run between high stone walls, and the feel of the place is quite similar to parts of the Old City of Jerusalem. In fact, after the Jews were exiled from their holy city in 70 AD, some found refuge in Egypt and the country's oldest existing synagogue is here in Coptic Cairo.

There are two entrances to the Coptic Cairo compound: one, a sunken staircase beside the pedestrian bridge over the metro, gives access to most churches and the syna-gogue, while the other, the main entrance, is for visiting the Coptic Museum and Church of the Virgin. Eventually, when restoration work is finished, the two parts of the compound will be reconnected.

Roman Towers

The main entrance to the compound is between the remains of the two round towers of Babylon's western gate. Built in 98 AD by Emperor Trajan, these were part of the waterside battlements and at the time, before it shifted half a kilometre to the west, the Nile would have lapped up right against them. Excavations on the southern tower have revealed part of the ancient quay, several metres below street level. The Greek Orthodox Church of St George has been built on top of the northern tower.

Coptic Museum

Beyond the towers is the verdant garden of the Coptic Museum. The ticket office is on the left as you enter the garden. Founded in 1908 the museum houses Coptic art from Graeco-Roman times to the Islamic era (300 to 1000 AD) and the collection draws not just from Cairo but also the desert monasteries and Nubia. It's split into two wings, the old and the new. From the entry hall the old wing is to the right and the new to the left. In the **new wing** the exhibits (stonework, manuscripts, woodwork, glass and ceramics) are housed on two floors and arranged in chronological order in an anti-clockwise direction. Explanations are in French and English.

The rooms themselves are very much part of the attraction, adorned with elaborately painted ceilings, fountains and mashrabiyya screens. The **old wing** is even finer, unfortunately it was badly damaged by the 1992 earthquake and won't reopen until 1999. The door from the entrance hall that leads out to the old wing's courtyard is usually unlocked and you can look out; chances are a custodian will then come over and lead you across and down the stairs to the flooded **Water Gate**. This was the southern gate of Roman Babylon, on top of which the Hanging Church was built.

The museum is open from 9 am to 5 pm daily. Admission is E£16 (E£8 for students); the camera fee is E£10 or E£100 for videos.

There's a pleasant but expensive cafe in the southern part of the garden where there is also a gate leading through to the Hanging Church; if this gate is locked, go back out onto the main street running parallel to the metro and there's another entrance south of the Roman tower.

Hanging Church

Dedicated to the Virgin Mary, this church is nevertheless more popularly called the Hanging Church (Al-Muallaqa – the suspended) because it is built on top of the Water Gate of Roman Babylon. It's the most famous, the most beautiful and possibly even the oldest Christian place of worship in Cairo, dating back in all likelihood to the 4th century.

A flight of stairs leads up into an interior courtyard festooned with icons where there are also several stalls selling cassettes and videos of Coptic sermons. The interior of the church, renovated many times over the centuries, has three barrel-vaulted, woodenroofed aisles. Ivory inlaid screens hide the three altar areas, but in front of them, raised on 13 slender pillars that represent Christ and his disciples, is a fine pulpit, used only on Palm Sunday each year. One of the pillars is darker than the rest, symbolising Judas. In the baptistery off to the right a panel has been cut out of the floor through which you can look down on the Water Gate below; however, it's hard to make anything out in the gloom so also look out of the window for a good view of one of the gate's twin towers and the violently green water stagnating about its foundations.

There is no admission fee because the church is still in use. Coptic mass is held on Friday from 8 to 11 am and on Sunday from 7 to 10 am. The ancient liturgical Coptic language is still used in most of the services.

Monastery & Church of St George

Back on Sharia Mari Girgis, the first doorway north of the main entrance leads through to the Greek Orthodox Monastery & Church of St George (in Arabic he's called Mari Girgis), named for one of the most popular Christian saints in the Middle East. He was a conscript in the Roman army who was executed in 303 AD for tearing up a copy of the Emperor Diocletian's decree that forbade the practice of Christianity. There has been a church dedicated to him in Coptic Cairo since the 10th century but this particular one dates from 1909. The interior is a bit gutted from past fires, but the stained glass windows are bright and colourful. The monastery next door is closed to the public.

Convent of St George

If you descend the sunken staircase by the footbridge, then the first doorway on your left along the alleyway leads into the courtyard of the Convent of St George. The convent is closed to visitors but you can step down into the main hall and the chapel. Inside the latter is a beautiful, wooden door, almost 8m high, behind which is a small room still used for the chain-wrapping ritual which symbolises the persecution of St George during the Roman occupation. Visitors wishing to be blessed are welcome to be wrapped by the patient nuns present who will then intone the requisite prayers.

Churches of St Sergius & St Barbara
To get to St Sergius, also called Abu Serga, leave the Convent of St George by the same door you entered, turn left and walk down the lane, following it round to the right and then take a left for the church entrance. This church is supposedly built over one of the spots where the Holy Family rested after fleeing from King Herod – the crypt in question is reached by descending some steps to the right of the altar but it's been flooded for some time now. Every year, on 1 June, a special mass is held here to commemorate the event. The church is open from 8 am to 4 pm daily.

Continuing on along the alley brings you to Ben Ezra on the right and to the Church of St Barbara on the left. St Barbara's is dedicated to the saint who was beaten to death by her father for trying to convert him to Christianity. Her relics supposedly rest in a small chapel to the left of the nave.

If you walk on past the church, an iron gate on the left leads through to a large **Greek Orthodox cemetery** the peace of which is usually shattered by the shouts and cheers from a neighbouring football pitch and sports field.

Ben Ezra Synagogue
Ben Ezra (Egypt's oldest synagogue) occupies the shell of a 4th century Christian church which the Copts were forced to sell in the 9th century in order to meet the tax demands of Ibn Tulun who was indulging in a bit of mosque building (see the Islamic Cairo section earlier in this chapter). In the 12th century the synagogue was restored by

---

The Jews of Cairo
From an all-time peak of 80,000, Egypt's Jews now number no more than 200, almost all of whom are elderly women. Contemporary sources show that as far back as 1168 there were 7000 Jews, who would have formed the backbone of the congregation at the Ben Ezra synagogue, living in Fustat. We know this for sure because of an amazing 19th century discovery. According to Jewish tradition any document that might bear the name of God could not be idly discarded and instead would be deposited in a special chamber known as a *geniza*. Renovations at Ben Ezra in the 1890s unearthed such a cache containing more than 10,000 documents that dated back to the earliest years of the synagogue. Included were items such as wills, bills of sale, letters of credit and even laundry lists, all of which contributed enormously to historians' knowledge of day-to-day life in medieval Cairo. The geniza documents are now scattered throughout academic institutions, libraries and museums worldwide.

As Cairo extended north so did the Jewish community and in Mamluk times there was a Jewish quarter, Haret al-Yahud, in the vicinity of the Al-Azhar mosque. The first four decades of this century constituted something of a golden age for Jews in Cairo as their numbers expanded and they came to play a bigger role in society and the affairs of state. Jews were responsible for the modernisation of Egypt's finances, including the founding of the national bank, the opening and running of most of the city's department stores, and major financial involvement in new urban developments.

The reversal began with the creation of Israel in 1948. Not long afterwards, the exodus received further impetus with the nationalisation that followed Nasser's seizure of power. In the present climate of media-led anti-Israeli hysteria mention of the 'J' word in connection with Cairo's history has been all but banished, but the evidence is there in Ben Ezra, Downtown's Sharia Adly synagogue, and in the Bassatine Jewish cemetery just north of the southern suburb of Maadi. ■

Abraham Ben Ezra, Rabbi of Jerusalem, from whom it takes its name. Centuries later it was allowed to fall again into disrepair until in the 1980s the American Jewish Congress stepped in to halt the rot and completely overhaul the place.

Several legends are connected with the synagogue. It is said that the temple of the prophet Jeremiah once stood on the same spot and that this is where he gathered the Jews after they fled from Nebuchadnezzar, destroyer of their Jerusalem temple. There is also a spring which is supposed to mark the place where the Pharaoh's daughter found Moses in the reeds, and where Mary drew water to wash Jesus.

FUSTAT (Map 11)

Fustat was founded in 642 AD as a garrison for the conquering armies of Amr ibn al-As. It gradually took on a more permanent aspect and became a thriving commercial city and the first Islamic capital of Egypt. Fustat was razed during the reign of the Fatimids (see History in the Facts about Cairo chapter). Under the Mamluks it became a rubbish dump and it has remained an uninhabited wasteland ever since.

The fact that Fustat has lain dormant and largely uninhabited for the 600 years since its destruction makes it one of the most important Islamic archaeological sites in the world. It was first excavated early this century and most of the finds – predominantly pottery – are on display in the Museum of Islamic Art. More recently, the excavations have been continued by an archaeological team from the American Research Centre. Although it takes enormous leaps of the imagination to make anything of the sun-baked earthen mounds and trenches, it's possible to identify traces of alleyways, houses, wells and water-pipe systems surrounded by a low wall. It costs E£6 to visit the site.

To get there from Coptic Cairo's main entrance, head north along Sharia Mari Girgis, and take the first road to the right (Sharia Ain as-Sirah), follow it for about half a kilometre until you see a large unmarked gate on

your left that opens onto a short path leading to the ruins.

Potters

Fustat has always been home to potters. The smoke you see rising across the moonscape is from kilns. Nestled beneath the smouldering mounds are hundreds of workshops turning out pots, urns, dishes and pipes for sewers and drainage. The pottery factories line the whole length of Sharia Ain as-Sirah and though they look unwelcoming the inhabitants don't mind visitors wandering around and observing. If you are looking to buy, then Sharia Mari Girgis in the area around the Mosque of Amr is lined with pottery stalls.

Mosque Of Amr ibn al-As

Although hardly any of the original structure remains, this mosque can claim direct descent from the first mosque ever built in Egypt. It was constructed in 642 AD by the victorious invader Amr (the general who conquered Egypt for Islam) and was founded on the site where he'd first pitched his tent. The original structure is said to have been made of palm trunks thatched with leaves but it was rebuilt and expanded until it reached its current size in 827. The reconstruction didn't end there and the mosque has continued to be amended and reworked until as recently as 1983. There's little of interest to see inside, although of the 200 or so columns supporting the ceiling no two are said to be the same. To the left of the entrance there's a pair of columns extremely close together which, according to a tale told to Gustave Flaubert when he visited in 1849, only a man who has never told a lie can pass between. Admission is E£6.

Beside the mosque is a bus station from which several buses run up to Midan Tahrir including Nos 134, 135, 412, 444 and 814. The fare is 25 pt.

From the Mosque If you are returning directly to town, you can either take one of the buses mentioned earlier, or you can retrace your steps to either the metro or the river bus landing. You could continue on the Old Cairo walk described earlier in this section, or you can head directly for Rhoda and the Nilometer. To get to Rhoda, walk back south to the footbridge over the metro. On the other side don't go south but head directly west along a narrow slightly wandering but essentially straight lane which will deposit you on the Corniche opposite the footbridge over to Rhoda.

RHODA & THE NILOMETER (Map 11)

Unlike the alluvial island of Gezira which was formed within the last thousand years, Rhoda is solid bedrock and was around during Pharaonic times when it was part of the territory of ancient Heliopolis. In the Roman era it was the site of a fortress, twin to that at Babylon. In the 13th century, Sultan as-Salih Ayyub quartered his Mamluk guard here and the island contained palaces, mosques, more than 50 towers and extensive gardens – the name Rhoda means 'garden' in Arabic. The place frequently pops up as an exotic setting in the tales of *The Thousand and One Nights*.

When power later shifted away from the Mamluks who lived on the island, Rhoda was abandoned and later quarried for stone. Until the middle of this century the island remained undeveloped and largely agricultural but during the post-Revolution period it experienced a building boom. Today it's an extremely drab and shabby residential district notable only for the Manial Palace Museum at the northern end and the Nilometer at the south. The distance between the two is quite substantial – a 45 minute walk at least. Manial is best visited from Garden City (see the Manial & The Palace Museum section earlier in this chapter) while the Nilometer is best reached from Old Cairo.

Nilometer

Built in the 9th century to measure the rise and fall of the Nile, the Nilometer helped predict the state of the annual harvest. If the Nile rose to 16 cubits (a cubit is about the length of a forearm) this held great promise for the crops, and people would celebrate.

The conical dome was added when the Nilometer was restored in the 19th century. The measuring device, a graduated column, is well below the level of the Nile in a paved area at the bottom of a flight of steps. The admission fee is E£6. The ticket also admits you to the neighbouring **Munasterli Palace**, built in 1851 and recently converted into an arts centre.

Gezira & Zamalek

Uninhabited until the mid-19th century, Gezira (which means 'island') was a 3.5km by 1km strip of alluvial land rising up out of the Nile opposite Bulaq. After Ismail had created his new city – modern-day Downtown – on the flood plain of the river's west bank, he built a great palace on the island and had much of it landscaped as a vast royal garden. In the early years of this century, as Cairo was experiencing a land development boom, the palace grounds were partitioned, sold off and built upon.

The island today divides almost equally into two: the southern part is largely green and leafy and retains the name Gezira (see Map 7), while the north is an upmarket residential district known as Zamalek (see Map 3).

GEZIRA (Map 7)

Gezira is best approached across the Tahrir Bridge from Midan Tahrir, which brings you to a small midan (Midan Saad Zaghloul) presided over by a statute of a stout man in a tarboosh, representing Saad Zaghloul the nationalist leader of the 1930s. To the right of the bridge is the beginning of a new Nile-side **pedestrian corniche** which will soon allow you to walk north up the shore of the island into Zamalek. Between the promenade and the main road is a narrow strip of greenery known as the **Andalusian Gardens**, a small park complete with Pharaonic obelisk that costs 50 pt to enter. Immediately south of the midan is the Casino el-Nil, a former weekly hang-out of writer Naguib Mahfouz. The road south beside the Casino leads down to the Gezira Sheraton.

Opera House & Museum of Modern Art

Immediately west of Midan Saad Zaghloul are the immaculately groomed grounds of the Opera House complex, a US$30 million complex that includes the Museum of Modern Art, the Hanagar Art Gallery, a music library, a planetarium (closed at present) and various performance spaces with modern technical equipment and superb acoustics. Opened only in 1988, the Opera House itself is a modern take on traditional Islamic designs, and was a gift from the Japanese – the inaugural kabuki performance left most Cairenes totally baffled.

Entry to the Opera House itself is only during performances but the grounds are pleasant to walk around. They contain the Museum of Modern Art (☎ 342 0592), home to a fairly limited collection of 20th century Egyptian painting, some of which is certainly worth seeing (see Art in the Facts about Cairo chapter). There are often also temporary exhibits.

The museum is open daily, except Monday, from 10 am to 1 pm and from 5 to 9.30 pm. Admission is E£10 (E£5 for students).

Mahmoud Mokhtar Museum

At the time of writing, this museum was in search of a new home and, consequently, was closed. Mokhtar (1891-1934) was the sculptor laureate of Egypt – he was responsible for Saad Zaghloul on the nearby midan and for the Mother of Egypt statue outside the entrance to the zoo. The museum's collection contains some of his lesser works. Check with the tourist office for its new location.

Cairo Tower

Legend has it that the tower, completed in 1961 and looking like a 185m-high wickerwork tube, was built as a thumb to the nose at the Americans who had given Nasser the money used for its construction to buy US arms. After the Pyramids it's now the city's most famous landmark. The view from the top is, of course, excellent – clearest in the early morning or late afternoon. There's an expensive revolving restaurant on top as well as a cheaper cafeteria. The entrance fee for the tower, if you're going to the top, is E£10 (plus E£10 for a video). Hours for the viewing area are 9 am to midnight, daily. You might find a bit of a queue at dusk.

ZAMALEK (Map 3)

Occupying the northern part of the island of Gezira, Zamalek is an attractive residential district with a continental European tinge. It has few tourist sites but it's a pleasant place to wander and an even better place to eat (Le Steak, Justine, La Piazza, L'Aubergine or Hana) or drink (L'Aubergine, Deals or the Cairo Marriott). See the Places to Eat chapter for more details.

The main street is 26th of July which cuts east-west across the island. The junction with Hassan Sabry/Brazil is the focal point of the area – there's good shopping around here, particularly at Sunny's (a supermarket on Aziz Osman that is something of an institution among Cairo's expat community), and three of the city's best newsstands are located at the crossroads. Just a couple of doors east of Hassan Sabry on 26th of July is **Simonds**, the best cafe in town at which to read your papers, if you can get a seat.

At the eastern end of 26th of July, beside the bridge over to Bulaq, is the **Akhnaton Centre of Arts** housed in a luxurious European style villa built earlier this century by an Egyptian aristocratic family. There are always several different exhibitions on, so it's worth dropping in – see Activities later in this chapter for opening hours.

Immediately south of 26th of July, overlooking the Nile is the salmon-pink **Cairo Marriott** (see the boxed text 'Cairo's Historic Hotels' in the Places to Stay chapter). It has a good bakery and an attractive garden terrace which is a good place for a beer. Behind the Cairo Marriott, on Al-Saraya al-Gezira, is the main entrance to the Gezira club, across from a beautiful little neo-Islamic villa which used to house the Mahmoud Khalil art collection before it was removed to Doqqi.

The Nile-side road on the west of the island is Sharia Umm Kolthum (formerly Sharia Gabaleyya), named after the legendary singer. When she died in 1975, the beautiful Zamalek villa in which she'd lived – which would have made a far better monument than a strip of tarmac – was hastily demolished by rapacious developers while parliament was discussing a bill to safeguard its preservation.

Lying between Sharia Umm Kolthum and Hassan Sabry is the **Fish Garden**, once part of the grounds of Ismail's Gezira Palace (now the Cairo Marriott). It's a small area of grassy hillocks and tree-shaded lovers' benches with an aquarium grotto where the fish swim (or float belly up) in tunnels that resemble bomb shelters. It's open from 9 am to 3.30 pm daily and entry costs 50 pt.

The **view** north from the 15th of May Bridge of a sweep of the Nile lined with houseboats and the Kitkat mosque in the background is beautiful.

Mohandiseen, Agouza & Doqqi

A map of Cairo in Baedecker's 1929 guide to Egypt shows nothing on the west bank other than a hospital and the road to the Pyramids. The hospital is still there, set back off the Corniche in Agouza, but it's now hemmed in on all sides by an unsightly rash of mid-rise housing blocks that shot up during the 1960s and 70s when Mohandiseen, Agouza and Doqqi were created as new suburbs for Egypt's emerging professional classes. The three districts have remained bastions of the middle classes, home largely to those families who made good during the years of Sadat's open-door policy.

Unless you happen to find concrete and traffic stimulating, the sole attraction of these areas is that they contain many of the city's better eating places. See the Places to Eat chapter for more details.

HOUSEBOATS (Map 2)

What little history there is here is on the river in the form of the **houseboats** moored off the Sharia el-Nil just north of the 15th of May Bridge. Known as *dahabiyyas*, these floating two storey wooden structures used to line the banks of the Nile all the way up from Giza to Imbaba forming an extensive waterborne neighbourhood. During the 1930s they were something of an interwar tourist attraction, especially when some of the boats were converted into casinos, music halls and bordellos. It was on one of them, owned by the belly-dancer Hekmat Fahmy, that the German spy John Eppler was arrested in 1943 (see the boxed text 'As if the Real Story isn't Enough: Cairo in Fiction' in the Facts for the Visitor chapter). Many of the houseboats continue to be rented out and they're popular with teachers at the British Council which is just a few hundred metres south down the street.

The small midan and mosque beyond the boats take their name from a famed wartime club that once existed there, the Kitkat.

The Nile-side attractions these days are a little more sedate – just the **Balloon Theatre**, a venue for farcical Egyptian plays, and the big top of the **Cairo Circus** (summers only; check with the tourist office or *Egypt Today*).

AGRICULTURAL MUSEUM (Map 6)

It sounds dull but this museum in Doqqi is actually quite fascinating, and verges on the bizarre. Apart from stuff on life in Egyptian villages, it has giant plastic fruits, glass cases packed full of stuffed birds, and a Pharaonic-era mummified bull from Memphis. The gardens are quite relaxing. There's also a more conventional **Museum of Cotton**. These two museums are off Sharia Wizaret al-Ziraa, to the west of the 6th of October Bridge. Both are open from 9 am to 2 pm, except on Monday, and admission is a mere 10 pt.

MAHMOUD KHALIL MUSEUM (Map 7)

This museum (☎ 336 2379) claims to have the Middle East's finest collection of 19th century European art. That's debatable, but it does have numerous sculptures by Rodin and a rich selection of French works by the likes of Delacroix, Gauguin, Lautrec, Monet and Pissaro. There are also some Reubens, Sisleys and a Picasso. The paintings are housed in a recently renovated villa that used to be the home of Mohammed Mahmoud Khalil, a noted politician during the 1940s, and was later taken over by Sadat as the official residence of the President of Egypt. It's on Sharia al-Giza on the border of Doqqi and Giza. The museum is open daily except Monday from 9.30 am to 6 pm; admission is a whopping E£25 (E£5 for students).

Giza

A former village on the west bank of the Nile, Giza is now a vast governorate in its own right. It stretches from the Nile 18km westwards to the Pyramids, adjoining Doqqi to the north and petering out into fields then desert to the south. To Cairenes it's best known as the site of their largest university, **Cairo University**. The plaza out in front of the domed main building is a favoured gathering point for demonstrations – more often than not against Israel whose embassy is about half a kilometre due east of here.

CAIRO ZOO (Maps 6 & 10)
Cairo's zoo has been in existence for more than 100 years – it celebrated its centennial in 1994. It was a legacy from Khedive Ismail, a part of his former Harem Gardens passed over to the state in partial settlement of his debts. The backbone of the animal collection was made up of his private menagerie. The only present-day survivors of the original gardens include a giant banyan, planted around 1871, and the light suspension bridge, built by Gustave Eiffel, that links two artificial hills.

Though bedraggled and badly lacking in funding, the zoo remains a popular excursion for local families and couples, especially on Friday and Saturday. It's not, however, a good place for anybody who cares about animals. Polar bears, for one, don't seem to cope too well with average daily temperatures of over 35°C. The zoo is near Cairo University, between Sharia Gamiat al-Qahira (Cairo University St) and Sharia al-Giza/Charles de Gaule. It's open from 9.30 am to 6 pm and admission costs 10 pt.

Across the road from the zoo is the small but well kept Al-Orman Park.

DR RAGAB'S PAPYRUS INSTITUTE (Map 7)
Dr Ragab's original Papyrus Institute is housed in a boat moored off the Corniche about a kilometre south of the Al-Galaa Bridge and Cairo Sheraton. It's very close to the University stop on the river bus route. On board you can see some displays on the ancient art of papyrus writing and painting, and you can buy some of the doctor's work. It's open from 9 am to 9 pm.

DR RAGAB'S PHARAONIC VILLAGE
For the time being (until Cinema City opens up – it's currently under construction 20km outside town) this is the city's sole shot at a Pharaonic theme park. Visitors get to float down the 'canal of mythology' and try to imagine that they've been thrown back a millennium or two. Actors and actresses in Pharaonic costume play out the fantasy by performing Pharaonic tasks. Dr Ragab is no Disney, but after paying E£40 admission (students E£20) you're probably going to be eager to encourage the illusion to work to get your money's worth. It's open from 9 am to 5 pm in winter, until 10 pm in summer. It's about 20 minutes walk south of the Giza Bridge.

PYRAMIDS RD
Pyramids Rd is known as Sharia al-Haram by the locals (even though *al-haram* means 'pyramid' and the plural, 'pyramids', is *al-ahram*). It starts just south of Midan Giza and runs more or less 10km south-west to reach the site of the ancient monuments (see the Around Cairo map on page 181). The road was laid down in the 1860s for the benefit of the Empress Eugenie, who was visiting

Egypt for the inauguration of the Suez Canal. Wayside houses and places of refreshment sprang up along the route to cater to the carriage loads of tourists that followed. These were soon joined by the nightclubs and casinos for which the Pyramids Rd has long been notorious. The most famous were burnt down in the 1972 riots but they were replaced and in the 70s the strip boomed, providing girlie entertainment for the oil-rich Arabs from the Gulf who began to flock over every summer. The Gulfies still come and Pyramids Rd is still full of dodgy nightclubs, but the shows these days are less risqué, more rip-off.

Off Pyramids Rd

Kerdassa Many of the scarves, galabeyyas, rugs and weavings sold in the bazaars and shops of Cairo are made in this touristic village near Giza (see the Around Cairo map on page 181). There is one main market street along which you'll find all of the above as well as a hideous collection of stuffed animals such as gazelles, jackals and rabbits. In fact, Kerdassa is almost as well known for its illegal trade in Egyptian wildlife as it is for crafts. The Egyptian Environmental Affairs Agency periodically raids the bazaar to try and halt this.

To get to Kerdassa, head down Pyramids Road towards the Pyramids, turn right at the Maryutia Canal, and follow the road for about 5km to the village. The minibus from Midan Tahrir to the Pyramids begins and ends its trips at the junction of the canal and Pyramids Road, and a local microbus does the stretch along the canal for 25 pt. You can also get bus No 116 from Midan Giza all the way to Kerdassa; the trip takes 20 minutes and costs 25 pt.

Wissa Wassef Art Centre This tranquil art centre is next to the Motel Salma in Harraniyya, on the Saqqara Rd, about 4km south of Pyramids Rd (see the Around Cairo map in page 181). It specialises in woollen and cotton tapestries, as well as batiks and ceramics, and features a museum, workshops and sales gallery.

The centre is the creation of Ramses Wissa Wassef. Believing that the imagination of children was unintentionally suppressed by teachers and parents, he founded a tapestry school in 1942 to allow young children to create freely. He ran it until his death in 1974 when the centre's management was taken over by his widow, Sophie Habib Gorgy.

Over the years, two generations of weavers have grown up with the school. Some of the original artists, now in their 40s and 50s, are still creating, as is the second wave of younger weavers. A lot of the tapestries are representational, depicting rural scenes, folklore, flora and fauna; others are pure imagination. Some superb pieces are showcased in the domed museum at the rear of the complex.

The centre is open daily from 10 am to 6 pm (summer) and from 9.30 am to 5 pm (winter); admission is free. If you particularly want to see tapestries being woven, don't come on Friday when the workshops are closed. To get there, take a microbus for Abu Sir down the Saqqara Rd from Pyramids Rd. It's the same stop as for the Motel Salma.

The Pyramids

Considered by the Ancient Greeks to be one of the Seven Wonders of the World, the Pyramids are also the world's oldest tourist attractions – they've been visited by Herodotus the Greek historian, climbed by Anthony lover of Cleopatra, and slept in by Napoleon. They were already more than 2500 years old at the time of the birth of Jesus Christ. Even more than their age, the wonder of the Pyramids lies in their twin mysteries: What were they built for? How were they built? The traditionally accepted notions that they are tombs built on the order of the Pharaohs by teams of slaves are constantly being challenged, and new theories ranging from the highly unlikely through to the wild and wacky are constantly being propounded. Pyramidologists – for the study of the vast structures has become a science in its own

EDDIE GERALD

EDDIE GERALD

EDDIE GERALD

EDDIE GERALD

In Cairo's Cities of the Dead (less sensationally known as the Northern and Southern Cemeteries) the living and the deceased cohabit side by side, and have done so for centuries in a practice which echoes ancient Pharaonic funerary traditions.

EDDIE GERALD

EDDIE GERALD

KRISTIE BURNS

EDDIE GERALD

Coptic Cairo, centred around the remains of the Roman fortress of Babylon, has been the focus of Egyptian Christianity since the religion was introduced into the country sometime around 40 AD. It remains to this day a small, time-locked enclave within the greater Muslim city.

right – point to such things as the millimetre-precise carving and placement of the stones and the cosmological significance of the structures' dimensions as evidence that the Pyramids were variously constructed by angels, the devil or visitors from another planet. (The only theory that really bothers the Egyptians is the one put forward by an Israeli academic that the Pyramids were built by the Jews before Moses led them out of Egypt.) It's easy to laugh at such seemingly out there ideas but visit the Giza Plateau and gaze on the Pyramids and you'll immediately see why so many people believe that such awesome structures could only come of unearthly origins.

The Pyramid Builders

It was not an obsession with death, or a fear of it, on the part of the ancient Egyptians that led them to build such incredible mausoleums as the Pyramids; it was their belief in eternal life and their desire to be one with the cosmos. A Pharaoh was the son of a god, and the sole receiver of the *ka*, or life force, that emanated from the god. The Pharaoh, in turn, conducted this vital force to his people, so in life and death he was worshipped as a god.

A pyramid was a sanctum for the preservation of the ka, and the apex of a much larger funerary complex that provided a place of worship for his subjects, as well as a visible reminder of the absolute and eternal power of the gods and their universe.

The mortuary complexes of Cheops, Chephren and Mycerinus, who were father, son and grandson, included: a pyramid, which was the Pharaoh's tomb as well as a repository for all his household goods, clothes and treasure; a funerary temple on the east side of the pyramid; pits for the storage of the Pharaoh's solar boats (known as barques), which were his means of transport in the afterlife; a valley temple on the banks of the Nile; and a causeway from the river to the pyramid.

In the case of the Pyramid of Cheops, the biggest of the trio, it supposedly took 10 years to build the causeway and the massive earth ramps used as a form of scaffolding, and 20 years to raise the pyramid itself. The stone was quarried locally and from the Muqqatam Hills – Napoleon calculated that the $2\frac{1}{2}$ million blocks of stone used in Cheops' pyramid alone were enough to build a 3m-high wall around the whole of France. The job was done by a highly skilled corps of masons, mathematicians, surveyors and stonecutters as well as about 100,000 slaves who carried out the back-breaking task of moving and laying the stones.

The Pyramids of Giza are only the most famous of a chain of around 70 pyramids which stretch the length of the Nile as far south as Sudan. Amazingly, all these structures were built over a period of just a few hundred years, referred to as the 'age of the Pyramids' – for more pyramids see the Saqqara, Dashur and Meidum sections in the Excursions chapter.

Recharging at a Price

While many of the coach loads rolling up at Giza just get the Pyramids as part of the package – Abu Simbel, tick; Valley of the Kings, tick; Egyptian Museum, tick; Pyramids, tick – there's a minority element for whom the Pyramids are the sole reason for and ultimate goal of a trip to Egypt. These people are the spiritual tourists, members of creeds with names like the Rosicrucians, the Red Shrine, the Friends of the Soul and the Twelve Twelvers. Modern-day pilgrims, they come for spiritual sustenance in the belief that the Pyramids emanate special forces that enhance health and bestow longevity.

The groups pay premiums to be permitted to descend into the Pyramids outside tourist hours, visiting at the break of dawn or arriving in darkness to spend the night in the burial chamber in meditation and in performing whatever rituals their particular creed requires. The current cost for a group of up to 15 is E£2000. 'After all,' said a guard quoted in the *Al-Ahram Weekly*, 'if someone was able to convince these weirdos to believe all this nonsense about spirits, we should be able to convince them to hand over a little bit of cash.' ∎

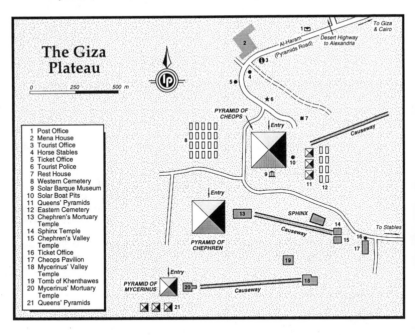

The Giza Plateau

0   250   500 m

1 Post Office
2 Mena House
3 Tourist Office
4 Horse Stables
5 Ticket Office
6 Tourist Police
7 Rest House
8 Western Cemetery
9 Solar Barque Museum
10 Solar Boat Pits
11 Queens' Pyramids
12 Eastern Cemetery
13 Chephren's Mortuary
    Temple
14 Sphinx Temple
15 Chephren's Valley
    Temple
16 Ticket Office
17 Cheops Pavilion
18 Mycerinus' Valley
    Temple
19 Tomb of Khenthawes
20 Mycerinus' Mortuary
    Temple
21 Queens' Pyramids

GIZA PLATEAU BASICS

See further on in this section for details of getting to the Pyramids, but whether you come by bus, minibus or taxi you're most likely to be dropped off at the end of Pyramids Road by the Mena House hotel. As you follow the road up to the Giza Plateau on which the Pyramids are sited, you'll pass the tourist office (open daily from around 9 am to 5 pm) off to the left, where you can check on the official rates for horse and camel rides. If anyone around here starts steering you towards the unmistakable stench of a stable, backtrack fast – ignore all the jabbering about them being able to get you onto the Plateau area without a ticket.

There's an admission fee of E£20 for the Plateau and then the same again to enter each of the Pyramids and for the Solar Barque Museum (plus E£10/100 for cameras/videos); tickets for the latter are sold at the museum itself. The Pyramid chambers are open from 8.30 am to 4 pm, but the site itself is open

from about 7 am to 7.30 pm. The Solar Barque Museum is open from 9 am to 4 pm (5 pm in summer). The best times to visit the Pyramids are at sunrise, sunset and night. During the day it can get very hot and crowded.

The Hassle

Every visitor to the Giza Plateau has to run the gauntlet of camel and horse hustlers, souvenir and soft drink hawkers, would-be guides, agonisingly persistent shop owners and sundry beggars. As writer Tony Horwitz comments in *Baghdad Without a Map*, it's difficult to gaze in awe at these ancient wonders with modern Egypt tugging so persistently at your sleeve. This is not a new phenomenon. Mark Twain who visited the Pyramids in 1866 wrote of the experience: 'We suffered torture that no pen can describe from the hungry appeals for baksheesh that gleamed from Arab eyes'. Unfortunately there is no foolproof way of sidestepping this dollar-driven mob. All we can say is be firm in your refusals and don't be drawn – 'No' is enough, so don't feel that you have to justify yourself.

Camels & Horses

One strategy to avoid the hassle is to hire a horse or camel and gallop, glide, or jolt through the desert around the Pyramids. At present the beasts can't be avoided as the area in front of the Pyramids resembles a chaotic, sandy paddock but there are plans for that to change and all animals to be shifted away from the immediate vicinity of the monuments. This may well have happened by the time you read this. Wherever they are, beware of the camel owners, who are a pretty unscrupulous lot. Bargain fiercely and be sure of what you have agreed on. A camel should not cost more than E£12 an hour but more than a few people have found themselves paying ridiculous amounts of money at the end of the ride to be let *off* their mounts. Single women should be particularly careful and *do not* allow the camel or horse owner to climb on the animal behind you.

Hiring a horse is a better option as once you're mounted you are away and off on your own. There are stables near the tourist office on Pyramids Rd but the animals here are often not in very good condition. If you head south of the entrance by the Sphinx (turn right on your way out), you'll come across several stables. MG stables (☎ 358 3832) on Sharia Abu al-Hol is owned by Mohammed Ghoneim and has been recommended for its well kept horses. Again, the hire of a horse should cost no more than E£12 per hour. The best time to go for a ride is at sunset, ending at the Cheops Pavilion just as the sound & light show illuminates the Pyramids and the Sphinx. Alternatively, some of the stables are open through the night and it's exhilarating to ride out at dawn and watch the sun rise over the desert.

GREAT PYRAMID OF CHEOPS

The oldest at Giza and the largest in Egypt, the Great Pyramid of Cheops stood 146.5m high when it was completed around 2600 BC.

After 46 centuries its height has been reduced by only 9m. About 2½ million limestone blocks, weighing around six million tonnes, were used in the construction.

Although there is not much to see inside the pyramid, the experience of climbing through such an ancient structure is unforgettable – though completely impossible if you suffer from even the tiniest degree of claustrophobia. The entrance, on the north face, leads to a descending passage which ends in an unfinished tomb (usually closed) about 100m along and 30m below the pyramid. About 20m from the entrance, however, there is an ascending passage, 1.3m high and 1m wide, which continues for about 40m before opening into the Great Gallery, which is 47m long and 8.5m high. There is also a smaller horizontal passage leading into the so-called Queen's Chamber.

As you ascend the Great Gallery to the King's Chamber notice how precisely the blocks were fitted together at the top. Unlike the rest of the pyramid, the main tomb chamber, which is just over 5m wide and 10m long, was built of red granite blocks. The roof, which weighs more than 400 tonnes, consists of nine huge slabs of granite, above which are another four slabs separated by gaps designed to distribute the enormous weight away from the chamber. There is plenty of air in this room, as it was built so that fresh air flowed in from two shafts on the north and south walls. Entry costs E£20.

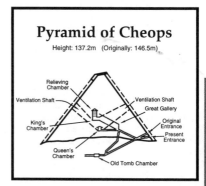

Pyramid of Cheops

Height: 137.2m (Originally: 146.5m)

Relieving Chamber
Ventilation Shaft
Ventilation Shaft
Great Gallery
King's Chamber
Original Entrance
Present Entrance
Queen's Chamber
Old Tomb Chamber

Still Taking Bookings

In the run-up to New Year's Eve 1999, millions of tourists are expected to head for party spots the world over to see in the new millennium. The big draws are the Chatham Islands, east of New Zealand (the first land mass to receive the rising sun of the year 2000); Bethlehem, birthplace of Christ; and Greenwich, UK, keeper of the world's official time. Cairo's in the running too. As early as 1979, New York's Millennium Society sent out invitations for a masked ball beneath the Great Pyramid.

However, at the time of writing the potential has barely been tapped. As of late 1997 the Mena House hotel, which overlooks the Pyramids, still had rooms free for the night of 31 December 1999. So had all the other hotels in the area that we checked with. But if you miss out, no problem – the Pyramids will be seeing out their fifth millennium and chances are they'll still be there for the celebrations for a sixth. ■

Climbing the outside of the Great Pyramid was, for centuries, a popular adventure despite the fact that every year a few people fell to their death. Scaling the pyramid is now forbidden.

On the eastern side of the pyramid are the Queens' Pyramids, three small structures about 20m high, which resemble little more than pyramid-shaped piles of rubble. They were the tombs of Cheops' wives and sisters.

Solar Barque Museum

Along the eastern and southern sides of the Pyramid of Cheops are five long pits which once contained the Pharaoh's boats. These solar barques may have been used to bring the mummy of the dead Pharaoh across the Nile to the valley temple, from where it was brought up the causeway and placed in the tomb chamber. The boats were then buried around the pyramid to provide transport for the king in the next world.

One of these ancient wooden vessels, possibly the oldest boat in existence, was

unearthed in 1954. It was restored and a glass museum was built over it to protect it from damage from the elements. For the same reason, visitors to the museum must don protective footwear in order to keep sand out.

The barque is 43m long and 8m high and sits in a 5m-deep pit. Entry costs E£20 (plus E£10/100 for cameras/videos); tickets are sold at the museum entrance.

PYRAMID OF CHEPHREN

South-west of the Great Pyramid, and with almost the same dimensions, is the Pyramid of Chephren. At first it seems larger than his father's because it stands on higher ground and its peak still has part of the original limestone casing which once covered the whole structure. It is 136.5m high (originally 143.5m).

The chambers and passageways of this pyramid are less elaborate than those in the Great Pyramid, but are almost as claustrophobic. The entrance leads down into a passage and then across to the burial chamber, which still contains the large granite sarcophagus of Chephren. Entry costs E£20.

Among the most interesting features of this pyramid are the substantial remains of Chephren's mortuary temple outside to the east. Several rooms can be visited and the causeway, which originally provided access from the Nile to the tomb, still leads from the main temple to the valley temple.

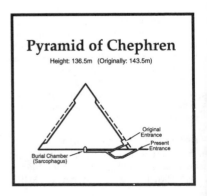

Pyramid of Chephren
Height: 136.5m (Originally: 143.5m)

Original Entrance
Present Entrance
Burial Chamber (Sarcophagus)

PYRAMID OF MYCERINUS

At a height of 62m (originally 66.5m), this is the smallest of the three pyramids. Extensive damage was done to the exterior by a 16th century caliph who wanted to demolish all the pyramids.

Inside, a hall descends from the entrance into a passageway, which in turn leads into a small chamber and a group of rooms. There is nothing particularly noteworthy about the interior, but at the very least you can have the thrill of exploring a seldom-visited site – again, it's another E£20 to enter. Outside are the excavated remains of Mycerinus' mortuary temple and, farther east, the ruins of his valley temple, still lying beneath the sand.

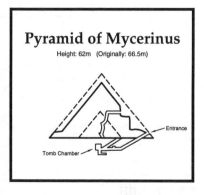

Pyramid of Mycerinus

Height: 62m (Originally: 66.5m)

Entrance

Tomb Chamber

THE SPHINX

Legends and superstitions abound about the Sphinx and the mystery surrounding its long-forgotten purpose is almost as intriguing as its appearance. English playwright Alan Bennett, however, was disappointed, noting in his diary, 'The Sphinx, like a personality seen on TV and then met in the flesh, is smaller than one had imagined.'

Known in Arabic as Abu al-Hol (Father of Terror), the feline man was called the Sphinx by the ancient Greeks because it resembled the mythical winged monster with a woman's head and lion's body who proposed a riddle to the Thebans and killed all unable to guess the answer.

Carved almost entirely from one huge piece of limestone left over from the carving of the stones for Cheops' pyramid, the Sphinx is about 50m long and 22m high. It is not known when it was carved but one theory is that it was Chephren who thought of shaping the rock into a lion's body with a god's face, wearing the royal headdress of Egypt. Another theory is that it is the likeness of Chephren himself that has been staring out over the desert sands for so many centuries.

One legend about the Sphinx is associated with the fact that it was engulfed and hidden by sand for several hundred years. The sun-god Ra appeared to the man who was to become Tuthmosis IV and promised him the crown of Egypt if he would free his image, the Sphinx, from the sand. The stelae found between the paws of the Sphinx recorded this first known restoration.

During the period of the Ottoman Empire the Turks used the Sphinx for target practice (though other sources have it that it was Napoleon), and its nose and beard were blasted off. Part of the fallen beard was carted off by 19th century adventurers and is now in the British Museum in London, UK. The Sphinx has been undergoing restoration for seven years but the scaffolding is due to disappear by 1998.

OTHER SITES

Tomb of Khenthawes

This rarely visited but imposing structure, opposite the Great Pyramid and north of Mycerinus' causeway, is the tomb of the daughter of Pharaoh Mycerinus. The tomb is a rectangular building cut into a small hill. You can go down a corridor at the back of the chapel room to the burial chambers, but the descent is a bit hazardous.

Cemeteries

Private cemeteries with several rows of tombs are organised around the pyramids in a grid pattern. Most of the tombs are closed to the public, but those of Qar, Idu and Queen Mersyankh III, in the eastern cemetery, are accessible, although it's sometimes difficult to find the guard who has the keys.

The Tomb of Iasen, in the western cemetery, contains interesting inscriptions and wall paintings which give us a glimpse of daily life during the Old Kingdom.

SOUND & LIGHT SHOW

The Sphinx takes the role of the narrator in this show, which is designed with the tourist in mind but definitely worth seeing. The booming narrative that accompanies the colourful illumination of the Pyramids and the Sphinx is an entertaining way to learn a little of Egypt's ancient history.

There are two or three shows each evening in English, French, German, Japanese, Italian, Spanish or Arabic. Show times are 6.30, 7.30 and 8.30 pm in winter and one hour later in summer. At the time of writing, the schedule was as follows:

Day	Show 1	Show 2	Show 3
Monday	English	French	–
Tuesday	English	Italian	French
Wednesday	English	French	–
Thursday	Japanese	English	Arabic
Friday	English	French	–
Saturday	English	Spanish	–
Sunday	Japanese	French	German

There is open-air seating on the terrace of the Cheops Pavilion, near the Sphinx and facing Chephren's valley temple. Admission costs E£30 (half for students). During the Ramadan period performance times can be different. If you are unsure call ☎ 385 2880/7320, or ask at the tourist office.

GETTING THERE & AWAY

For 25 pt you can have the bone-crushing experience of riding a bus from Midan Tahrir almost all the way to the Pyramids (see the Getting Around chapter for bus numbers). They will drop you at or near the turn-off to the Desert Highway to Alexandria, just short of the Mena House hotel on Pyramids Rd. From Ramses station you can take bus No 804 and from Midan Giza bus No 3. You can also get bus No 913 from Midan Tahrir to the Sphinx entrance. It is easier to catch a bus from the Pyramids to Central Cairo (rather than vice versa) because they start off empty.

Make sure you get a seat near the front so you'll be able to get out more easily.

A much more practical and comfortable alternative is to take a minibus. They leave from the bus station in front of the Nile Hilton on Midan Tahrir; the fare to the Pyramids is 35 pt and the trip takes about 30 minutes. Look for No 83 or the men standing next to minibuses and shouting 'Haram'.

There are also privately run microbuses from the Hilton station. They are far more frequent and cost 50 pt. You can also get one from Midan Giza for 25 pt.

Taking a taxi from Downtown will cost E£15 one way.

Ride to Saqqara

If you're after adventure you could rent a camel or horse for the ride across the desert to Saqqara. This trip is not really for inexperienced riders. By the end of the day you will have spent about six to seven hours atop a horse or camel and a few more hours roaming around the sites at Saqqara.

The trip takes about three hours each way, and costs anything from E£30 to E£50 for a horse and E£30 to E£70 for a camel, depending on how desperate the owners are and how well you can bargain. Don't forget that a camel can carry two people.

Heliopolis

By the beginning of this century the number of Europeans flooding into Egypt was so great that they undertook the building of their own suburb. Underwritten by a Belgian company and figureheaded by Baron Edouard Empain, a Belgian industrialist, Heliopolis was intended to be a garden city, isolated from the squalor of Cairo, that would house the European officials who ruled Egypt. Construction on a desert site north-east of the city began in 1906. The architectural style was an odd European-Moorish mix with wide avenues with grassy central strips, arcaded pavements, a racecourse, a club and a grand hotel.

A Walk Around Heliopolis

Assuming that you are heading to Heliopolis by tram the place to jump off is Roxy. The way you'll know that you have come to Roxy is that the tram stops twice here – after halting for a minute it moves forward 100m then stops again – this is where you jump off. Ask if you aren't sure: 'Fi Roxy?' Walk on along the route of the tram tracks until you reach the major traffic junction at which point you want to swing left along the wide avenue which leads up to **Midan Roxy**, which takes its name from the cinema on its east side. Following the road as it curves around to the right brings you onto **Ibrahim Laqqany** with its line of fantastic colonnaded facades book-ended by tear-drop turrets – European fantasies of the Orient cast in stone.

After about 350m Ibrahim Laqqany intersects with Sharia al-Ahram, originally the main street of Heliopolis (it has a tram line running up its centre). At this point, on your left is the **Amphitrion Cafeteria** while a block down to the right is a branch of **Groppi's**, the once-renowned patisserie. Over Al-Ahram street to the right is the former Heliopolis Grand Hotel, now the **Uruba Palace**, official residence of Egypt's president.

Sharia al-Ahram has suffered particularly badly from rapacious developers, but 300m to the east a cluster of grand old buildings remain including the one that houses the **Palmyra Cafeteria**. Both the Palmyra and the Amphitrion are as old as Heliopolis itself and were popular watering holes for the Allied soldiers during WWI and WWII. Today they're two of the very few places in Cairo where it's possible to drink a beer without having to skulk in some dingy room away from public eyes. Both terraces serve food and are great places to relax on a balmy evening.

Two blocks further east on Al-Ahram is Baron Empain's **Basilica** designed as a miniature version of Istanbul's famous Aya Sofya. Its distinctive shape has caused it to be known as the 'jelly mould' by local expats. Empain and his family are buried in the crypt. Unfortunately the place is usually kept locked. From the Basilica head south (right) down Shahid Tayyar Nazih Khalifa; a six minute walk brings you to Sharia Uruba, the airport road, at a point directly facing the Baron's Palace – see over the page.

After the Baron's Palace retrace your steps until you reach the point at which the road forks and bear left along Sawra until Baghdad; 200m west is **Le Chantilly**, about the best place up here to eat or, if you prefer, to take a beer in the garden out back. Continue on down Baghdad turning right at the bottom; two or three doors along on your right are the former **offices of the Heliopolis Company**, the founders and developers of Heliopolis. Just inside the entrance is the beautifully restored main chamber – the attendants are usually happy for visitors to poke their heads in.

You can catch a tram on Sharia al-Ahram back to the city centre. ■

The Basilica – designed by French architect Alexander Marcel as a small version of Istanbul's Aya Sofya.

EDDIE GERALD

THINGS TO SEE & DO

In addition to Europeans the new suburb, known in Egyptian as Masr al-Gedida or 'New Cairo', attracted the upper classes of Egyptians and spawned large Coptic, Jewish and Islamic communities. In the 1950s, however, overcrowding in Cairo caught up with this not-so-distant neighbour and the former desert barrier was breached by a creeping tide of middle-income high-rises.

These days Heliopolis (see Map 12) is still a fairly upmarket address. The president resides here as do most of his ministers and the odd deposed head of an African state. The ranks of apartment buildings festooned with satellite TV dishes now greatly outnumber the graceful, old villas, but Heliopolis still has an urbane charm. Were it to stand alone as a town apart from Cairo it would be considered a gem of northern Africa – as it is it's an elegantly faded suburb well worth the brief tram ride from Downtown.

Getting There & Away

There's a tram line which starts on Sharia Galaa, just north of Midan Abdel Moniem Riad, Downtown, and heads up through Midan Ramses to connect Heliopolis to Central Cairo. It's used by three tram routes (see the Getting Around chapter or Map 12), that diverge at Roxy to head for different parts of Heliopolis. The journey up to Roxy takes about 30 minutes and costs 25 pt.

BARON'S PALACE (Map 12)

Just off the modern-day airport road, the Baron's Palace (Qasr al-Baron) makes for a bizarre and incongruous sight – a Hindu-style temple looming up among the faceless apartment blocks. This was the personal residence of Baron Empain, the man who conceived Heliopolis. Built in 1910, it was commissioned from a French architect, Alexander Marcel (who had previously built an Oriental Pavilion for the King of Belgium), and is modelled – for no known reason – on the temples of Angkor Wat. Three generations of the Empain family inhabited the palace until it was sequestered by the state in the 1950s and allowed to fall into ruin. While a rich collection of sandstone

Buddhas, geishas, elephants and serpents still adorns the exterior, the interior has been gutted and is now home to large colonies of bats. Entry is not permitted but if you tip the bawwab (who lives in a shack in the grounds) a couple of pounds, he'll let you walk around the outside.

PALESTINIAN HERITAGE HOUSE (Map 12)

Occupying the ground floor of an apartment building at 5 Sharia Damascus, the Palestinian Heritage House (☎ 258 0318) was established in 1984 by Khadeja Arafat, Yasser Arafat's sister-in-law, as a centre where exiled Palestinian women could make and sell crafts. It's now a modest showcase of Palestinian history and culture as well as traditional and contemporary art, with century-old bridal gowns from Gaza and Galilee exhibited alongside richly embroidered shawls woven by women in a workshop situated out the back. The house is open daily from 8.30 am to 3 pm (until 1 pm on Thursday); admission is free.

OCTOBER WAR PANORAMA & SADAT'S TOMB (Map 1)

About 2km south-west of Qasr al-Baron, farther in towards the city in the suburb of Medinet Nasr (Victory City), is the October War Panorama. Coming in from the airport, it's off to the left on Sharia al-Uruba. Built with help from North Korean artists, this memorial to the 1973 'victory' over the Israeli occupation of Sinai is quite an extraordinary propaganda effort.

Inside at the centre of the cylindrical building, you climb two flights of stairs to a revolving dais which carries the audience around a three-dimensional mural depicting the breaching of the Bar Lev line on the Suez Canal by Egyptian forces and the initial retreats by the Israelis. A stirring commentary recounts the heroic victories but is short on detail on the successful Israeli counterattacks that pushed the Egyptians back before both sides accepted a UN-brokered cease-fire. Sinai was eventually 'liberated' – but by negotiation six years later.

The October War Panorama is closed on Tuesday. Admission is E£8 and performances, usually with an Arabic commentary, begin at 9.30 and 11 am and 6 pm. Groups can request a performance with an English commentary.

About a kilometre away, under the pyramid-shaped Victory Memorial, is the tomb of President Sadat who was assassinated just over the road as he sat in the reviewing stand observing a 6th of October anniversary parade in 1981.

Activities

ART GALLERIES

In addition to the Museum of Modern Art (see the Gezira section earlier this chapter) there are numerous small galleries around town where contemporary local and foreign artists and sculptors exhibit. *Al-Ahram Weekly* and *Egypt Today* have fairly comprehensive listings of what's on, or check some of the places below, which tend to show the most interesting stuff:

Akhnaton Centre of Arts (Map 3; ☎ 340 8211) 1 Maahad al-Swissri, Zamalek. Open 10 am to 1 pm and 5 to 7 pm, Saturday to Thursday. The official Ministry of Culture exhibition halls (four of them) housed in a grand villa on the banks of the Nile.

Atelier du Caire (Map 8; ☎ 574 6730) 2 Karim ad-Dawla, off Mahmoud Bassiouni one block west of Midan Talaat Harb. Open 10 am to 1 pm and 5 to 11 pm daily; closed Friday. Official artists' union exhibition halls.

The Basement Gallery (☎ 575 9451) in the German Church on Sharia Galaa, Downtown. Open Monday to Thursday, 10 am to 3 pm. Specialises in exhibiting works by African artists from the refugee community.

British Council (Map 2; ☎ 354 3281) 192 Sharia el-Nil, Agouza. Small gallery that often hosts visiting exhibitions from abroad.

Cairo-Berlin (Map 8; ☎ 393 1764) 17 Yousef al-Guindi, Downtown. Open 11 am to 9 pm daily; closed Saturday. Along with the Mashrabia, this place consistently hosts the most exciting works in town.

Espace Karim-Francis (☎ 393 1699) 1 Sherifeen, off Qasr el-Nil, Downtown. Open 10 am to 2 pm and 5 to 8 pm; closed Friday. Up on the 3rd floor of an apartment block.

Extra 3 Nesim, Zamalek. Open 10.30 am to 2 pm and 5 to 8 pm daily; closed Sunday. Tucked away right at the north-eastern tip of the island.

Mashrabia (Map 8; ☎ 578 4494) 8 Champollion, off Midan Tahrir. Open 11 am to 9 pm daily; closed Saturday. Cairo's most attractive gallery and one of the two best in terms of its stable of artists.

DIVE CLUBS

The Cairo Divers Group (☎ & fax 570 3242) organises monthly diving trips, rents equipment, offers interesting discounts and has plenty of information on the available dive sites. The club meets on the first Monday of each month at the Semiramis Intercontinental Hotel. The annual membership fee for divers is E£50.

The Maadi Divers is another group. They organise trips and sell and rent equipment as well. Membership is E£50 – call Magdy al-Araby (☎ 353 7144) for details.

Diving equipment is available at Scubatec (☎ 418 0118), at 9 Sharia Dr Hassan Eflatoun, Heliopolis, and Scuba Plus (☎ 574 7988), 1st floor, World Trade Centre, 1191 Corniche el-Nil, Bulaq.

FELUCCA RIDES

Feluccas are the ancient broad-sail boats that are seen everywhere up and down the Nile. They can be hired out by the hour from several places along the Corniche. One of the most pleasant things to do in Cairo is to go out on a felucca with a supply of beer and a small picnic just as sunset approaches. The best spot for hiring is the Dok Dok landing stage on the Corniche at Garden City just north of the Meridien Le-Caire. A boat and captain should cost about E£15 per hour irrespective of the number of people on board – this rate is, of course, subject to haggling. Other felucca mooring points are the south-east end of Gezira just north of the Tahrir Bridge, opposite the Helnan Shepheard's hotel (captains here tend to be more voracious in their demands for money) and in Maadi just north of the Felfela.

THINGS TO SEE & DO

HORSE RIDING

A horse ride out by the Pyramids, especially in the evening, can be a great way to escape the clamour of Cairo and vent some pent-up aggro. For details, see the Pyramids section.

HAMMAMS

There are several hammams (public bathhouses) still functioning in Islamic Cairo. They are mostly men-only institutions although at least one, the Hammam Beshtak, is open to women in the mornings. See the boxed text 'Hammam' in the Islamic Cairo section earlier in this chapter for information about which hammams you can visit.

SWIMMING

Finding a place to cool off is not easy in Cairo. Sporting clubs, the places that most Cairenes who can afford to go to swim, restrict access to members only for insurance reasons. The only option is to make for a hotel. Most of the five-star hotels allow day use of the pool. About the best value is the pool at the Meridien Le-Caire which has a fantastic Nile-side location and costs E£39 per person. The Cairo Marriott has a nice pool out in the garden and charges E£63 per person, but the one at the Mena House is unbeatable, surrounded by palm trees and with views of the Pyramids: it costs E£175 for two people.

At the cheaper end of the scale the Atlas Zamalek has a high-rise postage stamp plunge pool which costs E£28.50 (of which E£25 is a minimum charge against refreshments). Cheapest of all is the pool on the roof of the Fontana Hotel on Midan Ramses which is just E£10 for a day's use; trouble is it's not big enough to actually swim in.

Courses

LANGUAGE

Various institutions in Cairo offer Arabic courses. One of the best but most expensive is the Arabic Language Institute (Map 8; ☎ 357 5055) at the American University in Cairo (AUC). They offer instruction at elementary, intermediate and advanced levels and at the time of research the intensive course cost US$4500 per semester (20 hours per week over 14 weeks). The institute also offers intensive summer programs (20 hours per week for six weeks) for US$2240.

The British Council (Map 2; ☎ 345 3281), at 192 Sharia el-Nil, Agouza, has eight-week courses (two 90 minute lessons per week) for E£270. The two, unrelated International Language Institutes (ILI) both offer Arabic courses. The one at 3 Mahmoud Azmy, Sahafayeen (Map 2; ☎ 346 3087) and the other at 2 Mohammed Bayoumi, in Heliopolis (☎ 291 9295) both charge E£350/390 for a 60 hour program of Egyptian Arabic. They also offer residential summer courses (running from late June to late July) ranging from E£275 for 40 hours of tuition to E£500 for 100 hours.

The French Cultural Institute offers a number of courses, all of a reasonable standard, through its Département de l'Étude d'Arab du Caire (Map 8; ☎ 355 9517) in Garden City.

The Goethe Institut (Map 8; ☎ 575 9877), 5 Bustan, offers relatively inexpensive Arabic lessons, but generally concentrates on not overly demanding courses in colloquial Egyptian Arabic.

The Egyptian Centre for International Cultural Cooperation (ECICC) (☎ 341 5419), 11 Shagaret ad-Durr, Zamalek, offers courses in classical Arabic. Intensive courses (96 hours over 12 weeks) cost US$220 and regular courses (48 hours over the same period) US$110. Contact Mrs Abla Ghoneim any day between 10 am and 1 pm.

Check the magazine *Egypt Today* for a list of other organisations that offer Arabic courses, but be wary of quality and cost.

THE AMERICAN UNIVERSITY IN CAIRO

The AUC is one of the premier universities in the Middle East. Some 4300 students, the bulk of whom are Egyptian, study at its campus on Midan Tahrir in the heart of Cairo. The curriculum, and a third of the full-time faculty are American and accredited in the USA.

The AUC offers degree, nondegree and summer-school programs. Any of the regular courses offered can be taken. Popular subjects include Arabic Language and Literature, Arab History & Culture, Egyptology, Islamic Art and Architecture, Middle East Studies and Social Science courses on the Arab world. Up to 15 unit hours can be taken per semester at the undergraduate level.

Summer programs offer similar courses. The term lasts from mid-June to the end of July. Two three-unit courses can be taken and several well-guided field trips throughout Egypt are usually included.

The largest programs at the AUC are for bachelor's and master's degrees; they offer more than 29 subjects ranging from Anthropology to Teaching English as a Foreign Language.

Applications for programs with the Arabic Language Institute (previously detailed) and undergraduate and graduate studies at the university are separate. Specify which you want when requesting an application form. A catalogue and program information can be obtained from: The Office of Admissions, The American University in Cairo, 866 United Nations Plaza, New York, NY 10017 (☎ (212) 421-6320; fax 688-5341); or you can write to PO Box 2511 in Cairo (☎ 354 2964, ext 5011/2/3; fax 355 7565).

EGYPTIAN UNIVERSITIES

It is also possible to study at Egyptian universities such as Al-Azhar, Ain Shams and Cairo. Courses offered to foreign students include Arabic Language, Islamic History, Islamic Religion, and Egyptology. For information on courses, tuition fees and applications, contact: The Cultural Counsellor, The Egyptian Educational Bureau (☎ (202) 296-3888), 2200 Kalorama Rd NW, Washington DC 20008. In London, contact the Cultural Affairs Office (☎ (0171) 491 7720).

Places to Stay

Cairo offers visitors the full spectrum of accommodation, from the big international five-star chains to flea-ridden dives. The more expensive hotels usually quote prices in US dollars. In most cases, however, there is no problem paying in Egyptian pounds.

Almost all of the world's major hotel chains are represented in Cairo; in the centre, out near the Pyramids, up in Heliopolis or close to the airport. While their prices and amenities are usually up to international standards, their service hardly ever is. A few of the more expensive hotels are interesting to visit (see the boxed text 'Cairo's Historic Hotels' later in this chapter) and are pleasant places in which to seek refuge from the chaos and cacophony of Cairo's streets.

Unless otherwise indicated, the prices quoted for budget and mid-range hotels include breakfast and taxes. However, don't have any great expectations about breakfast – it usually consists of no more than a couple of pieces of bread, a chunk of frozen butter, a dollop of jam, and tea or coffee. Also, just because the room rates in these places are displayed in a glass frame on the wall, it doesn't mean they are untouchable – haggling will sometimes get you significant discounts.

Note On arrival at the airport, if you're not with a group, you may be approached by a man or woman with an official-looking badge that says 'Egyptian Chamber of Tourism' or something similar. Such people are not government tourism officials, they are hotel touts. They'll tell you all sorts of porkies, such as the hotel where you want to stay is 'no good', 'full' or has quadrupled its prices. Steer clear of these people.

RENTED ACCOMMODATION

If you are planning on staying in Cairo for a couple of months or more, it's easy to find a flat to rent. However, if you're on a budget, then a month's rent on the cheapest flat works out to cost a lot more than 30 nights at a cheap hotel. It depends on the area you're looking at, but the lowest price you can expect to pay (say in an area like Bab al-Luq which is cheap and close to the centre) is about E£500 per month. This will get you a one or two bedroom place, old and none too clean, with a horrible bathroom and kitchen. For the same figure you could perhaps find a room, in a more decent, two or three bedroom shared-flat, somewhere like Doqqi, Agouza or Zamalek. A good flat in any of these three areas with two or three rooms, a good kitchen and bathroom, and a balcony goes for between E£1200 and E£2000, depending on the size and how well it is kitted out. If you don't mind being out of the centre, flats in Heliopolis tend to be extremely large, often with spacious balconies, and lower rents than those Downtown.

By far the easiest way to find a flat is to use a *simsar* (flat agent). Every street has one of these guys; he's generally a *bawwab* (doorman) who makes it his business to know who is renting what in his area. Choose the neighbourhood you want to live in and then ask any bawwab for directions to the local simsar. The last time we did this we were shown nearly a dozen flats in neighbouring streets, in the space of just a couple of hours. The finders' fee should be about 10% of the rent. If nothing takes your fancy, then a little baksheesh is in order for the simsar's time.

Flat hunters should also consult the classifieds in the *Middle East Times* and check the notice board at Sunny's supermarket at 11 Aziz Osman in Zamalek.

PLACES TO STAY – BUDGET
Camping

The *Motel Salma* (☎ 384 9152; fax 385 1010) is next to the Wissa Wassef Art Centre at Harraniyya, south of Giza – and is miles and miles from anywhere else. Camping costs E£7 per person with your own tent or camper

The Bawwab

Every apartment block comes with a *bawwab*, or porter. His role – for they're all male, invariably elderly, and often Nubian or Upper Egyptian – is to keep the corridors and stairs clean, run errands for the tenants and perform the function of a security guard. As a tenant, much depends on your bawwab, who can be closest ally or your worst enemy – this will usually be determined by the amount of baksheesh you dole out. ∎

van. You can also get a stuffy two/four person cabin for E£30/40, or E£50 with your own shower. Overland tour companies occasionally use this place which has views of the Pyramids from the back of the camp site.

To get there, take a microbus for Abu Sir from Pyramids Rd. It's about a 4km trip; ask the driver about the best place to alight. Be prepared for a mosquito attack at sunset.

Hostels

The *HI – Manial Youth Hostel* (Map 7; ☎ 364 0729; fax 984 107), at 135 Abdel Aziz el-Saud on Rhoda Island, is one of the cheapest options in Cairo. It's in reasonable nick with clean toilets, although the beds are nothing great. Each dorm room sleeps either three or

six people; there are no rooms for couples or families. Mosquitoes and cats are plentiful enough to ensure constant companionship of a sort. For HI members it costs E£12 in three-bed dorms or E£8 in the six-bed dorms; nonmembers pay E£4 more. Breakfast is included.

From Midan Tahrir, take minibus No 82 from the Nile Hilton bus station, get off just before the Al-Gamaa bridge and head about 100m down the river-side street. There's an 11 pm curfew.

The offices of the Egyptian Youth Hostels Association (Map 7; ☎ 354 0527; fax 355 0329) are at 1 Ibrahimy, Garden City.

Hotels & Pensions

The inexpensive hotels and pensions are concentrated Downtown, mainly on and around Talaat Harb. This is the most convenient place to stay for getting around, eating and entertainment. Most of the hotels tend to be on the upper floors of old, and often fairly decrepit, apartment blocks. Rooms tend to be large, but are also musty and sparsely furnished. In this price range there is no air-conditioning, but sometimes there may be a ceiling fan. Shared bathrooms are the norm, usually with a Pharaonic-era plumbing system that delivers a highly erratic water supply.

There are also several cheap places around Midan Ramses, but the traffic noise and pollution is much worse there than the heart of Downtown. For somewhere quiet, look to Zamalek.

The prices given here for budget accommodation can be deceiving because they aren't always accurate indicators of the hotel's quality and they are often negotiable – consider the following room rates as estimates. If you are staying for more than a week, then it's definitely worth pushing for a discount.

The following list, while far from exhaustive, covers some of the better options.

Central Cairo Backpacker central is the area around the Tawfiqiyya souq off the top end of Talaat Harb (see Map 4). One particular

Hotel with Wildlife

For years the Oxford Hotel at 32 Talaat Harb – up on the 6th floor and reached by a rickety lift, with its back kicked out, that always felt uncomfortably like a coffin – was the sleaziest, most flea infested, motley collection of stained, flattened mattresses that ever dared to call itself a hotel. The walls were nicotine-coloured, the showers spouted only rusty trickles and some of the 'rooms' weren't rooms at all, just widenings in the corridor. It had its devotees, however. Among would-be bohemians and travellers in search of misadventure, the Oxford was something of a cult, a place to make contacts and connections, buy some hash, trade your Walkman for some cash, sell your passport, or pick up a bit part in an Egyptian soap.

Given such a transient cast of wilfully eccentric characters, the Oxford accumulated a patina of legends which were passed from each long-term resident to the next over Stellas in the stale-smoke smelling flophouse of a reception. Just for the record here's our addition to the canon: Larry (name changed to protect the far from innocent) taught English in a cowboy school where the pay didn't allow for anything more than a bed at the Oxford. To brighten up his room Larry bought 10m of red cloth from the bazaar and draped it over the ceilings and walls. For company he added Miss Fifi, a white rabbit bought for E£1 from a poultry shop. Months later when Larry left, the management decided to let his room as it was – any guests getting number seven got it complete with boudoir décor, rabbit shit and Miss Fifi.

The Oxford remains, but on our last visit it was undergoing a complete makeover under a new management that is eager to shed past associations. When it reopens, rooms will have TVs, fridges, sinks, toilets and even beds. Miss Fifi, needless to say, has long since checked out. ■

---

block on this colourful market street is home to – at last count – four very similar establishments: the *Tawfikia Hotel* (☎ 755 514), the *Safary Hotel* (☎ 575 0752), the *Sultan Hotel* (☎ 772 258) and the *Hotel Venice*. All offer cramped dorms (from E£7 to E£9 for a bed), a communal kitchen, a couple of bathrooms, and a small reception area with a TV.

Two other backpacker favourites are down by Midan Tahrir. One is the *Sun Hotel* (Map 8; ☎ 578 1786) at 2 Talaat Harb, on the 9th floor – with an up-only elevator. It has decent-sized singles/doubles with big comfortable beds for E£25/40, or you can pay E£15 per person in a four bed room. The clean, communal bathrooms have hot water and there's a lounge room with satellite TV and a small, spotless kitchen. This place arranges a tour to the Birqash camel market every Friday. The second favourite is the *Ismailia House Hotel* (Map 8; ☎ 356 3122) on the 8th floor at 1 Midan Tahrir (the elevator here will take you up *and* down). The bright, whitewashed rooms are clean and the linen is regularly changed. There's also satellite TV in the lounge and, perhaps

best of all, several bathrooms, all with electric water-heaters ensuring hot showers. Singles, a few of which are pretty dingy, cost E£25. Doubles without/with private bathroom are E£40/45 and are the best value. A bed in a share room (a double room with two extra rickety beds crammed in) costs from E£12 to E£15, depending on the room. Most of the rooms have balconies overlooking the midan.

We also like the *Hotel Minerva* (Map 4; ☎ 392 0600/1/2), hidden in an alley opposite the À l'Américaine Café at the top of Talaat Harb. Reception is at ground level, but the hotel occupies the 6th floor. The rooms are kept clean as are the communal showers and toilets. Single/double rooms are E£16/28; doubles with bath are E£32.

The *Pension Roma* (Map 4; ☎ 391 1088), at 169 Mohammed Farid (down a side alley next to the Gattegno department store), has long been popular for its 1940s charm – shiny hardwood floors, antique furniture and a wonderful lounge and breakfast room. That said, many of the rooms have slipped beyond charm into plain shabbiness, and the shared bathrooms are appalling. Reservations though are still necessary. Single/double/triple rooms without a bath are E£23/42/54.

Also overtrading on its old-world charm is the *Anglo-Swiss Hotel* (Map 8; ☎ 575 1497), 6th floor, 14 Champollion. While it's generally clean and comfortable, it is very creaky when it comes to things like toilets, hot water and a functioning lift. Rooms cost E£25 for a big single, E£20 for a poky one, and E£45/50 for doubles without/with bathroom. Still, it's not bad and certainly not to be confused with the grotty *Pensione Suisse* nearby on Mohammed Bassiouni which, according to one traveller, has a 'major wildlife problem'.

For some peace and quiet, try the *Hotel Select* (Map 4; ☎ 393 3707) next door to the synagogue at 19 Adly. This is a small and friendly family-run place tucked away at the back of the 8th floor. While it's a little dark and gloomy inside, the rooms are clean and the beds have fresh sheets. Singles/doubles cost E£20/40 without bathroom.

A small distance away from the established travellers' areas is the *Amin Hotel* (Map 8; ☎ 393 3813) at 38 Midan Falaki, Bab al-Luq. It has big and fully carpeted rooms with fans, and some have bathrooms. The shared bathrooms tend to get rather messy. Single rooms without/with bathroom cost E£26/33; doubles cost E£37/41.

Around Midan Ramses The *Everest Hotel* (Map 4; ☎ 574 2707) on Midan Ramses occupies the 14th, 15th and 16th floors of the tallest building on the square; the reception desk and cafeteria are on the 15th floor. The low prices (singles/doubles E£14/20), proximity to the railway station and the fantastic views from the balcony once made this hotel a popular place, but the badly deteriorating conditions have begun to discourage people from staying.

Across the road from the Al-Fath mosque is the *Cairo Palace* (Map 4; ☎ 590 6387) which occupies the upper floors of a modern, 12 storey block. It's in better condition than the Everest and has an OK cafe on the top

floor. Prices seem to be negotiable; we were offered a double with bathroom for E£33.

Zamalek The *Mayfair Hotel* (Map 3; ☎ 340 7315) at 9 Aziz Osman has singles/doubles without bath for E£20/24, or air-con doubles with bath for E£60 (E£45 for sole occupancy). There are also a few triples starting from around E£50. Despite being just off a busy shopping street and next door to a supermarket, it's a very tranquil and friendly place with deck chairs and a shady terrace.

One block south at 6 Salah ad-Din is the *Zamalek Pension* (Map 3; ☎ 340 9318). If you desire quiet and privacy, this is the place to be; there are only about five rooms and you feel like a house guest rather than a hotel resident. Price wise it's really heading into the middle range, with singles/doubles costing E£50/70, or more with air-conditioning.

PLACES TO STAY – MIDDLE
Central Cairo

The *Garden City House* (Map 7; ☎ 354 4969), 23 Kamal ad-Din Salah, is opposite the back of the Semiramis Intercontinental. Look for the small sign at 3rd-floor level and the bronze plaque at the front of the building. This hotel was, for a long time, a favourite among Egyptologists and Middle Eastern scholars, but it's now more popular with young students from the American University in Cairo (AUC). It's a bit dusty and overpriced, but a lot of people love it and keep coming back. Singles/doubles range from E£51/94 (without bath) to E£64/102 (with bath), breakfast and supper included.

There are three other hotels with character in this price range. The *Cosmopolitan Hotel* (Map 8; ☎ 392 3663; fax 393 3531) is a gorgeous, old Art Deco building tucked away in a little alley (Sharia ibn Taalab), just off Qasr el-Nil. It has plush, old rooms with dark lacquered furniture, central air-conditioning and tiled bathrooms with tubs. Singles/doubles cost E£135/175 (tax included) and despite the hotel's very central location, it's surprisingly quiet.

Pre-1952 the *Hotel Windsor* (Map 4; ☎ 591 5277; fax 592 1621) at 19 Alfy was the British Officers' Club. It retains a great deal of colonial charm, particularly in the reception area with its beautifully ornate lift and walls hung with ancient Swissair posters. While the dining room's not up to much, the bar is one of the best in town. In 1991, former Monty Python member, Michael Palin, stayed here while filming the BBC series *Around the World in 80 Days*, describing the place as possessing an 'almost unreal individuality ... which represents Cairo in a microcosm'. There's a wide variety of rooms with all combinations of bathroom types – cramped or the size of a tennis court, with or without shower/toilet/tub, newly tiled or well-worn antique, hot water or no water. Prices range from E£75 to E£102 for singles and E£102 to E£140 for doubles.

Not too far from the Windsor, and about 800m north of Midan Opera at 66 Al-Gomhuriyya, the *Victoria Hotel*, (Map 4; ☎ 589 2290; fax 591 3008) dates back to the 1930s and still retains plenty of period charm, particularly in the foyer. There's also a nice garden cafe with a gurgling fountain. Singles/doubles cost E£120/170.

Recommended, but with less character, is the *Lotus Hotel* (Map 8; ☎ 575 0966; fax 575 4720) at 12 Talaat Harb, opposite Felfela Takeaway. It is one of the best hotels in this price range. The elevator to the reception desk (on the 7th floor) is reached through an arcade which almost faces Sharia Hoda Shaarawi. The rooms are clean and comfortable and they all have air-conditioning and large balconies. You'll pay E£47/67 for a single without/with bath. A double without/with bath costs E£67/87.

Another good place is the *Odeon Palace Hotel* (Map 4; ☎ & fax 776 637) at 6 Abdel Hamid Said, off Talaat Harb. It is a very comfortable, upper-middle range hotel where all rooms have a mini-fridge, TV, telephone and air-con. Singles/doubles cost E£115/146. Breakfast is E£10 extra. The rooftop 24 hour bar is popular with the city's night owls.

Other reasonable Downtown alternatives include a string of four hotels along 26th of July. Cheapest of the bunch is the *Carlton Hotel* (Map 4; ☎ 575 5022; fax 575 5323).

It's a nice old place but is showing its age; singles/doubles cost E£65/85. It's just off 26th of July, one block west of the junction with Talaat Harb, entered via the side street that runs down by the Rivoli cinema. Beyond the Rivoli, and opposite the law court building, the *Ambassador* (Map 4; ☎ 578 3225; fax 574 3263) offers recently refurbished singles/doubles for E£150/190. The views are great and there's an OK restaurant and cafe.

The *Grand Hotel* (Map 4; ☎ 575 7509; fax 575 7662) is right on the junction of 26th of July and Talaat Harb. It has clean and comfortable rooms with Art Deco-style furniture. There is a wide variety of rooms – singles and doubles, with and without bathrooms and air-con. Prices start from E£117/153.

The *Cairo Khan* (Map 4; ☎ 392 2015; fax 390 6799), on the corner of 26th of July and Mohammed Farid, is also quite comfortable, although the rooms are a little small. Singles/doubles with the usual facilities cost E£170/220. The owners seem keen to do deals – without even asking we were offered a 25% discount.

Around Midan Ramses

Tucked away down a quiet backstreet off Sharia Emad ad-Din (behind the Karim Cinema) the *Happyton Hotel* (Map 4; ☎ & fax 592 8671/00) is another good value-for-money option. It's a relaxed place with a restaurant and a small, open-air rooftop bar. Singles/doubles with air-con cost E£40/52.

The *Fontana Hotel* (Map 4; ☎ 592 2321; fax 592 2145), to the north-west of Midan Ramses, is hardly in an inviting location, but the views from the clean rooms are impressive. There's a pleasant roof-terrace cafe/bar with a small pool for cooling off; there's also a disco on the 8th floor. Singles/doubles cost E£57/84.

Islamic Cairo

Just off Midan Hussein, the *Hotel al-Hussein* (☎ 591 8089) is right in the thick of things in the Khan al-Khalili bazaar. The rooms are clean and the restaurant on the roof has a fantastic view of medieval Cairo – unfortunately the food is lousy. Singles/doubles with bath and views over the midan cost E£60/70. Smaller rooms without bath or views cost E£35/45. Air-conditioning, telephone, mini-fridge and hot water are included, but a TV or fan is extra.

Diagonally opposite is the *Radwan Hotel* (☎ 590 1311). It has OK rooms for E£45/70 with breakfast and bath. Be aware that in either of these places you're almost sure to be woken by the early calls to prayer.

Zamalek

The *Flamenco Hotel* (Map 3; ☎ 340 0815; fax 340 9312), at 2 Geziret al-Wusta, is highly recommended for anyone who doesn't mind being a little out of the centre. It overlooks the branch of the Nile between Zamalek and Mohandiseen and the views from the balconies are intoxicating. The service is good and there are two OK bars and a very good restaurant. Singles/doubles cost E£220/292.

Over towards the Bulaq side of the island, the *New Star Hotel* (☎ 340 0928; fax 341 1321) at 34 Yehia Ibrahim is also quite appealing. Fully carpeted doubles with modern bathrooms, air-con and large balconies with Nile views cost E£170.

Mohandiseen

The *Atlas Zamalek* (Map 2; ☎ 346 6569; fax 437 6958) at 20 Gamiat ad-Dowal al-Arabiyya suffers for being on one of the city's main drags. As well as being noisy into the early hours, it's not very picturesque (which is why, presumably, none of the Atlas' rooms have balconies). However, the hotel is quite pleasant inside, and there's a small pool on the roof. It also has one of Cairo's most popular discos. Rooms cost E£282/358. On the same street, the *Al-Nabila Hotel* (Map 2; ☎ 347 3384; fax 347 5661) is very clean and appealing and has an attractive coffee shop. Singles/doubles cost E£289/340 including breakfast.

Heliopolis

If you want to be relatively close to the airport but don't wish to spend top dollars, you could try the three star *Hotel Beirut* (Map 12; ☎ 291 6048) at 43 Baghdad. It is a sombre place where singles/doubles cost E£204/272. Alternatively there's the *Baron Hotel* (Map 12; ☎ 291 5757; fax 290 7077) which overlooks the incredible Hindu-styled Baron's Palace. Rooms cost E£135/170.

PLACES TO STAY – TOP END

All of Cairo's five-star hotels come with the complete complement of amenities such as restaurants, bars, executive suites, business centres, shops and banks, plus a few Egyptian touches like belly-dancing nightclubs and weekly wedding receptions in the foyer. The following prices generally don't include breakfast and taxes – typically 19% plus a further 5% service tax. Rates are supposedly the same year round, but they usually go up in October.

Central Cairo

The *Nile Hilton* (Map 6; ☎ 578 0444; fax 578 0500), on Midan Tahrir, was Cairo's first new, post-Revolution luxury hotel and remains one of the best places to stay for those with the money. It has terrific river views from the Nile-facing rooms and is, of course, very central – next door to the Egyptian Museum. The Ibis Cafe on its terrace is popular with city residents and its secluded pool is one of the best in town. Rooms are large and clean, although the plumbing can be unreliable. The better singles/doubles cost about US$175/210.

Just north of the Nile Hilton, on the Corniche, is the newer *Ramses Hilton* (Map 3; ☎ 574 4400; fax 575 7152). It's one of the blandest and most characterless of the city's hotels, but much worse, it's surrounded by flyovers and is adjacent to a city bus station. Unless you take a taxi from the door every time, walking anywhere involves negotiating at least half a dozen of Cairo's most lethal roads. Rooms range from US$140 for a standard single to US$2030 for a three bed suite.

Still on the Corniche but this time south of the Nile Hilton, is the glitzy, orange and brass *Semiramis Intercontinental Hotel* (Map 7; ☎ 355 7171; fax 356 3020). The location is good – not far from Midan Tahrir and with only one road to be crossed to get to the Egyptian Museum or Downtown. The foyer area is the most attractive of all the newer hotels and the places to eat are very pleasant with lots of glass, greenery and Nile views. Rooms with views cost US$170/200; rooms overlooking the city are US$20 cheaper.

One block south is *Helnan Shepheard's* (Map 7; ☎ 355 3800; fax 355 7284), which

other than the name has nothing to do with the celebrated Shepheard's of yesteryear (see the boxed text 'Shepheard's Hotel' in the History section of the Facts about Cairo chapter). Aside from the good location, this gloomy place has little to recommend it. Singles/doubles fronting the Nile cost US$134/160, while those at the back cost US$90/105, taxes included.

Cairo's Historic Hotels

The inauguration of the Suez Canal in 1869 inspired Ismail, Egypt's reigning khedive, to initiate a flurry of building activity to provide suitable accommodation for the invited heads of state and royalty. The guest of honour was to be the Empress Eugenie of France for whom he constructed the Gezira Palace – a baroque three-winged building modelled on the Alhambra in southern Spain. The building which originally had two storeys, was painted with yellow and maroon horizontal stripes and was set in gardens that spread over most of the island of Gezira. Today, it has three storeys, is salmon pink and is better known as the Cairo Marriott. To appreciate its former splendour, peer into some of the ballrooms up on the 1st floor or the reception rooms at garden level.

While attending the Suez Canal opening, Eugenie was taken to visit Ismail's hunting lodge, built in the 1860s beside the Pyramids. By the time she revisited Egypt 40 years later, Ismail had lost Egypt and his one-time lodge was now a hotel owned by an English couple. Large terraces and verandahs had been added. 'At tea hour,' according to a pre-WWI description of the hotel, 'the Mena House terraces are crowded with a gay and brilliant throng.' By this time there was also an open-air pool, tennis courts, a golf course and a croquet lawn. Being so grand and, until the 1960s, the only hotel in the vicinity of the Pyramids, Mena House was host to an array of the great and famous, including Roosevelt and Churchill who met here in 1943 to hammer out plans for the defeat of Germany.

Since 1952 both hotels have been owned by the Egyptian government, from whom the Marriott and Oberoi chains lease them. ■

EDDIE GERALD

Bask in the shadows of the Pyramids while sipping something cool on the terrace of the Mena House hotel.

The *Meridien Le-Caire* (Map 7; ☎ 362 1717; fax 368 1555) is the large, curving block at the northern tip of the central island of Rhoda. Its views are fantastic, its restaurant, Champollion, is reckoned to be one of the three best restaurants in town, and its pool-side terrace is a great place for a sunset cocktail. However, the hotel is showing its age and it's a 1.5km walk – albeit a beautiful one – to Midan Tahrir. Spacious single/double rooms with all facilities cost US$180.

Gezira & Zamalek
Enjoying a similar sort of position to the Meridien, the *Gezira Sheraton* (Map 7; ☎ 341 1333; fax 340 5056) is the big round tower that is perched on the very southern tip of the island of Gezira. It too has several river-side restaurants and bars, but other than that – and of course the views – it's fairly unexceptional. Standard singles/doubles cost US$185/210.

In our view, the *Cairo Marriott* (Map 3; ☎ 340 8888; fax 340 8240), at the other end of the island, is the best of the city's top-end hotels. As a former khedival palace (see the boxed text 'Cairo's Historic Hotels') which has been tastefully extended and added to, it boasts a classy reception, exquisite dining areas and a serene garden with bar, cafe, pool and tennis courts. Single/double rooms are both US$180.

Doqqi
Several hundred metres from the same company's Gezira property, the *Cairo Sheraton* (Map 7; ☎ 348 8600; fax 336 4601) squats on the west bank of the Nile with views across to Helnan Shepheard's, the Semiramis, the Nile and Ramses Hilton hotels and perhaps a bit of Cairo behind. It is poorly located beside a couple of busy roads and the interior of the hotel has very little going for it either. Single/double rooms start from US$152/176.

The *Pyramisa* (Map 7; ☎ 336 7000; fax 360 5347), behind the Sheraton at 60 Sharia al-Giza, does at least have a quality of intimacy and, for a five star hotel, reasonable rates – US$100/120.

Giza
We'd rate the *Mena House* (☎ 383 3444; fax 383 7777) as the city's second best hotel. It's actually regarded as one of the best in the world, but what lets it down for us is that it's some 10km out of the centre, next to the Pyramids – which for some might prove more than ample compensation. The interior is like an opulent Oriental fantasy, and there are beautiful gardens with a large, deep pool in which you can float and regard the looming presence of Cheops' Great Pyramid. Prices start at US$130/160.

Also with Pyramid views are the elegant *Forte Grande* (☎ 383 0827; fax 384 1993), with singles/doubles from US$125/160, and the slightly more downmarket *Mövenpick Jolie Ville* (☎ 385 2555; fax 383 5006), with singles/doubles at US$115/145.

Heliopolis
There are several five-star establishments in the Heliopolis area, none of which make a good base for a visit to Cairo. They include:

Le Meridien Heliopolis Airport Rd (☎ 290 5055; fax 417 2492). Singles/doubles US$150/190.
Mövenpick Heliopolis Cairo Airport (☎ 247 0077; fax 418 0761). Singles/doubles US$140/170.
Novotel Cairo Airport (☎ 291 8577; fax 291 4794). Singles/doubles US$129/163.
Sheraton Heliopolis Airport Rd (☎ 290 2027; fax 290 4061).

Places to Eat

For a city of its size and cosmopolitan flavour, Cairo has very little to excite in the way of restaurants. The large numbers of Greeks and Lebanese that Egypt has traditionally been home to are all but invisible when it comes to dining out, and while the architectural legacies of the French and Italians are omnipresent, their influence on the city's menus is sadly lacking. As for the local cuisine, while there are many wonderful things about Egypt, none of them are gastronomic. In fact, Egypt can lay claim to having introduced the world to one of the most revolting dishes of all time – *molokhiyya*. Made by stewing the leaf of a particular plant in chicken stock, molokhiyya looks like green algae and has the consistency of mucus. The 11th century caliph, Al-Hakim, found the stuff so repulsive he had the dish banned from Cairo.

Egyptian meals largely do away with rice, potatoes and pasta, and concentrate on meat (no pork of course) with salads (usually chopped tomato and cucumber in vinegar). The meat that is served is usually lamb, in the form of *kebab* (roast meat) or *kofta* (ground meat peppered with spices, skewered and grilled over a fire). Chicken (*firekh*) is common, roasted on a spit and, in restaurants, ordered by the half. Pigeon (*hamam*) is extremely popular and usually served stuffed with rice. It's also served as a stew cooked in a deep clay pot, known as a *tagen*, with onions, tomatoes, and rice or cracked wheat.

Aside from salad there are quite a few good side dishes to be ordered with meat. *Mashi* consists of various vegetables such as vine leaves (in summer), cabbage (in winter), peppers, or white and black aubergines, which are stuffed with minced meat, rice, onions, parsley and herbs. *Baba ghanoug* is a thick paste made of mashed eggplant with garlic, and is similar in appearance to *houmos* (cooked chickpeas ground into a paste and mixed with garlic and lemon) and

tahina (a thinner paste made from sesame seeds). Pickled vegetables known as *torshi* are usually served complimentary.

EGYPTIAN STAPLES
Fuul & Taamiyya

Fuul and *taamiyya* are unofficially the national staples of Egypt. Fuul is mashed fava beans, usually ladled into a piece of *shammy* bread (like pitta) and sells for about 50 pt. You can often also get egg or garlic mixed in with it. Taamiyya is mashed chickpeas and spices fried in a patty – known elsewhere as felafel – and stuffed into a piece of shammy with salad and tahina. Again, a taamiyya sandwich costs about 50 pt and two make a substantial snack.

There are fuul and taamiyya places on nearly every street in Cairo but, of course, some are better than others. Three stand out above the rest. *At-Tabie ad-Domyati* at 31 Orabi, north of 26th of July, near the Orabi metro station (see Map 4), is a personal favourite. They do fuul with tomatoes and onions, egg and pasturma, or clarified butter. They also serve a fuul platter (E£6) with salad, tahina, taamiyya and French fries to accompany your beans. They also have a branch in Mohandiseen, south-west of Midan Mustafa Mahmoud (see Map 2). *Naama* on the Corniche in Agouza, just north of the 6th of October bridge (see Map 3), is a favourite for taxi drivers and is open 24 hours. The *Felfela Takeaway* on Talaat Harb (see Map 8) beats all other competition Downtown – place your order, pay at the tills, then present your ticket at the busy counter, way at the back, to get your food.

Kushari

Second only to fuul & taamiyya, *kushari* (a mix of noodles, rice, black lentils, fried onions and tomato sauce) is the other streetfood staple. The ingredients are served up altogether, in a bowl (small, *suraiyyar*; medium, *metawasit*; or large, *kebir)* for sit-down meals, or spooned into a polythene bag for takeaway. A medium serve, containing more than most people can eat, costs from E£1 to E£1.50. There are plenty of kushari joints about town (identified by the great tureens of noodles and rice in their windows), but the best are all Downtown: *At-Tahrir* at 19 Abdel Khalek Sarwat, east off Talaat Harb, and on Sharia Tahrir, in Bab al-Luq (see Map 8); the nearby *Abu Tarek* at 40 Champollion (see Map 8); and the *Lux* distinguishable by its red-painted window frames: the first, on the corner of Emad ad-Din and Alfy (see Map 4), and the second on the south side of Midan Falaki (see Map 8).

Shawarma

Shawarma is the Egyptian equivalent of the Greek *gyros* sandwich or the Turkish *doner kebab*. Strips of lamb or chicken are sliced from a spit, sizzled on a hot plate with chopped tomatoes and garnish, and then stuffed in a pocket of shammy bread. A lot of fuul and taamiyya places do shawarma, but rarely is it good – the meat is often unappetisingly fatty. A few good places for shawarma are *Abu Shaqra* and *Al-Omda* in Mohandiseen (Map 2; see Places to Eat – Budget later in this chapter), and the *Felfela Takeaway*, Downtown (see Fuul & Taamiyya opposite).

Kofta & Kebab

While kofta and kebab dominate many Cairo menus, there are several places which sell nothing else. Each evening, Sharia Ezbek-iyya, just north of 26th of July, Downtown, is choked with smoke from the charcoal braziers of half a dozen meat merchants. None, however, are particularly good. It would be better to go to Midan Hussein near the Khan al-Khalili. *Al-Dahan* on Muski near the Hotel al-Hussein is excellent, as is *Al-Agaty*, which is on Sharia Makassisse, just off Sharia al-Muizz li-Din Allah – from Muski head north and take the first left. Kofta and kebab are always ordered by weight – 250g is usually sufficient for one person. They come with salad, bread and tahina and cost from E£9 to E£12. Both these restaurants are open from noon to midnight.

Serious carnivores should head for the Zein al-Abdin district which was, until recently, the site of the city's slaughterhouses. On Midan Zein al-Abdin (see Map 8), *Ouf* is a fairly traditional kebab house distinguished by fine meat and excellent offal, particularly the kidneys (*kellawi*). For a real meat-eating experience head for the nearby *Abu Ramy's*. It is nothing more than benches and tables on open ground beside the old slaughterhouse buildings. Sheep are tethered behind the ramshackle kitchens, so there are no illusions about where your supper is coming from. As well as kofta and kebab, they serve liver (*kebda*), kidneys, sausage and strongly flavoured, succulent lamb chops (*rayesh*). This place only opens after evening prayers (about 8 pm) and serves food until dawn. To get there, take a taxi to Midan Zein al-Abdin, locate Ouf, and then head down the street to the left of it. At the bottom of the street, past the stalls selling butchers' knives, bear left and Abu Ramy's is 50m on the right.

Middle-class Cairenes, who wouldn't be seen dead in Zein al-Abdin, prefer the more sanitary *Abu Shaqra*, at 69 Qasr al-Ainy (about 1.5km south of Midan Tahrir; see Map 7). It was named for Ahmed Abu Shaqra, who was known as the 'the King of Kebab' after he opened his place in 1947. Prices here are quite high. Abu Shaqra also has branches in Mohandiseen (see Places to Eat – Budget later in this chapter) and on Mirghani in Heliopolis.

There is also a good late-night kofta and kebab place, *Ar-Rifai*, just off Midan Sayyida Zeinab, up the alleyway to the left of the garish sabil-kuttab of Sultan Mustafa opposite the mosque.

Fiteer

Fiteer is a kind of pizza made with a flaky pastry base. The filling can be served as a topping or stuffed inside, and can be sweet or savoury. The place that serves fiteer is called a *fatatri*. Part of the attraction of eating fiteer is watching it being made – after being pounded, the dough is stretched and whirled around the cook's head like a lasso. There's a good fatatri on Midan Hussein called *The Egyptian Pancake House*. A medium fiteer, either with cheese, egg, tomato, olives and ground meat, or with raisins, coconut and icing sugar, is E£8. One fiteer is usually enough for a complete meal. Downtown, at 166 Sharia Tahrir, close to Midan Tahrir, is the 24 hour *Fatatri at-Tahrir* where, sweet or savoury, it's E£6 for small fiteer, E£8 for medium and E£10 for large. The cheapest – and arguably the best – fiteer of all are served at *Haram Zeinab* on the corner of Sharia Abdel Meguid and Midan Sayyida Zeinab (see Map 8). It's open 24 hours.

Fruit Juices

On practically every street corner, in every town throughout Egypt, there is a juice stand where you can get a drink squeezed out of just about any fruit or vegetable that is in season. Standard *asiir*, or juices, include: banana (*moz*); guava (*guafa*); lemon (*limoon*); mango (*manga*); orange (*bortuaan*); pomegranate (*rumman*); strawberry (*farawla*); and sugar cane (*asab*). Depending on the type of fruit, a glass costs from 50 pt to E£1.50 – you can also take along an empty mineral water bottle and get that filled up.

BETHUNE CARMICHAEL

Exploring Cairo is a thirsty business –
fortunately a refreshing apple, orange or
pomegranate juice is never far away.

SUPERMARKETS & SELF-CATERING

There are a few western-type mini-markets around but none are in the city centre. Probably the most convenient is *Sunny's supermarket* at 11 Aziz Osman in Zamalek (see Map 3). This place is something of an institution among expats who long for a little taste of home. It also has a community notice board that advertises flats for rent, language tutors, missing pets and the like. There's a second Sunny's in Mohandiseen, where Sharia Syria intersects with Gamiat ad-Dowal al-Arabiyya.

There's also a number fruit and vegetable markets around town. Try the *Tawfiqiyya souq*, off the top end of Talaat Harb, Downtown (see Map 4), or the *Souq Mansour*, off Midan Falaki (see Map 8). Of the two, the Tawfiqiyya souq has a larger range of produce and it's open until late at night. When buying fruit and vegetables check that the vendors don't try and slip in any rotten stuff. The Tawfiqiyya souq is also home to several bakeries and numerous *ba'aals*, the all-purpose grocers, where you can stock up on things like bread, cheese and yoghurt.

The general term for bread is *aysh* – which in Arabic also means 'life'. The basic form of bread is *aysh baladi* (country bread), which is coarse, flat and dinner-plate sized. The other main bread is called *aysh fransawi*, or French bread (baguette). There are two main types of cheese: *gibna beyda* (white cheese), which tastes like Greek feta; and *gibna rumi* (Turkish cheese), which is a hard, sharp, yellow cheese that is something of an acquired taste. Most ba'aals also stock a fairly bland, European-style cheese, generically known as 'cheddar'.

Takeaway alcohol supplies can be bought from the liquor stores that are irregularly dotted round the city. There are several at the top end of Talaat Harb including: *Nicolakis*, next to the Casablanca Restaurant; and another place, just round the corner on Sharia 26th of July (near the alley leading to Ash-Shams). In Zamalek there's *Ambrosio* on Sharia Brazil (see Map 3) or *Maison Thomas* at 157 Sharia 26th of July, near the Cairo Marriott (see Map 3). Foreign beers are not available, there's only Stella which goes for E£4.50 with 50 pt refundable on return of the bottle. For more information about alcohol and where to buy it, see Egyptian Alcohol under Nightlife in the Entertainment chapter.

BAKERIES & PATISSERIES

You can always smell these places long before you see them. Typical products include tiny French loaves, sesame-covered bagels, almond or date biscuits, and the coronary-inducing *basboosa*, *kanafe* and *baklava* (different kinds of pastries all dripping with syrup).

Cairo's best bakery is *El-Abd* with two branches Downtown – one on Talaat Harb, and the other at the junction of 26th of July and Sherif – which are virtually mobbed until midnight every day. For excellent cheesecake and crusty French bread, try the *Marriott Bakery*, either at the Cairo Marriott itself, in Zamalek (see Map 3), or in Mohandiseen on Gamiat ad-Dowal al-Arabiyya (see Map 2).

BREAKFAST

The average Egyptian is happy to make do with fuul sandwiches for breakfast, but there are alternatives. The Marriott Bakery (see under Bakeries & Patisseries) offers a variety of excellent French-bread sandwiches and slices of quiche from E£5.50 to E£6.50. *Maison Thomas* (see Places to Eat – Budget later in this chapter) in Zamalek offers a set breakfast of orange juice, fried eggs, bacon, bread, croissants and tea or coffee for E£17. Downtown, the Swiss restaurant *La Chesa*, at 21 Adly, opens at 7 am and serves various egg-based dishes (omelettes from E£6; scrambled eggs on toast, E£5), along with croissants, Danishes and rolls. *Lappas*, the delicatessen/mini-market at 17 Qasr el-Nil, has an upstairs cafeteria that serves a fairly unexciting Egyptian breakfast (croissant, tub of jam, cheese spread and tea) from 8 am.

All the big five-star hotels do breakfast buffets, probably the best of which is offered at *Omar's Cafe* at the Cairo Marriott – it costs E£27.50 with Middle Eastern, western and Japanese choices. The Nile Hilton has two

types of breakfast buffet, both served in the *Ibis Cafe* from 5 to 11 am. There's an open buffet for E£27 or the all-you-can-eat hot and cold buffet for E£35. The *Mena House* is a wonderful place to have breakfast before touring the Pyramids. At E£19, its continental breakfast is skimpy, but the special breakfast buffets are not bad at E£34.

CAFES
Downtown

Groppi's, on Midan Talaat Harb (see Map 8), used to be one of the most popular places in Cairo for taking tea and cakes (see the boxed text 'Groppi's of Cairo' in the Things to See & Do chapter) but these days it's for real nostalgia buffs only. For a tolerable cappuccino there's *Simonds* on Sharia Sherif (see

---

Tea & Coffee

Shay and *ahwa* – tea and coffee – are served strong and sugary. Specify how much sugar you want, otherwise in most nonwestern places, staff will automatically dump three or four heaped teaspoons of the stuff into your glass. To moderate that, order your tea *sukhar shwayya*, with 'a little sugar'. If you don't want any sugar at all, ask for *sukhar minrayer*. If you take your tea with milk, ask for *bi-laban*. Far more refreshing, when it's in season, is tea served with mint leaves – ask for *shay naana*.

If you ask for coffee, you will probably get Turkish coffee, which comes in a two-sip sized cup. It is gritty and *very* strong. Let the grains settle before drinking it. As with tea, you have to specify how much sugar you want: *ahwa mazboot* comes with a moderate amount of sugar but is still fairly sweet; if you don't want any sugar ask for *ahwa saada*. Coffee is often flavoured with cardamom. If you want something more like western-style instant coffee, ask for *nescaf*.

The best place to drink tea and coffee is at one of Cairo's multitudinous coffeehouses (see the boxed text 'The Ahwa' in the Entertainment chapter), but if you want to munch while sipping you'll need to look elsewhere. ∎

Map 8), sister outlet to the much better place of the same name in Zamalek. *La Chesa* at 21 Adly (see Map 4) does good coffee and has an appetising selection of pastries and cakes. Ibis Cafe at the Nile Hilton (see Map 7) has a popular garden terrace with an E£7.50 minimum charge – which you will have absolutely no problem covering – and it also serves Stella.

Zamalek

The closest thing you'll find to a real Italian cafe this side of the Mediterranean is *Simonds* at 112 Sharia 26th of July (see Map 3). For more than 40 years, it's been serving up the city's best cappuccino (E£2) and a decent espresso, as well as fruit juices and savoury pastries. It's open from 7.30 am to 9.30 pm daily.

FAST FOOD

Fast-food chains are mushrooming in Cairo quicker than you can say 'Big Mac and fries'. There are now over 30 international franchises in town and it's estimated that there will be 500 outlets in Cairo by the year 2000. The term fast food is something of a misnomer though, as young Egyptians spend hours at a time hogging the tables in these joints, which are considered some of the trendiest places in town to hang out. Mohandiseen's Gamiat ad-Dowal al-Arabiyya has become the street to cruise down – Cairo's smog-choked, six-lane, concrete Sunset Boulevard – largely because of its heavy concentration of fast-food outlets.

The following list mentions only the Downtown branches, but many chains aren't represented Downtown – the main fast-food centres are found in the affluent suburbs of Maadi and Heliopolis, along Pyramids Rd and, of course, on Gamiat ad-Dowal al-Arabiyya in Mohandiseen.

House of Donuts (see Map 4) on Adly, next to La Chesa.
KFC (see Maps 8 & 4) on Mohammed Mahmoud, opposite the American University in Cairo (AUC), and on Abdel Khalek Sarwat.

McDonald's (see Maps 4 & 8) on Talaat Harb, on Mohammed Mahmoud opposite the AUC and on the top floor of the Ramses Hilton shopping mall.
Pizza Hut (see Map 8) on Mohammed Mahmoud, across from the AUC.
Texas Fried Chicken (see Map 4) 31 Sharia 26th of July, west of Talaat Harb.
Wimpy on Sharia Hoda Shaarawi, near Midan Falaki; on Talaat Harb; and just off Sharia Sherif, north of the junction with Qasr el-Nil.

VEGETARIAN FOOD

Although there are few vegetarian restaurants – just one in fact – non-meat eaters shouldn't have too much trouble. Salads, dips, pulse-based dishes and stuffed vegetables feature heavily on most menus, as do the staples of fuul and taamiyya. Try places like *At-Tabie ad-Domyati*, *Felfela* or *Maroosh* Downtown or in Mohandiseen, or *Chabrawi's* in Heliopolis (see Places to Eat – Budget and Places to Eat – Middle, for information about all of these).

Happily, Cairo's one vegetarian restaurant, *L'Aubergine*, at 5 Sayed al-Bakry, Zamalek, is a good one. The extensive menu is constantly changing but the dishes are invariably excellent and prices range from E£15 to E£25.

PLACES TO EAT – BUDGET
Bab al-Luq

The area around the Souq Mansour has a wide variety of cheap places to eat, taking in everything from sandwich places to fatatris, kushari joints, juice stands and bakeries. One of the better places is the *Cafeteria ash-Shaab*, about halfway along Sharia Mansour (see Map 8). You can get a serve of makarone and potato stew for E£2. The fatatri next door does a good fiteer for E£3. *Al-Guesh* on the corner of Falaki and Sharia Tahrir is a traditional restaurant that does things like grilled liver, kofta and kebab for about E£15 to E£20.

Downtown

Thronged by tourists and coach parties, *Felfela* at 15 Hoda Shaarawi (see Map 8) does deserve its popularity. The quirky décor (tree-trunk tables, stuffed animals, aquariums, trellises and lanterns) creates a fun dining environment and, depending on your choices, the all-Egyptian food is excellent and moderately priced. Give the meat dishes a miss, as they are all overpriced and done better elsewhere. Instead order a selection of fuul, taamiyya, salads and other side dishes like tahina and baba ghanoug. A bill for two will come in under E£20. You can also get beer here. Felfela has branches along Pyramids Rd, on Rhoda and on the Corniche in Maadi.

Not far from the Felfela, midway down Mahmoud Bassiouni and a few doors shy of the Thomas Cook office, is *La Pasha* (no sign, just look for the stained wood frontage and push open the door; see Map 8) which serves simple but very good and filling Egyptian fare; recommended are the liver and rice (E£4) and the macaroni bechamel (E£3.50).

The *Excelsior*, on the corner of Talaat Harb and Adly (see Map 4), serves terrible food for very high prices, although the makarone or cannelloni (both around the E£5 mark) are possibilities. However, it is one of only a handful of places Downtown where it's possible to drink Stella and observe the street outside. The seedy and unappetising *Amira*, lurking in the alley across the road from the Excelsior, is worth mentioning for its decent lentil soup (E£1.50) and because it's open round the clock.

Also open 24 hours, the *Akher Saa* at 8 Alfy (sign in Arabic only – it's next to the Christian bookshop; see Map 4) is a fuul and taamiyya takeaway joint with a sit-down restaurant next door. The menu is limited but you can get things like omelettes (with pasturma is good) and tahina and bread. The bill is never more than a couple of pounds. *Restaurant GAD* on Adly, opposite the synagogue, is popular at lunch time with Downtown office workers; it has an extensive all-Egyptian menu or you can choose one of the three-course set meals for E£12 to E£15.

Around Midan Ramses

One of the best places for a cheap meal in Cairo is *At-Tabie ad-Domyati*, at 31 Orabi (see Map 4). The portions are large, the service is fast and friendly, the setting is clean and the food is excellent. It's predominantly vegetarian and has a wonderful salad bar with a choice of about 15 prepared salads and a variety of pickles – a large platter costs just E£3. Other specialities include a good lentil soup (don't be put off by the classic misspelt menu which promotes lentils as 'a type of Egyption legune which we lick and cook very well'). A filling meal for two can cost from as little as E£6 to E£8.

Rhoda

Just 100m south of the youth hostel is a *Felfela* restaurant. The food is more or less the same as the Downtown branch, and its river-side location makes it the perfect place to sit and drink a relaxing beer. There is one or two other similar places as you continue down the same street.

Zamalek

Cheap dining is not one of Zamalek's fortes but there are a couple of possibilities. The excellent *Maison Thomas* (see Map 3) – Cairo's only continental-style deli – does the best pizza in Cairo, with prices ranging from E£15 to E£20 for a 'regular', which is easily enough for two. It has imaginative – though pricey – sandwiches and salads too. Eat in or take out. It's at 157 Sharia 26th of July and is open 24 hours.

Al Dente at 26 Bahgat Aly (see Map 3), is a tiny Italian place frequented by students from the nearby AUC hostel. It's pasta only – choose the type and the sauce. Portions are small and cost between E£6 and E£10. The *Zamalek Restaurant* (see Map 3) on Sharia 26th of July, just east of the junction with Shagaret ad-Durr, does kofta, kebab or half a spit-roasted chicken, with bread or rice for under E£10.

Mohandiseen

Unless you stick with the fast-food places, dining out in Mohandiseen is rarely cheap. However, just off Gamiat ad-Dowal al-Arabiyya, down the street beside the Atlas Zamalek Hotel, is the excellent *Al-Omda* (see Map 2), a fuul, taamiyya and kushari place with a sit-down restaurant. It is towards the end of the block, up a flight of stairs. Not all of the items on the menu are cheap, but a meat-filled fiteer is only E£8.

Abu Shaqra, renowned for its pricey kebab, also has a variety of other cheaper dishes such as pigeon stuffed with rice and served with chips, and fatta moza tagen (lamb on a bed of baked rice with pieces of bread in a vinegary sauce), both of which cost less than E£15. It's at 17 Gamiat ad-Dowal al-Arabiyya, just south-west of Midan Mustafa Mahmoud (see Map 2).

Heliopolis

Chabrawi's (see Map 12) is a fuul and taamiyya place on Sharia Damascus. It also has a 1st floor dining room with an extensive salad bar and serves extras like omelettes. Other than pasturma the place is completely vegetarian. It's extremely clean and highly recommended. Look for the cherry-red window frames and mock Islamic frontage.

Traditional Egyptian fare such as kebab, kofta, shawarma and spit-roasted chicken is served at the *Amphitrion* and *Palmyra*, the two terrace cafeterias on Al-Ahram, and at the *Kashef*, at the bottom of Sharia Damascus, near the intersection with Ibrahim Laqqany (see Map 12).

PLACES TO EAT – MIDDLE

Unless stated otherwise most kitchens tend to be open until about 11 pm. Reservations are generally not needed anywhere except at the top-end places.

Downtown

There are few really good restaurants in Central Cairo, those we mention here are the best of a fairly uninspiring bunch. The *Estoril* (see Map 8) has its fans, probably as much for the atmosphere as the food – although what others might term period charm we consider to be dour and gloomy. Meals are a combination of French and Middle Eastern cuisine and generally cost from E£19 to E£30, although there are cheaper items such as the cannelloni for E£7.60. It's

at 12 Talaat Harb, in the alley next to the American Express office.

Nearby, at 6 Sharia Qasr el-Nil, between Midan Talaat Harb and Midan Tahrir, *Arabesque* (see Map 8) scores highly for its décor and surroundings. It's entered through a small art gallery and the restaurant is intimate with mashrabiyya screens, columns and a small gurgling fountain. Unfortunately the food – a mix of traditional Egyptian, seafood and steaks – is often mediocre and, as such, is overpriced (main meals range from E£25 to E£30).

Better value for money is offered at the far more modest *Alfy Bey Restaurant* on Sharia Alfy (see Map 4). Open since 1938, it has seen better days, but while the table-cloths are not as spotless as they could be and the service is less than brisk, the food is quite decent – lamb chops, kebab, chicken, pigeon and a good assorted dolma platter of stuffed peppers, courgettes (zucchinis) and vine leaves. Its prices are in the E£10 to E£20 range.

Similar fare at similar prices is offered at *Ali Hassan al-Hatti* (see Map 4), a place to fill up at and not really one to visit for a dining experience. There are two Al-Hattis, only one of which is good – that's the one tucked down an alleyway south of No 8 Sharia 26th of July. The second Al-Hatti, just south of the Hotel Windsor, has a gem of a dining hall that almost feels like the interior of a mosque, with chandeliers, suspended from a 5m-high ceiling, hanging to almost head height. It has a menu which is an absolute delight, including – and we're not making this up – 'drilled shops', but the food is appalling.

As an alternative to Egyptian cuisine, the *Peking* at 14 Ezbekiyya, just north of 26th of July (see Map 4), is a very passable Cantonese restaurant. Don't be put off by the shabby exterior, inside the place is smart, yet cosy. Fortunately, the food has largely managed to escape the 'Egyptianisation' that has afflicted the kitchens of the other Pekings in town (in Mohandiseen, Zamalek, Heliopolis and Maadi). Expect to spend from E£20 to E£30 per head, without drinks.

The pseudo-Swiss *La Chesa*, at 21 Adly (see Map 4), is not a bad place for lunch, with plenty of options under E£20 and self-service salads at E£4.50. Entrees cost from E£25 to E£30, but the food is fairly bland. A better option is *Le Bistro* at 8 Hoda Shaarawi, not far from the Felfela (see Map 8). The cooking is Gaelic enough to ensure that the place is heavily patronised by the French-speaking community. The menu features some good salads (all under E£10) and plenty of beef and chicken dishes for around the E£20 mark. While the restaurant is fairly busy at lunchtime, it's like a morgue in the evening. It's open daily from 11 am to 11 pm.

Islamic Cairo
The *Naguib Mahfouz Cafe*, right at the heart of Khan al-Khalili, is done out in a kind of 'Disneyfied Orientalism'. Despite the name it's not a cafe at all, but an upmarket restaurant. However, the menu is extremely limited and the food, though quite good, is way overpriced.

Zamalek
L'Aubergine, the vegetarian restaurant at 5 Sayed al-Bakry (see Vegetarian Food earlier in this chapter), also incorporates the *Cafe Kurnovsky* upstairs. It has an ever changing menu which is loosely Mediterranean, but occasionally wanders further afield. The food is often excellent and is moderately priced. While Cafe Kurnovsky is a restaurant that doubles as a popular bar (see Bars under Nightlife in the Entertainment chapter), *Deals*, on the same street, close to the junction with Maahad al-Swissri, is a busy bar that moonlights as a restaurant. The food on offer ranges from burgers and chilli con carne to calamari and large salads. Check the blackboard for daily specials. As bar food goes, it's very good and not expensive, but if you're planning to eat make sure you get there before 8 pm to stand a chance of finding some table space.

A personal favourite *Hana* is an unpretentious, smoky, little Korean restaurant that serves up fairly authentic South-East Asian food. Dishes are substantial and cost around

E£20, rice is another E£3. Beer is served. It's on Sharia Brazil, about 400m north of 26th of July.

South of 26th of July, on the 3rd floor of 4 Hassan Sabry, is *Four Corners*, a collection of four restaurants/bars. Of these, *La Piazza* is an OK place to have lunch in. It has a light and airy dining room with plenty of greenery, and some of the items on the menu are quite good (though not the pastas). The onion soup is excellent as is the liver pâté mousse, and the salads are usually a good bet.

Mohandiseen & Doqqi
Though bland and flavourless in appearance, Cairo's grey-concrete suburbs contain some of the city's better restaurants. Top of the list for many expat residents is *Tia Maria* at 32 Sharia Jeddah (see Map 6), to the west of the Shooting Club (Nadi as-Seid). It has an incredibly chintzy interior, all frilly, pink curtains and whatnot, but the food is superb and served in huge helpings. We can thoroughly recommend the spaghetti carbonara (E£12), the seafood pasta (E£18) and the crespelle Argentine – crêpes with ice cream smothered in caramel sauce.

Le Tabasco (Map 6; ☎ 336 5583), at 8 Midan Amman, is run by the same people as Zamalek's L'Aubergine and is every bit as popular. Again, the menu changes regularly, but ranges over a wider culinary field stretching beyond the Mediterranean to include, on occasion, dishes from Mexico and Eastern Europe. Prices are more expensive here (in the E£25 to E£40 range), and you usually need to make reservations.

Although, by all accounts, it's not up to the standards of its namesake in Beirut, Mohandiseen's *Maroosh*, at 64 Midan Libnan, has excellent mezze which can be enjoyed while lounging in rattan chairs on a streetside terrace. Skip the main meat dishes (it shouldn't be too hard with the 'lamb scrotum sandwich') and fill the table with bread and dips which cost from E£3 to E£5 each. For those who don't know their tabouleh from their fatoush, everything is well described in English on the menu.

For more alfresco dining, *Prestige* at 43 Sharia Geziret al-Arab is two restaurants in one – a cheerful, cheap pizzeria (prices in the E£12 to E£20 range) and a more expensive Italian*ish* place specialising in steaks and fresh fish (E£30 to E£40) – with pavement seating under large sun-brellas. Beer is served, but only inside. If you're heading west along Gamiat ad-Dowal al-Arabiyya, Geziret al-Arab is the street on the right at Wimpy Corner (see Map 2).

Mohandiseen also has two very good Indian restaurants, and one, the Tandoori, which should be avoided. There's not much to choose between them, but the *Taj Mahal* (Map 2; ☎ 302 5669) at 5 Libnan, entered off Sharia Hegaz, is possibly the better of the two. The cool, white and grey interior is a great counterpoint to some deliciously hot and spicy cuisine. There are also plenty of dishes for vegetarians. Expect to pay around E£40 per head. The cooks in the kitchen at *Kandahar* (Map 2; ☎ 344 3773) go a little easier on the hot stuff and the curries are much more subdued. Prices are roughly similar to the Taj Mahal. It's on the 4th floor of 3 Gamiat ad-Dowal al-Arabiyya, just south of Midan Sphinx – take the golden lift. Reservations are recommended at both these places.

Heliopolis

There are not too many places to eat here. The usual fall-back is the Swiss-style *Le Chantilly* at 11 Baghdad (see Map 12). The food is fine, if unexciting, but the surroundings are very pleasant if you can find seating in the garden at the back. Entrees are in the E£25 to E£35 range, although there are a few cheaper options, and beer is served.

Giza & Pyramids Rd

There's a *TGI Friday's* (Map 7; ☎ 570 9690) on a boat moored at 26 Sharia el-Nil, between the University (Al-Gamaa) and Giza (Abbas) bridges. TGI Friday's is a shamelessly manufactured American feel-good franchise and the Egyptians love it. The menu offers a broad range of American cuisine and it's possible to eat for under E£20, if you can resist dessert. Reservations are recommended at the weekend when it's at its liveliest and loudest. On the deck above TGI's is *The Fish Market*, one of Cairo's best seafood restaurants.

There are several options along the Maryutia Canal road, off to your right (heading towards the Pyramids) from Pyramids Rd. *Andrea's* is a famed chicken restaurant. Seating is out in a large garden, which would be quite pleasant if it weren't for the constant attention of clouds of mosquitoes – last time we were there, one of our party who had come in sandals had to spend the evening with her feet in her handbag. There is no menu – it's spit-roasted chicken only (there's sometimes quail too) with a selection of very good mezze as starters. The cost is about E£20 per head. Kids are well catered for with a large wooden playframe and donkey rides. Andrea's is about 1.5km north of the Pyramids Rd. If you're taking a taxi here from Central Cairo, you can expect it to cost about E£15.

The *Felfela Village* is several hundred metres further down the road from Andrea's on the right bank. If you're after a packaged Middle Eastern atmosphere with everything that is supposedly exotic, then this is the place. This restaurant and circus has everything – dancing horses, camel rides, acrobats, snake charmers, and a playground and small zoo for the kids – and is very popular with Egyptians. Massive amounts of traditional Egyptian food are served here.

There are only a few options close to the Pyramids. At the turn off for the Desert Highway from Pyramids Rd is an overpriced fish restaurant called *Christo's*. There's no menu – after making your selection from the catch that is laid out just inside the entrance, head up to the 2nd floor for a seat with a view of the Pyramids. Prices range from E£25 to E£42. At the Cheops Pavilion, directly in front of the Sphinx, is the *Sphinx House* restaurant/cafe. It has a shaded terrace with unobstructed views of the Sphinx but, as you'd expect with such a prime position, prices are way over the top.

PLACES TO EAT – TOP END

There aren't too many French restaurants in Cairo, but there are two that rank among the finest places to eat in town. At *Justine* (Map 3; ☎ 341 2961), part of the Four Corners complex at 4 Hassan Sabry in Zamalek, the cuisine is said to be both creative and exquisite. The menu at *Champollion* (Map 7; ☎ 362 1717), at the Meridien Le-Caire hotel, is said to be more traditional, but the food is every bit as exceptional. There's also the option here of dining on the terrace overlooking the Nile.

For a close-up view of the Nile, try for a window seat at *Le Steak* (Map 3; ☎ 340 6730) on Le Pache 1901, the river bus moored off Al-Saraya al-Gezira on Gezira. The décor is a little oppressive, but there's no faulting the slabs of beef that the restaurant is known for. Prices are also quite reasonable, with most entrees in the E£30 to E£35 range.

Also highly recommended is the *Moghul Room* (☎ 383 3222) at the Mena House hotel, which serves up Cairo's best Indian food. The dining room is completely over the top and it feels like you're sitting in a jewellery box, but the service is relaxingly friendly. The food is superb and the portions are generous; one main dish each, plus a couple of side orders, is sufficient for two and the bill will come to around E£150 without drinks. Afterwards, have a beer in the hotel's garden, with its awesome view of the floodlit Pyramid of Cheops rising above the palm trees.

It is advisable to make reservations at all the restaurants mentioned here.

Cruising Restaurants

The MS *Scarabee* and its more modern stable mate, the MS *Aquarius* (Map 7; ☎ 354 3198), are usually moored alongside the Corniche by Helnan Shepheard's hotel. The MS *Scarabee* has three cruises each day – at 2.30 pm for a 1½ hour lunch cruise that costs E£48; at 6 pm for a sunset cruise (E£21); and at 8 pm for a two hour voyage, including a buffet dinner, belly-dancing and band, for E£65. None of these prices include the cost of drinks. At the time of writing, the MS *Aquarius* was in dry dock but, once back on the water, it should be offering similar but more expensive services.

The classier *Nile Maxim* (☎ 340 8888 ext 8340) is operated by the Cairo Marriott. It has lunch cruises from 2 to 4 pm every Friday, Saturday and Sunday, and dinner cruises nightly from 8 to 10 pm and 11 pm to 1.30 am. The night cruises include entertainment and belly dancing. All-inclusive prices per head start at E£125 and go up to E£175.

In all cases, it's advisable to book a few days ahead.

Entertainment

Western-style discos, cinemas with English-language movies and nightclubs with floor shows abound in Cairo. With bucks to burn you can head to the casinos at many of the five-star hotels. If, on the other hand, you've already blown your budget, there are thousands of coffeehouses where you can while away the hours over a game of backgammon and a glass of tea.

For information about activities such as felucca trips, gallery visits, golf, horse riding, swimming, tennis and walking, see the Activities section at the end of the Things to See & Do chapter.

NIGHTLIFE
It's at night that Cairo really buzzes. The city only starts to come to life as the sun sets. During the summer months, families don't head Downtown to shop until 8 or 9 pm, when the heat of the day is less intense, and the smarter set never make dinner reservations before 10 pm. Bars get busy only towards midnight and the witching hour is long past before any discos start to fill. It's after 1 am before the bands kick in and the belly-dancers take to their five-star stages, and 3 or 4 am when the last ones bow out. For those still unwilling to call it a night,

The Ahwa
The coffeehouse or *ahwa* (the Arabic word means both coffee and the place in which it's drunk) is one of the great Cairo social institutions. Typically just a collection of cheap tin plate-topped tables and wooden chairs in a sawdust strewn room open to the street, the ahwa is a relaxed and unfussy place where the average Joe, or Ahmed, will hang out for part of each day reading the papers, meeting friends, sipping tea and whiling away the hours. The hubbub of conversation is usually accompanied by the incessant clacking of slammed *domina* (dominoes) and *towla* (backgammon) pieces, and the burbling of smokers drawing heavily on their *sheeshas*, the cumbersome waterpipes.

You'll notice that ahwa-going is something of an all-male preserve. With few exceptions Egyptian women do not frequent ahwas. That said, there is absolutely no reason why a foreign women shouldn't do so – although if you are unaccompanied by a male choose your ahwa wisely.

What to Order In the hot summer months some ahwa-goers forgo the tea and coffee (see the Cafes section in the Places to Eat chapter for a description of Egyptian coffee and tea) for cooler drinks like iced *karkadey* (made from boiled hibiscus leaves), *limoon* (a lemon drink) or *zabaady* (yoghurt). In winter many prefer *sahleb*, a warm drink made with semolina powder, milk and chopped nuts, or *yansoon* (a medicinal-tasting aniseed drink).

With the sheesha there's usually a choice of two types of tobacco: the standard *maasil*, which is soaked in molasses, or *tofah*, which is soaked in apple juice and has a sweet aroma but a slightly sickly taste. Filtered by the water in the glass bowl, the smoke is mild but the effort required to draw it can leave you quite light-headed. A good sheesha can last

there are places that just don't close at all –
some have never closed in the last 200 years.

Bars

Egyptian Alcohol For beer in Egypt say
'Stella'. Sold in dark-green 75 cL bottles,
Stella has been produced since the turn of the
century. It's a yeasty lager, the taste of which
varies enormously depending on the batch.
In a bad month it used to be that you would
send back bottle after bottle until the waiter
came up with something that wasn't flat or
vinegary. However, since privatisation in
early 1997 the quality has improved immeas-
urably. In 1998 the new producers of Stella
are also set to launch a locally brewed Carls-
berg on the as yet under-beered Cairo market,
and at least one other beverage company

may also be getting in on the act. Happy
times are ahead.

There are no plans, however, to improve
the Egyptian wine industry. From its vine-
yards in the Delta region, Egypt produces
red, rosé and white wines (with names like
Omar Khayyam, Rubis d'Egypte and Cru
des Ptolemies) but they are nearly undrink-
able, especially the reds. At E£30 a bottle
they are not cheap either. Unfortunately, outrageous import taxes mean that bottles of
imported wine, when available, sell for a
minimum of E£125.

Egypt also produces its own spirits – gin,
whisky, vodka, brandy (they all taste roughly
the same, which is to say dreadful) – which
are marketed to resemble foreign imports.
The whiskies include Johnny Wadie and

---

15 to 20 minutes. When the tobacco is burnt out or the coals have cooled, the *raiyis* (waiter) will
change the little clay pot of tobacco (the *hagar* or 'stone') for a fresh one. Each hagar costs 50 pt
to E£1. Most Egyptians will smoke two or three hagars per sitting.

When it comes time to pay, catch the eye of the raiyis and shout *Filoos!* (money).

Where to Go Other than in the newer suburbs like Mohandiseen, Doqqi and Agouza, almost every
street in Cairo has at least one ahwa. One of the oldest, and certainly the most famous, is *Fishawi's*
in Khan al-Khalili to the west of Midan Hussein. Despite frequently being swamped by foreign
tourists and equally wide-eyed Egyptians from out of town, Fishawi's manages to shrug it all off
(no waiters in fancy headgear or Fishawi keyrings for sale) and play the role of a regular ahwa,
serving tea, coffee and sheesha to all-comers. The place is open 24 hours and the best time to
visit is late at night.

More colourful than Fishawi's in terms of décor, if not atmosphere, is *Ash-Shams*, tucked away
in a courtyard alleyway between Sharia 26th of July and the Tawfiqiyya souq, Downtown (see
Map 4). Its walls are adorned with gilt stucco and kitschy mock-classical paintings. Just along the
alley are towering piles of onion sacks belonging to a stall in the market, and a blue barrel into
which the chopped heads of chickens are thrown by the poultry store on the corner. Since several
budget hostels opened in a single building in the souq, Ash-Shams has become a popular
backpackers' haunt.

Further down the market towards Sharia Ramses, in the last alley on the left, is the *Cafe
al-Agaty*, frequented by musicians, actors and journalists. It has a smoky 'Islamic' room with
mashrabiyya (carved wooden screens) and couches, and a rooftop terrace – it's another of those
places that only really gets going after midnight.

Although domina, towla and occasionally cards are the standard games played at ahwas, there
are a couple of places popular with the chess crowd, notably the *Cafeteria Horeyya* on Midan
Falaki in Bab al-Luq (see Map 8) and *Zahret al-Midan* on Midan Sayyida Zeinab at the junction
with Sharia Abdel Meguid (see Map 8). Also in the Sayyida Zeinab district are a cluster of what
are, as far as we know, Cairo's only 'video ahwas'. These are four or five large ahwas, each with
one, two or three TVs, which screen nonstop Arabic movies on video. The deal is that you have
to buy at least one tea or coffee for every film you watch. They're all on Sharia Nasriyya which
runs from Sayyida Zeinab north towards Bab al-Luq (see Map 8). ■

Black Tabel, while Garden's Gin carries a bold claim to the effect that 'The Queen drinks this'. We do not recommend that you drink any of this stuff as a bad aftertaste and a hangover could be the least of your worries – see the boxed text 'Deadly Drinks'.

Baladi Bars The local spit-and-sawdust bars are euphemistically known as 'cafeterias', though the only food present is usually a small plate of *fuul* (beans) or *termis* (small yellow beans that you nip with your teeth and squeeze out through their skin) which are used to salt the palate and quicken the down flow of beer. These places are discreet and don't advertise themselves, but if you know what you're looking for, they're pretty easy to spot – saloon-type doors leading into a dark interior are pretty good pointers. There are several on and around Sharia Alfy, Downtown (see Map 4), including the *Cafeteria Port Tawfiq* on Midan Orabi and the *Cafeteria Orabi* just 150m north on the left-hand side of Sharia Orabi. On Abdel Khalek Sarwat the *Cap d'Or* is a little more salubrious and people here are quite used to seeing foreigners, the same applies to the cramped *Stella Bar* on the corner of Hoda Shaarawi and Talaat Harb. None of these places are suitable for women on their own and the toilets are pretty foul in all of them (at the Stella you can at least nip a few doors down to use the ones at the Felfela restaurant on Hoda Shaarawi). Although primarily a coffeehouse, the *Cafeteria Horeyya* on Midan Falaki (see Map 8) also serves Stella.

All of these places charge from E£5 to E£6 for a beer and are open daily from around 11 am and close anywhere between 1 and 4 am. They all close completely during the month of Ramadan (see Public Holidays in the Facts for the Visitor chapter for dates).

Western-Style Bars Like any other busy city, bars and hang-outs open and close and go in and out of favour. At the time of writing the most popular place to go is upstairs at *L'Aubergine* restaurant at 5 Sayed al-Bakry in Zamalek (see Map 3). The crowd is largely thirtysomething, expat residents and the

atmosphere is cool jazz and candlelight. It gets busy from 11 pm onwards and closes about 2 am. The same management runs *Le Tabasco* at 8 Midan Amman in Doqqi (see Map 6) which pulls in a younger, trendier and mainly Egyptian crowd. The music and general all-round volume is loud and the décor is smart and hip. Many of the same comments – young, trendy crowd and loud music – apply to *Deals* restaurant back in Zamalek on Sayed al-Bakry (see Map 3). However, it's a little too small and claustrophobic for comfort.

Pub 28 on Shagaret ad-Durr in Zamalek is, as the name suggests, a pseudo-British pub. It has its regulars but it's gloomy and something of a lonely hearts club. *Harry's Pub* at the Cairo Marriott (see Map 3), another home for Brits away from home, is at least more cheery and patrons can catch major sports fixtures on the cable TV. A beer costs E£10 and there's a cover charge on Thursday for karaoke and Friday for the disco.

All the big hotels have bars but, other than Harry's, the only one worth patronising might be the *Taverne du Champs de Mars* at the Nile Hilton (see Map 7) which is a 1920s pub transposed in total from Belgium to Cairo. Imported beers are available on tap for the outrageous price of E£24, while Stella costs E£12. The *Windows on the World* bar, on the 36th floor of the Ramses Hilton (see Map 3), offers superb views of the city, especially at sunset, but the minimum charge of E£35 and 'no jeans' policy deters many – which is no doubt what these rules are designed for.

Much more welcoming, and in fact one of the most relaxing places to drink in Cairo, is the creaky *Lounge Bar* at the Hotel Windsor (see Map 4). Seating is on sofas or remodelled and padded barrels and the décor is post-colonial. A lot of locals use the place – particularly those in the theatre and cinema business – and solo women travellers should feel quite comfortable here. It's open until 1 am and beer is E£7.50. The rooftop bar at the *Odeon Palace Hotel* on Abdel Hamid Said (off Talaat Harb) draws a local crowd similar

ADAM MCCROW

KRISTIE BURNS

KRISTIE BURNS

EDDIE GERALD

For the first time in what seems like millennia, the Sphinx is free of scaffolding – see it while you can. The plateau around the Pyramids is also being cleared of the centuries-old detritus of hawkers and camel and horse owners whose persistent touting for trade has always been an unfortunate detraction from the spectacle of the monuments.

EDDIE GERALD

EDDIE GERALD

Much of life in Cairo takes place on the street, from the hours many men spend daily socialising in the city's pavement coffeehouses (top) to the elaborate 'tents' set up in alleys and side streets for weddings, parties and funerals (bottom).

Deadly Drinks

For years, tales have circulated among Middle Eastern travellers and Cairo residents of deaths caused by drinking local Egyptian spirits. They were usually considered to be apocryphal until a few years ago when the Canadian embassy issued a circular to its nationals stating that a couple of deaths had proven to be the result of a lethal bottle of locally produced whisky. So, perhaps the story of three Swedes going blind after sharing a bottle of brandy was true after all! The sensible advice has to be to leave this stuff well alone. At best it will churn up your stomach and have you spending two days feeling nervous anywhere out of immediate sight of a toilet; at worst the consequences are too unpleasant to contemplate. ■

---

to that at the Windsor, though its main appeal is the fact that it's open 24 hours every day. The minimum charge is E£10 and a beer is just over half that. There are also rooftop terrace bars at the *Carlton Hotel*, on 26th of July, Downtown, and at the *Fontana Hotel*, which has a fantastic view of the chaos down below on Midan Ramses.

Casinos

A number of Cairo's five-star hotels have casinos, open to non-Egyptians only (take your passport). All games are conducted in US dollars or other major foreign currencies, with a minimum stake of US$1. Smart casual attire is required. These casinos are not to be confused with local *casinos*, the name given for certain restaurants popular with families on a day out.

Discos

Thursday, Friday and Saturday nights are the most popular disco nights. During the rest of the week most places are a little on the quiet side. That isn't necessarily the case with *Casanova's* in the Hotel Burg on Midan Saad Zaghloul (see Map 7) which is pounding most nights. It's patronised by a fairly sleazy mix of young expats, Russians, gays and

wideboy Egyptians on the make. The admission charge is E£30 which includes a free beer. Also colourful is *Africana* on Pyramids Rd where, as you might guess, African-oriented sounds feature heavily on the play-list. It's hot and sweaty and there's the occasional punch-up and high velocity chair show, but it's all part of the charm. It's open weekends only – don't get there before midnight. Admission is E£25 which gets you one beer. The club is not easy to find – it's on the right as you head towards the Pyramids, beyond the Haram Theatre and then one block past the KFC.

The *Tamango Disco* in the Atlas Zamalek hotel in Mohandiseen (see Map 2) has a couples-only door policy, but foreigners can usually get around it. More off-putting is the E£40 admission charge for men; while it's only E£1.25 for women. Inside it's handbags and high heels with a mix of westerners and trendy, well-off Egyptians. The seriously wealthy head for *Jackie's* at the Nile Hilton. Again, most nights it's couples-only but it does host the occasional 'house' evening – check *Egypt Today* for information. The really seriously rich rattle their jewellery at *Piano Piano* or *Upstairs*, both in the World Trade Centre on the Corniche el-Nil at Bulaq.

Nightclubs

Nightclub in the Egyptian sense means a place that you go to sit down and eat, or possibly just drink, and watch a floor show. The floor show can feature folkloric dancing or a star singer, but the ones that really pull in the crowds concentrate on belly-dancing.

The best dancers perform at Cairo's five-star hotels. Dina, reckoned to be *the* best belly-dancer has an annual summer residency at the Cairo Sheraton's *Alhambra* nightclub (see Map 7) for which she's reputed to be paid E£10,000 per performance. It's no surprise then that a seat for the show, which starts at around 2.30 am and goes through to 4 am, costs E£150 per head (buffet included). One of the other big names, the legendary Fifi Abdou, dances at the *Gezira Sheraton* – the cost of admission is only slightly cheaper and the performance times are just as unsociable. The audiences for such shows are predominantly Gulf Arabs and the few high-rolling tourists who don't have an appointment with a tour guide at 7 am the next morning.

At the other end of the scale, it is possible to watch belly-dancing for just a few pounds. There are several places Downtown – plus plenty more along Pyramids Rd (generally expensive rip-off joints) – that cater mainly to Egyptians. It has to be said that these places are fairly seedy and most of the dancers have the appearance and grace of amateur wrestlers, but it can be fun especially when the inebriated patrons join in – as they invariably do. The *Palmyra*, south off 26th of July, is a cavernous place with the full Arab music contingent, belly-dancers (from about 1 to 4 am) and, occasionally, other acts like acrobats. There is an entry charge of E£3 and a Stella costs E£12. On Sharia Alfy there's the *New Arizona* and the *Shererazad Nightclub*, the latter is above the Alfy Bey Restaurant, but neither of these is as entertaining as the Palmyra.

CINEMAS

There was a time, just a few years back, when all that was on offer at Cairo's movie houses were Roger Moore-era James Bond movies and perpetual reruns of *Cobra*, *Predator* and *Rocky*. But the cinema business is now booming and new deals mean that Cairo gets first-run Hollywood blockbusters soon after their US release. Many of the city's cinemas have also recently been refurbished and revamped, and there are several new multi-cinema complexes on the way. Films are subtitled rather than dubbed, which means that the audience doesn't have to listen to the soundtrack and is free to chatter all the way through. Cairo cinema-goers are also big on audience participation which can be great fun on the opening night of something like *Independence Day*, but the whooping, cheering and clapping is a bit distracting if you're trying to settle into something like *The English Patient*. Films are subject to censorship. How heavy-handed this is depends on the mood of the moment. Even the most

seemingly innocuous movies often arrive on screen with a few tell-tale hiccups indicating scissor cuts.

One thing to beware of is that Egypt's anti-terrorism laws mean that no one is allowed to leave a cinema before the film ends. So if you wandered into some godawful talking-baby film because the ticket cost peanuts and you had nothing better to do, then you're stuck with it for the whole 90 minutes or more.

Screenings are usually at 1.30, 3.30, 6.30 and 9.30 pm. A few cinemas also have midnight shows on Friday and Saturday. Tickets range from E£8 to E£18 depending on the venue and seating. Check the daily *Egyptian Gazette* for details of what's showing.

Of course, not all of Cairo's cinemas screen English-language films but the following do:

Cairo Sheraton (Map 7; ☎ 360 6081) Sharia al-Giza, Doqqi. The closest Cairo has to an 'art house' cinema, in that it tends to forgo blockbusters for Merchant Ivory films and the like.

Horeyya I & II (Map 12; ☎ 452 9980) 6th floor Horeyya Mall, Sharia al-Ahram, Heliopolis. Currently Cairo's best cinema in terms of sound and comfort.

Karim I & II (Map 4; ☎ 591 6095) Emad ad-Din, Downtown. Old cinema recently refurbished. The programming and cheap tickets make it popular with young Egyptian males – not a place for women to go unaccompanied.

Metro (Map 4; ☎ 393 7566) 35 Talaat Harb, Downtown. Once Cairo's finest, now one of its scruffiest – see comments on Karim above.

MGM (☎ 352 3066) Maadi Grand Mall, Maadi. Fine if you live in Maadi, otherwise way, way out of town.

Normandy (Map 12; ☎ 258 0254) 32 Sharia al-Ahram, Heliopolis

Radio (Map 8; ☎ 575 6562) 24 Talaat Harb, Downtown. See comments on Karim.

Ramses Hilton I & II (Map 3; ☎ 574 7436) 7th floor Ramses Hilton Mall. Two relatively new screens, well maintained, although II is a bit small.

Swissotel al-Salam (Map 12; ☎ 293 1072) 65 Abdel Hamid Badawi, Heliopolis. Very difficult to get to without a car, unless you take a taxi from the centre of Heliopolis.

Tahrir (Map 6; ☎ 335 4726) 122 Sharia Tahrir, Doqqi. A fairly modern cinema that is rapidly moving downmarket.

THEATRE, MUSIC & DANCE

The *Cairo Opera House* (Map 7; ☎ 342 0598) on Gezira is the city's premier performing arts venue. Well-known international troupes sometimes perform here – the Bolshoi Ballet visits almost annually – and at other times the recitals by local companies, such as the Cairo Opera Ballet Company and the Cairo Orchestra, are worth catching too. In addition to a main hall and small hall, the Opera House also has an open-air theatre and summer amphitheatre. Check *Egypt Today* and *Al-Ahram Weekly* for what's on, or pass by and pick up a program. Jacket and tie are required by males for main hall performances, but less well-dressed travellers have been known to borrow them from staff.

There are often music recitals and plays of varying quality at the *Ewart Hall* and *Wallace Theatre*, both part of the American University in Cairo (AUC) campus. In Islamic Cairo theatre performances and music evenings are held at the House of Zeinab Khatoun and the Al-Ghouri complex (see Map 9), especially during Ramadan. It's worth attending something at each of these places at least once, if only for the setting. Also worth checking, especially if you have kids, is the *Cairo Puppet Theatre* in the Ezbekiyya Gardens, just north of Ataba (see Map 4). Performances are usually held late in the morning from Sunday to Thursday – October through to May. Again, check the two publications mentioned above for notices of events.

Sufi Dancing

On Wednesday and Saturday nights from 9 pm (9.30 pm in winter) the Al-Tannoura Egyptian Heritage Dance Troupe gives a 1½ hour display of Sufi dancing in the Madrassa of al-Ghouri in Islamic Cairo (see Map 9). The troupe has toured overseas, and their colourful performances are extremely popular (see Dance under Facts about Cairo for more information about Sufi dancing).

Admission is free and it's advisable to come early, especially in winter, as the small auditorium can get quite crowded.

CLUBS

The club (*al-nadi*) is the great social institution of Cairo's upper and middle classes. Anyone who can afford to do so and has the right connections is a member of a club, which gains them access to a private swathe of the city's precious green. The most extensive and exclusive is the *Gezira Club* (see Map 3), followed closely by Doqqi's *Shooting Club* (see Map 6) and the Heliopolis *Sporting Club* (see Map 12). It can take years to gain membership to a club (and thousands of pounds) but day passes are usually available for E£10 to E£20. These give the holder access to the tennis courts, jogging track, golf course (in the case of the Gezira) and whatever other facilities the club possesses but does not always include access to the pool.

SPECTATOR SPORT

Football is king in Egypt. Of the Arab nations, Egypt is the one country with players of international capacity (Hazem Emam formerly of Zamalek now currently plays for Udinese of Italy), and although they won't be taking part in the 1998 World Cup, they did qualify in 1990, but were knocked out in the first round – in a group that included Holland and England. In conversation with any Egyptian male, Cairo's premier teams – Zamalek and Al-Ahly – arouse greater passions than almost any other subject. Demand for tickets makes them hard to get hold of, especially for derbies. You could try at the box offices of the two teams' home grounds, Ahly, next to the Cairo Tower on Gezira (see Map 7) and Zamalek, south off 26th of July in Mohandiseen (see Map 2). The season begins in September and continues until May. The big matches are held in the Cairo Stadium in Medinet Nasr (see Map 1).

Shopping

Cairo is both a budget souvenir and a kitsch-shoppers' paradise. Tourists with shelf space to fill back home can indulge in an orgy of alabaster pyramids, onyx Pharaonic cats, sawdust stuffed camels, and the ubiquitous painted papyrus. Hieroglyphic drawings of Pharaohs, gods and goddesses embellish and blemish everything from leather wallets to engraved brass tables. The best place for this sort of stuff is Khan al-Khalili, although you will have to be prepared to bargain hard (see the boxed text below).

The Art of Bargaining
Almost all prices are negotiable in Cairo, especially in the souqs and bazaars where bargaining is expected. Prices of souvenirs are always inflated to allow for it. Bargaining can be a hassle, but keep your cool and remember it's a game, not a fight.

The first rule is never to show too much interest in the item you want to buy. Secondly, don't buy the first item that takes your fancy. Wander around and price things, but don't make it obvious otherwise when you return to the first shop the vendor will know it's because they are the cheapest.

Decide how much you would be happy paying and then express a casual interest in buying. The vendor will state their price and you should state a figure somewhat lower than that you have fixed in your mind. So the bargaining begins. The shopkeeper will inevitably huff about how absurd your offer is and then tell you the 'lowest' price. If it is still not low enough, be insistent and keep smiling. Tea or coffee might be served as part of the bargaining ritual – accepting it doesn't place you under any obligation to buy. If you still can't get your price, then walk away. This often has the effect of closing the sale in your favour. If not, there are thousands more shops in the bazaar.

If you do get your price or lower, never feel guilty – no vendor, no matter what they say, ever sells below cost. ■

Away from the touristy sales patter of the Khan vendors there are plenty of other good places to shop for quality crafted goods – where the items for sale come with price tags affixed for those who like their transactions kept simple. Try the fantastic souvenir shop-cum-bazaar in Coptic Cairo opposite the Church of St Sergius – probably the biggest in the city. Some of the gift shops in the Nile Hilton and Semiramis hotels are also no more expensive than the Khan.

For more general shopping, there are several malls around town. These include the Ramses Hilton Mall, beside the hotel of the same name (see Map 3); the downmarket Bustan Centre on Sharia Bustan, Downtown (see Map 8); and the way, way upmarket World Trade Centre on the Corniche el-Nil in Bulaq (see Map 3).

ANTIQUES
There are few real antique bargains around, and it is illegal to export anything of antique value out of Egypt without a licence from the Department of Antiquities. But, if you're interested in browsing start on Sharia Hoda Shaarawi, Downtown (see Map 8). There are also several expensive places in Zamalek such as Nubi Antiquaire at 157 Sharia 26th of July and Galerie Odeon on the same street at No 110 (see Map 3). For smaller items like old jewellery and ceramics, try Senouhi on the 5th floor at 54 Abdel Khalek Sarwat, just off Midan Opera, Downtown.

For anyone who knows what they're doing, Osiris (Map 2; ☎ 392 6609) at 15 Sharia Sherif, opposite the Banque Masr, Downtown is the city's best auction house. Unmonopolised by commercial antique dealers, the occasional genuine bargain can be had. Auctions are held every few weeks, preceded by three days of viewing.

ARTS & CRAFTS
For general handicraft emporiums try the Khan Misr Touloun (Map 8; ☎ 365 2227)

opposite the entrance to the Mosque of ibn Tulun and run by a pleasant French lady. The cave-like interior is crammed with Bedouin rugs and cushions, pottery from the Western Desert Oases, locally made glazed dishes and plates, blown glass, woven items and wooden dolls and puppets. There are also more unusual items such as traditional wooden benches and chests. It's open Monday to Friday from 10 am to 5 pm.

Mameluke on Sharia Hassan Assem just south-east of the junction with Mansour Mohammed in Zamalek (see Map 3) has more of the same, particularly patterned ceramics. Nomad (Map 3; ☎ 341 1917) at 14 Al-Saraya al-Gezira, up on the 1st floor, is an enchanting place specialising in Bedouin crafts, dress and jewellery. It's open from 10 am to 3 pm only, Monday to Saturday.

It is also worth checking the artisans studios at the Wikala of al-Ghouri by Al-Azhar mosque (see Map 9) and, when it reopens, Beit as-Sennari south of Midan Sayyida Zeinab (see Map 8 and the Things to See & Do chapter).

Appliqué

The place to go for appliqué is the Street of the Tentmakers (Sharia al-Khayamiyya), south of Bab Zuweyla in Islamic Cairo (see Map 9), where a dozen or more workshops are clustered in a medieval, covered market. The colours are bright and the patterns range from arabesques and calligraphy to the more figurative like dervish dancers or Pharaonic motifs. The price depends on the intricacy of the pattern (arabesques and calligraphy cost the most), the quality of the work, and the size: as a guide a small cushion cover costs E£20; a larger one E£40. Wall hangings of about 1.5sq metres range from E£80 to almost E£200.

Brass & Copperware

The best place for this sort of thing is Khan al-Khalili, particularly An-Nahassin (Street of the Coppersmiths) – that part of Sharia al-Muizz li-Din Allah just south of the Qalaun complex. Also, for tin-lined copper cookware, go up the stairway located 50m along the alley opposite the Naguib Mahfouz Cafe. Engraved trays and plates start at around E£30 for one 30cm in diameter. Be wary of claims that the object in your hand is a hundred years old – more often than not it rolled off the production line a couple of weeks ago.

Inlaid Boxes

Second only in popularity to papyrus as souvenir items are the mother-of-pearl inlaid boxes piled high in most of the Khan's stores. They are incredibly inexpensive, a small one selling for as little as E£6. For that price you'll get something of fairly poor quality but it is possible to pay a higher price for something much more beautifully crafted – like a mirror frame or jewellery casket.

Inlay is also used to decorate backgammon boards (some with chess on the reverse side) which can cost over E£100 – an unadorned board can be bought for as little as E£20 on Al-Muizz li-Din Allah. Counters and chess pieces are sold separately; the poorer ones are made of plastic, the better of bone. A mother-of-pearl chess board together with camel bone pieces would sell for somewhere in the region of E£240 to E£300. You may be offered ivory – see the boxed text below.

Responsible Shopping

Although, in line with international treaties, Egypt no longer imports ivory, large quantities still continue to be smuggled into the country. Most of it comes from Sudan and Kenya, where elephant populations were decimated during the 1970s and 80s in order to meet demands for ivory jewellery and trinkets. Many countries – Australia, the UK and the US included – prohibit the import of ivory in any form or quantity, including souvenirs.

Other animals which have fallen victim to illegal trading are birds and desert creatures. You'll see plenty of these stuffed and sold at Kerdassa, a village near the Pyramids, as well as in the Khan al-Khalili. ■

SHOPPING

Mashrabiyya

Virtually nobody these days is in the business of making complete mashrabiyya screens. What you get instead are things that look like magazine racks (actually Quran holders) or table bases. It is still possible to find large screens in some of the antique stores, but they'll be prohibitively expensive. The one exception is NADIM (the National Art Development Institute for Mashrabiyya; ☎ 348 1075), which is a craftshop that is dedicated to keeping the art of mashrabiyya alive. It has all manner of mashrabiyya products, screens included (from E£2000 to E£3000) and visitors are welcome to watch the artisans at work with no obligation to buy. It's on Sharia al-Mazaniyya, off Sudan behind the Coca Cola plant, Doqqi.

BOOKS

Cairo has a reasonably good selection of bookshops, particularly if it's Egypt-oriented titles that you're after. If you've got the time, it's worth shopping around as prices can vary considerably – although all prices are far higher than in Europe and the US.

The best of the lot is the American University in Cairo (AUC) Bookshop (see Map 8; ☎ 357 5377), reached via the Mohammed Mahmoud gate and in the building to the right. Being an academic outlet, it has stacks of material on the politics, sociology and history of Cairo, Egypt and the Middle East. It also has by far the largest selection of fiction, both popular and the classics and it also carries Lonely Planet titles. It's open Sunday to Thursday from 9 am to 4 pm and Saturday from 10 am to 3 pm. It's closed on Friday and during the month of August. There is also a much smaller branch (Map 3; ☎ 339 7045) at the AUC Hostel at 16 Sharia Mohammed ibn Thakeb in Zamalek.

Other bookshops with very good selections of books about Cairo and Egypt are Lehnert & Landrock (Map 4; ☎ 393 5324) at 44 Sharia Sherif and Livres de France (Map 8; ☎ 393 5512) at 36 Qasr el-Nil. The former has plenty of books in German and the latter has shelves of French titles. Lehnert & Landrock is also one of the better places for maps and it also has a large collection of old postcards and prints. It's open from 9.30 am to 2 pm and 4 to 7.30 pm, but is closed Saturday afternoon and Sunday. Livres de France is open 10 am to 7 pm, closed Saturday afternoon and Sunday.

Cairo's most intriguing bookshop is the Anglo-Egyptian (Map 4; ☎ 391 4337) at 165 Mohammed Farid. Books are piled floor to ceiling and need to be unearthed and excavated. Most of the titles are academic but if you dig around at the back you'll find plenty of English literature. Books are priced by multiplying the publisher's price by the current exchange rate – as a lot of the stock has been hanging around for 10 or more years it makes for some bargains.

Other places worth checking are the Zamalek and Romantica bookshops opposite each other on Shagaret ad-Durr, Zamalek (see Map 3), both of which carry plenty of airport novels. In Heliopolis the Everyman Bookshop at 12 Baghdad (see Map 12) has more Collins, Grisham, King et al upstairs.

L'Orientaliste at 15 Qasr el-Nil, opposite Groppi's restaurant (see Map 8), is an antiquarian bookshop specialising in Egypt. It also sells 19th century prints. It's open daily Monday to Saturday, from 10 am to 7.30 pm.

Second-Hand Books

There are no second-hand bookshops in Cairo. There was a second-hand book market in the Ezbekiyya Gardens but it was forced to clear out a few years ago. All there is now is a guy with a spread of tatty paperbacks and magazines on Talaat Harb 20m north of Cinema Radio (see Map 4). The newsstands outside Groppi's restaurant and across from the AUC's Mohammed Mahmoud gate also do a little trade in used reads (see Map 8).

Newsstands

The three best newsstands are right next to each other in Zamalek, at the junction of 26th of July and Hassan Sabry (see Map 3). You can get just about anything from these guys, provided there are no bare breasts or buttocks involved. You will pay a premium though – a magazine which sells for UK£2.60

costs the equivalent of UK£6 in Cairo, while a daily that costs 40p in the UK is E£6 here.

Downtown, the places with the best selections include the guy on Midan Talaat Harb out front of Groppi's restaurant; the newsstand on Sharia Mohammed Mahmoud, opposite the entrance to the AUC; and the place on the opposite side of Midan Tahrir from the Hilton, next to TWA (see Map 8). Of the hotel bookshops, those at the Cairo Marriott and Semiramis hotels are the best for periodicals and papers.

JEWELLERY

Gold and silver jewellery can be made to specification for not much more than the cost of the metal. A cartouche with the name of a friend or relative spelled out in hieroglyphs makes a great gift.

Although gold shops are concentrated on Sharia al-Muizz li-Din Allah just north of the junction with Muski (an area called Souq as-Sagha or Goldsmiths' Bazaar), gold can be bought all over Khan al-Khalili. It is generally sold by weight. Buying gold and jewellery is always a little fraught. The Assay Office in Birmingham, UK, says that hallmarking for gold of at least 12 carats and silver of 600 parts per thousand or more is compulsory in Egypt – verifying this is another matter. The hallmark contains a standard mark showing where a piece was assayed and a date mark in Arabic. Foreign goods cannot be resold, in the UK at least, unless they are first assayed there. Storekeepers have an irritating habit of weighing the gold out of sight. Insist that they put the scales on the counter and let you see what's happening. This doesn't eliminate the chances of cheating, but does reduce them. Flat rates per gram at the time of writing were E£31 for 18k; E£36 for 21k. You can check the day's gold prices in the *Egyptian Gazette*.

Much the same cautionary rules apply to silver and other jewellery. An endless assortment of rings, bracelets, necklaces and the like can be found all over Islamic Cairo. One jeweller who has been recommended to us is Mihran Yazejian, almost opposite the Naguib Mahfouz Cafe in the Khan.

Away from Khan al-Khalili, the Midan Opera end of Abdel Khalek Sarwat, Downtown (see Map 4) is the other area with a high density of gold and silver. For ethnic jewellery, see the general arts & crafts shops mentioned earlier in this chapter.

MUSIC
Music Cassettes & CDs

Cassette kiosks dot the city but the highest concentration is along Sharia Shawarby which runs between Qasr el-Nil and Abdel Khalek Sarwat, Downtown (see Map 8). There's also a good kiosk in a little alleyway off the top end of Talaat Harb, just a few doors up from McDonald's.

As well as cassettes by Egyptian and other Arab artists (see the boxed text 'Recommended Listening' on page 176) most places have a very limited selection of pirated, poor quality tapes of western artists – fine if you're a big fan of bland, sanitised pop sung through a bucket. It's the done thing to ask to listen to a tape before buying it.

Imported western CDs, and a growing number by Egyptian artists, are available from Maestro and Juke Box both at the World Trade Centre shopping mall on the Corniche el-Nil, Bulaq. Some of the cassette kiosks on Shawarby also have a small selection of CDs.

Musical Instruments

Traditional musical instruments such as the *oud* (a type of lute), *kamaan* (violin), *nay* (flute), *tabla* (hand drum) and various others, are made and sold in about a dozen shops on Sharia Mohammed Ali (also known as Sharia al-Qalaa) which runs south-east from Midan Ataba to the Museum of Islamic Art (see Map 8). Gamil Georges at No 170 sells ouds, for example, with prices ranging from E£150 to E£300.

PAPYRUS

You can pick up cheap, poor quality papyrus all over Cairo for virtually nothing, but many well-heeled visitors continue to part with ridiculous sums of money for garbage. Look long and hard at what you are getting.

Recommended Listening

There are no music charts in Cairo, but you know when something is big because you just can't escape it. The following list is not based on bestsellers or what we consider the best cassettes – it is purely intended as a very selective sample, offering a tiny inroad into the vast array of sounds available. For more information on Egyptian music see the Facts about Cairo chapter.

- **Zahma** by Ahmed Adawiyya
  From the 1970s when Adawiyya's irreverent backstreet sound was at the peak of its popularity. The title means 'crowded'.
- **Shababik** or **Al-Malik** by Mohammed Mounir
  Dubbed the 'thinking person's pop star', Mounir, a Nubian, fuses traditional Arabic music with jazz to create a fairly sophisticated sound that's very accessible to western ears.
- **Nazra** by Hakim
  One of the most popular shaabi singers of the moment. This is his first and best album.
- **Lo Laki** by Ali Hameida
  Lo laki (which means 'Without you') dominated Cairo's airwaves for several years after its release in 1988. It was the song that crystallised the al-jeel formula – rasping synthesizer and catchy, nonsensical lyrics. Listen at your peril.
- **Awaddaak** by Mohammed Fuad
  Hugely popular al-jeel pop from 1994.
- **Omar Khayrat**
  Primarily a composer of scores for films and TV, Khayrat mixes classical and Arabic motifs to create what some would call Egyptian lift music.
- **Yalla**
  A cassette/CD compilation of Egyptian street music of which half is al-jeel, half shaabi. It has excellent sleeve notes. Released by Mango Records, a division of Island, in 1990.
- **Songs from the City Victorious**
  A collaboration between Jaz Coleman (Killing Joke), Anne Dudley (Art of Noise) and a bunch of Egyptian musicians with fantastic results – the Egyptians like it so much that it's all over state TV.
- **Diaspora** by Natacha Atlas
  Another east-west collaboration, this time between trance vocalist Atlas and her band, and a bunch of Cairo musicians. It's successful only in parts.

The last three are not available in Cairo, but major stores in the west such as Tower, HMV or Virgin should stock, or at least be able to order, them. ∎

Is it machine printed? Has it rolled off a sweatshop production line? Or has it been masterfully hand-painted? And is it papyrus, which will not be damaged by rolling, or is it in fact banana leaf which will crack?

The name Dr Ragab has long been associated with papyrus, and he has a floating 'institute' moored on the Nile just off the Sharia el-Nil in Doqqi. His stuff is good quality but it's also expensive. A good alternative is Said Delta Papyrus Centre (Map 9; ☎ 512 0747) in Islamic Cairo. Said learnt his craft from the famed Dr Ragab, and some of his work is stunning. The posted prices seem to be negotiable. The shop is on Sharia al-

Muizz li-Din Allah, north of Bab Zuweyla. It's on the 3rd floor above a shoe shop – look for a yellow sign at 1st floor level.

PERFUMES

Egypt is a big producer of many of the essences that make up French perfume, hence it's no surprise that part of Cairo's Khan al-Khalili is devoted to a perfume bazaar. Here you can buy pure essence (anywhere from E£8 to E£20 an ounce) as well as cheaper substances diluted with alcohol or oil. Some of the perfume traders have price tags on their goods, but that doesn't mean you can't haggle.

Intricate perfume bottles are also a big seller but, once again, there are expensive and cheap varieties. Small glass bottles start at about E£3; the heavier and more durable Pyrex bottles cost from E£10.

SPICES

Every conceivable herb and spice, and many you will never have heard of or seen before, can be bought around the Khan al-Khalili. Generally they are fresher and of better quality than any of the packaged stuff you'll find in the west, and four to five times cheaper – exactly how much cheaper will, of course, depend on your bargaining prowess. Many of the spice stalls are on the stretch of Al-Muizz li-Din Allah between Muski and Al-Azhar, known as the Souq Attarine. Far better – more colourful, more aromatic and cheaper – is the narrow alleyway behind the Mosque-Madrassa of al-Ghouri (see Map 9).

DUTY-FREE SHOPS

It is possible to buy a wide range of articles duty-free, either on, or within a month of, entry. Imported beer and alcohol are the main draw. You are allowed either three bottles or two bottles and a box of cans. Take your passport. The two main duty-free outlets are at 106 Gamiat ad-Dowal al-Arabiyya in Mohandiseen (see Map 2) and at the Cairo Sheraton. There is also a duty-free shop on Talaat Harb, Downtown, but it doesn't have any booze.

SHOPPING

Excursions

The region around Cairo (see the Excursions and Around Cairo maps) offers some interesting attractions, including the ancient tombs and pyramids of Saqqara, the Birqash camel market, Al-Fayoum – one of the world's largest oases – and the medieval monasteries of Wadi Natrun. Most of the destinations described in this chapter can be visited on day trips from Cairo, but some, such as Alexandria and Al-Fayoum, are better visited on overnight trips.

ALEXANDRIA, ISMAILIA & PORT SAID

All three of these cities, while some distance away from Cairo, are served by regular and fairly speedy buses and trains, and all three make very easy day trips. For further transport details see the Getting There & Away chapter.

The best short trip out of Cairo is up to the Mediterranean port city of **Alexandria**. Cairenes flock up here in their thousands every summer to escape the stifling heat of the capital and settle like seabirds on the beaches to the west of the centre. In fact the city's beaches aren't overly enticing – the thing to do in Alex is book a hotel room overlooking the bay, take long breakfasts on the balcony and then while away the days walking the Corniche and idling in cafes. For atmospheric accommodation try the *Hotel Acropole* (☎ 805 980) or *Hotel Triomphe* (☎ 807 585), both in the E£20 to E£30 range. They are both just west of Midan Saad Zaghloul, behind the far more pricey *Cecil Hotel* (☎ 483 7173), an Alexandrian institution, that has at one time or another played host to Somerset Maugham, Winston Churchill and, of course, Lawrence Durrell, author of *The Alexandria Quartet*. Singles/doubles start at E£114/140.

The other two day trips that are popular with Cairo residents are to the Suez Canal towns of Ismailia and Port Said. **Ismailia** has attractive examples of late 19th and early 20th century colonial-style architecture but most people just go to swim in the lakes and watch the ships glide languorously down the canal. While there are a couple of little hotels few people stay overnight.

The allure of **Port Said** lies in some attractive canal-side streets and beautiful tiered-balcony buildings which look like they'd be more at home in New Orleans. There's a sprawling souq here and also a very good National Museum with a decent collection of artefacts from all stages of Egyptian history – it merits more visitors than it gets. A good place to stay is the *Akri Hotel* (☎ 221 013), at 24 Sharia al-Gomhurriya, which has clean singles/doubles for about E£15/21.

BIRQASH CAMEL MARKET

Egypt's largest camel market (Souq al-Gamal) is held at Birqash, about 35km north-west of Cairo. Up until 1995, this famous market was located among run-down tenements and overcrowded streets in Imbaba, one of Cairo's western suburbs, but a burgeoning population squeezed out the animals and traders to the edge of the Western Desert.

Hundreds of camels are sold here every day, most having been brought up the 40 Days Road from western Sudan to just north of Abu Simbel by camel herders. From here, they're hobbled and crammed into trucks for the 24 hour journey to Birqash. By the time they arrive, many are emaciated while others are fit only for the knackery.

In addition to those from Sudan, there are camels from various parts of Egypt (including Sinai, the west and the south) and sometimes from as far away as Somalia. They are traded for other livestock such as goats, sheep and horses or sold for farm work or slaughter – yes, your kofta is probably camel meat. If you're interested in buying, the going rate is around E£1500 for a smaller beast or E£3000 for something bigger. Females go for slightly more. The market is

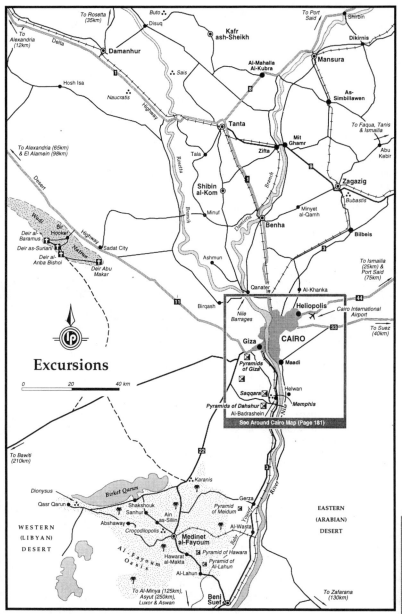

Excursions

0   20   40 km

See Around Cairo Map (Page 181)

most lively on Friday and Monday mornings, from about 6 to 9 am. As the day wears on, the bargaining activity subsides and by early afternoon it becomes quite subdued.

For a long time a question mark has hung over whether or not there is an official entrance fee for tourists to the market, but the practice has established itself and admission is E£3 plus another E£2 for cameras.

Getting There & Away

The cheapest way to get to the market involves getting yourself to the site of the old camel market at Imbaba, from where microbuses filled with galabeyya-clad traders and potential buyers shuttle back and forth to Birqash. To get to the old camel market take bus No 99 from Midan Tahrir (next to the Nile Hilton), or minibus No 72 from Ramses station, to Midan Libnan (in Mohandiseen) and then catch a microbus from there. It's much easier to simply take a taxi from central Cairo all the way to the old site (about E£3 to E£5) – ask for Imbaba airport (*Imbaba matar*) as it's the closest landmark. From Imbaba, microbuses to Birqash (E£1) leave from a cafe (look for the sign 'Modern Cairo House') opposite the old souq site (which has become, for the time being, a garbage dump-cum-playground).

From Imbaba, the road winds through fields dotted with date palms, dusty villages and orange orchids before climbing the desert escarpment to the market. In all, it's a 45 minute taste of rural Egypt. Microbuses from Birqash back to Imbaba leave when full so, depending on the time of the day, you may have to wait an hour or so.

Alternatively, on Friday only, the Sun Hotel (☎ 578 1786) at 2 Sharia Talaat Harb organises a minibus tour to the souq, leaving the hotel at 7 am and returning at about noon. The charge is E£20 per person (minimum five people); you must book a day or two in advance.

The final option is to hire a taxi to take you all the way there and back. Depending on your bargaining skills, you'll be looking at around E£60; make sure to negotiate waiting time.

MEMPHIS

Memphis (Mit Rahina), once the glorious Old Kingdom capital of Egypt, has almost completely vanished. It is believed that the city was founded around 3100 BC, probably by King Menes, when Upper and Lower Egypt were first united. It had many splendid palaces and gardens, and was one of the most renowned and populous cities of the ancient world. Even as late as the 5th century BC, long after Thebes had taken over as the capital of Egypt, Memphis was described by the Greek historian Herodotus as a 'prosperous city and cosmopolitan centre'.

Today there are few signs of the grandeur of Memphis. It's extremely difficult to imagine that a city once stood where there is now only a small museum and a scattering of statues in a garden. The partly open-air museum contains a prone, colossal limestone statue of Ramses II. In fact, by the time you read this it should contain two, as a twin Ramses II, which at the time of writing stands at the centre of Midan Ramses in Cairo, is due to be moved to Memphis before the end of 1997 (see the boxed text 'Ramses II to Go' in the Things to See & Do chapter). Also in the museum garden are yet more statues of Ramses II, an eight tonne alabaster sphinx, the sarcophagus of Amenhotep and the alabaster beds on which the sacred Apis bulls were mummified before being placed in the Serapeum at Saqqara.

Admission is E£14, half price for students plus E£10/50 for a camera/video. It's open from 8 am to 5 pm.

Getting There & Away

Memphis is 24km south of Cairo and 3km from Saqqara. The cheapest way to get there from Cairo is to take a 3rd class train from Ramses station to Al-Manashy, and get off at Al-Badrashein village. The trip takes about two hours (to go 24km) and costs 35 pt. From the village, you can either walk for about half an hour, catch a Saqqara microbus for 25 pt or take a taxi.

Rather than catch the slow train, you could just as easily go via Helwan on the metro, get a microbus (don't believe it if you're told

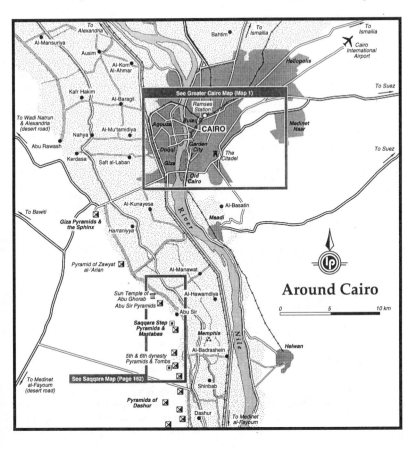

Around Cairo

there are none) from Helwan station to the boat landing (ask for *markib lil-Badrashein*; 15 pt). Get a boat across the Nile to Al-Badrashein and then take another microbus from there. This way, however, will still take you a good 1½ hours to get to Memphis. Note that the reverse procedure may be a little tricky, as there does not always seem to be any transport waiting at the boat landing on the Al-Badrashein side of the Nile. If this is the case, you can take a microbus from Al-Badrashein to Al-Tabbim a few kilometres further south and then backtrack to Helwan.

The easiest way of getting to Memphis is to gather about six or seven people and hire a service taxi (for about E£60 to E£70) for a day trip that also includes Saqqara, or go on one of the tours organised by Mohammed Abdel Hafez. For more details on this, and transport to and from this area in general, see the Saqqara Getting There & Away section later in this chapter.

SAQQARA

When Memphis was the capital of Egypt, during the Old Kingdom period, Saqqara was its necropolis. Deceased pharaohs, family

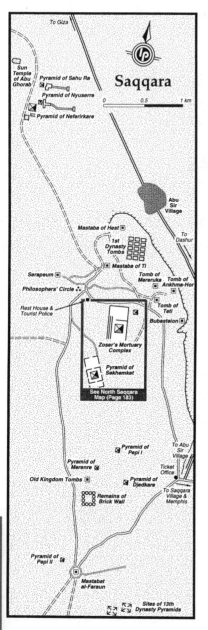

To Giza

Sun Temple of Abu Ghorab

Pyramid of Sahu Ra

Saqqara

Pyramid of Nyuserre

0   0.5   1 km

Pyramid of Neferirkare

Abu Sir Village

Mastaba of Hesi

1st Dynasty Tombs

To Dashur

Mastaba of Ti

Serapeum

Tomb of Mereruka

Tomb of Ankhma-Hor

Philosophers' Circle

Rest House & Tourist Police

Tomb of Teti

Bubasteion

Zoser's Mortuary Complex

Pyramid of Sekhemket

See North Saqqara Map (Page 183)

Pyramid of Pepi I

To Abu Sir Village

Pyramid of Merenre

Ticket Office

Old Kingdom Tombs

Pyramid of Djedkare

To Saqqara Village & Memphis

Remains of Brick Wall

Pyramid of Pepi II

Mastabat al-Faraun

Sites of 13th Dynasty Pyramids

members and sacred animals were ceremoniously transported from Memphis to be permanently enshrined in one of the myriad temples, pyramids and tombs at Saqqara.

In terms of the value of what has been and has yet to be uncovered, there are few archaeological sites in the world that compare with Saqqara. Yet, apart from the Step Pyramid, the necropolis was virtually ignored by archaeologists until the mid-19th century, when Auguste Mariette found the Serapeum. Even the massive mortuary complex surrounding Zoser's Step Pyramid wasn't discovered and reclaimed from the sand until 1924, and it is still being restored.

The very worthwhile visit to Saqqara will definitely take more than one day. Because of its size it seems that other visitors are few and far between, apart from the organised tour groups that are rushed through in the mornings.

Orientation & Information

The main places of interest are in North Saqqara. Other sites are scattered further north, such as the pyramids of Abu Sir, and to the south, at South Saqqara. Most travellers start their visit in North Saqqara (Zoser's Step Pyramid area) and, if they are up to it, continue by taxi, donkey or camel to Abu Sir and/or South Saqqara. It's imperative to have some form of transport to get around here as the tombs and sites are spread over a vast distance and walking is not feasible. Make sure you bring some water as it gets very hot. Before setting off, ask first at the ticket office, which is at the base of the plateau of North Saqqara, about which monuments are open.

Most of the pyramids and tombs at Saqqara can be officially visited between 7.30 am and 4 pm (5 pm in summer). The guards start locking the monument doors at about 3.30 pm, although some have been known to lock up even earlier. The admission fee for all North Saqqara sights is E£20, or E£10 for students, plus another E£10 for the new tombs. There is a E£5 fee for using a camera, collected only at the entrance to Zoser's Step Pyramid.

Step Pyramid

When it was constructed by Imhotep, the Pharaoh's chief architect, in the 27th century BC, the Step Pyramid of King Zoser was the largest stone structure ever built. The pyramid began as a simple mud-brick mastaba (the flat tomb superstructure common at the time), but Imhotep added five more mastabas on top, each one smaller than the last.

The resulting Step Pyramid dominates Zoser's mortuary complex, which is 544m long and 277m wide and was once surrounded by a magnificent bastioned and panelled limestone wall. Part of the enclosure wall survives and a section near the south-eastern corner has been restored, with stones found in the desert, to its original 10m elevation. In the enclosure wall, the many false doors which were carved and painted to resemble real wood with hinges and sockets allowed the Pharaoh's *ka*, or attendant spirit, to come and go at will.

For the living there is only one entrance, on the south-eastern corner, via a vestibule and along a colonnaded corridor into the broad hypostyle hall. The 40 pillars in the corridor are the original 'bundle columns' – ribbed to resemble bundles of palm or papyrus stems. The walls have been restored, but the protective ceiling is modern concrete. The roof of the hypostyle hall is supported by four impressive bundle columns and there's a large, false, half-open ka door. Here you will be accosted by a bevy of would-be guides eager to show you around.

The hall leads into the Great South Court, a huge open area flanking the south side of the pyramid, with a rebuilt section of wall featuring a frieze of cobras. The cobra, or *uraeus*, was a symbol of Egyptian royalty, a fire-spitting agent of destruction and protector of the king. A rearing cobra, its hood inflated, always formed part of a Pharaoh's headdress.

Near the frieze is a shaft that plunges 28m to the floor of Zoser's Southern Tomb, which is similar in decoration to the main tomb beneath the Step Pyramid. Originally, it probably stored the Canopic jars containing the Pharaoh's preserved internal organs.

In the centre of the Great South Court are two stone altars representing the thrones of Upper and Lower Egypt. Similarly, on the eastern side of the pyramid are the House of the South and House of the North, representing the shrines of Upper and Lower Egypt, which symbolise the unity of the country. The House of the South, faced with proto-Doric columns, features the oldest known examples of tourist graffiti. The vandalism of visiting 12th century BC Theban scribes, who scrawled their admiration for Zoser on the wall in a cursive style of hieroglyphs, is now protected under a piece of transparent plastic just inside the entrance. To the north of the pyramid is the Pyramid of Userkef, now little more than a mound of rubble.

The *serdab*, a stone structure right in front of the Step Pyramid, contains a slightly tilted wooden box with two holes drilled into its north face. Look through these and you'll have the eerie experience of coming face to face with Zoser himself. Inside is a life-size,

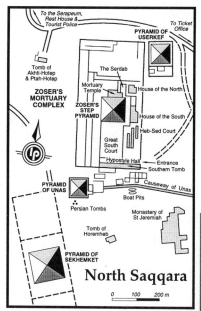

North Saqqara

lifelike painted statue of the long-dead king, gazing stonily out towards the stars. Although it's only a copy (the original is in the Egyptian Museum), it is still quite haunting. Serdabs were designed so that the Pharaoh's ka could communicate with the outside world. The original entrance to the Step Pyramid is directly behind the serdab, but is closed to the public.

Pyramid & Causeway of Unas

What appears to be a big mound of rubble to the south-west of Zoser's tomb is actually the Pyramid of Unas, the last Pharaoh of the 5th dynasty. Built only 350 years after the inspired creation of the Step Pyramid, and after the perfection of the Great Pyramids of Giza, the Pyramid of Unas marked an important new trend in funerary architecture, in that it was the first structure to feature hieroglyphs on its interior walls. Carved into the huge slabs of white alabaster, these so-called Pyramid Texts are the earliest known examples of decorative writing in a Pharaonic tomb chamber. The texts record the rituals, and prayers that accompanied the Pharaoh's burial to enable the release of his ka, and list the articles, like food and clothing, necessary for his existence in the afterlife.

This is one of the easiest pyramids to visit at Saqqara, which means if there's a tour group in the area it will probably be crowded. However, at the time of writing, it was closed for restoration.

Part of the 1km causeway, which ran from the east side of the Pyramid of Unas, has been restored. More than 200 mastabas have been excavated around it and there are several well-preserved tombs with wall paintings, some of which can normally be visited.

Persian Tombs

The tombs of three Persian noblemen, just south of the Pyramid of Unas, are some of the deepest subterranean burial chambers in Egypt. The entrance is covered by a small inconspicuous wooden hut, to which a guard in the area has the key. If you don't have your own torch, the guard will lead you the 25m down the winding staircase to the vaulted

tombs of Psamtik, Zenhebu and Pelese. According to the ancient wall drawings, which are colourful and fantastic, Zenhebu was a famous Persian admiral, Psamtik was chief physician of the Pharaoh's court and Pelese was Psamtik's son. The tombs were built deep to prevent grave robbers from stealing the contents. It didn't work – it was thieves who cut the spiral entrance passage.

Monastery of St Jeremiah

The half-buried remains of this 5th century AD monastery are up the hill from the Causeway of Unas and south-east of the boat pits. There's not much left of the structure because it was ransacked by invading Arabs in 950 AD and, much more recently, the Egyptian antiquities people transferred all the wall paintings and carvings to the Coptic Museum in Cairo.

Tomb of Horemheb

This tomb, built for the last Pharaoh of the 18th dynasty while he was still a general, was replaced by another located in the Valley of the Kings.

Pyramid of Sekhemket

The unfinished Pyramid of Sekhemket is a short distance to the west of the ruined monastery. It was abandoned before completion, for unknown reasons, when it was only 3m high. There's an unused alabaster sarcophagus in one of the underground passageways, but no one is permitted to enter this pile of rubble because of the danger of a cave in.

Tomb of Akhti-Hotep & Ptah-Hotep

Akhti-Hotep and Ptah-Hotep, who were father and son officials during the reign of Djedkare (a 5th dynasty Pharaoh), designed their own tomb complex which consists of two burial chambers, a chapel and a hall of pillars. The reliefs in their chambers are some of the best at Saqqara and depict everyday life during the 5th dynasty. You'll see: Akhti-Hotep in the marshes building boats, fighting enemies and crossing rivers; a splendid scene of wild animals with Ptah-Hotep and other hunters in hot pursuit;

PATRICK HORTON

EDDIE GERALD

GEERT COLE

EDDIE GERALD

EDDIE GERALD

Shopping is fascinating – the goods on offer are usually colourful, if not outright bizarre –
but as intiguing as some of this stuff is, there's very little that even the most ardent
shopper would ever be inclined to actually buy.

PATRICK HORTON

PATRICK HORTON

BETHUNE CARMICHAEL

Although less visited than the Pyramids of Giza, the Step Pyramid of Saqqara (top left) is one of Egypt's most significant archaeological sites and has yielded great finds such as the Serapeum wall painting (bottom). The statue of Ramses II (top right) was discovered at Memphis and is displayed at the open-air museum there.

people playing games, collecting food and eating; and Ptah-Hotep having a manicure while being entertained by musicians. The dual tomb is south of the main road, between the Step Pyramid and the rest house.

Philosophers' Circle
Down the slope, to the north-west of the rest house, are several statues of Greek philosophers and poets, arranged in a circle beneath a protective roof. From left to right, the statues are Plato (standing), Heraclitus (seated), Thales (standing), Protagoras (seated), Homer (seated), Hesiod (seated), Demetrius of Phalerum (standing against a bust of Serapis) and Pindar. The circle was set up, during the Ptolemaic period, at the eastern end of a long avenue of sphinxes running from the Temple of Ptah, where a live Apis bull was worshipped, to the Serapeum, where the bulls of this strange animal cult were buried.

Serapeum
The sacred Apis bulls were by far the most important of the cult animals entombed at Saqqara. The Apis, it was believed, was an incarnation of Ptah, the god of Memphis, and was the calf of a cow struck by lightning from heaven. Each calf was kept in the Temple of Ptah and worshipped as a god. The Apis was always portrayed as black, with a distinctive white diamond on its forehead, a sun disc between its horns, the image of an eagle on its back and a scarab on its tongue. When it died, the bull was mummified, then carried on an alabaster bed to the subterranean galleries of the Serapeum at Saqqara, and placed in a huge sarcophagus.

The Apis catacombs date from the 13th century BC, when Ramses II began the first gallery, which reached a length of 68m. The catacombs were extended by subsequent rulers and remained in use until around 30 BC. Twenty-five Apis were embalmed and stabled in perpetuity here in monolithic granite coffins weighing up to 70 tonnes each.

Until 1851, the existence of the sacred Apis tombs was known only from classical references. Having found a half-buried sphinx at Saqqara, and following the description given by the Greek historian Strabo in 24 BC, the French archaeologist Auguste Mariette began digging, and uncovered the avenue of sphinxes leading to the Serapeum. His great discovery sparked the extensive and continuing excavation of Saqqara. Only one chamber, walled up during the reign of Ramses II, had escaped the notice of tomb robbers and its mummified bull is now in Cairo's Agricultural Museum. On finding the tomb intact, Mariette wrote:

The finger marks of the Egyptian who had inserted the last stone in the wall built to conceal the doorway were still recognisable on the lime. There were also the marks of naked feet imprinted on the sand which lay in one corner of the tomb chamber. Everything was in its original condition in this tomb where the embalmed remains of the bull had lain undisturbed for 37 centuries.

The Serapeum is near the rest house, just off the main road, west of the Philosophers' Circle. You'll probably experience the same feeling as Mariette, for this place is definitely weird and gets stranger still as you wander along galleries lit only by tiny lanterns that cast a murky light over the vaults and the enormous black sarcophagi they contain.

Mastaba of Ti
This tomb, or mastaba, is one of the main sources of knowledge about life in Egypt towards the end of the Old Kingdom. Ti, an important court official who served under three pharaohs, collected titles like his kings collected slaves. He was Lord of Secrets, Superintendent of Works, Overseer of the Pyramids of Abu Sir, Counsellor to the Pharaoh and even Royal Hairdresser. He married a woman of royal blood and the inscriptions on the walls of his tomb reveal that his children were rated as royalty. One of the best reliefs depicts Ti standing regally on a boat sailing through papyrus marshes, while others show men and women at various jobs like ploughing, ship-building, reaping grain and feeding cranes. The tomb,

continued on page 188

EXCURSIONS

Ancient Egyptian Funerary Architecture

The earliest Egyptian burial sites were a far cry from their well-known dynastic descendants, being little more than shallow pits in the desert containing few, if any, grave goods. Over time, with the desire to create a more protected dwelling for the dead, the graves became deeper and were covered with a mound of rocks and sand. For the majority of the population this continued to be the standard type of burial until modern times. However, with the rise in the belief that the tomb was the 'house of eternity' for the spirit of the deceased, the graves of the wealthy slowly became more and more elaborate in order to create a satisfactory eternal dwelling for their spirit bodies.

In order to protect the body from grave robbers and create a more comfortable abode for the afterlife, the burial pits of wealthy peoples' graves became deep shafts lined with matting, mud-brick or wood, and more chambers were added to house the growing collections of grave goods. The simple covering mound also grew greatly in size and developed a low, rectangular mud-brick superstructure which, because of its resemblance to the mud-brick seat found outside many Egyptian peasant houses, was given the name mastaba, which means bench in Arabic.

Mastabas

The building of mastabas, used to house the ka of the affluent, was well established by the beginning of the 1st dynasty. By this time, the tomb's enclosing mud-brick superstructure regularly rose to a height of 6m and inside contained a labyrinth of storage rooms for burial goods and subterranean burial chambers. Royal tombs could be easily distinguished from those of the nobles which surrounded them by their size and by the elaborate palace-facade motif dominating their retaining walls.

A stone, or less frequently wood, stele was placed against one of the faces of early mastabas, acting both as a tombstone and as the focus for the funerary cult of the deceased. Priests and relatives could come here on certain days and leave offerings on a small altar near the stele. In time, with the development of the palace-facade niche design, these stelae were moved to the southernmost niche in the mastaba's eastern external wall. This was the origin of the false door stele, the 'dummy' door through which the ka or spirit could pass between the tomb and the world of the living.

With the rise to power of the 3rd dynasty and the introduction of stone as a building material at the Step Pyramid complex at Saqqara, more extensive changes to mastaba design developed. Stone replaced the mastaba's mud-brick outer-casing and the external offering niche was moved to become the focus of a chapel built inside the mastaba super-

The Step Pyramid was the earliest model of the pyramid. Imhotep engineered this incredible architectural feat in the 27th century BC; a series of stone mastabas were placed on top of each other in a graduated design, and then sheathed in fine limestone.

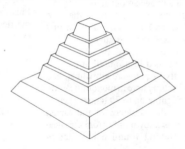

structure. The contents of the stelae, depicting the deceased sitting at a table laden with offerings of food and beer or lists of grave goods, were transferred to a panel above the false door, which had itself become more elaborate in design and decoration. Sometimes a ka-statue (substitute body) of the tomb owner stood in front of the false door. Both it and the increasingly detailed reliefs decorating the tombs were meant to ensure that the deceased enjoyed a comfortable existence in the afterworld. Statues were also sometimes placed in a small room near the chapel called a serdab. This chamber was completely sealed except for a small window through which the statue (and thus the deceased inhabiting it) could view the commemorative offering ceremonies.

Artwork in tombs represented much more than just a decorative record of each individual's life. Each carving, painting and statue was meant to guarantee that everything depicted in the tomb would come to life in the afterlife. This had a very practical reason behind it, for if the mummy was destroyed, the ka could continue to survive through the likenesses of the deceased as represented in stone and wood. In order to make this possible, priests performed a ritual in the tomb after all the carving and painting was finished, which caused everything depicted in the tomb 'to come to life' and fulfil their role in the afterlife.

Over time, the walls of these mastaba tombs were elaborately decorated with fine painted bas-reliefs. The floor plan also became more complex, comprising the burial shafts, chapels and storage rooms of other family members. One particular mastaba at Saqqara, belonging to Mereruka, a vizier of the first king of the 6th dynasty, had 31 rooms – 21 for his own funerary purposes and the rest for his wife and son.

Pyramids

Architecturally, the pyramid exemplified the culmination of the mortuary structures developed from the Early Dynastic period. Egypt's first pyramid, in Pharaoh Zoser's mortuary complex at Saqqara, was a 62m-high marvel of masonry completed in the 27th century BC. It was a product of the technical brilliance of Imhotep, the Pharaoh's chief architect. In this early model, a series of stone mastabas were placed on top of one another in a graduated design, and finally sheathed in fine limestone. This was the first time stone had been used to such an extent and with such artistry and precision. It became known as the Step Pyramid. Other step pyramids were built shortly after Zoser's reign, and have been found at Zawiyet el-Mayitin, Sheila, el-Kula, Edfu and at Elephantine Island.

The first true pyramid was built at Meidum at the end of the Third Dynasty, however, the style attained its highest form in the great Pyramids at Giza – see the Things to See & Do chapter. ∎

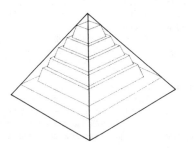

Early models of the true pyramid can be found at the Meidum and Dashur, however it was at Giza that the style attained its highest form. The true pyramid was built as a step pyramid which was then cased in polished stone.

continued from page 185

discovered by Mariette in 1865, is a few hundred metres to the north-east of the Philosophers' Circle.

Tombs of Teti, Mereruka & Ankhma-Hor

The avenue of sphinxes excavated by Mariette in the 1850s has again been engulfed by desert sands, but it once extended as far east as the Tomb of Teti. To get to this somewhat weathered tomb now, you must follow the road from the rest house, heading a little to the north once you've passed the Step Pyramid. The interior is often closed to the public but is worth seeing if you can get in.

Nearby is the Tomb of Mereruka, which has 31 rooms, many with magnificent wall inscriptions. Egyptologists have learned a great deal about the wildlife of ancient Egypt from these drawings.

The Tomb of Ankhma-Hor, a little further east, contains some very interesting scenes depicting 6th dynasty surgical operations, including toe surgery and a circumcision.

Mummified Animals

Excavations in this area have also uncovered several temples but they may be closed to the public. They include the Anubieion, sacred to the jackal-headed Anubis, god of embalming and the dead, which has a gallery for dogs; the Bubasteion, sacred to the cat-goddess Bastet, which is filled with mummified cats; as well as other galleries with thousands of mummified birds and monkeys.

Abu Sir

The pyramids of Abu Sir, at the edge of the desert and surrounded by a sea of sand dunes, formed part of a 5th dynasty necropolis. There were originally 14 but only three main pyramids survive – the rest are mostly just mounds of rubble. Originally excavated from 1902 to 1908 by a German expedition, the pyramids had long been closed to the public but were reopened in mid-1996.

Pyramid of Sahu Ra This is the northernmost and best preserved of the group. The ground-level entrance is only half a metre high and you have to crawl along on your stomach for about 75m to get into the tomb. The remains of Sahu Ra's mortuary temple still stand nearby with relief carvings depicting a military campaign against the Libyans.

Pyramids of Neferirkare & Nyuserre Neferirkare's tomb now resembles Zoser's Step Pyramid but, like the Giza pyramids, it originally had an outer casing of stone. The most dilapidated of these three tombs, the Pyramid of Nyuserre, has a causeway that runs southeast to what's left of Nyuserre's mortuary temple.

Other Monuments North of Nyuserre's temple there are other interesting monuments, including several mastabas and the **Tomb of Ptahshepses**, who was a court official and relative of King Nyuserre. If you happen to be going to Abu Sir by camel, horse or donkey across the desert from Giza, then stop off at the 5th dynasty **Sun Temple of Abu Ghorab**. It was built by King Nyuserre in honour of the sun-god Ra. The huge altar is made from five big blocks of alabaster and once served as the base of a large solar obelisk. Very few travellers ever make it this far off the beaten track.

Mastabat al-Faraun

The oldest structure in the South Saqqara area is the unusual mortuary complex of the 4th dynasty king Shepseskaf, believed to be a son of Mycerinus. Shepseskaf's tomb is neither a mastaba nor a pyramid. The Mastabat al-Faraun, or 'Pharaoh's Bench', is an enormous stone structure resembling a sarcophagus topped with a rounded lid. The complex once covered 700sq metres and the interior consists of long passageways and a burial chamber. It is possible to enter the tomb if you can find a guard.

Southern Pyramids

The pyramids of the 6th dynasty Pharaohs Pepi I, Merenre and Pepi II, who made the move to South Saqqara, have been cleared of sand and feature some interesting hieroglyphic texts. The crumbling southernmost pyramids, built of sun-dried bricks, belong to 13th dynasty Pharaohs.

A little north-west of the Mastabat al-Faraun is the **Pyramid of Pepi II**, a 6th dynasty Pharaoh, who allegedly ruled for 94 years. Pepi II's tomb contains some fine hieroglyphs. The ruins of his mortuary temple, immediately adjacent to the pyramid and once connected to it by a causeway, can also be explored. Nearby, to the west, are the remains of the **Pyramids of Queen Apuit** and **Queen Neith**.

North-east of what's left of Pepi II's valley temple is the **Pyramid of Djedkare**, a 5th dynasty Pharaoh. Known as Ahram ash-Shawaf, or 'Pyramid of the Sentinel', it stands 25m high and can be entered through a tunnel on the north side.

Organised Tours

For details on organised tours to this area – there's a good, inexpensive one arranged by Salah Mohammed Abdel Hafez – see the Organised Tours section in the Getting Around chapter.

Getting There & Away

Saqqara is about 25km south-west of Cairo and about 3km north-west of Memphis. Although it is possible to get within 1.5km of the Saqqara ticket office using public transport, this is a very time consuming business and, once there, you'll be stuck unless you try to hitch a ride up onto the plateau and then haggle for a camel or donkey. They can be hired at the rest house near the Serapeum. After bargaining, a trip around North Saqqara on camel or horse should cost E£4. However, don't be surprised if it's more as the handlers are well aware that you're in need of the extra legs and you have little bargaining power.

The site is really best combined with a visit to Memphis and the whole lot covered by taxi. You'll have to arrange this option in Cairo as there are no taxis hanging around the site. A taxi from Central Cairo will cost about E£70 shared between a maximum of seven people. However, make sure you know what you want to see and stipulate how long you want to be out – it's not unknown for taxi drivers to simply skip the main sights (like the Step Pyramid!) and dump unsuspecting visitors at a few of the lesser monuments before whisking them back to Cairo.

If you are coming from Cairo or Giza and are determined to do it on your own, you have several unappealing options.

Train Refer to the Memphis Getting There & Away section for details on the train. The train from Cairo to the village of Al-Badrashein also goes to Dashur; a taxi from either place to North Saqqara should cost about E£5. You can arrange a microbus from Memphis, to the turn-off to the Saqqara site on the Giza-Memphis road, from where it's about a 1.5 km walk to the Saqqara ticket office. There is usually a bit of traffic along the Giza-Memphis road, so you can usually get a lift.

From Al-Badrashein there are (sometimes) direct microbuses to Giza.

Bus One of the cheapest ways of getting to Saqqara without going via Memphis is to take a bus or minibus (25 pt to 50 pt) to the Pyramids Rd (see the Giza section) and get off at the Maryutia Canal (Saqqara Rd) stop. From the canal, you can get a microbus to the turn-off to the Saqqara site (don't ask for Saqqara village as you'll end up in the wrong place), from where you'll probably have to walk the last 1.5km to the ticket office. Once at the ticket office, you'll have to try and hitch to the main sights.

Horse or Camel The most adventurous (although physically strenuous) option is to hire a camel or horse and cross the desert from the Pyramids of Giza to Saqqara. This takes about six to seven hours for a round trip so make sure you're prepared for it. Unless you're accustomed to it, that amount of time spent in a saddle will make sitting down rather difficult for a few days. Also keep in mind that you won't have much time left to explore Saqqara unless you start off very early and make it one very long day.

Animals can be hired from the stables near the Mena House hotel and the Giza Pyramids – see that section in the Things to See & Do chapter for more details.

DASHUR

Though visible in the distance from Saqqara, for decades Dashur was off limits to most foreigners. However, the military's decision to relinquish the area means that it has been open to visitors since mid-1996. A southern extension of the necropolis of Memphis, the main attraction of Dashur (named for the village 3.5km east) is more pyramids.

Bent Pyramid

This is the most conspicuous of the four pyramids at Dashur. Although its rather strange shape seems to suggest otherwise, this tomb and the Pyramid of Meidum (see later this chapter), also built (or at least completed) by Sneferu, demonstrate the design transition from step pyramid to true pyramid.

For some reason though, just a little over half way up its 105m height, the angle of the exterior of this pyramid was reduced from 52 to 43.5°, giving it its distinctive blunt shape. The reason for the change in design is not known, but perhaps it was believed that the initial angle was too steep to be stable. It could explain why Sneferu built another tomb only 2km away, the so-called **Red Pyramid**, which rises at a constant angle of 43.5°.

Most of the Bent Pyramid's outer casing is still intact and it is unique in having two entrances. Nearby are the remains of the mortuary temple and further north are the ruins of Sneferu's valley temple, which yielded some interesting reliefs.

The other two dilapidated pyramids at Dashur, which belong to 12th dynasty Pharaohs Amenemhet III and Sesostris III, are less interesting and really only for those with pyramid fever. Around all the pyramids there are also the customary tombs of the members of the royal families, court officials and priests.

Getting There & Away

See the Saqqara Getting There & Away section for details. You can get a microbus to Dashur along the Giza-Memphis road.

AL-FAYOUM OASIS

About 100km south-west of Cairo is Al-Fayoum, Egypt's largest oasis. The region of Al-Fayoum is about 70km wide and 60km long, and includes the lake known as Birket Qarun. Home to more than two million people, it is an intricately irrigated and extremely fertile basin watered by the Nile via hundreds of capillary canals.

The oasis became a favourite vacation spot for Pharaohs of the 13th dynasty, and many fine palaces were built. The Greeks later called the area Crocodilopolis, because they believed the crocodiles in Birket Qarun were sacred. A temple was built in honour of Sobek, the crocodile-headed god, and during Ptolemaic and Roman times pilgrims came from all over the ancient world to feed the sacred beasts.

Al-Fayoum has been called the garden of Egypt: lush fields of vegetables and sugar cane, and groves of citrus fruits, nuts and olives produce abundant harvests; the lake, canals and vegetation support an amazing variety of bird life (some of which is unfortunately hunted by groups of tourists); and the customs, living conditions and agricultural practices in the mud-brick villages throughout the oasis have changed very little over the centuries.

Medinet al-Fayoum

Within the oasis is the rather grimy town of Medinet al-Fayoum, a microcosm of everything that is bad about Cairo: horn-happy drivers, choking fumes and dust, and overcrowded streets.

The canal acts as the city's main artery; most of the commercial activities take place around it and the further you wander away from the canal, the quieter things become. The bus and taxi stations, unfortunately, are all a bit of a hike from the centre.

At the rear of the governorate building there is a tourist office (☎ 342 313) which is

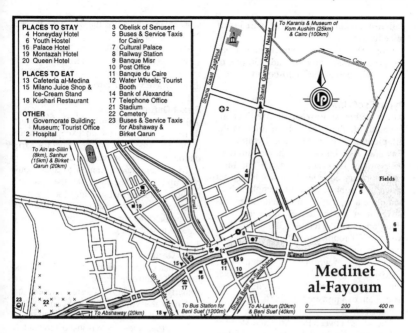

Medinet al-Fayoum

PLACES TO STAY
4 Honeyday Hotel
6 Youth Hostel
16 Palace Hotel
19 Montazah Hotel
20 Queen Hotel

PLACES TO EAT
13 Cafeteria al-Medina
15 Milano Juice Shop & Ice-Cream Stand
18 Kushari Restaurant

OTHER
1 Governorate Building; Museum; Tourist Office
2 Hospital
3 Obelisk of Senusert
5 Buses & Service Taxis for Cairo
7 Cultural Palace
8 Railway Station
9 Banque Misr
10 Post Office
11 Banque du Caire
12 Water Wheels; Tourist Booth
14 Bank of Alexandria
17 Telephone Office
21 Stadium
22 Cemetery
23 Buses & Service Taxis for Abshaway & Birket Qarun

open daily (except Friday) from 8 am to 2 pm. There's also a booth (☎ 325 211), by the water wheels in the centre of town, which is open daily from 8 am to 5 pm. The **water wheels** are four functioning models of the 200 or so *shadouf* still in use around the oasis. Irrigation water has to be obtained from the Nile rather than from Birket Qarun, as the lake is salty.

Other things to see include the 13m-high **Obelisk of Senusert** placed at a roundabout to the north-east of town – supposedly the only one in Egypt with a rounded top – and the **museum**, housed in the governorate building, with a variety of interesting displays on the history and fauna of the oasis, and on its future as a tourist destination.

Getting There & Away Regular buses connect Medinet al-Fayoum's eastern station with Ahmed Helmy station behind Ramses railway station in Cairo. The bus costs E£3 and takes about two hours. There are also five trains a day (2nd and 3rd class only) between the two places but the journey takes an agonising four or more hours. The quickest option of all is to hop in a service taxi. They depart from the bus stations and a seat is E£4.

Karanis
At the edge of the oasis depression, 25km north of Medinet al-Fayoum on the road to Cairo, are the ruins of the old city of Karanis and two temples from the Graeco-Roman period. Some of the painted portraits found here are now in the Egyptian Museum in Cairo. Entry to the Karanis site (including the two temples) is E£16.

The nearby Museum of Kom Aushim has good displays of Old and Middle Kingdom objects including sacred wooden boats, Canopic jars, and wooden and ceramic statuettes entombed to serve the deceased in the afterlife. The Graeco-Roman period, and later history, is exhibited on the 1st floor. It is open

EXCURSIONS

daily from 8 am to 4 pm; entry is E£3 (half price for students).

From Medinet al-Fayoum there's a bus (50 pt) to Karanis at 7 am and 2.30 pm, or simply take one of the Cairo-bound buses.

Pyramid of Hawara

About 12km south-east of Medinet al-Fayoum, off the road to Beni Suef, is the dilapidated 58m mud-brick Pyramid of Hawara, also known as the Pyramid of Amenemhet III (12th Dynasty). His once vast mortuary complex is now nothing but mounds of rubble. Even his temple, which had quite a reputation in ancient times, has suffered at the hands of stone robbers. Herodotus said the temple (300m by 250m) was a 3000 room labyrinth that surpassed even the pyramids.

At the time of writing, it was not possible to go into the pyramid as rising ground water had blocked the entrance. The site is open from 7 am to 5 pm; entry is E£16, or E£8 for students.

The buses between Beni Suef and Medinet al-Fayoum pass through Hawarat al-Makta, from where it's a short walk to the pyramid. Just ask the driver to let you off.

Nine kilometres south of the Pyramid of Hawara is the Pyramid of Al-Lahun, also known as the Pyramid of Senusert II. Although it once gave up a horde of fantastic jewellery (now in the Egyptian Museum) it's now little more than rubble.

Ain as-Siliin

The spring waters and gardens here, about 8km north-west of Medinet al-Fayoum around a branch of Bahr Yusef, merit an excursion if only to see their location amid a lovely lush valley. The spring water itself is sweet to taste and is said to help in the prevention of arteriosclerosis (hardening of the arteries) because of the traces of titanium found in it. One of the springs recently dried up, supposedly due to the earthquake of 1992. There are a few cafes, restaurants and little stores for water, biscuits and the like. Farmers from the adjacent gardens sell their seasonal produce along the walkway. It costs 25 pt to get in.

From Medinet al-Fayoum, get a Sanhur service taxi or a bus (hourly) from the station in the west of the town (50 pt) and tell the driver where you want to get off.

Birket Qarun

This is another pleasant enough spot where there is really nothing to do, except sit at one of the lake-side cafes or hire a boat for a trip out on the lake for about E£5 an hour.

To get here, take a Sanhur to Shakshouk pick-up (E£1). When you see the lake and the hotel Auberge du Lac, you've arrived; get off wherever you choose. It's easy enough to get another pick-up going either way along the south bank road.

Qasr Qarun

The ruins of the ancient town of Dionysus, once the starting point for caravans to Bahariyya Oasis in the Western Desert, are just near the village of Qasr Qarun at the western end of Birket Qarun.

The Ptolemaic temple is just off to the left of the road shortly before the village, and was erected to the god of Al-Fayoum, Sobek, in the 4th century BC. It was partly restored in 1956. You can ask to go down to the underground chambers and climb up to the top for a view of the desert, the sparse remains of Ptolemaic and Roman settlements and the oasis. Entry is E£8 (half price for students).

Getting out here is a bit of an ordeal, considering the relatively small distances involved. From Medinet al-Fayoum, take a service taxi or pick-up to the town of Abshaway (55 pt; one hour) and from there take another for the 40km on to Qasr Qarun (E£1.20; another hour). There are also some pick-ups plying the road along the south side of the lake to Qasr Qarun, but they are few and far between.

Places to Stay

You can pitch a tent in the grounds of the Museum of Kom Aushim at Karanis for E£4. It is also possible to camp at Birket Qaran;

get a permit from the tourist police. Bring mosquito repellent.

In Medinet al-Fayoum the *Youth Hostel* (☎ 323 682), near the Cairo bus station and almost 1km from the centre, is cheap (E£5 for a dorm bed) but not recommended – the building looks like it has been bombed out. Much better is the quiet *Montazah Hotel* (☎ 328 662), 1km north-west of the centre, which has fairly good singles/doubles with bath and fan for E£30/35. Also in the same area is the *Queen Hotel* (☎ 326 819) with basic rooms for E£33/55; with air-con, TV and fridge E£53/75. Breakfast is included. Closer to the centre, the *Palace Hotel* (☎ 321 222) is keeping its standards up by providing soap and towels. It has good, clean singles/doubles (including breakfast) without bath for E£20/35, and with bath for E£30/45. The *Honeyday Hotel* (☎ 341 205; fax 340 105) has good rooms for E£40/60, including breakfast. It also has a bar, coffee shop and restaurant.

At Ain as-Siliin the *Hotel-Chalet Ain as-Siliin* (☎ 522 113) is pleasantly located amid the greenery near the springs. Its simple rooms are quite big and boast some sort of a terrace. They cost E£38 and breakfast is included. Arriving at the lake, the place you'll pass first is the four star *Auberge du Lac* (☎ 700 002; fax 700 730), a former royal hunting lodge. Singles/doubles are E£233/287; breakfast is another E£10.

PYRAMID OF MEIDUM

Standing beyond the vegetation belt, about 32km north-east of Medinet al-Fayoum and 45km north of Beni Suef, is the ruin of the first true pyramid attempted by the ancient Egyptians. The Pyramid of Meidum is impressive, although it looks more like a stone tower than a pyramid, rising abruptly as it does from a large hill of rubble. This is one case, however, where the apparent state of disrepair was not caused by time or centuries of stone robbers, but was actually the result of design flaws. The pyramid began as an eight-stepped structure; the steps were then filled in and the outer casing was added, forming the first true pyramid shell. How-

ever, sometime after completion (possibly as late as the time of the Ptolemaic rulers in the last centuries before Christ's birth) the pyramid's own weight caused the sides to collapse, leaving just the core that still stands today.

Entrance to the site is E£16 (half price for students). Ask the guard at the nearby house to unlock the entrance of the pyramid for you. You can follow the steps down 75m to the empty underground burial chamber.

Getting There & Away

It is much easier to get to the pyramid from Beni Suef, about 45 km to the south, than from Medinet al-Fayoum. Get a pick-up from Beni Suef to Al-Wasta for 75 pt (45 minutes). From there take another to Meidum village (35 pt), from where you'll have to walk a couple of kilometres – unless you can get a ride.

Alternatively, you could get one of the service taxis or buses running between Beni Suef and Cairo and ask to get off at the Meidum turn-off, from where you still have about 6km to go. The reverse of this is probably the easiest way to get back to Beni Suef (or to Cairo for that matter) – just flag down a service taxi or hitch a ride.

WADI NATRUN

Wadi Natrun is a partly cultivated valley, about 100km north-west of Cairo, that was important to the Egyptians long before the Copts took refuge there. The natron used in the mummification process came from the large deposits of sodium carbonate left when the valley's salt lakes dried up every summer. Those deposits are now used on a larger scale by the chemical industry.

A visit to the monasteries of Wadi Natrun should explain the endurance of the ancient Coptic Christian sect. It is the desert, in a sense, that is the protector of the Coptic faith, for it was there that thousands of Christians retreated to escape Roman persecution in the 4th century AD. They lived in caves, or built monasteries, and developed the monastic tradition that was later adopted by European Christians.

EXCURSIONS

St Makarios retreated with his pupils to Wadi Natrun in 330 AD, and soon there were more than 50 monasteries. These originally isolated, unprotected communities were fortified after destructive raids in 817 by Arabs who were on their way to conquer North Africa.

While only four of the monasteries survived the Romans, the Bedouin raids and the coming of Islam, the religious life they all protected is thriving. The Coptic pope is still chosen from among the Wadi Natrun monks, and monasticism is experiencing a revival, with younger Copts again donning hooded robes to live within these ancient walls in the desert.

As a general rule, you can visit all of the monasteries. You will need to arrange permission in advance for overnight stays and visits to Deir Abu Makar (Makarios). You can arrange this through the monasteries' Cairo residences: Deir al-Anba Bishoi (☎ 591 4448); Deir as-Suriani (☎ 929 658); Deir al-Baramus (☎ 922 775); Deir Abu Makar (☎ 770 614). Women may not be allowed to stay overnight in some of the monasteries.

Deir al-Anba Bishoi

St Bishoi founded two monasteries in Wadi Natrun, this one (which bears his name) and the nearby Deir as-Suriani. Deir al-Anba Bishoi – a great place to watch a desert sunset – contains the saint's body, which is said to be perfectly preserved under a red cloth. The monks there claim that it is not uncommon for St Bishoi to perform miracles for true believers.

Deir as-Suriani

Deir as-Suriani, or the 'Monastery of the Syrians', is named after a wealthy Syrian who founded it in the 8th century, and after the many Syrian monks who subsequently came to live here; it's about 500m north-west of Deir al-Anba Bishoi. In the 17th century the monastery, and its valuable manuscript collection, was taken over by the Copts. There are several domed churches in the gardens and courtyards of this tranquil monastery. Ask the monks to show you St

Bishoi's private cell where he stood for nights on end with his hair attached to a chain dangling from the ceiling. It was during one of these marathon prayer vigils that Christ is said to have appeared before Bishoi, allowing him to wash his feet and then drink the water.

Deir Abu Makar (Makarios)

This monastery is nearly 20km south-east of Deir al-Anba Bishoi and was founded around the hermit's cell where St Makarios spent his last 20 or so years. Although structurally it has suffered worst at the hands of raiding Bedouins, it is perhaps the most renowned of the four monasteries, as over the centuries most of the Coptic popes have been selected from among its monks. It is the last resting place of many of those popes and also contains the remains of the '49 Martyrs', a group of monks killed by Bedouins in 444 AD. It is also the most secluded of the monasteries, and permission even to visit must be organised in advance.

Deir al-Baramus

Deir al-Baramus was the most isolated of the Wadi Natrun monasteries until recently when a good road was built between it and Deir al-Anba Bishoi to the south-east. Despite this, it still has an isolated feel, and is probably the best monastery to stay at, as it's a little less austere than the others.

Getting There & Away

From Midan Abdel Moniem Riad in Cairo, near the Ramses Hilton, you can get a West Delta Bus Co bus to Wadi Natrun for E£3. They depart every hour from 6.30 am. From Bir Hooker you have to negotiate for a taxi.

If you have your own vehicle and you're coming from Cairo, take the Pyramids Rd through Giza and turn right onto the Desert Highway just before the Mena House. About 95km from Cairo (just after the rest house) turn left into the wadi, go through the village of Bir Hooker and continue on, following the signs indicating the monasteries. The first one is Deir al-Anba Bishoi. Deir as-Suriani is about half a kilometre to the north-west,

Deir Abu Makar is 20km via a paved road to the south-east, and Deir al-Baramus is off to the north-west.

NILE BARRAGES (QANATER)

The Nile Barrages and the city of Qanater (which simply means barrages) lie 16km north of Cairo where the Nile splits into the eastern Damietta branch and the western Rosetta branch. The barrages, begun in the early 19th century, were successfully completed several decades later. The series of basins and locks, on both main branches of the Nile and two side canals, ensured the vital large-scale regulation of the Nile into the Delta region, and led to a great increase in cotton production.

The Damietta Barrage consists of 71 sluices stretching 521m across the river; the Rosetta Barrage is 438m long and has 61 sluices. Between the two is a 1km-wide area filled with beautiful gardens and cafes. It's a superb place to rent a bicycle or a felucca and take a relaxing tour. The place is an incredibly popular day trip with Egyptian students and best avoided on public holidays and weekends.

The town of Qanater, at the fork of the river, is officially the beginning of the Delta region.

Getting There & Away

To get to the barrages from Cairo you can take a river bus for 50 pt from the terminal in front of the Radio & Television building (Maspero terminal), just north of the Ramses Hilton. The trip takes about two hours. A faster but less relaxing way to get there is by taking bus No 930 from Midan Ataba bus station or No 950 from Ahmed Helmy bus station behind Ramses railway station.

Glossary

For a glossary of Islamic architecture terms see page 27. For Egyptian food types and words connected with food, see the Places to Eat chapter.

abd – servant of
abeyya – women's version of the *galabeyya*
abu – father, saint
ahwa – coffee and coffeehouse
ain – well, spring
al-jeel – synthesised pop music

bahr – river
baksheesh – tip
baladi – local, rural
bawwab – doorman
bey – term of respect
bir – spring, well
birket – lake
Book of the Dead – ancient theological compositions, or hymns, that were the subject of most of the colourful paintings and reliefs on tomb walls

caliph – Islamic ruler; also spelt khalif
Canopic jars – pottery jars which held the embalmed internal organs and viscera (liver, stomach, lungs, intestines) of the mummified Pharaoh
cartouche – oblong shaped box enclosing the hieroglyphs of royal or divine names

dahabiyya – houseboat
darb – track, street
deir – monastery, convent
domina – dominoes

eid – feast
emir – Islamic ruler, military commander or governor

fellaheen – the peasant farmers or agricultural workers who make up the majority of Egypt's population. Fellaheen literally means ploughman or tiller of the soil.
fenous – Ramadan lantern

filoos – money

galabeyya – light full-length robe worn by men
gebel – mountain or mountain range
gezira – island
guinay – Egyptian pound

haj – pilgrimage to Mecca. All Muslims should make the journey at least once in their lifetime.
hamman – bathhouse
hantour – horse-drawn carriage
harah – small lane, alley
haramlik – women's quarters
hieroglyphs – ancient Egyptian form of writing, which used pictures and symbols to represent objects, words or sounds

ibn – son of
iftar – breaking of the fast during Ramadan
imam – man schooled in Islam who often doubles as the *muezzin*
irsh – piastre (pt)

ka – spirit, or 'double', of a living person which gained its own identity with the death of that person. The ka was also the vital force emanating from a god and was transferred through the Pharaoh to his people.
karkadey – drink made from boiled hibiscus leaves
khamseen – hot wind emanating from the Western Desert
khedive – Egyptian viceroy under Ottoman suzerainty (1867-1914)
khwaga – foreigner
kubri – bridge

limoon – a lemon drink
lotus – white waterlily which was regarded as sacred by the ancient Egyptians

maasil – tobacco soaked in molasses
mahatta – station
makwagee – laundry man

Masr – another name for Egypt and Cairo; also written as Misr

mastaba – a mud-brick structure above tombs from which the Pyramids evolved. Taken from the Arabic word for 'bench'.

midan – town or city square

moulid – festival celebrating the birthday of a local saint or holy person

muezzin – mosque official who calls the faithful to prayer five times a day from the minaret

mugzzabin – Sufi followers who participate in *zikrs* in order to achieve unity with Allah

nai – reed pipe

natron – whitish mineral of hydrated sodium carbonate that occurs in saline deposits and salt lakes and acts as a natural preservative. It was used in ancient Egypt to pack and dry the body during mummification.

Nilometer – pit descending into the Nile containing a central column marked with graduations. The marks were used to measure and record the level of the river, especially during the inundation.

obelisk – monolithic stone pillar, with square sides tapering to a pyramidal, often gilded, top; used as a monument in ancient Egypt

oud – a sort of lute

papyrus – plant identified with Lower Egypt; writing material made from the pith of this plant; a document written on such paper

pasha – ruler of Egypt, but also used more generally to denote someone of standing

porphyry – from Greek *porphyros* (purple); a reddish-purple rock highly resistant to erosion. Many sarcophagi were made from this rock.

Pyramid Texts – paintings and reliefs on the walls of the internal rooms and burial chamber of pyramids and sometimes also on the sarcophagus itself. The texts recorded the Pharaoh's burial ceremonies, associated temple rituals, the hymns vital to his passage into the afterlife and, sometimes, major events in his life.

qanun – zither

qarafa – cemetery ('q' is unvocalised)

qasr – castle or palace ('q' is unvocalised)

raiyis – waiter

Ramadan – ninth month of the lunar Islamic calendar during which Muslims fast from sunrise to sunset

sahleb – warm drink made with semolina powder, milk and chopped nuts

salamlik – men's quarters

sarcophagus – huge stone or marble coffin used to encase other wooden coffins and the mummy of the Pharaoh or queen

scarab – dung beetle regarded as sacred in ancient Egypt and represented on amulets or in hieroglyphs as a symbol of the sun-god Ra

serdab – hidden cellar in a tomb, or a stone room in front of a pyramid, containing a coffin with a life-size, lifelike, painted statue of the dead king

shaabi – working class or 'popular' music which has satirical or politically provocative lyrics and is cruder than *al-jeel*

shadouf – water wheels used for irrigation purposes

sharia – road or street

Shari'a – Islamic law, the body of doctrine that regulates the lives of Muslims

sharm – bay

shay – tea

sheesha – waterpipe

simsar – agent who can help people find flats

solar barque – wooden boat placed in or around a Pharaoh's tomb

souq – market

stele (pl: stelae) – stone or wooden commemorative slab or column decorated with inscriptions or figures

Sufi – follower of any of the Islamic mystical orders which emphasise dancing, chanting and trances in order to attain unity with Allah

tabla – small hand-held drum

tarboosh – hat, elsewhere known as a fez

tofah – tobacco soaked in apple juice

towla – backgammon

umm – mother of
uraeus – cobra used to symbolise Egyptian royalty. A rearing cobra, hood inflated always formed part of the Pharaoh's headdress.

wadi – desert watercourse, dry except during the rainy season

wahah – oasis

yansoon – medicinal-tasting aniseed drink

zabaady – drink made from yoghurt
zikr – long sessions of dancing, chanting and swaying usually carried out by Sufi *mugzzabin* to achieve oneness with Allah

Index

MAPS

BOXED TEXT

TEXT

See also Islamic Monuments
　index on pages 204-5.

Colour map references are in
　bold type.

ISLAMIC MONUMENTS

LONELY PLANET PHRASEBOOKS

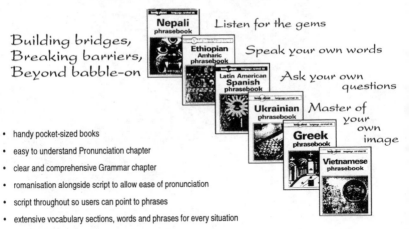

Building bridges,
Breaking barriers,
Beyond babble-on

Listen for the gems

Speak your own words

Ask your own
questions

Master of
your
own
image

- handy pocket-sized books
- easy to understand Pronunciation chapter
- clear and comprehensive Grammar chapter
- romanisation alongside script to allow ease of pronunciation
- script throughout so users can point to phrases
- extensive vocabulary sections, words and phrases for every situation
- full of cultural information and tips for the traveller

'...vital for a real DIY spirit and attitude in language learning' – Backpacker

'the phrasebooks have good cultural backgrounders and offer solid advice for challenging situations in remote locations' – San Francisco Examiner

'...they are unbeatable for their coverage of the world's more obscure languages' – The Geographical Magazine

---

Arabic (Egyptian)
Arabic (Moroccan)
Australia
  Australian English, Aboriginal and Torres Strait languages
Baltic States
  Estonian, Latvian, Lithuanian
Bengali
Brazilian
Burmese
Cantonese
Central Asia
Central Europe
  Czech, French, German, Hungarian, Italian and Slovak
Eastern Europe
  Bulgarian, Czech, Hungarian, Polish, Romanian and Slovak
Ethiopian (Amharic)
Fijian
French
German
Greek

Hindi/Urdu
Indonesian
Italian
Japanese
Korean
Lao
Latin American Spanish
Malay
Mandarin
Mediterranean Europe
  Albanian, Croatian, Greek, Italian, Macedonian, Maltese, Serbian and Slovene
Mongolian
Moroccan Arabic
Nepali
Papua New Guinea
Pilipino (Tagalog)
Quechua
Russian
Scandinavian Europe
  Danish, Finnish, Icelandic, Norwegian and Swedish

South-East Asia
  Burmese, Indonesian, Khmer, Lao, Malay, Tagalog (Pilipino), Thai and Vietnamese
Spanish (Castilian)
  Basque, Catalan and Galician
Sri Lanka
Swahili
Thai
Thai Hill Tribes
Tibetan
Turkish
Ukrainian
USA
  US English, Vernacular, Native American languages and Hawaiian
Vietnamese
Western Europe
  Basque, Catalan, Dutch, French, German, Irish, Italian, Portuguese, Scottish Gaelic, Spanish (Castilian) and Welsh

---

LONELY PLANET JOURNEYS

JOURNEYS is a unique collection of travel writing – published by the company that understands travel better than anyone else. It is a series for anyone who has ever experienced – or dreamed of – the magical moment when they encountered a strange culture or saw a place for the first time. They are tales to read while you're planning a trip, while you're on the road or while you're in an armchair, in front of a fire.

JOURNEYS books catch the spirit of a place, illuminate a culture, recount a crazy adventure, or introduce a fascinating way of life. They always entertain, and always enrich the experience of travel.

THE GATES OF DAMASCUS
Lieve Joris

Translated by Sam Garrett

This best-selling book is a beautifully drawn portrait of day-to-day life in modern Syria. Through her intimate contact with local people, Lieve Joris draws us into the fascinating world that lies behind the gates of Damascus. Hala's husband is a political prisoner, jailed for his opposition to the Assad regime; through the author's friendship with Hala we see how Syrian politics impacts on the lives of ordinary people.

Lieve Joris, who was born in Belgium, is one of Europe's leading travel writers. In addition to an award-winning book on Hungary, she has published widely acclaimed accounts of her journeys to the Middle East and Africa. *The Gates of Damascus* is her fifth book.

'Expands the boundaries of travel writing' – Times Literary Supplement

KINGDOM OF THE FILM STARS
Journey into Jordan
Annie Caulfield

Kingdom of the Film Stars is a travel book and a love story. With honesty and humour, Annie Caulfield writes of travelling in Jordan and falling in love with a Bedouin. Her book offers fascinating insights into the country – from the traditional tent life of nomadic tribes to the first woman MP's battle with fundamentalist colleagues. *Kingdom of the Film Stars* unpicks some of the tight-woven Western myths about the Arab world, presenting cultural and political issues within the intimate framework of a compelling love story.

Annie Caulfield, who was born in Ireland and currently lives in London, is an award-winning playwright and journalist. She has travelled widely in the Middle East.

'Annie Caulfield is a remarkable traveller. Her story is fresh, courageous, moving, witty and sexy!' – Dawn French

LONELY PLANET TRAVEL ATLASES

Lonely Planet has long been famous for the number and quality of its guidebook maps. Now we've gone one step further and in conjunction with Steinhart Katzir Publishers produced a handy companion series: Lonely Planet travel atlases – maps of a country produced in book form.

Unlike other maps, which look good but lead travellers astray, our travel atlases have been researched on the road by Lonely Planet's experienced team of writers. All details are carefully checked to ensure the atlas corresponds with the equivalent Lonely Planet guidebook.

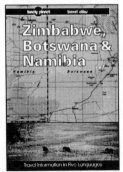

The handy atlas format means no holes, wrinkles, torn sections or constant folding and unfolding. These atlases can survive long periods on the road, unlike cumbersome fold-out maps. The comprehensive index ensures easy reference.

- full-colour throughout
- maps researched and checked by Lonely Planet authors
- place names correspond with Lonely Planet guidebooks
  – no confusing spelling differences
- legend and travelling information in English, French, German, Japanese and Spanish
- size: 230 x 160 mm

Available now:
Chile & Easter Island • Egypt • India & Bangladesh • Israel & the Palestinian Territories •Jordan, Syria & Lebanon • Kenya • Laos • Portugal • South Africa, Lesotho & Swaziland • Thailand • Turkey • Vietnam • Zimbabwe, Botswana & Namibia

---

LONELY PLANET TV SERIES & VIDEOS

Lonely Planet travel guides have been brought to life on television screens around the world. Like our guides, the programmes are based on the joy of independent travel, and look honestly at some of the most exciting, picturesque and frustrating places in the world. Each show is presented by one of three travellers from Australia, England or the USA and combines an innovative mixture of video, Super-8 film, atmospheric soundscapes and original music.

Videos of each episode – containing additional footage not shown on television – are available from good book and video shops, but the availability of individual videos varies with regional screening schedules.

Video destinations include: Alaska • American Rockies • Australia – The South-East • Baja California & the Copper Canyon • Brazil • Central Asia • Chile & Easter Island • Corsica, Sicily & Sardinia – The Mediterranean Islands • East Africa (Tanzania & Zanzibar) • Ecuador & the Galapagos Islands • Greenland & Iceland • Indonesia • Israel & the Sinai Desert • Jamaica • Japan • La Ruta Maya • Morocco • New York • North India • Pacific Islands (Fiji, Solomon Islands & Vanuatu) • South India • South West China • Turkey • Vietnam • West Africa • Zimbabwe, Botswana & Namibia

The Lonely Planet TV series is produced by:
Pilot Productions
The Old Studio
18 Middle Row
London W10 5AT UK

For video availability and ordering information contact your nearest Lonely Planet office.

Music from the TV series is available on CD & cassette.

PLANET TALK

Lonely Planet's FREE quarterly newsletter

We love hearing from you and think you'd like to hear from us.

When...is the right time to see reindeer in Finland?
Where...can you hear the best palm-wine music in Ghana?
How...do you get from Asunción to Areguá by steam train?
What...is the best way to see India?

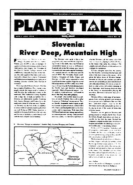

For the answer to these and many other questions read PLANET TALK.

Every issue is packed with up-to-date travel news and advice including:

- a letter from Lonely Planet co-founders Tony and Maureen Wheeler
- go behind the scenes on the road with a Lonely Planet author
- feature article on an important and topical travel issue
- a selection of recent letters from travellers
- details on forthcoming Lonely Planet promotions
- complete list of Lonely Planet products

To join our mailing list contact any Lonely Planet office.

Also available: Lonely Planet T-shirts. 100% heavyweight cotton.

LONELY PLANET ONLINE

Get the latest travel information before you leave or while you're on the road

Whether you've just begun planning your next trip, or you're chasing down specific info on currency regulations or visa requirements, check out Lonely Planet Online for up-to-the minute travel information.

As well as travel profiles of your favourite destinations (including maps and photos), you'll find current reports from our researchers and other travellers, updates on health and visas, travel advisories, and discussion of the ecological and political issues you need to be aware of as you travel.

There's also an online travellers' forum where you can share your experience of life on the road, meet travel companions and ask other travellers for their recommendations and advice. We also have plenty of links to other online sites useful to independent travellers.

And of course we have a complete and up-to-date list of all Lonely Planet travel products including guides, phrasebooks, atlases, Journeys and videos and a simple online ordering facility if you can't find the book you want elsewhere.

www.lonelyplanet.com
or
AOL keyword: lp

LONELY PLANET PRODUCTS

Lonely Planet is known worldwide for publishing practical, reliable and no-nonsense travel information in our guides and on our web site. The Lonely Planet list covers just about every accessible part of the world. Currently there are eight series: *travel guides, shoestring guides, walking guides, city guides, phrasebooks, audio packs, travel atlases* and *Journeys* – a unique collection of travel writing.

EUROPE

Amsterdam • Austria • Baltic States phrasebook • Britain • Central Europe on a shoestring • Central Europe phrasebook • Czech & Slovak Republics • Denmark • Dublin • Eastern Europe on a shoestring • Eastern Europe phrasebook • Estonia, Latvia & Lithuania • Finland • France • French phrasebook • Germany • German phrasebook • Greece • Greek phrasebook • Hungary • Iceland, Greenland & the Faroe Islands • Ireland • Italian phrasebook • Italy • Lisbon • Mediterranean Europe on a shoestring • Mediterranean Europe phrasebook • Paris • Poland • Portugal • Portugal travel atlas • Prague • Russia, Ukraine & Belarus • Russian phrasebook • Scandinavian & Baltic Europe on a shoestring • Scandinavian Europe phrasebook •Slovenia • Spain • Spanish phrasebook • St Petersburg • Switzerland •Trekking in Spain • Ukrainian phrasebook •Vienna •Walking in Britain • Walking in Switzerland • Western Europe on a shoestring • Western Europe phrasebook

Travel Literature: The Olive Grove: Travels in Greece

NORTH AMERICA

Alaska • Backpacking in Alaska • Baja California • California & Nevada • Canada • Florida • Hawaii • Honolulu • Los Angeles • Mexico • Miami • New England • New Orleans • New York City • New York, New Jersey & Pennsylvania • Pacific Northwest USA • Rocky Mountain States • San Francisco • Southwest USA • USA phrasebook • Washington, DC & the Capital Region

CENTRAL AMERICA & THE CARIBBEAN

Bermuda • Central America on a shoestring • Costa Rica • Cuba •Eastern Caribbean •Guatemala, Belize & Yucatán: La Ruta Maya • Jamaica

SOUTH AMERICA

Argentina, Uruguay & Paraguay • Bolivia • Brazil • Brazilian phrasebook • Buenos Aires • Chile & Easter Island • Chile & Easter Island travel atlas • Colombia • Deep South • Ecuador & the Galápagos Islands • Latin American Spanish phrasebook • Peru • Quechua phrasebook • Rio de Janeiro • South America on a shoestring • Trekking in the Patagonian Andes • Venezuela

Travel Literature: Full Circle: A South American Journey

ANTARCTICA

Antarctica

ISLANDS OF THE INDIAN OCEAN

Madagascar & Comoros • Maldives• Mauritius, Réunion & Seychelles

AFRICA

Africa - the South • Africa on a shoestring • Arabic (Moroccan) phrasebook • Cape Town • Central Africa • East Africa • Egypt • Egypt travel atlas• Ethiopian (Amharic) phrasebook • Kenya • Kenya travel atlas • Malawi Mozambique & Zambia • Morocco • North Africa • South Africa, Lesotho & Swaziland • South Africa, Lesotho & Swaziland travel atlas • Swahili phrasebook • Trekking in East Africa • West Africa • Zimbabwe, Botswana & Namibia • Zimbabwe, Botswana & Namibia travel atlas

Travel Literature: The Rainbird: A Central African Journey • Songs to an African Sunset: A Zimbabwean Story

MAIL ORDER

Lonely Planet products are distributed worldwide.They are also available by mail order from Lonely Planet, so if you have difficulty finding a title please write to us. North American and South American residents should write to Embarcadero West, 155 Filbert St, Suite 251, Oakland CA 94607, USA; European and African residents should write to 10a Spring Place, London NW5 3BH; and residents of other countries to PO Box 617, Hawthorn, Victoria 3122, Australia.

NORTH-EAST ASIA

Beijing • Cantonese phrasebook • China • Hong Kong • Hong Kong, Macau & Guangzhou • Japan • Japanese phrasebook • Japanese audio pack • Korea • Korean phrasebook • Mandarin phrasebook • Mongolia • Mongolian phrasebook • North-East Asia on a shoestring • Seoul • Taiwan • Tibet • Tibet phrasebook • Tokyo

Travel Literature: Lost Japan

MIDDLE EAST & CENTRAL ASIA

Arab Gulf States • Arabic (Egyptian) phrasebook • Central Asia • Central Asia phrasebook • Iran • Israel & the Palestinian Territories • Israel & the Palestinian Territories travel atlas • Istanbul • Jerusalem • Jordan & Syria • Jordan, Syria & Lebanon travel atlas • Lebanon • Middle East • Turkey • Turkish phrasebook • Turkey travel atlas • Yemen

Travel Literature: The Gates of Damascus • Kingdom of the Film Stars: Journey into Jordan

ALSO AVAILABLE:

Travel with Children • Traveller's Tales

INDIAN SUBCONTINENT

Bangladesh • Bengali phrasebook • Delhi • Hindi/Urdu phrasebook • India • India & Bangladesh travel atlas • Indian Himalaya • Karakoram Highway • Nepal • Nepali phrasebook • Pakistan • Rajasthan • Sri Lanka • Sri Lanka phrasebook • Trekking in the Indian Himalaya • Trekking in the Karakoram & Hindukush • Trekking in the Nepal Himalaya

Travel Literature: In Rajasthan • Shopping for Buddhas

SOUTH-EAST ASIA

Bali & Lombok • Bangkok • Burmese phrasebook • Cambodia • Ho Chi Minh City • Indonesia • Indonesian phrasebook • Indonesian audio pack • Jakarta • Java • Laos • Lao phrasebook • Laos travel atlas • Malay phrasebook • Malaysia, Singapore & Brunei • Myanmar (Burma) • Philippines • Pilipino phrasebook • Singapore • South-East Asia on a shoestring • South-East Asia phrasebook • Thailand • Thailand's Islands & Beaches • Thailand travel atlas • Thai phrasebook • Thai audio pack • Thai Hill Tribes phrasebook • Vietnam • Vietnamese phrasebook • Vietnam travel atlas

AUSTRALIA & THE PACIFIC

Australia • Australian phrasebook • Bushwalking in Australia • Bushwalking in Papua New Guinea • Fiji • Fijian phrasebook • Islands of Australia's Great Barrier Reef • Melbourne • Micronesia • New Caledonia • New South Wales • New Zealand • Northern Territory • Outback Australia • Papua New Guinea • Papua New Guinea phrasebook • Queensland • Rarotonga & the Cook Islands • Samoa • Solomon Islands • South Australia • Sydney • Tahiti & French Polynesia • Tasmania • Tonga • Tramping in New Zealand • Vanuatu • Victoria • Western Australia

Travel Literature: Islands in the Clouds • Sean & David's Long Drive

THE LONELY PLANET STORY

Lonely Planet published its first book in 1973 in response to the numerous 'How did you do it?' questions Maureen and Tony Wheeler were asked after driving, bussing, hitching, sailing and railing their way from England to Australia.

Written at a kitchen table and hand collated, trimmed and stapled, *Across Asia on the Cheap* became an instant local bestseller, inspiring thoughts of another book.

Eighteen months in South-East Asia resulted in their second guide, *South-East Asia on a shoestring*, which they put together in a backstreet Chinese hotel in Singapore in 1975. The 'yellow bible', as it quickly became known to backpackers around the world, soon became *the* guide to the region. It has sold well over half a million copies and is now in its 9th edition, still retaining its familiar yellow cover.

Today there are over 240 titles, including travel guides, walking guides, language kits & phrasebooks, travel atlases and travel literature. The company is the largest independent travel publisher in the world. Although Lonely Planet initially specialised in guides to Asia, today there are few corners of the globe that have not been covered.

The emphasis continues to be on travel for independent travellers. Tony and Maureen still travel for several months of each year and play an active part in the writing, updating and quality control of Lonely Planet's guides.

They have been joined by over 70 authors and 170 staff at our offices in Melbourne (Australia), Oakland (USA), London (UK) and Paris (France). Travellers themselves also make a valuable contribution to the guides through the feedback we receive in thousands of letters each year and on our web site.

The people at Lonely Planet strongly believe that travellers can make a positive contribution to the countries they visit, both through their appreciation of the countries' culture, wildlife and natural features, and through the money they spend. In addition, the company makes a direct contribution to the countries and regions it covers. Since 1986 a percentage of the income from each book has been donated to ventures such as famine relief in Africa; aid projects in India; agricultural projects in Central America; Greenpeace's efforts to halt French nuclear testing in the Pacific; and Amnesty International.

'I hope we send people out with the right attitude about travel. You realise when you travel that there are so many different perspectives about the world, so we hope these books will make people more interested in what they see. Guidebooks can't really guide people. All you can do is point them in the right direction.'

– Tony Wheeler

---

lonely planet

LONELY PLANET PUBLICATIONS

Australia
PO Box 617, Hawthorn 3122, Victoria
tel: (03) 9819 1877 fax: (03) 9819 6459
e-mail: talk2us@lonelyplanet.com.au

USA
Embarcadero West, 155 Filbert St, Suite 251,
Oakland, CA 94607
tel: (510) 893 8555 TOLL FREE: 800 275-8555
fax: (510) 893 8563
e-mail: info@lonelyplanet.com

UK
10a Spring Place,
London NW5 3BH
tel: (0171) 428 4800 fax: (0171) 428 4828
e-mail: go@lonelyplanet.co.uk

France:
71 bis rue du Cardinal Lemoine, 75005 Paris
tel: 1 44 32 06 20 fax: 1 46 34 72 55
e-mail: 100560.415@compuserve.com

World Wide Web: http://www.lonelyplanet.com
or *AOL keyword: lp*

CAIRO MAP LIST

EDDIE GERALD

The minaret of the Al-Fath mosque towers majestically over the multi-layered mayhem below that is Midan Ramses.

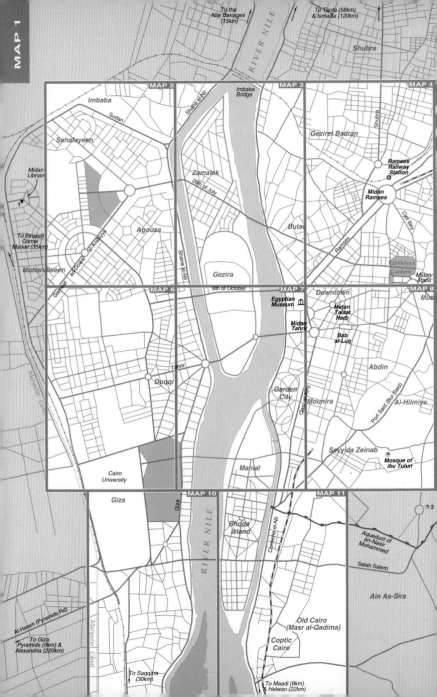

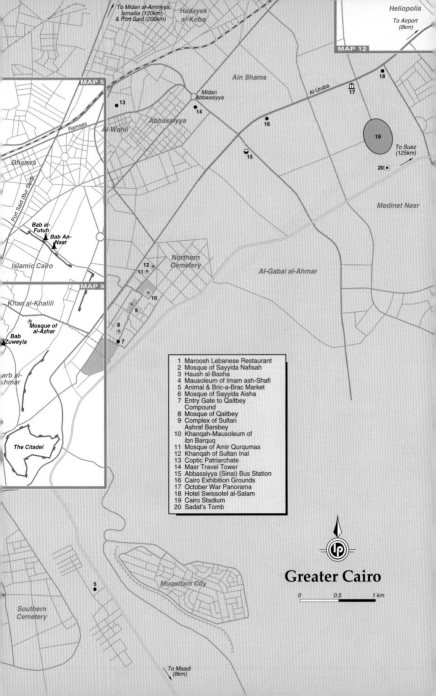

To Midan al-Aminiyya,
Ismailia (120km)
& Port Said (200km)

Hadayek
al-Koba

Heliopolis

To Airport
(8km)

MAP 12

Ain Shams

Al-Uruba

17

18

MAP 5

● 13

Midan
Abbassiyya

14

Ramses

Al-Wahli

Abbassiyya

16

To Suez
(125km)

19

Ghamra

15

20

Medinet Nasr

Port Said (Bur Said)

Bab al-
Futuh

Bab An-
Nasr

Islamic Cairo

MAP 9

Northern
Cemetery

12
11

Al-Gabal al-Ahmar

Khan al-Khalili

10

Mosque of
al-Azhar

9

Bab
Zuweyla

8

7

arb al-
ahmar

1 Maroosh Lebanese Restaurant
2 Mosque of Sayyida Nafisah
3 Haush al-Basha
4 Mausoleum of Imam ash-Shafi
5 Animal & Bric-a-Brac Market
6 Mosque of Sayyida Aisha
7 Entry Gate to Qaitbey
   Compound
8 Mosque of Qaitbey
9 Complex of Sultan
   Ashraf Barsbey
10 Khanqah-Mausoleum of
   ibn Barquq
11 Mosque of Amir Qurqumas
12 Khanqah of Sultan Inal
13 Coptic Patriarchate
14 Masr Travel Tower
15 Abbassiyya (Sinai) Bus Station
16 Cairo Exhibition Grounds
17 October War Panorama
18 Hotel Swissotel al-Salam
19 Cairo Stadium
20 Sadat's Tomb

The Citadel

Muqattam City

Greater Cairo

0   0.5   1 km

5

Southern
Cemetery

To Maadi
(8km)

MAP 2

IMBABA

SAHAFAYEEN

as-Sudan

Midan
Kitkat

Ahmed Orabi

**Mohandiseen
& Agouza**

0   200   400 m

Tirsana
Club

26th of July

Midan
Sphinx

Shaira el-Nil

15

20

23

22

MOHANDISEEN

Wedi el-Nil

Zamalek
Club

AGOUZA

14

16

13

19

Gamat ad-Dowal al-Arabyya

To Midan
Librian

Falouga

12

17

18

Midan
Aswan

Shahab

Librian

Hedgez

3

Wimpy
Corner

9

11

10

Gezirat el-Arab

Feric Abdel Montem Riad

Abdel Hamid Lothy

8

7

Midan
Mustafa
Mahmoud

Mahrouki

Batal Ahmed Abdel Aziz

Syria

4

5

6

Neshni

Suleyman Abaza

Abdel Rahman
ar-Rifai

MAP 6

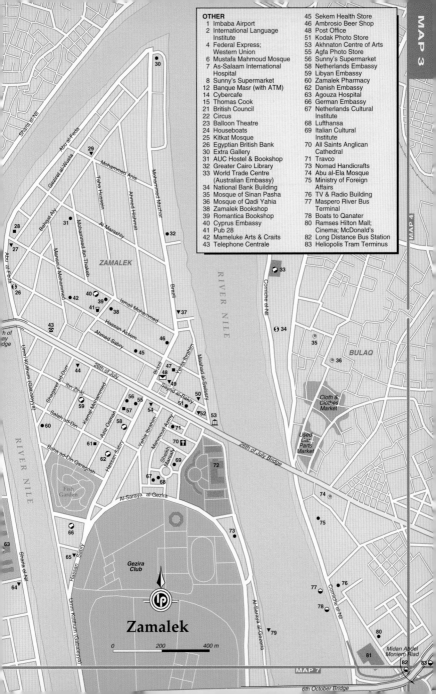

MAP 3

MAP 4

OTHER

1	Imbaba Airport	45	Sekem Health Store
2	International Language Institute	46	Ambrosio Beer Shop
4	Federal Express; Western Union	48	Post Office
6	Mustafa Mahmoud Mosque	51	Kodak Photo Store
7	As-Salaam International Hospital	53	Akhnaton Centre of Arts
8	Sunny's Supermarket	55	Agfa Photo Store
12	Banque Masr (with ATM)	56	Sunny's Supermarket
14	Cybercafe	58	Netherlands Embassy
15	Thomas Cook	59	Libyan Embassy
21	British Council	60	Zamalek Pharmacy
22	Circus	62	Danish Embassy
23	Balloon Theatre	63	Agouza Hospital
24	Houseboats	66	German Embassy
25	Kitkat Mosque	67	Netherlands Cultural Institute
26	Egyptian British Bank	68	Lufthansa
30	Extra Gallery	69	Italian Cultural Institute
31	AUC Hostel & Bookshop	70	All Saints Anglican Cathedral
32	Greater Cairo Library	71	Travco
33	World Trade Centre (Australian Embassy)	73	Nomad Handicrafts
34	National Bank Building	74	Abu al-Ela Mosque
35	Mosque of Sinan Pasha	75	Ministry of Foreign Affairs
36	Mosque of Qadi Yahia	76	TV & Radio Building
38	Zamalek Bookshop	77	Maspero River Bus Terminal
39	Romantica Bookshop	78	Boats to Qanater
40	Cyprus Embassy	80	Ramses Hilton Mall; Cinema; McDonald's
41	Pub 28	82	Long Distance Bus Station
42	Mameluke Arts & Crafts	83	Heliopolis Tram Terminus
43	Telephone Centrale		

ZAMALEK

RIVER NILE

BULAQ

Cloth & Clothes Market

Used Car Parts Market

RIVER NILE

Fish Garden

Gezira Club

Zamalek

0   200   400 m

MAP 7

6th October Bridge

PLACES TO STAY
7 Fontana Hotel
8 Cairo Palace
12 Everest Hotel
19 Victoria Hotel
21 Happyton Hotel
30 Ambassador Hotel
33 Carlton Hotel
35 Tawfikia, Safary,
   Sultan & Venice
   Hotels
36 Grand Hotel
43 Hotel Windsor
48 Pension Roma
49 Cairo Khan
52 Hotel Minerva
58 Oxford Hotel
61 Odeon Palace
   Hotel
70 Hotel Select

PLACES TO EAT
24 At-Tabie ad-Domyati

39 Alfy Bey Restaurant;
   Shererazad Nightclub
40 Akher Saa
41 Lux Kushari
   Restaurant
42 Peking
45 Ali Hassan al-Hatti
47 Ali Hassan al-Hatti
51 El-Abd Bakery
54 Excelsior
56 McDonald's
57 Amira Cafe
60 Abu Tarek Kushari
   Restaurant
62 El-Abd Bakery
64 At-Tahrir Kushari
   Restaurant
65 KFC
66 Simonds
69 Restaurant GAD
72 La Chesa
75 Groppi's Garden
   Terrace

OTHER
1 Masarra Metro Station
2 Service Taxi Station
3 Egyptian National
   Railways Museum
4 Post Traffic Centre
5 Tram Stop to Heliopolis
6 Superjet Port
   Said Buses
9 Sabil of Umm
   Mohammed Ali
10 Al-Fath Mosque
11 Mubarak Metro Station
13 Service Taxis
14 Bus Station
15 Telephone Centrale
16 Orabi Metro Station
17 Cinema Posterboard
   Painter
18 Open-Air Cinema
20 St Mark's Cathedral
22 Karim II Cinema
23 Karim I Cinema
25 Cafeteria Orabi
26 German Church
27 Isaaf Pharmacy
28 Nasser Metro Station
29 Entomological Society
   Museum
31 Cafe al-Agaty
32 Rivoli Cinema

Around Midan Ramses

0   200   400 m

SHUBRA

To Alexandria

Ahmed Helmy Bus Station

Ramses Railway Station

Midan Ramses

Midan Ulali

Midan Orabi

BULAQ

Ezbekiyya Gardens

Midan Khazindar

Midan Opera

Midan Ataba

Midan Mustafa Kamel

Midan Abdel Moneim Riad

MAP 3

MAP 8

MAP 5

The Northern Walls & Beyond

0   200   400 m

GHAMRA

Ramses

Ibn Haldun

Al-Zahir

Al-Abbassiyya

Al-Abbassiyya

Al-Khaliq al-Masri

Al-Geish

To Northern
Cemetery
(600m)

Al-Baghdali

Bab an-Nasr
Cemetery

Al-Galal

Al-Gamaliyya

Al-Geish

Port Said (Bur Said)

Darb al-Asfar

Darb at-Tablawi

Al-Muizz li-Din Allah

See Al-Azhar & Khan al-
Khalili Map (Page 103)

MAP 9

GAMALIYYA

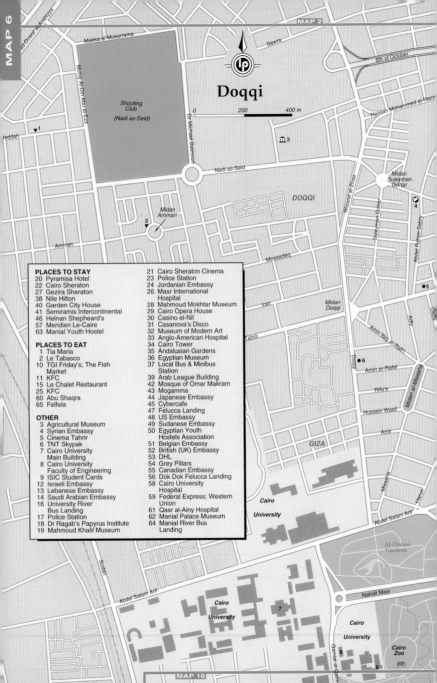

MAP 6
MAP 2

Doqqi

Shooting
Club
(Nadi as-Seid)

6th of October

Hassan Mohammed al-Razz

Jeddah

Makka al-Mukarrama

Sawra

Morty Al-Din Abu al-Ezz

Dr Michael Bakhoum

0   200   400 m

Nadi as-Seid

Midan
Suleyman
Gohar

DOQQI

Midan
Amman

Amman

Mossadeq

Wizarat az-Ziraa

Suleyman Gohar

Abdel Rahim Sabry

PLACES TO STAY
20 Pyramisa Hotel
22 Cairo Sheraton
27 Gezira Sheraton
38 Nile Hilton
40 Garden City House
41 Semiramis Intercontinental
46 Helnan Shepheard's
57 Meridien Le-Caire
63 Manial Youth Hostel

PLACES TO EAT
1 Tia Maria
2 Le Tabasco
10 TGI Friday's; The Fish
  Market
11 KFC
15 Le Chalet Restaurant
25 KFC
60 Abu Shaqra
65 Felfela

OTHER
3 Agricultural Museum
4 Syrian Embassy
5 Cinema Tahrir
6 TNT Skypak
7 Cairo University
  Main Building
8 Cairo University
  Faculty of Engineering
9 ISIC Student Cards
12 Israeli Embassy
13 Lebanese Embassy
14 Saudi Arabian Embassy
16 University River
  Bus Landing
17 Police Station
18 Dr Ragab's Papyrus Institute
19 Mahmoud Khalil Museum

21 Cairo Sheraton Cinema
23 Police Station
24 Jordanian Embassy
26 Masr International
  Hospital
28 Mahmoud Mokhtar Museum
29 Cairo Opera House
30 Casino el-Nil
31 Casanova's Disco
32 Museum of Modern Art
33 Anglo-American Hospital
34 Cairo Tower
35 Andalusian Gardens
36 Egyptian Museum
37 Local Bus & Minibus
  Station
39 Arab League Building
42 Mosque of Omar Makram
43 Mogamma
44 Japanese Embassy
45 Cybercafe
47 Felucca Landing
48 US Embassy
49 Sudanese Embassy
50 Egyptian Youth
  Hostels Association
51 Belgian Embassy
52 British (UK) Embassy
53 DHL
54 Grey Pillars
55 Canadian Embassy
56 Dok Dok Felucca Landing
58 Cairo University
  Hospital
59 Federal Express; Western
  Union
61 Qasr al-Ainy Hospital
62 Manial Palace Museum
64 Manial River Bus
  Landing

Midan
Doqqi

Iran

Amin Bey ar-Rafei

Dok

Amin ar-Rafei

Midan al-Messaha

Rifa'a

Hussein Wasif

Amir

GIZA

Cairo
University

Al-Orman
Gardens

Abdel Salam Arif

Abdel Salam Arif

Cairo
University

7

Nahdit Masr

Gamrat al-Qahra

Cairo
University

Cairo
Zoo

8

9

MAP 10

Gezira & Manial

MAP 3

Gezira Club

6th of October   6th ↘

GEZIRA

RIVER NILE

Hadeyek al-Zuhreya

33

34

35

Ahly
Stadium

Umm Kolthum (Gabalayya)

Shari'a el-Nil

32

31

Tahrir Bridge

29

Midan
Saad
Zaghloul

30

MAP 8

Champollion

21
28

37

39

40

42

41

Midan Simon
Bolivar

46

45

43

Abdel-Kader
Hamza

47

48

Ismail Abu al-Fotoh

Al-Saraya

26

Midan
Fini

25

Saad al-Aly

Ismail Abu al-Fotoh

Galaa
Bridge

Midan
al-Galaa

23

22

22

21

Abi Emama

20

19

Nady al-
Qahira
Garden

28

27

Latin America

52

Lazoughli

Ibrahim

51

50

49

Gohainy

Missalla

Al-Giza

18

Kamel ash-Shennawi

Gam al-Din Abu al-Mahasin

53

Al-Birgas

Al-Saraya al-Kubra

Ibrahim Naguib

GARDEN
CITY

56

57

54

55

Aisha
at-Taimuriyya

Corniche al-Nil

Qasr al-Aini

MAP 8

Shari'a el-Nil

Gezira
& Manial

0   200   400 m

RIVER NILE

58

59

Ismail Sirry

60

Al-Saray

MANIAL

61

University (Al-Gamaa) Bridge

16

14

15

13

12

Midan al-
Gamaa

11

10

64

65

63

62

Abdel Aziz al-Saud

Al-Manial

Saafil al-Roda

Ali Basha Ibrahim

Charles de Gaulle

MAP 11

Central Cairo

MAP 4

Midan
Mustafa
Kamel

Midan
Ataba

MAP 7

MAP 11

BAB
AL-LUQ

Midan
Tahrir

Midan
Falaki

Midan
Talaat
Harb

ABDIN

HILMIYYA

Midan
Al-Gomhuriya

Abdin
Palace

Hassan al-Akhbat

Midan Bab
al-Khalq

MOUNIRA

Midan
Lazoghli

SAYYIDA
ZEINAN

Sayyida
Zeinab
Cultural
Park

Midan
Sayyida
Zeinab

ZEIN-AL-ABDIN

Midan Zein-
al-Abdin

To Abu
Ramy's

To YHA Office

Zainhum
Gardens

0   200   400 m

MAP 9

MAP 5

101
104
102
103
105
106
GAMALIYYA
Bayn al-Qasreyn
107
KHAN AL-KHALILI
108
109
Al-Mu'izz li-Din Allah
Muski
Port Said (Bur Said)
Midan
Hussein
116
Al-Azhar
117
113
115
118
114
110
See Al-Azhar & Khan al-
Khalili Map (Page 103)
119
Khushqadam
111
Al-Mu'izz li-Din Allah
120
112
121
122
123
Ahmed Mahir
124
125
BAB
AL-KHALQ
126
Darb al-Ahmar
To Mosque
of Qaitbey
see Map 1
128
127
129
130
DARB
AL-AHMAR
131
Al-Khayamiyya
Mohammed Ali
132
133
At-Tabbana
Northern
Cemetery
134
135
136
Walls of Salah ad-Din
137
Suq as-Silah
138
Sayudiyya
139
Bab al-Wazir
143
140
142
144
141
See The Citadel
Map (Page 118)
146
145
Midan Salah
ad-Din
The
Citadel
The
Citadel
147
148
Sayyida Aisha
149
Al-Imam
Salah Salam
To Muqattam
(1.5km)

Khan al-Khalili
to the Citadel

To Mosque of
Sayyida Aisha
To Southern Cemetery
0   200   400 m

CAIRO – MAPS 8 & 9

PLACES TO STAY
16 Cosmopolitan Hotel
27 Anglo-Swiss Hotel
34 Sun Hotel
37 Lotus Hotel
50 Amin Hotel
64 Ismailia House Hotel

PLACES TO EAT
1 Abu Tarek Kushari Restaurant
2 El-Abd Bakery
4 Simonds
23 Groppi's
25 La Pasha
29 Arabesque
39 Estoril
45 Felfela Restaurant
46 Felfela Takeaway
52 Le Bistro
57 Cafeteria ash-Shaab
59 Lux Kushari Restaurant
60 Al-Guesh
61 At-Tahrir Kushari Restaurant
62 Fatatri at-Tahrir
65 KFC; Pizza Hut
66 McDonald's
76 Wimpy
81 Ar-Rifai Kebab & Kofta
85 Haram Zeinab Fatatri
87 Ouf

OTHER
3 French Consulate & Cultural
  Centre
5 Cap d'Or
6 Turkish Airlines
7 Meat Market
8 Banque Masr (with ATM)
9 1920 Banque Masr Building
10 St Joseph's Church
11 Osiris Auction House
12 Tourist Friends Association
13 Livres de France Bookshop
14 Italian Insurance Building
15 Olympic Airways
17 Photo Centre
18 Karim-Francis Espace Gallery
19 Western Union Office
20 Lappas Delicatessen/Minimarket
21 Cinema Radio
22 Atelier du Caire Gallery
24 Thomas Cook
26 Middle East Airlines
28 Mashrabia Gallery
30 Local Bus & Minibus Station
31 British Airways

32 Goethe Institut
33 Telephone Centrale
35 Masr Travel
36 KLM
38 De Castro Tours
40 American Express
41 Air France
42 Site of Former Cafe Riché
43 Stella Bar
44 Zahret al-Bustan Coffeehouse
47 EgyptAir
48 Bustan Centre; EBB ATM
49 Cairo-Berlin Gallery
51 Cafeteria Horeyya
53 Ministry of Waqf
54 Antar Photostore
55 Cairo Chamber of Commerce
56 Telephone Centrale
58 Souq Mansour
63 Aly Baba Cafeteria
67 American University in Cairo
  & Bookshop
68 Mogamma
69 Sadat Metro Station
70 Mosque of Omar Makram
71 Banque Masr (with ATM)
72 US Embassy
73 Sudanese Embassy
74 People's Assembly (Maglis
  ash-Shab)
75 Post Office
77 Saad Zaghloul Metro Station
78 Saad Zaghloul Museum
79 French Cultural Institute
80 Beit as-Sennari
82 Sabil-Kuttab of Sultan Mustafa
83 Mosque of Sayyida Zeinab
84 Police Station
86 Zahret al-Midan Chess
  Coffeehouse
88 Mausoleum of Shagaret
  ad-Durr
89 Gayer-Anderson Museum
90 Khan Misr Touloun Arts & Crafts
  Emporium
91 Mosque of ibn Tulun
92 Mosque of Sarghatmish
93 Khanqah of Sheikhu
94 Mosque of Sheikhu
95 Mosque of Taghribardi
96 Post Office
97 Video Coffee Shops
98 Market
99 Cairo Governorate
100 Museum of Islamic Art
101 Madrassa & Mausoleum of
  Barquq
102 Qasr Beshtak

Colourful billboards displaying the latest efforts of the Egyptian film industry adorn walls and scaffolding throughout Cairo, promoting an extensive range of uniquely Arabic film experiences.

MAP 10

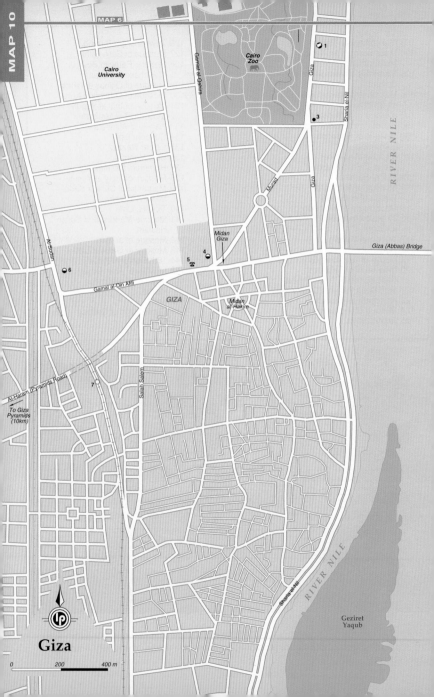

MAP 6

Cairo
University

Cairo
Zoo

Garnet al-Qahira

Giza

Sharia el-Nil

R I V E R   N I L E

1

3

Murad

Giza

Midan
Giza

Giza (Abbas) Bridge

4

5

At-Sudan

6

Gamal al-Din Afifi

GIZA

Midan
al-Hakim

Salah Salem

Al-Haram (Pyramids Road)

7

To Giza
Pyramids
(10km)

Sharia el-Nil

R I V E R   N I L E

Geziret
Yaqub

Giza

0   200   400 m

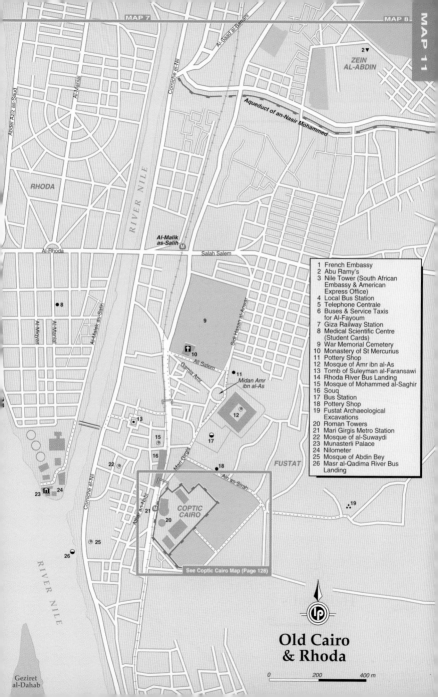

MAP 7   MAP 8

MAP 11

ZEIN
AL-ABDIN

2▼

Aqueduct of an-Nasir Mohammed

RIVER NILE

RHODA

Al-Malik
as-Salih

Al-Rhoda
Salah Salem

●8

9

✝10

Ali Salem

●11
Midan Amr
ibn al-As

12

17

13

15

16

22●

23 ▥ 24

●18

COPTIC
CAIRO

21

20

FUSTAT

19

●25

26

See Coptic Cairo Map (Page 128)

RIVER NILE

Geziret
al-Dahab

1 French Embassy
2 Abu Ramy's
3 Nile Tower (South African
   Embassy & American
   Express Office)
4 Local Bus Station
5 Telephone Centrale
6 Buses & Service Taxis
   for Al-Fayoum
7 Giza Railway Station
8 Medical Scientific Centre
   (Student Cards)
9 War Memorial Cemetery
10 Monastery of St Mercurius
11 Pottery Shop
12 Mosque of Amr ibn al-As
13 Tomb of Suleyman al-Faransawi
14 Rhoda River Bus Landing
15 Mosque of Mohammed al-Saghir
16 Souq
17 Bus Station
18 Pottery Shop
19 Fustat Archaeological
   Excavations
20 Roman Towers
21 Mari Girgis Metro Station
22 Mosque of al-Suwaydi
23 Munasterli Palace
24 Nilometer
25 Mosque of Abdin Bey
26 Masr al-Qadima River Bus
   Landing

Old Cairo
& Rhoda

0   200   400 m

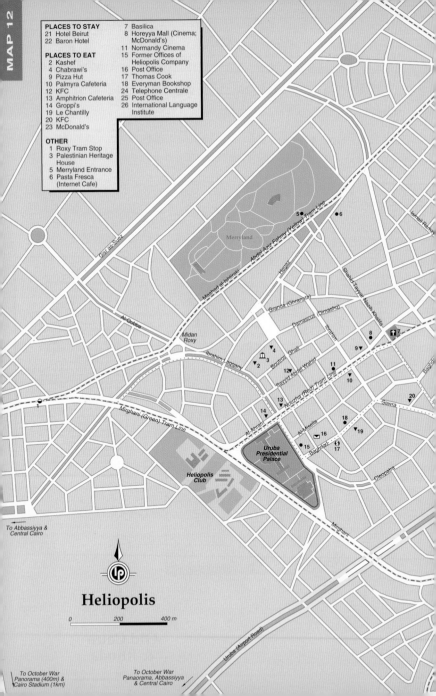

Heliopolis

MAP 12

PLACES TO STAY
21 Hotel Beirut
22 Baron Hotel

PLACES TO EAT
2 Kashef
4 Chabrawi's
9 Pizza Hut
10 Palmyra Cafeteria
12 KFC
13 Amphitrion Cafeteria
14 Groppi's
19 Le Chantilly
20 KFC
23 McDonald's

7 Basilica
8 Horeyya Mall (Cinema; McDonald's)
11 Normandy Cinema
15 Former Offices of Heliopolis Company
16 Post Office
17 Thomas Cook
18 Everyman Bookshop
24 Telephone Centrale
25 Post Office
26 International Language Institute

OTHER
1 Roxy Tram Stop
3 Palestinian Heritage House
5 Merryland Entrance
6 Pasta Fresca (Internet Cafe)

Merryland

Midan Roxy

Heliopolis Club

Uruba Presidential Palace

To Abbassiyya & Central Cairo

To October War Panorama (400m) & Cairo Stadium (1km)

To October War Panaorama, Abbassiyya & Central Cairo

Uruba (Airport Road)

Gisr as-Suez

Al-Qubba

Ibrahim Laqqany

Mirghani (Green) Tram Line

Al-Ahram

Mirghani

Cleopatra

Baghdadi

Sawra

Baghdadi

Al-Nosha

Sayyid Abdel Wahab

Nuzha (Red) Tram Line

Boutros Ghali

Damascus (Dimashq)

Ibrahim

Granda (Ghranata)

Shahid Hayyad Nazm Khalifa

Abdel Aziz Fahmy (Yellow) Tram Line

Meshad el-Ishfirak

Hijaz

Ismail Ramzy

0   200   400 m

Al-Nasr Club

Abu Bakr as-Sadiq

Harun ar-Rashid

Al-Ghaba Club

Omar ibn al-Khattab

Harun ar-Rashid

Nouzha (Red) Tram Line

Midan Salah ad-Din

Osman Ibn Affan

Salah ad-Din

21

Beirut

Cleopatra

Uruba (Airport Road)

Sawri

Baron's Palace

Mirghani (Green) Tram Line

23

■22

24 ☎

25 ✉

26 ●

Mirghani

EDDIE GERALD

EDDIE GERALD

The bizarre and somewhat incongruous Baron's Palace (top) combines with a more European style of architecture to give Heliopolis a very different appearance to the rest of Cairo.

Map Legend

ROUTES

.... Train Route, with Station
.... Tramway
.... Walking Tour

.... Freeway
.... Primary Road
.... Secondary Road
.... Unsealed Road
.... Minor Road
.... City Freeway
.... City Primary Road
.... City Secondary Road
.... City Minor Road
.... City Lane

AREA FEATURES

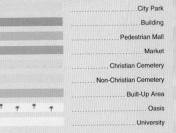

.... City Park
.... Building
.... Pedestrian Mall
.... Market
.... Christian Cemetery
.... Non-Christian Cemetery
.... Built-Up Area
.... Oasis
.... University

HYDROGRAPHIC FEATURES

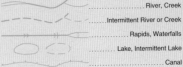

.... River, Creek
.... Intermittent River or Creek
.... Rapids, Waterfalls
.... Lake, Intermittent Lake
.... Canal

SYMBOLS

○ **CAPITAL** ..... National Capital	✈ .... Airport	🏛 .. Museum or Art Gallery
◉ **Capital** ..... Regional Capital	▬▬ Ancient or City Wall	)(........Pass, Tunnel
● **City** .... City	⚓ ....Archaeological Site	₽ .... Petrol Station
● **Town** .... Town	❸ .... Bank	★ .... Police Station
● **Village** .... Village	⌁ 🛈 .. Cathedral, Church	✉ .... Post Office
	☾ ... Contemporary Mosque	✕ ....Pyramid
■ .... Place to Stay	☊ .... Embassy	A25 ..... Route Number
▼ .... Place to Eat	↦ ..... Escarpment	❖ ...Shopping Centre
🍺 .... Pub or Bar	🏛 .... Fort	🏛 .... Stately Home
☕ .... Coffeehouse	❋ ‡ .... Gardens	🛏 .... Swimming Pool
	ⓗ .... Hammam	✡ .... Synagogue
	🏛 ... Historic Building	☎ .... Telephone
	✛ .... Hospital	🚻 .... Toilet
	◉ .. Islamic Monument	■ .... Tomb
	Ⓜ ...... Metro Station	❶ ..Tourist Information
	⚑ ...... Monument	❍ .... Transport
	▲ ..... Mountain, Hill	🐘 .... Zoo

Note: not all symbols displayed above appear in this book